Hotel Modernisms

This collection of essays explores the hotel as a site of modernity, a space of mobility and transience that shaped the transnational and transcultural modernist activity of the first half of the twentieth century. As a trope for social and cultural mobility, transitory and precarious modes of living, and experiences of personal and political transformation, the hotel space in modernist writing complicates binaries such as public and private, risk and rootedness, and convention and experimentation. It is also a prime location for modernist production and the cross-fertilization of heterogeneous, inter- and trans-literary, cultural, national, and affective modes. The study of the hotel in the work of authors such as E. M. Forster, May Sinclair, Mary Butts, and Joseph Roth reveals the ways in which the hotel nuances the notions of mobilities, networks, and communities in terms of gender, nation, and class. Whereas H.D., Djuna Barnes, Anaïs Nin, and Denton Welch negotiate affective and bodily states which arise from the alienation experienced at liminal hotel spaces and which lead to new poetics of space, Vicki Baum, Georg Lukács, James Joyce, and Elizabeth Bishop explore the socio-political and cultural conflicts which are manifested in and by the hotel. This volume invites us to think of "hotel modernisms" as situated in or enabled by this dynamic space. Including chapters which traverse the boundaries of nation and class, it regards the hotel as the transcultural space of modernity par excellence.

Anna Despotopoulou is Professor in English Literature and Culture at the National and Kapodistrian University of Athens.

Vassiliki Kolocotroni is Senior Lecturer in English Literature at the University of Glasgow.

Efterpi Mitsi is Professor in English Literature and Culture at the National and Kapodistrian University of Athens.

Among the Victorians and Modernists
Edited by Dennis Denisoff

This series publishes monographs and essay collections on literature, art, and culture in the context of the diverse aesthetic, political, social, technological, and scientific innovations that arose among the Victorians and Modernists. Viable topics include, but are not limited to, artistic and cultural debates and movements; influential figures and communities; and agitations and developments regarding subjects such as animals, commodification, decadence, degeneracy, democracy, desire, ecology, gender, nationalism, the paranormal, performance, public art, sex, socialism, spiritualities, transnationalism, and the urban. Studies that address continuities between the Victorians and Modernists are welcome. Work on recent responses to the periods such as Neo-Victorian novels, graphic novels, and film will also be considered.

Critical Essays on Arthur Morrison and the East End
Edited by Diana Maltz

Writers at War
Exploring the Prose of Ford Madox Ford, May Sinclair, Siegfried Sassoon and Mary Borden
Isabelle Brasme

Hotel Modernisms
Edited by Anna Despotopoulou, Vassiliki Kolocotroni, and Efterpi Mitsi

Legal Narratives in Victorian Fiction
Joanne Bridget Simpson

For more information about this series, please visit: www.routledge.com/Among-the-Victorians-and-Modernists/book-series/ASHSER4035

Hotel Modernisms

Edited by Anna Despotopoulou,
Vassiliki Kolocotroni, and Efterpi Mitsi

NEW YORK AND LONDON

First published 2023
by Routledge
605 Third Avenue, New York, NY 10158

and by Routledge
4 Park Square, Milton Park, Abingdon, Oxon, OX14 4RN

Routledge is an imprint of the Taylor & Francis Group, an informa business

© 2023 selection and editorial matter, Anna Despotopoulou, Vassiliki Kolocotroni, and Efterpi Mitsi; individual chapters, the contributors

The right of Anna Despotopoulou, Vassiliki Kolocotroni, and Efterpi Mitsi to be identified as the authors of the editorial material, and of the authors for their individual chapters, has been asserted in accordance with sections 77 and 78 of the Copyright, Designs and Patents Act 1988.

All rights reserved. No part of this book may be reprinted or reproduced or utilised in any form or by any electronic, mechanical, or other means, now known or hereafter invented, including photocopying and recording, or in any information storage or retrieval system, without permission in writing from the publishers.

Trademark notice: Product or corporate names may be trademarks or registered trademarks, and are used only for identification and explanation without intent to infringe.

ISBN: 978-1-032-08127-4 (hbk)
ISBN: 978-1-032-08128-1 (pbk)
ISBN: 978-1-003-21307-9 (ebk)

DOI: 10.4324/9781003213079

Typeset in Sabon
by Newgen Publishing UK

Contents

List of Figures viii
List of Contributors ix
Acknowledgements xiii

Introduction 1
ANNA DESPOTOPOULOU, VASSILIKI KOLOCOTRONI,
AND EFTERPI MITSI

1 Hotel Trouble 11
VASSILIKI KOLOCOTRONI

Hospitalities, Communities 31

2 "Blank, blond horror": The Hotel as Medical Facility 33
ROBBIE MOORE

3 Hotel Performance and Its Remains: Jean Cocteau and
Mary Butts at the Welcome 49
JOEL HAWKES

4 Performing Belonging in Early Twentieth-Century
Literary Hotels and the Case of Rich Americans 65
BETTINA MATTHIAS

5 "No longer a hotel": Colonial Decadence in
Lawrence Durrell's *The Alexandria Quartet* 79
ATHANASIOS DIMAKIS

Rooms, Views 93

6 Landslide at the Pension Bertolini: Anti-tourism versus Groundless Transculturalism in E. M. Forster's *A Room with a View* 95
SHAWNA ROSS

7 H.D.'s Hotel Visions 110
POLLY HEMBER

8 Carnivorous Flowers and Poisoned Webs: Surrealist Experimentation in Djuna Barnes's *Nightwood* and Anaïs Nin's *House of Incest* 124
JOSIE CRAY

9 "Found his anxiety frothing": Denton Welch's *In Youth Is Pleasure* and the Hotel as Camp Allegory 137
ALLAN PERO

Labour, Love 153

10 "The hotel story he made up": Hotel Life, Death, and Work in James Joyce's *Ulysses* 155
EMMA SHORT

11 Life and Work in Interwar "Cathedrals of Modernity" 168
ULRIKE ZITZLSPERGER

12 White Women and Cheap Hotels 182
TYLER T. SCHMIDT

Theory, Design 199

13 *Rota Moderna*: Vortex Force in Viennese Hotel Lobbies 201
RAJESH HEYNICKX

14 Grand Hotel Theory   213
    JOHN HOFFMANN

15 Prototype Hotels for the Jet Age   229
    BRUCE PETER

    Index   244

Figures

2.1	A bathroom in the Ritz Hotel, London, 1910. Chronicle/Alamy Stock Photo	35
2.2	An operating theatre in the requisitioned Flandria Palace Hotel, Ghent, during the German occupation, c. 1915–16. Photo: Kommandantur Gent, Photographische Abteilung. Collectie Archief Gent	41
11.1	Thomas Mann at Hotel Adlon, Berlin 1929. © Bundesarchiv, photo 183-H27032. No named photographer, 1929	179
13.1	The lobby of Hotel Royal in 2019. © Wolfgang Thaler	202
13.2	The Corso on the Ringstrasse in Vienna. Print after a painting by Theo Zasche, c. 1900. © Schloss Schönbrunn Kultur and Betriebsges.m.b.H	203
13.3	The Grand Hotel National advertisement. © Vienna Museum	204
13.4	Theophilus van Kannel, the revolving door design. www.google.com/patents/US387571?hl=d	209
15.1	Hotel Statler, Washington, DC. Bruce Peter personal collection	232
15.2	Hotel Jaragua, Ciudad, Trujillo, poolside view. Bruce Peter personal collection	234
15.3	Caribe Hilton exterior, San Juan, Puerto Rico. Bruce Peter personal collection	239

Contributors

Josie Cray is a doctoral student at the School of English, Communication and Philosophy, Cardiff University. Her thesis examines the relationship between Anaïs Nin's work and Surrealism, placing the writer in conversation with Surrealist women artists through her experimentation with and redeployment of surrealist aesthetics. Cray's work has been supported by the Sir Richard Stapley Educational Trust and the Reid Trust.

Anna Despotopoulou is Professor in English Literature and Culture at the National and Kapodistrian University of Athens. She is the author of *Women and the Railway, 1850–1915* and of articles on nineteenth-century literature in journals such as *Modern Fiction Studies, The Henry James Review,* and *Studies in the Novel*. Books she has co-edited include *Ruins in the Literary and Cultural Imagination* and *Henry James and the Supernatural*. Her collaborative research project "Hotels and the Modern Subject, 1890–1940" was funded by the Hellenic Foundation for Research & Innovation (2020–2022).

Athanasios Dimakis is a postdoctoral researcher at the National and Kapodistrian University of Athens, working on the project "Hotels and the Modern Subject: 1890–1940" (funded by the Hellenic Foundation for Research & Innovation). He holds an MA from the University of London (Goldsmiths), and a PhD from the University of Athens. He has published essays on E. M. Forster, Lawrence Durrell, and Iris Murdoch. In June 2020, he was awarded the William Godshalk Prize for new Durrell scholarship by the International Lawrence Durrell Society, and he has recently been elected Board Member of the same society.

Joel Hawkes lectures in English at the University of Victoria. His research is interested in the practices and performances that create the physical and literary spaces we inhabit, and the ritual nature of these. Mary Butts has long been a focus of his work. His edited collection of Butts's essays was published by McPherson & Co in 2021. He is now working on Butts's letters.

x   *Contributors*

Polly Hember is a Techne-funded PhD student at Royal Holloway, University of London. Her thesis explores the work of the POOL group, focusing on modernism, early cinema, and queer affective networks. She is a former co-editor of the *Modernist Review*, a former postgraduate representative for the British Association of Modernist Studies, and her article on H.D. and Robert Herring is forthcoming in *Modernist Cultures*.

Rajesh Heynickx is Professor of Architectural Theory and Intellectual History at the Faculty of Architecture and Vice-Chair of the Department of Architecture at KU Leuven. Current research topics include twentieth-century architectural theory and art philosophy; architectural pedagogy; and knowledge transfer. He recently co-edited the volumes *Architecture Thinking across Boundaries: Epistemological Transfers in the Postwar World (1965–1995)* (Bloomsbury), *The Figure of Knowledge: Conditioning Architectural Theory, 1960s-1990s* (Leuven UP), and *Architectural Education through Materiality: Pedagogies of 20th Century Design* (Routledge).

John Hoffmann is a postdoctoral fellow in the Institute for Media Studies at the University of Marburg. His work focuses on German and Anglophone culture, and he has published essays in journals such as *Diacritics*, *Modernism/Modernity*, *Film History*, and *New Literary History*. His work has been supported by the Germany Research Foundation, the Modernist Studies Association, and the Max Kade Center for Modern German Thought.

Vassiliki Kolocotroni is Senior Lecturer in English Literature at the University of Glasgow. She is the General Editor of *The Routledge Encyclopedia of Modernism*, and the co-editor of *Modernism: An Anthology of Sources and Documents* and *The Edinburgh Dictionary of Modernism*. She has published numerous articles and book chapters on a range of topics in international modernism, theory, and film; co-edited an anthology and a collection of essays on women's travel in Greece, as well as two books on the Surrealist theorist, poet, and art historian Nicolas Calas. She is an international research member in the project "Hotels and the Modern Subject: 1890–1940," funded by the Hellenic Foundation for Research & Innovation.

Bettina Matthias is the Maurice R. Greenberg Professor of Language and Linguistics and Professor of German at Middlebury College in Vermont (USA). A specialist in early twentieth-century literature, she has published books and articles on Austrian and German modernist authors and culture as well as on teaching German as a Foreign Language. Her monograph *The Hotel as Setting in Early 20th Century German and Austrian Literature* (Camden House, 2006) is generally considered one of the first systematic discussions of this setting in US German Studies.

Efterpi Mitsi is Professor in English Literature and Culture at the National and Kapodistrian University of Athens. She is the author of *Greece in Early English Travel Writing, 1596–1682* (2017), editor of *Troilus and Cressida: A Critical Reader* (2019), and co-editor of *Ruins in the Literary and Cultural Imagination* (2019), and other four collections of essays. Her collaborative research project "Representations of Modern Greece in Victorian Popular Culture" is funded by the Hellenic Foundation for Research & Innovation.

Robbie Moore is Senior Lecturer in English at the University of Tasmania. His research focuses on space and place in late-Victorian and modernist literature and culture. His book, *Hotel Modernity: Corporate Space in Literature and Film*, was published by Edinburgh University Press in 2021. He has also published work on hotels in *The Henry James Review* and *Modernist Cultures* and on "Corporate Space" in *The Routledge Companion to Literature and Economics*.

Allan Pero is Associate Professor at the University of Western Ontario. He is Editor-in-Chief of *English Studies in Canada*, co-editor of and contributor to *The Many Façades of Edith Sitwell* (2017), and the author of two dozen other articles and chapters. He is currently working on *An Encyclopedia of Cultural Theory* for the University of Toronto Press, an edition of Wyndham Lewis's *The Childermass* for Oxford University Press, and a book-length project on Camp and Modernism.

Bruce Peter is Professor of Design History at the Glasgow School of Art. His research interests focus on modern environments designed for leisure, entertainment, and travel. Previous subjects on which he has published have included the architecture and interiors of cinema buildings, the design of modern passenger ships and their interiors, and, most recently, modernist hotel design. He is half-Danish and lives in Edinburgh.

Shawna Ross is Associate Professor of English at Texas A&M University, where she researches and teaches on transatlantic modernism, Victorian literature, and the digital humanities. Her most recent books include the second edition of *Using Digital Humanities in the Classroom* and *Charlotte Brontë at the Anthropocene* (SUNY Press, 2020). She is also co-editor of *Reading Modernism with Machines* and *Humans at Work: Histories of Digital Textual Labor*. She is currently at work on a study of popular modernist scholarship conducted through memes and Web 1.0 technologies.

Tyler T. Schmidt is Associate Professor of English at Lehman College, City University of New York. The author of *Desegregating Desire: Race and Sexuality in Cold War American Literature* (2013), Dr. Schmidt is currently completing a book on Midwestern Queer Modernism that re-imagines the cultural borders of the Chicago Black Renaissance,

Cold War racial aesthetics, and queer art in the mid-twentieth-century Midwest. His critical work has appeared in *African American Review*, *Women Studies Quarterly*, *Radical Teacher*, and *Postmodern Culture*.

Emma Short is Assistant Professor in Modern and Contemporary Literature at Durham University. She is the author of *Mobility and the Hotel in Modern Literature: Passing Through* (Palgrave, 2019), and her research interests span from the late nineteenth century to the present day, focusing on the intersections of space, mobility, embodiment, and gender in literature and culture.

Ulrike Zitzlsperger is Associate Professor of German at the University of Exeter. Her published research includes the exploration of the 1920s and 1990s culture and history of Berlin (in *Journal of Urban Cultural Studies*, 2021); hotels, train stations, coffeehouses, and department stores in German and European film and literature (including *Topografien des Transits. Die Fiktionalisierung von Bahnhöfen, Hotels und Cafés im zwanzigsten Jahrhundert*, 2013); and souvenirs within the wider context of tourism and cultural history (in *The International Journal of the Inclusive Museum*, 2021).

Acknowledgements

This book was conceived during our collaboration on a research project entitled "Hotels and the Modern Subject, 1890–1940" (HOTEMS), which ignited lively discussion as well as an opportunity for reaching out to other scholars interested in hotel topics. We would like to thank the contributors to this volume for their collegiality, creativity, generosity, and shared commitment, which made editing this book a pleasure. We are grateful to Dennis Denisoff for warmly embracing the idea behind this volume from the start and for his encouragement and support. We also appreciate the professionalism of the editorial and production teams at Routledge, their patience and guidance throughout the publishing process.

For financially supporting our collaboration, research, editing, and writing, we gratefully acknowledge the funding that the HOTEMS project received from the Hellenic Foundation for Research & Innovation (H.F.R.I.) under the "1st Call for H.F.R.I. Research Projects to support Faculty Members & Researchers and the Procurement of High-Cost Research Equipment Grant" (Project Number: 1653).

Introduction

Anna Despotopoulou, Vassiliki Kolocotroni, and Efterpi Mitsi

For Walter Benjamin the twentieth century "put an end to dwelling in the old sense" (2002, 221). Reflecting on domestic interiors, in his notes for *The Arcades Project*, Benjamin defined the old sense of dwelling as the tight encasement of the individual in a house which he dubbed a "shell" and a "receptacle" (220) and concluded that "[t]oday this world has disappeared entirely, and dwelling has diminished: for the living, through hotel rooms; for the dead, through crematoriums" (221). His notes on "dwelling" foreshadow his life as an expatriate and exiled writer, staying in cheap hotels and rented apartments. The binary life/hotels—death/crematoriums forms an apposite, albeit ominous, opening for this volume which reflects on the role of hotels in modernist writing and culture. Before Benjamin, it was Henry James who, having grasped the impact of hotels on the American architectural and cultural landscape, wrote in *The American Scene* (1907) that "the present is more and more the day of the hotel" (1994, 79). James stressed the spatial and temporal ubiquity of hotels in the beginning of the twentieth century, associating the hotel "genius" or "spirit" with many of what he viewed as the evils of modern American life: publicity, mobility, ephemerality, promiscuity, and monotony (79–81). Venerated or vilified, hotels in modernism both invoke and defy such a vocabulary, straddling the lines between the public and the intimate, mobility and inertia, transience and permanence, daring and convention. *Hotel Modernisms*, then, checks into some of these iconic, absolutely modern spaces to explore the complex imaginaries they may have fostered.

As architectural landmark and emblem of urban life, the hotel occupied the real and imaginary spaces of modernism, becoming a new setting and trope which complicated issues of community, social and cultural mobility, gender, and sexuality. In a period of increased travel and mobility, the hotel became a site that inspired the exploration of national, transnational, and transcultural networks, bonds, and conflicts. At the same time, hotels provided the infrastructure that enabled modernist production and new aesthetic modes fed by cultural exchange and experimentation. The essays in this volume, featuring hotels from Harlem to Vienna and Alexandria to Villefranche, examine the extent to which

DOI: 10.4324/9781003213079-1

hotels bring cultures and individuals into proximity, across nation, language, and class, and trace the tense dynamics of such encounters.

Visiting various hotel spaces, from the welcoming revolving door and the authoritative lobby to the mystical recesses of the private room, this book invites us to think of "hotel modernisms" through a variety of methodological approaches.[1] The hotel setting accommodates and concretizes critical modes and concerns, ranging from politics and form, phenomenology and affect, gender and queer perspectives, and working independently and in confluence to produce original readings. The study of the hotel in the work of authors such as May Sinclair, Joseph Roth, Robert Musil, Mary Butts, and Lawrence Durrell reveals the ways in which the hotel nuances the notions of mobility, networks, and communities in terms of nation, empire, gender, sexuality, and class. Djuna Barnes, Anais Nin, H.D., and Denton Welch negotiate affective and bodily states which arise from the vacillation of familiarity and alienation experienced in hotel spaces and which may lead to new queer poetics of space; Vicki Baum, Georg Lukács, James Joyce, Stefan Zweig, Elizabeth Bishop, and Ann Petry explore the sociopolitical and racial conflicts that are manifested in and by the hotel. For Marcel Proust, André Breton and W.G. Sebald hotels are sites of haunting, memory, and risk.

Until recently, most book-length critical analyses of hotels in literature had concentrated on the nineteenth century, exploring the histories and nomenclature of hotels, from coaching inns to lodging houses and from the railway hotel to the Grand (Elbert and Schmid 2017; Black 2019). One of the first scholars to focus on twentieth-century literary hotels was Bettina Matthias, a contributor to this volume, whose *The Hotel as Setting in Early 20th-Century German and Austrian Literature* (2006) introduced the hotel's importance as an experimental and stage-like setting that witnesses socio-historical change and generates class and gender anxieties. For Matthias the hotel in German and Austrian texts is largely a symbol of "existential estrangement" (2006, 6). More recently, Emma Short and Robbie Moore, also contributors to this book, in their respective monographs *Mobility and the Hotel in Modern Literature: Passing Through* (2019) and *Hotel Modernity: Corporate Space in Literature and Film* (2021), discuss the significance of hotels in the work of Anglophone writers of the first half of the twentieth century, centring on mobility, gender, class, and capital. The works of European and American authors examined in this volume connect modernity to the hotel by shedding light on the cultural interrelations and intersections spawned by hotel stays.

This volume contributes to the understanding of modernist spaces, building on historical and cultural studies of the hotel (Sandoval-Strausz 2007; Berger 2011; James 2018; Davidson 2018), which have discussed the ways in which it reflected and reproduced the diversity and density of city life, becoming a microcosm of the city and society in general.

Recording his 1904–1905 impressions of American hotels, Henry James, a pioneer of hotel criticism, was one of the first authors to emphasize their impact on urban space in terms of mobility and publicity, which are as pervasive in the city street as in the hotel interiors (Despotopoulou 2018, 502). James discerns a similarity between hotels and moving vehicles, the Pullmans (1994, 300), in that they both suspend the distinction between movement and stasis: "the Pullmans [...] are like rushing hotels and the hotels [...] are like stationary Pullmans" (300). James's critique introduces many of the paradoxes examined in this volume. On the one hand, the insular and claustrophobic, for James, "hotel-world" generates "sameness" and "monotony" despite its affected variety created by publicity, consumption, and luxury (78, 80). On the other hand, as many chapters in this volume show, the sameness is counteracted by transformation, dissonance, and modernist experimentation, and the insularity is challenged by restless guests escaping its confines. The hotel seems to be at the same time socially and architecturally bound and culturally and conceptually unbound. As a writer whose work centres on travel and transcultural encounters, James seems to have also been especially attuned to the hotel's double-edged power of inclusion and exclusion, cultural expansion and alienating narrowness, as illustrated most poignantly in the hotel scenes of his early story "Daisy Miller" (1878), where the young American girl rejects and is rejected by the community of hotel guests and their conservative values. E. M. Forster, Mary Butts, Stefan Zweig, H.D., Denton Welch, Anaïs Nin, and other authors discussed in the chapters that comprise this collection confront such hotel paradoxes and bear out Kevin J. James's definition of hotels as "sites in which ambivalences associated with the modern condition are played out" (2018, 2). The volume's contributors explore the ways in which bureaucratic or corporate normativity alternates with decadent fantasy, and work with leisure; displacement is countered by belonging, and alienation by inclusivity; hospitality is transformed into surveillance; the mundane is interrupted by the marvellous.

Tensions emerging from hotel living may lead to inner conflicts but also self-expansion, self-transformation, and even self-invention. Unlike the home, the hotel may be seen as a traversable threshold, encouraging diverse cultural, social, and sexual becomings and ruptures. For Barnes, the hotel is a site of queer transformation, in Petry, of racial transgression, and in Welch, of psychic reformation. Guests may find themselves existing outside the boundaries of definable time and space: for H.D. hotels invoke a waking-dream state, an in-between state of consciousness. Allowing chance encounters and sexual escapades, the hotel room in Barnes and Nin is a fluid space, transformed by desire. Short defines the hotels as a "vital imaginative space," especially for women writers who explore sexual freedom in its premises (2019, 22). The desiring subjects challenge the impersonality and uniformity of the room, forming affective relations with this temporary space: "Already from the moment I begin to unpack my luggage, I observe that I have started to expand in this room," writes the Dutch psychologist David Jacob van Lennep in his essay "The Hotel Room" (1987, 212); "I find myself transformed through the anonymity of the hotel room" (213).

In turn, hotels themselves change to accommodate new subjectivities and activities; their meaning, for Kevin J. James "is produced and reproduced, contested and reconfigured" (2018, 4). In May Sinclair's World War I journals, hotels and hospitals in Belgium are interchangeable, and the line between hospitality and containment is crossed. For Lawrence Durrell, the colonial hotel in Egypt operates as an embassy and a brothel. For Jean Cocteau, the hotel in the South of France is the stage for a collaborative performance of life and art. Robert Davidson has emphasized the performative nature of hotel spaces which privilege a visual economy of seeing and being seen (2018, 7). Hotel guests play roles and negotiate new modes of being, being liberated, as Matthias has argued, "from the restrictions that their everyday life imposes" (2006, 5). Yet, hotel experience may also lock one in the fixity of social and cultural roles that are performed there, as in the case of rich Americans in European hotels. The anonymity of guests and the impersonality of the rooms may be welcomed by some—Joseph Roth, the "hotel patriot" (2015, 158), for example—but loathed by others who feel reduced to the number on their door. For Moore, hotel texts suggest that "the individual hotel guest exists within larger corporate, architectural, informatic and technological networks" (2021, 186); this becomes even more obvious in the first jet-age hotels and their architectural uniformity, a development treated by Bruce Peter in this volume.

Yet, when entering a hotel room, there is a sense of familiarity created not only by the uniformity but also by the traces of previous guests imprinted on objects of everyday use. Although twentieth-century hotels may have put an end to dwelling in the old sense, as Benjamin wrote, these mostly invisible traces create a new sense of dwelling, if "to dwell means to leave traces" (Benjamin 2002, 9). These traces haunting hotel rooms disturb or inspire the hotel guests of many modernist texts. When Peter Walsh returns to his Bloomsbury hotel, in Virginia Woolf's *Mrs Dalloway*, feeling dejected after having received a letter from Clarissa, he awakens to a sense of being a permanent guest in impermanent rooms:

> These hotels are not consoling places. Far from it. Any number of people had hung up their hats on those pegs. Even the flies, if you thought of it, had settled on other people's noses. As for the cleanliness which hit him in the face, it wasn't cleanliness, so much as bareness, frigidity; a thing that had to be. Some arid matron made her rounds at dawn sniffing, peering, causing blue-nosed maids to scour, for all the world as if the next visitor were a joint of meat to be served on a perfectly clean platter. For sleep, one bed; for sitting

in, one armchair; for cleaning one's teeth and shaving one's chin, one tumbler, one looking-glass.

([1925] 1981, 155)

The system of enforced cleanliness designed to erase all traces of previous occupants fails. The material and immaterial features shared by countless former guests haunt him, while he is doomed to also repeat the same hotel rituals. While Clarissa's (now Mrs Dalloway's) home hosts the traces of her life, Peter's hotel room is a palimpsest of the traces of the lives of others. Feeling dehumanized, a "joint of meat" to be devoured by commercial hotel interests, a victim of the "highly standardised and rationalised machine offering efficient accommodation" (Avermaete and Massey 2013, 1), Peter sees his few personal possessions—his books, his letters, and his dressing gown—as "incongruous impertinences" ([1925] 1981, 155), unable to warm up the 'frigid' impersonality of his room. In a novel that explores the permeability of subjective states of being in its constant juxtaposition of private musings and public happenings, Peter's thoughts on the unconsoling effect of the non-private yet also non-public hotel rooms may be seen to corroborate the porosity of enclosed hotel space, even when it is secure under lock and key. The lingering presence of former guests who have repeated the same routines countless times in the room confirms his loneliness, rather than bringing him comfort or any sense of community.

On the other hand, for Edith Wharton in her erotically charged poem, "Terminus" (1909),[2] the "dull impersonal furniture" of a hotel room may kindle "a mystic flame" in the room mirror which has reflected innumerable faces and the bed which has borne the weight of countless tired or ecstatic bodies (2005, 160). The hotel room comes to epitomize a timeless space of mobility and desire, an evocative palimpsest on which every new passion, thought, or disappointment is superimposed on the previous one. For Wharton's speaker, the echo of experiences of past guests in the otherwise "passive & featureless room" (161) is exhilarating: "I was glad as I thought of those others, the nameless, the many, / who perhaps thus had lain and loved for an hour on the brink of the world" (161). The poem associates the hotel room with the trains that can be heard from the adjacent station, conflating the intensity of passion with the intensity of modern technological mobility as well as poignantly connecting the repetition of everyday routines with the transience of love: hotel guests, whether travellers or lovers, are "faces innumerous & vague," like "automata" experiencing momentary mobility and subsequent erasure (160). The sounds of love-making in the private space of the room merge with the shriek of the trains in the urban space, and the enduring embrace on the bed is followed by the inevitable farewell performed on the station platform the next morning. The image of "the night-long shudder of traffic" (161) connects the sexual traffic that railway hotels accommodated with the urban circulation as well as with the traffic of traces of the past, all conjured in the temporary hotel room.

Such "traffic" of experience and emotion, and the thrill of a secret life that can momentarily flourish in a hotel room, underlies the modernist texts explored in this volume. In the opening chapter titled "Hotel Trouble," Vassiliki Kolocotroni probes into the cognitive, emotional, personal, and political trouble residing in modernism's grand and little hotels, providing an entry point to the collection. In Kolocotroni's reading, Marcel Proust stages games of love, memory, and forgetting in his hotel life, W. G. Sebald and Walter Benjamin trace in hotel sites sightings of modernity's historical ruins, while surrealist pursuits of the marvellous are sampled briefly through mysterious and still resonant hotel settings.

As a site that hosts and generates modes of living dictated by tourism, leisure, and new technologies of transport, the hotel, in its semi-private/semi-public capacity, connects the notions of hospitality, mobility, and community with issues of gender, nation, and class, explored in the first section, "Hospitalities, Communities." During and after World War I, the hotel enables but also limits mobility, becoming a biopolitical threshold and a multi-purpose space functioning as camp, prison, and hospital, as Robbie Moore shows in his account of the Rotterdam NASM hotel for immigrants on their way to the USA, as well as the hotel turned into war hospital in May Sinclair's *A Journal of Impressions in Belgium*. Although both hotels are preoccupied with cleanliness, discipline, and control, they also might become, as Sinclair suggests in her journal, thresholds to the new, a new state of being or even a form of transcendence. After the war, the hotel provides a setting for and an insight into avant-garde mobilities and collaborative modernisms. Focusing on Mary Butts's short story "The House-Party," Joel Hawkes discusses the Hotel Welcome in the French Riviera in the 1920s, which hosted Butts, Cocteau, and other modernist artists. Constituting a type of artwork, the Hotel Welcome is in Butts's story an embodied, multi-media performance and a stage of layered and intersecting practices that enable both intellectual exchange and aesthetic innovation.

In the work of other modernist authors, hotels become the stage for performances of wealth and leisure, creating a hotel culture that purports to transcend national, cultural, and individual differences. For Bettina Matthias, such performances of status exceed traditional ways of belonging and reveal a European "reckoning" with what could be labelled the Americanization of "good society" at the turn of the century. Reading hotels in authors such as Henry James, Stefan Zweig, and Meinrad Inglin, Matthias shows that the European leisure class often snubbed the newly rich American elite despite Europe's dependence on American money, thus undermining the hotels' transnational promise. The section ends in 1940s Egypt, in the colonial hotels of Durrell's *Alexandria Quartet*, which, as Athanasios Dimakis argues, express the author's conflicted stance towards empire. In the tetralogy, mobility and hospitality become imbued with decadence and morbidity. Durrell's Alexandrian hotels are spaces that evoke both progress and deterioration, colonial authority and its decline, through their transformation into imperial spaces of decadence and waste.

The second section, "Rooms, Views," zooms into the interior spaces of the hotel and then looks out again from within. In the hotel room, affective, embodied states and personal and political visions generate a modernist poetics of space. Explored here is the premise that experimentation with form is integrally related to the distinctive spatial and temporal experience of the hotel. At the same time, hotel rooms are sites of performance of the self, of transgression and transformation. In Shawna Ross's analysis of Forster's *A Room with a View,* the hotel is a space of transcultural transformation for the British abroad, who negotiate national sentiment, recreated in Italian settings, with feelings of displacement and groundlessness. For Lucy, Forster's protagonist, the pension's failure to offer authentic experience, the view she wishes to possess, paradoxically generates transcultural awakenings, and transforms her into a proxy "Forsterian liberal humanist." Displacement, on the other hand, leads to visionary experience in H.D.'s hotel stays and stories. As Polly Hember shows, for H.D., hotel rooms become conduits for visions and subsequently for intermedial states of consciousness which blur the boundaries between dream and reality, past and present. The visions recorded in *Notes on Thought and Vision* and *Tribute to Freud* as well as in the short story "Mira-Mare" lead to intense moments of revelation. The relation between the hotel room and gendered subjectivity also features in the work of Djuna Barnes and Anaïs Nin. According to Josie Cray, in Barnes's *Nightwood* and Nin's *House of Incest,* the hotel room with its excessive features becomes a queer space of sexual agency and transgression. Here surrealist images and motifs convey the submergence of bodies in hotel rooms and point to the room's ambivalent potential for flux, violence, and change shaping its transient inhabitants. Excess and performance also define Denton Welch's Camp fiction in which the hotel develops into a space of queer becomings. As Allan Pero argues, in Welch's *In Youth Is Pleasure,* the liminal space of the hotel mirrors the liminal age of adolescence, bringing confusion, loss, and anxiety rather than pleasure. The hotel in his reading becomes an allegorical space of Camp form and aesthetic.

The third section of the volume, "Labour, Love," deals with sociopolitical, emotional, and sexual conflicts manifested in and by the hotel as literal and metaphorical space. James Joyce's Ormond Hotel, as a space of work, birth, and death, is for Emma Short paradigmatic of the modernist interest in the mundane, shattering the illusion of glamour, opulence, and exclusivity that grand hotels of the same period purveyed. Joyce's hotels in *Ulysses* connect class, sexuality, and morality to question existing power structures. Whether grand or modest, hotels are related to consumerism, and, like department stores, they impose themselves on the urban landscape exposing modernity's material base. In Ulrike Zitzlsperger's analysis of Vicki Baum and Joseph Roth, hotels are not places of wealth and leisure but systems of labour, with "invisible" members of staff moving from the marginal to the central spaces of the hotel and applying pressure to the conservative insularity that hotels try to retain. Both writers allow for representative case studies of the connections between the hotels and the department store, with Baum showcasing the interaction between "types" of guests and employees in 1920s Germany and Roth reflecting on post-World War I European spaces that served as markers of transience. Similarly, as Tyler Schmidt argues, Elizabeth Bishop and Ann Petry negotiate tensions between guest and employees, exposing racial and class transgressions and conflicts. They also raise questions about African-American manual and affective labour in the hotel industry as well as the ethics of interracial intimacy and the articulations of whiteness. Bishop's poem "In a cheap hotel" and Petry's novel *The Narrows* illustrate the material conditions of the Harlem hotel, a microcosm of the opposition between white privilege and commodified blackness in postwar New York.

The fourth section, "Theory, Design," examines the architecture and design of hotels as a way of reflecting on modernity and modernism. Hotels suggest for many central European authors the cultural decline associated with bourgeois society before World War I but also the rise of a new era of increased mobility and mass tourism. Focusing on the revolving door at the hotel entrance, Rajesh Heynickx sees the lobby as a vortex, a place of unending and unsettling movement in authors such as Roth and Robert Musil, for whom the spaces of Viennese hotels after the war evoke the decline of Europe's imperial grandeur and the emergence of an era of generalized uncertainty. In Vienna lobbies were spaces of nostalgia for a decaying empire, but they also created a hub which promised to facilitate connections between its remote parts. The revolving door symbolizes these connections as well as the flow and sharp changes of modern life. The relation between hotel and cultural decline is also broached in John Hoffmann's reading of Georg Lukács's metaphor of the "Grand Hotel Abyss," inspired by Vienna's grand establishments. In his reading, the hotel functions as a trope for understanding the fusion of ethical radicalism with conservatism born of material luxury and political privilege. Hoffmann interprets Lukács's design of the "Hotel Abyss" through the critic's earlier writings, *The Theory of the Novel* and *The Destruction of Reason*, arguing that the imaginary hotel serves as a basis for exploring Lukács's critique of modernism. The last essay of the section looks forward to the Jet Age. Approaching the topic from the perspective of modernism's architectural history, Bruce Peter explores the origins of the International Style, American-financed hotels, and the hybridization of architectural styles which reflected the hotels' new, diverse clienteles and the global mobilities that business or tourist guests embodied. The architecture and interior design of these hotels of the late 1940s quickly spread from American cities to Caribbean resorts and elsewhere embodying the transcultural spaces of modernity.

This volume positions this distinctive space within the broader map of modernism's dynamic life and legacy, and proposes it as a site of generative and multidimensional critical engagement. Enveloping the traces of presences or absences, hotels are key landmarks in the intellectual geography of modernism. The hotel narratives explored through the chapters evoke personal and political crises that derive from or unfold in dynamic hotel spaces. Shared by all the contributions to this volume is the recognition of modernism's peculiarly troubled, daring, performative, aesthetically and politically transformative hotel experiences, or in other words what this volume calls *hotel modernisms*.

Notes

1 While in the contexts of the New Modernist Studies and Spatial Humanities scholars have focused on the connections between modernism and mobility (Chalk 2014, Burden 2015, and Bradshaw et al. [eds.] 2016), modernism and community from a cosmopolitan or transnational perspective (Berman 2001 and Pollentier and Wilson [eds.] 2019), or urban and global geographies (Thacker 2003 and Riquet and Kollman [eds.] 2018), none have focused on the hotel as a distinctive modernist setting. A notable exception is perhaps Fredric Jameson's *Postmodernism, or the Logic of Late Capitalism* that inaugurated the "spatial turn" in critical theory (1991, 154), and featured a now emblematic reading of the Bonaventura Hotel.
2 Edith Wharton is said to have written this poem after a night spent with her lover William Morton Fullerton at the Charing Cross Hotel in London (Suite 92) on the 4th of June 1909 (Lee 2008, 336; Borish 1995, 30). On Wharton's extensive and colourful life in travel, see Lee (2008) as well as her own travel writing, such as *A Motor-Flight through France* (1908) and *In Morocco* (1919).

Works Cited

Avermaete, Tom, and Anne Massey. 2013. Introduction—Hotel Lobbies: Anonymous Domesticity and Public Discretion. In *Hotel Lobbies and Lounges: The Architecture of Professional Hospitality*, edited by Tom Avermaete and Anne Massey, 1–2. London: Routledge.
Benjamin, Walter. 2002. *The Arcades Project*. Translated by Howard Eiland and Kevin McLaughlin. Cambridge, MA: Belknap Press of Harvard University Press.
Berger, Molly W. 2011. *Hotel Dreams: Luxury, Technology, and Urban Ambition in America, 1829–1929*. Baltimore: Johns Hopkins University Press.
Berman, Jessica. 2001. *Modernist Fiction, Cosmopolitanism and the Politics of Community*. Cambridge: Cambridge University Press.
Black, Barbara. 2019. *Hotel London: How Victorian Commercial Hospitality Shaped a Nation and its Stories*. Columbus, OH: Ohio State University Press.
Borish, Elaine. 1995. *Literary Lodgings*. 2nd ed. Boulder, CO: Fidelio Press.

Bradshaw, David, Laura Marcus, and Rebecca Roach, eds. 2016. *Moving Modernisms: Motion, Technology, and Modernity*. Oxford: Oxford University Press.
Burden, Robert. 2015. *Travel, Modernism and Modernity*. Farnham: Ashgate.
Chalk, Bridget T. 2014. *Modernism and Mobility: The Passport and Cosmopolitan Experience*. New York: Palgrave Macmillan.
Davidson, Robert A. 2018. *The Hotel: Occupied Space*. Toronto: University of Toronto Press.
Despotopoulou, Anna. 2018. "'Monuments of an Artless Age': Hotels and Women's Mobility in the Work of Henry James." *Studies in the Novel* 50 (4): 501–22.
Elbert, Monika M., and Susanne Schmid, eds. 2017. *Anglo-American Travelers and the Hotel Experience in Nineteenth-Century Literature*. New York: Routledge.
James, Henry. 1994. *The American Scene*. New York: Penguin.
James, Henry. [1878] 1999. "Daisy Miller." *Complete Stories, 1874–1884*, 238–95. New York: Library of America.
James, Kevin J. 2018. *Histories, Meanings and Representations of the Modern Hotel*. Bristol: Channel View Publications.
Jameson, Fredric. 1991. *Postmodernism, or, the Cultural Logic of Late Capitalism*. Durham: Duke University Press.
Lee, Hermione. 2008. *Edith Wharton*. New York: Vintage.
Matthias, Bettina. 2006. *The Hotel as Setting in Early Twentieth-Century German and Austrian Literature: Checking in to Tell a Story*. London: Camden House.
Moore, Robbie. 2021. *Hotel Modernity: Corporate Space in Literature and Film*. Edinburgh: Edinburgh University Press.
Pollentier, Caroline, and Sarah Wilson, eds. 2019. *Modernist Communities across Culture and Media*. Gainesville: University of Florida Press.
Riquet, Johannes, and Elizabeth Kollman, eds. 2018. *Spatial Modernities: Geography, Narrative, Imaginaries*. New York: Routledge.
Roth, Joseph. 2015. *The Hotel Years*. Edited and translated by Michael Hofmann. London: Granta.
Sandoval-Strausz, A. K. 2007. *Hotel: An American History*. New Haven: Yale University Press.
Short, Emma. 2019. *Mobility and the Hotel in Modern Literature: Passing Through*. Cham: Palgrave.
Thacker, Andrew. 2003. *Moving through Modernity: Space and Geography in Modernism*. Manchester: Manchester University Press.
van Lennep, D. J. 1987 [1969]. "The Hotel Room." In *Phenomenological Psychology: The Dutch School*, edited and translated by Joseph J. Kockelmans, 209–15. Dordrecht: Martinus Nijhoff.
Wharton, Edith. 1908. *A Motor-Flight through France*. New York: Scribner's.
Wharton, Edith. 1919. *In Morocco*. New York: Scribner's.
Wharton, Edith. 2005. "Terminus." In *Selected Poems*, edited by Louis Auchincloss, 160–63. New York: Library of America.
Woolf, Virginia. 1981. *Mrs Dalloway*. New York: Harcourt.

1 Hotel Trouble

Vassiliki Kolocotroni

Grand

Vacationing in the Cabourg beach hotel as a 15-year-old, the French Surrealist writer-to-be Philippe Soupault was introduced to a "singular" man "who sometimes strolled through the casino in the evening. His name was Marcel Proust." Soupault recalled in 1923 how Proust "always managed to astonish":

> Towards six in the evening, at sunset, a rattan armchair was brought out onto the terrace of the Grand Hotel of Cabourg. It remained empty for a few minutes. The staff waited. Then Marcel Proust slowly drew near, parasol in hand. He watched inside the glass door for night to fall. When they passed near his chair, the bellboys communicated with signs, like deaf-mutes. […] All the hotel guests talked about how Monsieur Proust rented five expensive rooms, one to live in, the other four to "contain" the silence.
>
> (2016, n.p.)

The hotel was crucial to the material production of Proust's work. He first stayed there in July 1908, a year after the hotel opened, and returned for seven consecutive summers. As Jean-Yves Tadié notes, it was at the hotel in July 1911 that Marcel "discovered a 'highly competent' typist, Cecilia Hayward, who would type out the first 700 pages of *À la recherche*" (2000, 557). "Since she doesn't know French and I don't know English," Proust joked in a letter to Gaston Calmette, editor of *Le Figaro*, "my novel turns out to be written in an intermediary language" (quoted in Tadié 2000, 557).

The witty remark is apposite for our purposes, as the hotel too may be said to perform an intermediary function by definition, facilitating serendipitous encounters, the products of which are in turn inflected by that mediation. In Proust's case, as we will see, the language, loss, and memory of others reverberate in hotel spaces and structures, from rooms to façades, contributing to the cognitive and emotional dissonance that so persistently and poignantly troubles his work.

DOI: 10.4324/9781003213079-2

Still standing, the Grand Hôtel Cabourg MGallery by Sofitel predictably trades on its Proustian pedigree:

> Is it the pomp of the hotel, or the poetry of his room that whispered to the author a few lines of his celebrated book? [...] Taste the gastronomy of the Balbec Restaurant, facing the sea, and offer yourself a parenthesis of wellbeing. In your luxurious room or suite, try some house *madeleines* in front of the ocean or garden view. This delicacy symbolizes for us the sweetness of memory and of the moment, timeless refinement and the art of living. In one word, your Grand Hotel![1]

One can only imagine what Proust would have made of this lugubrious pitch, composed in the deathless prose of luxury marketing, complete with choice servings of literary cliché. In a sense, it wouldn't come as a shock. His stays at the Cabourg (or "Balbec," as he renamed it in *À la recherche du temps perdu*) were always a kind of literary field trip, providing him with opportunities for social observation, and the kind of visual and auditory detail that would be grist to his budding authorial mill. According to Tadié, Proust "amused himself [in the hotel] by collecting clichés [...] that made one want to gnash one's teeth" (2000, 558). The hotel manager is the most consistent of such providers of cliché, spouting earnestly a mixture of hospitality copy and comical malapropisms. Proust's description in the second volume of *À la recherche* is pretty arch, if not outright grotesque:

> [...] a dumpy little person whose face and voice were covered in the scars left by the removal of many pimples and the addition of many accents betokening distant origins and a cosmopolitan upbringing, who was wearing tails like a fashionable gentleman, whose acute psychological glances at those who stepped off the "omnibus" usually enabled him to take a duke for a skinflint and a hotel thief for a duke [...] Class was the only thing the manager paid attention to, or rather he was impressed by anything which he believed showed high class [...] He sprinkled his commercial patter with choice expressions, which he misused.
>
> ([1918] 2003a, 241–42)[2]

Beyond the astute anatomy of snobbery, however, and the attuning of the ear and eye to the vicissitudes of forced interaction in what the hotel brochure calls, as if ventriloquizing the Proustian *patron*, "a parenthesis of wellbeing," the Cabourg/Balbec Grand is the site of a productive form of trouble for young Marcel. His very being there with his grandmother is but confirmation of one of those epiphanies that beset his formative years, and drive that Freudian *fort da* game of a book forward: "I was beginning to realize for the first time that it was possible for my mother to live without me, to live for reasons unrelated to me, to lead a life of her own" (2003a, 227). Even when not focused on animate subjects of strangeness (the manager, "the lift," as Proust refers to the attendant, fellow guests, or the maids, potential objects of desire), Marcel's gaze finds hostility in everything:[3]

> In that room of mine at Balbec, "mine" in name only, there was no space for me: it was crammed with things which did not know me, which glared my distrust of them back at me, noting my existence only to the extent of letting me know they resented me for disturbing theirs. [...] I was tormented by the presence of low glass-fronted bookcases which ran all round the walls, and especially by a tall cheval-glass which stood athwart a corner of the room and which I knew would have to be taken away if I was ever to enjoy any possibility of calm. Constantly glancing or staring upwards [...], I looked at the vast height of the ceiling in this belvedere stuck on the very top of the hotel, which my grandmother had selected for me; and in that part of me which is more private than those used for seeing and hearing, that part where one is aware of shades of smell, almost inside the self, an assault by vetiver threw me back on my deepest defences as I tried to repel it, in my tiredness, with a pointless, repeated and apprehensive sniffing. Deprived of my universe, evicted from my room, with my very tenancy of my body jeopardized by the enemies about me, infiltrated to the bone by fever, I was alone and wished I could die.
>
> (245)

The synaesthetic assault of the hotel room dramatizes the precocious passivity of the experience, replaying the motif already established in the first volume of abandonment and impending loss. It also sets up the moment of release from that bondage, however, and the salutary promise of another bond: "It was then that my grandmother entered the room and, as my shrivelled heart expanded, broad vistas of hope opened to me" (246). The grandmother's solicitations reverse the alienation, introducing one of those rituals of confirmed presence that punctuate the novel: having untied his shoelaces and helped him undress, she asks him to knock on the adjoining wall if he needs anything during the night. The three little knocks on the wall, answered by her with another three, turn the hotel room into an echo chamber of the call and response of maternal love. Though never a complete substitute, the grandmother's ready proximity on the other side of the hotel room wall amplifies through contiguity and simulation the yearned for heeding of Marcel's call by his absent mother.

Soon, in a similar game of always imperfect, precarious substitution, the Balbec hotel room will become the site of yet another kind of grace, with the advent of Albertine, one of the "young girls in flower" with whom Marcel will play at love:

> My room suddenly seemed new to me. [...] [I]t was merely the room I had lived in for so many days that I had stopped seeing it. But now my eyes had just begun to open to it again, seeing it from the selfish viewpoint which is that of love. I fancied that, if Albertine should ever visit me here, the fine slanting cheval-glass and the handsome glass-fronted book-cases would give her a high opinion of me. Instead of being a mere place of transit, [...] my room had once more become real and dear to me, had been renewed, because I could see and appreciate all its contents through the eyes of Albertine.
> (Proust [1918] 2003a, 502)

By volume 4, where Proust's narrator has been exposed to a metaphorical Sodom and Gomorrah, again in Balbec/Cabourg, Albertine will be sidelined, kept waiting by a grudging and melancholy Marcel, now visited by the spectre of what he calls the "true memory" of his dead grandmother ([1921–22] 2003b, 158), striking him in the involuntary act of untying his own shoelaces. The hotel is now the setting for a double reversal, as Marcel, at last comforted by his mother, realizes through the visible signs of her grief that she has in fact taken his grandmother's place.

In *À la recherche*, grand hotel rooms are mini memory-mazes; there the material traces of the presence or absence in the mind of the loved one (objects, sounds, smells) form both an inventory of loss and recovery, to be tallied against the threat of forgetfulness, but paradoxically too, to return to the maze, they are threads in the heart's handiwork of spooling and unravelling, gathering together and letting go, so important to forgetting. For as Walter Benjamin points out in his reading of Proust,

> the important thing to the remembering author is not what he experienced, but the weaving of his memory, the Penelope work of recollection [*Eingedenken*]. Or should one call it, rather, a Penelope work of forgetting? Is not the involuntary recollection, Proust's *mémoire involontaire*, much closer to forgetting than what is usually called memory?
> ([1929] 1999b, 238)

The work of forgetting takes Marcel to the second of his Grand Hotels, in Venice, a site defined by the work of another of his beloved ghosts.

As in Cabourg/Balbec, Proust's time in Venice was not wasted. Having embarked on a project of translating John Ruskin's *The Bible of Amiens* and *Sesame and Lilies* into French with the aid of his mother and two other translators in 1900, the year of Ruskin's death, he approached his first of two trips there in the same year as "a Ruskinian pilgrimage" (Ellison 1988, 432; see also Simon 2001); "[a]rmed with a library of Ruskin's works," as Tadié reports, "Marcel and his mother put up at the Hotel [Europa], which was then at the Palazzo Guistiniani" (2000, 365). Now used as the head office of the Venice Biennale and a museum, the erstwhile Hotel Europa has rather sensational pedigree. A mere 20 years before the Prousts' arrival, George Eliot had her honeymoon in the hotel in 1880, during which her husband, John Cross, made a failed suicide attempt. Richard Wagner wrote *Tristan and Isolde* there, and Ruskin's favourite painter, J. M. W. Turner, had stayed in the Europa in 1840. But Venice for Proust was about more than its roster of visiting artists and intellectuals—as he put it in an essay on Ruskin in 1900: "I set off for Venice in order, before I died, to approach, to touch, to see embodied, in palaces that were decaying yet still upright, still pink, Ruskin's ideas on the domestic architecture of the Middle Ages" (2008, 58–59). He finishes the piece with an extraordinary analogy:

> But if we are unable to relight the fires of the past, we would like at least to gather up their ashes. [...] And so it is not the accents of our faith or of our love that you will come to know, but our piety alone that you will perceive here and there, stealthy and impassive, busied, like the Theban virgin, on the restoration of a tomb.
>
> (61)

More than a labour of love, the work of translation, and the pilgrimages-*cum*-field trips to Ruskin's Venice are presented here as expressions of piety of the highest order: "stealthy and impassive," Proust rather theatrically poses as another Antigone. The occasion of the Victorian sage's death may partly account for the grandiloquence, and Proust's reverence for Ruskin's work pervades his writing and thinking about art, but the statement has further resonance through its refashioning in the Venice episode of *À la recherche*. In *The Fugitive*, with Albertine gone (*"disparue"*) and reeling from the news of her fatal riding accident, Marcel delays the trip to Venice while dealing with the complex emotional aftermath, before landing on the inevitable insight:

> The problem with people is that for us they are no more than prints in our mental museum, which fade on exposure. And it is precisely because of this that they form the basis of projects illuminated by our thoughts, but thoughts tire and memories collapse: the day would come when I would happily give Albertine's room to the first girl who wanted it.
>
> ([1923] 2003c, 522–23)

As we (and the novel) already know, however, the work of mourning is never done. In Venice's Hotel Europa at last, in the company of his mother, herself still grieving, Marcel's at times dazzled, at times dejected, moods and reflections never stray too far from that task:

> Sometimes at dusk on my return to the hotel I felt that the Albertine of former times, although invisible, was none the less locked deep inside me, as if in the lead-lined cells of some inner Venice, where from time to time an incident would shake the heavy lid enough to give me a glimpse into the past.
>
> (603)

Readers of a Freudian disposition will make much of this Proustian "as if," but it is the "inner Venice" that detains me here. This is not the place for a detailed tour of the mental architecture of Proust's Venice,[4] but it is in his retracing of Ruskin's steps in the city of palaces and dungeons that Marcel's voluntary and involuntary bouts of memory and forgetting do their work, providing an idiosyncratic, intimate gloss on every architectural detail. In turn, the stones of Venice speak to Marcel, as they did to Ruskin, and unsurprisingly in his case, they speak of remembrance in fugitive times. In this striking passage, it is the hotel window that addresses him—I quote it in full:

> I glimpsed this ogive [window] from far away, when I had only just passed by San Giorgio Maggiore, and as it caught sight of me, its soaring lancet arches supplemented its welcoming smile with a distinguished, superior, almost impenetrable gaze. And, because, behind its multicoloured marble balustrade, Mama waited for me, her face, while she read, surrounded by a light veil of tulle (as heart-rendingly white for me as her hair) which I sensed that my mother, on drying her eyes, had pinned to her straw hat partly in order to seem "properly dressed" in the eyes of the hotel residents, but above all to seem to me to be less in mourning, less sad, almost consoled for the death of my grandmother; because, having not recognized me straight away, as soon as I called out to her from my gondola, she sent her love winging its way towards me, from the depths of her heart, a love that would cease only when it had no object left to sustain it, on the surface of the passionate gaze which she cast intensely in my direction, which she sought to enhance by forming her lips into a smile which seemed, within the frame and beneath the canopy of the more discreet smile of the ogive illuminated by the midday sun, to lean forward to embrace me,—because of that, this window has taken on in my memory the sweetness of things that played their part beside us just as a particular hour chimed, the same for us and them; and, however replete with admirable form its mullions may be, this illustrious window bears for me the familiar features of a man of genius frequented by chance for a month at a holiday resort and led to strike up a friendship with us, and if thereafter, each time I see a

cast of this window in a museum, I have to fight back my tears, it is because it tells me quite simply the thing that I find most moving of all, "I remember your mother very well."

(589–90)

The window to which we are introduced via a Ruskinian architectural gaze frames and reflects back Marcel's mother as a patient, loving figure;[5] it is she now who waits for Marcel, and not the other way around, and it is she, rather than Albertine, that casts on him a "passionate gaze." These subtle substitutions evidence the work of both memory and forgetting. With his grandmother still mourned, the love for the fugitive, elusive Albertine in the vault, and his mother's emblematic presence confirmed against the luminous setting of the hotel's "illustrious window," Proust's "inner Venice" is for a moment at peace.

Ghost

"In October 1980," reports the narrator of W. G. Sebald's *Vertigo*, he travelled from England to Vienna, "hoping that a change of place would help [him] get over a particularly difficult period in [his] life." The account of his journey "All' estero" [abroad, or to a foreign land] is recorded in the Proustian double time of retracing one's steps along the elusive route of recollection:

> Early every morning I would set out and walk without aim or purpose through the streets of the inner city [...] Later, when I looked at the map, I saw to my astonishment that none of my journeys had taken me beyond a precisely defined sickle- or crescent-shaped area [...] If the paths I had followed had been inked in, it would have seemed as though a man had kept trying out new tracks and connections over and over, only to be thwarted each time by the limitations of his reason, imagination or will-power, and obliged to turn back again. My traversing of the city, often continuing for hours, thus had very clear bounds, and yet at no point did my incomprehensible behaviour become apparent to me.
>
> (Sebald [1990] 2002, 33–34)

This metafictional *dérive* takes the narrator on journeys within journeys, from Vienna to Venice, Verona, Milan, and back. He is accompanied by spectres—of people "he had not thought of for years," and some illustrious dead: Dante, walking ahead of him in the street, unnoticed by passers-by, King Ludwig II of Bavaria, Franz Grillparzer, and Franz Kafka. Compounding the malaise, the causes of which he keeps to himself, this protracted drifting exposes the narrator to consecutive, ostensibly serendipitous, but cumulatively resonant and recurrent blasts from the past. To borrow Susan Sontag's phrase from her essay on Elias

Canetti, Sebald's world represents "a complex mental geography" (1981, 183) in which, I argue, hotels are coordinates of restlessness, not respite, of uncanny repetition and often unwelcome recognition. They are in that sense spatializations of a form of trouble that is structural to the Sebaldian atmosphere, and to his peculiar rendition of a time regained without redemption. Three hotel scenes interest me in this respect; the first is set in Vienna during a stay marked by aimless, solitary wandering:

> In the ten days or so I spent in Vienna I visited none of the sights and spoke not a word to a soul except for waiters and waitresses. [...] The fact that I still lived in a hotel was at ever increasing variance with the woeful state I was now in. [...] Returning from my excursions at a late hour, I felt the eyes of the night porter at my back subjecting me to a long and questioning scrutiny as I stood in the hotel lobby waiting for the lift, hugging the bag to my chest. I no longer dared switch on the television in my room, and I cannot say whether I would ever have come out of this decline if one night as I slowly undressed, sitting on the edge of the bed, I had not been shocked by the sight of my shoes, which were literally falling apart.
> (2002, 36–37)

Unlike young Marcel's boots, the lacing and unlacing of which in the Balbec hotel room conjures up the presence and later "true"—because involuntary—memory of the beloved grandmother, Sebald's narrator's shoes seem a reminder of a ravaged state of being, and as the passage goes on to suggest, perhaps a reminder and remainder too of a collective fate:

> I felt queasy, and my eyes dimmed as they had once before on that day, when I reached the Ruprechtplatz after a long trail round the Leopoldstadt that had finally brought me through Ferdinandstrasse and over the Schwedenbrücke into the first district. The windows of the Jewish community centre, on the first floor of the building which also houses the synagogue and a kosher restaurant, were wide open, it being an unusually fine, indeed summery autumn day, and there were children within singing, unaccountably, "Jingle Bells" and "Silent Night" in English. The voices of singing children, and now in front of me my tattered and, as it seemed, ownerless shoes. Heaps of shoes and snow piled high—with these words in my head I lay down.
> (37–38)

Crystallized in the image of the "heaps of shoes and snow piled high," which, viewed historically, is a freeze frame of horror, made more poignant by the sound of children's voices, this association relies on scale for its effect, but also its vicariousness, its randomness. In a sense too, the "ownerless" shoes, of an exhausted stranger in an anonymous hotel room compound the melancholy passivity of the mental image. For Marianne

Hirsch, this might be a case of an involuntary "postmemory," the term she coined for the affective experience of unwitnessed historical trauma by the "generation after" (2008, 105), but for our purposes it could be argued that it is the hotel setting that both houses and accentuates this instance of generational trouble.

Vicariousness presides over the next hotel episode too: in "Dr K. Takes the Waters at Riva," the book's third section, the narrator records the peregrinations of another troubled traveller: "In Vienna Dr K. takes a room at the Hotel Matschakerhof, out of sympathy with Grillparzer, who always dined there. [...] For most of the time, Dr K. is extremely unwell. He is suffering from dejectedness, and his sight is troubling him" (Sebald 2002, 142).

Kafka, for it is he,

> sits like a ghost at table, suffers bouts of claustrophobia, and imagines that every fleeting glance sees right through him. By his side, close enough to touch, as it were, sits Grillparzer, a man now so ancient that he has almost faded away.
>
> (142)

The plaque on the wall of the 5 Spiegelgasse address, where the Matschakerhof operated until 1960, memorializes the frequent stays there of the man considered the leading Austrian dramatist of the nineteenth century, but their imaginary co-existence, like Kafka's occasional haunting of Sebald's narrator collapses temporal distance into a continuum of encounters under the sign of Saturn. Similarly, the postcard sent by Kafka to his fiancée from the Sandwirth Hotel in Venice, which Sebald reproduces in that section, though it seems at first sight but a signature move of adding a visual clue to the text, a fragment in the word-image collage of his writing, is also another doubling, or ghosting device:

> Towards evening, in the sombre lobby, he writes once more to Felice. Now he no longer makes any reference to exploring the city. Instead, set down in hasty lines underneath the hotel's letterhead with its pretty steam yachts, there are references to his mounting despair. That he was alone and exchanged not a word with a living soul excepting the staff, *that the misery within him was almost overflowing*, and that—this much he could say with certainty—he was in a condition in keeping with his nature and ordained for him by a justice not of this world, a condition that he could not transcend and which he would have to endure till the very last of his days.
>
> (147–48; emphasis added)

Almost word for word, Kafka's writing repeats Sebald's narrator's own account of his solitude and mounting despair when in Vienna and Venice:

> the memories (at least so it seemed to me) rose higher and higher in some space outside of myself, until, having reached a certain level, *they overflowed from that space into me*, like water over the top of a weir.
>
> (82; emphasis added)

Is this a writer-epigone's subliminal mimicry, or the writing off of an unpaid, irredeemable debt? Or is it the sleight of hand of recollection itself, a kind of swindle, a fraudulent projection of the present into the past—after all, how else can history be experienced? The suggestion is built into the German title for the book, *Schwindel. Gefühle*, with its double meaning, "Giddiness" or "Swindle" (*Schwindel*), followed by "Feeling" (*Gefühle*).[6]

Finally, far from a nostos or an escape from the alienating effects of wandering, Sebald's narrator's "Ritorno in Patria" [Return to the Fatherland], in the book's final section, features probably the most subtly troubling of hotel experiences. For his stay in "W." (that is, Wertach, the southern Bavarian town that was Sebald's childhood home), at the Engelwirt inn (now the Gasthof zum Engel), the narrator reserves the most detailed, animated prose and forensic recollections:

> What now presented itself, in the pseudo-Alpine style which has become the new vernacular throughout the Federal Republic, as a house offering refined hospitality to its patrons, in those distant days was a hostelry of disrepute where the village peasants sat around until deep into the night and, particularly in winter, often drank themselves senseless.
>
> (2002, 186)

Registered on the hotel form as a "foreign correspondent," the narrator revisits the spaces of the inn that was once his family's rented home. He lingers particularly on the hotel's prized function room, "in which long tables could be set up for weddings and funerals, with enough seating for half the village" (186). There, he remembers the screenings of feature films and newsreels:

> almost every week we saw the mountains of rubble in places like Berlin or Hamburg, which for a long time I did not associate with the destruction wrought in the closing years of the war, knowing nothing of it, but considered them a natural condition of all larger cities.
>
> (187)

The phrase "Knowing nothing of it" echoes the "ownerless shoes" and the general feeling of dizziness, fraudulence, and confusion that besets, but does not absolve, the narrator. For Sebald in *Vertigo*, the great fires that turn cities into rubble never go out, and what remains, however hospitable or refined, cannot be forgiven for having witnessed the conflagration.

Ruin

Seeing, wandering, thinking, "as if through a veil of ash,"[7] as one of Sebald's emblematic phrases has it, returns us to the troublesome work of recognition. There is a paradoxical concreteness to this metaphorical logic of abiding destruction, which makes of spaces and edifices that surround or shelter us sites of memory and forgetting. Such sites may be actual *lieux de mémoire*, Pierre Nora's figure for the focal points of a national habitus that "anchor, condense and express the exhausted capital of our collective memory" (1989, 24),[8] or in a literal sense as the material base for the sighting of a past (personal or political) that may have become invisible but whose power remains. Hotels contribute to that concrete dynamic of encountering the past in the present, often in reassuring, preservative ways, but they also lend themselves to the kind of through-a-veil-of-ash scrutiny that engages the Saturnine imagination of writers like Sebald and Benjamin.

As Sontag puts it, "Benjamin, the translator of Proust, wrote fragments of an opus that could be called *À la recherche des espaces perdues*" (1979, 13). Indeed, Benjamin translated Proust in Paris, while staying at the Hôtel du Midi in Montparnasse from March through to August 1926 (Leslie 2007, 72), but Sontag is punningly referring to his unfinished magnum opus, *Das Passagen-Werk* (*The Arcades Project*), in the 1935 exposé of which, composed during another of his productive visits to Paris,[9] Benjamin cites one such lost space:

> "Turning back toward the Quartier Latin, one ran into the virgin forest of the Rue d'Enfer, which extended between the Rue du Val-de-Grâce and the Rue de l'Abbé-de-L'Epée. There, one found the garden of an old hotel, abandoned and in ruins, where plane trees, sycamores, chestnut trees, and intertwined acacias grew haphazardly. In the center, a deep shaft gave access into the catacombs. It was said that the place was haunted. In reality, it served for the romantic gatherings of the Carbonari and of the secret society Aide-Toi, le Ciel t'Aidera <God Helps Him Who Helps Himself> ." Dubech and d'Espezel, *Histoire de Paris* (Paris, 1926), p. 367. Gardens, The Seine. [VI,4].
>
> (1999a, 603)

Staying at the Hôtel Floridor, at Place Denfert-Rochereau, opposite the still-standing Barrière d'Enfer, Benjamin wouldn't have failed to note the palimpsestic trace in the address (Denfert-Rochereau was previously known as Place d'Enfer [Hell]).[10] But what interests me here is the snapshot of the ruined hotel that caught his eye, a portal to the catacombs

(Hell) and meeting place of secret societies (Revolution). Like Ruskin and Proust to Venice, Benjamin was drawn to the stones of Paris, though not as fast-disappearing examples of what Ruskin called the "heart-work" of Venice's builders (1853, 170), but as "ruined matter" to be "confronted by dialectical thinking," as Esther Leslie puts it (2007, 155). In this sense, the hotel in ruins above may be proffered as an example of the "dialectical image" that Benjamin was developing at the time;[11] as he put it in Proustian terms in the notes to his theses on history: "In drawing itself together in the moment—in the dialectical image—the past becomes part of humanity's involuntary memory" (2003, 403).[12]

This of course applies to a range of spaces of modernity, and specifically in Benjamin's project, the modernity of nineteenth-century Paris, stomping ground of commodity fetishists, urban planners, and revolutionaries. In that context, the hotel has dialectical image potential, and through a Benjaminian lens may achieve its full effect through its ruined state. Benjamin, whose life in flight had inevitably great hotel form, amounting to what Paul Fussell would call "hotel consciousness" (1980, 53),[13] provided the tools in his thinking for capturing that resonance, and in the citational form of the *Arcades Project* he recorded the remnants of the dreamworld of the nineteenth century captured in the moment of their passing. For Benjamin, "[t]he nineteenth century, like no other century, was addicted to dwelling. [...] Today this world has disappeared entirely, and dwelling has diminished: for the living, through hotel rooms; for the dead, through crematoriums. I4, 4" (1999a, 220–21). As Fredric Jameson notes, "[r]ooms are, indeed, always of heightened significance for Benjamin, as though the angel had driven Adam and Eve from the garden straight into a boarding house" (2022, 113–14). Through the excavation work of the Paris project, the waning of the "privileged spatial expression of a classical European bourgeoisie" (Jameson 2022, 114) would be traced in a sampling of a burgeoning modernism vicariously glimpsed. Emblematic for the project, and increasingly by 1937 its main focus, was the memory of Charles Baudelaire.[14] For Benjamin, Baudelaire was "a secret agent—an agent of the secret discontent of his class with its own rule" (cited by Jennings, in Benjamin 2006, 12). During his residence in the Hôtel Pimodan (now the Hôtel de Lauzun), one of Paris's *hôtels particuliers* or free-standing private mansions, as a man of letters, Baudelaire took pains to de-bourgeoisify his living environment, and instead, as Benjamin put it, "he set out to conquer the streets—in images. Later, when he abandoned one part of his bourgeois existence after another, the street increasingly became a place of refuge for him" (2006, 99–100). And in a fragment from the *Arcades Project*, Benjamin cites the poet's vision of futurity in a gesture of telling spatialization: "'The coarsest hangings plastering the walls of cheap hotels will deepen into splendid dioramas.' Baudelaire, *Paradis artificiels*, p. 72. <G,2>" (1999a, 841).

For Benjamin, the morphing of the sordid into the splendid required an allegorical, truly modern gaze, or, in another formulation, equally important to Benjamin's prospectus, a "profane illumination" ([1929] 1999c, 209), of the kind he identified in Surrealism,[15] and most notably in the quest of the marvellous in Louis Aragon's "incomparable" 1926 *Le Paysan de Paris* (*Paris Peasant*), which as he later recalled in a 1935 letter to Theodor Adorno, he had read with a pounding heart (Benjamin 1994, 408). Aragon's Paris peregrinations in search of a new mythology mapped for Benjamin routes and sightings of the superannuated, now unreadable signs and detritus of an outmoded world whose "latent revolutionary energy" could only be parsed by "that privileged interpreter, the surrealist *flâneur*," as Johanna Malt puts it (2011, 47).[16] In turn, hotels play a privileged role in the pursuit of the "profane illumination," especially those *maisons de passe*, cheap hotels where prostitutes purveyed their custom, and which for Benjamin stood in direct analogy to commodities on display in "those human aquariums," in Aragon's phrase ([1926] 1971, 28), that is, Paris's outmoded arcades, sites of passage and signs of the obsolescence Benjamin would go on meticulously to trace in his *Passagen-Werk*.

Sphinx

Hotels are enabling sites for Surrealism as one of modernism's most polemical fronts against bourgeois living. The relationship is symbiotic: not only did many of the Surrealists live in hotels, "or in hotel-like transient digs," as James Clifford noted (1992, 104), but their creative process and writings are testimony to that lived experience in a formal sense. As Wayne Koestenbaum puts it, "[a]leatory or chance-based literature exemplifies hotel liberties, the freedoms of anonymous address, of quick decampings and relocations, of dodges and sequestrations" (2007, 18). Arguably the most paradigmatic record of such aleatory pursuits, André Breton's *Nadja* (1928) bears out this observation. Through the "swing-door" (*porte battante*) that is his book arrives trouble in the form of a modern Sphinx.[17] In a sense, the figure is already anticipated: it features in passing in Breton's 1924 manifesto "Soluble Fish" (1969, 56–57) and in Aragon's *Paris Peasant*: "Our cities are peopled with unrecognized sphinxes which will never stop the passing dreamer and ask him mortal questions unless he first projects his meditation, his absence of mind" (1971, 28).[18] In *Nadja*, the eponymous anti-muse, a real-life,[19] deracinated, *déclassée flâneuse* is one of Surrealism's emblematic Sphinxes. Nadja is a poser of questions, but also the answer that defies all enigmas, at once a haunter and a hauntee, conjured up by Breton's opening Oedipal question: "Who am I? If this once I were to rely on a proverb, then perhaps everything would amount to whom I 'haunt'" (1960, 11). A "Paris peasant" of sorts, having moved there from her native Lille, Nadja moves with a "frivolity which is hers alone," with "that freedom" (71) and speaks the language of the timeless wanderer: "'Who are you?' And she, without a moment's hesitation: 'I am the soul in limbo'" (71). Displaying the features of a "fugitive sensibility or character, often 'feminine,' reprieved from the rigors of fixed address," Nadja is also a "hotel woman," in Koestenbaum's terms (2007, 70). In Breton's account in fact, a tellingly named hotel appears to have hailed her:

> We wander through the streets together, but quite separately. She repeats several times this sentence whose syllables she emphasises more and more heavily: "Time is a tease. Time is a tease—because everything has to happen in its own time." It is exasperating to see her reading the menus outside restaurants and punning with the names of certain dishes. I am bored. We pass the Sphinx-Hôtel, Boulevard Magenta. She shows me the luminous sign with the words that made her decide to stay here the night she arrived in Paris.
> (1960, 102, 105)

Though arguably a Surrealist in her own right,[20] Nadja is cast in the role of the evanescent spectre-to-be, and Breton's increasingly impatient reaction to her inscrutable promptings only confirms her fate as one of the casualties of the dangerous enterprise that living life as a riddle can be.[21] Her legacy, however, has not gone unnoticed. In the *Journal du dehors* [Diary of the Outside], Annie Ernaux retraces Nadja's memories. On the Boulevard Magenta she seeks number 106, the Hôtel de Suède, "once the *Sphinx Hôtel*," now a building site, its interior completely gutted (1993, 79; my translation). To the amused workers, Ernaux speculates, her gaze fixed on the hotel from across the street must have seemed as if she "were returning to the place of her memories, of love or of whoring" (79; my translation). The sexual interpellation of Ernaux by the builders' taunting laughter is at first glance a banal instance of everyday gender trouble, but perhaps too a conjuring of the elemental "free" energy of Nadja, once accommodated in the hotel. That the space is now vacated of any trace of that troubled residence, but still potent enough to effect the kind of transmission Ernaux set out to receive, adds an uncanny nuance and direct echo of Nadja's evanescent but lingering memory. Moving on, Ernaux reports the sensation of "follow[ing] on the steps of Nadja in a stupour that gives the impression of living intensely" (80; my translation).

Hotels in modernism cater for this impression of (re)living, intensely, vicariously (knowingly or not) the life of others; and there is something about the life of insignificant others in hotels, such as the Sphinx, that lends itself particularly to this experience—not only as a base for vanguard pursuits, or a remembrance of lives lost, but as a retracing, an inking in of faded lines of flight, a brush with the danger of unmoored existence. From the Grand to the little, then, hotels host modernism's trouble, and, in turn, as this essay suggests, may be approached productively as placeholders of its distinctive, persistent legacies.

Notes

1 www.grand-hotel-cabourg.com/un-peu-dhistoire/ (my translation).
2 This account of the disconcertingly "cosmopolitan" manager is reminiscent of Joseph Roth's 1929 sketch of "The *Patron*," in *The Hotel Years*:

> He is fluent in very many languages. There is not one in which he can write an error-free letter. [...] It may be that this is only natural, and comes with the territory. But what is unnatural is his way of always uttering the same banalities and asking unanswerable questions. "Have you come from very far away? Did you have a good time?"
> (2015, 182, 183)

For a discussion of Roth's hotel worlds, see the essays by Ulrike Zitzlsperger and Rajesh Heynickx in this volume (Chapters 11 and 13 respectively).
3 The social awareness and sensual assault recorded by Marcel may also echo the experiences of the self-declared "hotel child" on whose case the American sociologist Norman S. Hayner reports in a pioneering essay:

> "What I am is a hotel child," she continues. "I am a product of the hotel, just as surely as one speaks of a southerner or New Englander, or as a girl bears the imprint of a certain school or college." As a child she came to understand "certain aloofnesses and social differences between ladies in the hotel—certain abrupt departures and looks of intelligence" exchanged between her mother and other women. "In fact, I suffered as a sensitive child must suffer through coming at knowledge prematurely."
> (1928, 794)

4 For that, see Spurr 2012.
5 As Christopher Prendergast notes, Proust's "art of the image" often takes the form of a view framed by a window to varying psychic effects (2013, 130–31). In this instance, the practice pays an indirect homage to Ruskin too, whose texts, as Emily Eells puts it, were for Proust "an optical instrument offering an informed, illuminating view of the world" (2020, para 1).
6 On the fraught issue of the presumed responsibility of the postwar German-speaking writer to attend to historical guilt and generational trauma, and Sebald's self-positioning within that lineage and debate, see Caruth 2013, Huyssen 2003, Prager 2005, Sebald 2003, and Ward 2006.
7 The phrase appears in *Vertigo*, in the description of Giambattista Tiepolo's *Saint Tecla at Este*, a painting which the narrator

> ha[d] often looked at for hours. It shows the plague-ravaged town of Este on the plain seemingly unscathed. In the background are mountains, and a smoking summit. The light diffused through the picture seems to have been painted through a veil of ash.
> (Sebald 2002, 51)

8 Nora's monumental, multi-volume edited collection on the sites of France's collective memory (*Les lieux de mémoire*, published between 1984 and 1992) features Proust's *À la recherche* as one such *lieu*—see Compagnon 1997.

26 Vassiliki Kolocotroni

9 On the 1935 exposé, Benjamin's process and the structure of the *Passagen-Werk*, see Tiedemann 1999.
10 On the Benjaminian motif of the nineteenth century as hell, see Buck-Morss 1989, 53–54, 96–99, 102–104.
11 In fact, the concept seems to have had its own brief "hotel life": as Theodor Adorno put it in a 1935 letter to Max Horkheimer,

> In that memorable conversation in the Hotel Carlton [in Frankfurt]) which you, Benjamin, and I had about dialectical images, together with Asja Lacis and Gretel, it was you who claimed that feature of a historical image as central for the commodity; since that conversation, both Benjamin's and my thoughts on this matter have been reorganized in a decisive way.
>
> (Benjamin 1999, 1014)

12 For expansive discussions of the "dialectical image," see Buck-Morss 1989, Jennings 1987, and Tiedemann 1999.
13 As the editors of *Walter Benjamin's Archive* note, from 1924 onwards Benjamin "spent most of his life traveling" (Benjamin 2007, 328). See also Eiland and Jenkins 2014; Leslie 2007.
14 At the behest of Max Horkheimer and the Institute for Social Research, in 1937, Benjamin began to synthesize material from the Arcades Project into a book-length study of Paris after 1848 with Baudelaire as the central figure. "The Paris of the Second Empire in Baudelaire" was the only section completed and submitted for publication (Benjamin 2006, 46–133).
15 On Benjamin's mining of Surrealism as a Marxist project, see Cohen 1993. On Surrealism's revolutionary politics, see Spiteri and LaCoss 2003.
16 In James Clifford's terms, surrealist *flânerie* is a form of ethnography:

> The surrealists were intensely interested by exotic worlds, among which they included a certain Paris. Their attitude, while comparable to that of the fieldworker who strives to render the unfamiliar comprehensible, tended to act in the reverse sense, by making the familiar strange.
>
> (1981, 542)

17 As Breton declares at the outset: "I insist […] on being interested only in books left ajar, like doors [*portes battantes*]; I will not go looking for keys" (1960, 18). Benjamin found the analogy telling:

> [Breton] calls *Nadja* "a book with a banging door." (In Moscow I lived in a hotel in which almost all the rooms were occupied by Tibetan lamas who had come to Moscow for a congress of Buddhist churches. I was struck by the number of doors in the corridors that were always left ajar. What had at first seemed accidental began to be disturbing. I found out that in these rooms lived members of a sect who had sworn never to occupy closed rooms. The shock I had then must be felt by the reader of *Nadja*).
>
> (1999c, 209)

18 For a discussion of this key motif, see Mahon 2013; for figurations of the Sphinx in modern art and thought, see Regier 2004; for a deployment of the Sphinx as metaphor for women's participation in the urban life of modernity, see Wilson 1991.

19 Léona ("Lena") Camille Ghislaine Delcourt adopted the name "Nadja" because, as she told Breton, "in Russian it's the beginning of the word hope, and because it's only the beginning" (Breton 1960, 66). By the time she met Breton in 1926 she had worked as a sales clerk, actor, chorus girl, and prostitute.
20 For Penelope Rosemont, who included Nadja's poetic statements in a pioneering anthology, this "single nonconformist woman" was a "vital, active force in surrealism and did much to shape its mature outlook" (1998, 7, 28). Rosemont's view is echoed by Spiteri (2003, 61–62).
21 Nadja was interned in a mental asylum in March 1927 for having committed certain "eccentricities" in her hotel hallway. She was staying at the Hôtel du Théâtre at the time. See Breton (1960, 136) and Spiteri (2003, 61).

Works Cited

Aragon, Louis. [1926] 1971. *Paris Peasant*. Translated by Simon Watson Taylor. London: Jonathan Cape.
Benjamin, Walter. 1994. *The Correspondence of Walter Benjamin 1910–1940*. Translated by Manfred R. Jacobson and Evelyn M. Jacobson. Chicago: University of Chicago Press.
Benjamin, Walter. 1999a. *The Arcades Project*. Translated by Howard Eiland and Kevin McLaughlin. Cambridge, MA and London: The Belknap Press of Harvard University Press.
Benjamin, Walter. [1929] 1999b. "On the Image of Proust." In *Selected Writings Vol. 2, Part 1 1927–1930*. Translated by Rodney Livingstone and Others, edited by Michael W. Jennings, Howard Eiland, and Gary Smith, 237–47. Cambridge, MA and London: The Belknap Press of Harvard University Press.
Benjamin, Walter. [1929] 1999c. "Surrealism: The Last Snapshot of the European Intelligentsia." In *Selected Writings Volume 2, Part 1 1927–1930*. Translated by Rodney Livingstone and others, edited by Michael W. Jennings, Howard Eiland, and Gary Smith, 207–21. Cambridge, MA and London: The Belknap Press of Harvard University Press.
Benjamin, Walter. [1940] 2003. "Paralipomena to 'On the Concept of History.'" In *Selected Writings Volume 4, 1938–1940*, edited by Michael W. Jennings, translated by Edmund Jephcott and Howard Eiland, 401–11. Cambridge, MA and London: The Belknap Press of Harvard University Press.
Benjamin, Walter. 2006. *The Writer of Modern Life: Essays on Charles Baudelaire*, edited by Michael W. Jennings, translated by Howard Eiland, Edmund Jephcott, Rodney Livingstone, and Harry Zohn. Cambridge, MA and London: The Belknap Press of Harvard University Press.
Benjamin, Walter. 2007. *Walter Benjamin's Archive: Images, Texts, Signs*. Translated by Esther Leslie. Edited by Ursula Marx, Gudrun Schwarz, Michael Schwarz and Erdmut Wizisla. London and New York: Verso.
Breton, André. [1928] 1960. *Nadja*. Translated by Richard Howard. New York: Grove Press.
Breton, André. 1969. *Manifestoes of Surrealism*. Translated by Richard Seaver and Helen R. Lane. Ann Arbor: The University of Michigan Press.
Buck-Morss, Susan. 1989. *The Dialectics of Seeing: Walter Benjamin and the Arcades Project*. Cambridge, MA and London: The MIT Press.

Caruth, Cathy. 2013. *Literature in the Ashes of History*. Baltimore: Johns Hopkins University Press.
Clifford, James. 1981. "On Ethnographic Surrealism." *Comparative Studies in Society and History* 23, no. 4 (October): 539–64.
Clifford, James. 1992. "Traveling Cultures." In *Cultural Studies*, edited by Lawrence Grossberg, Cary Nelson and Paula A. Treichler, 96–116. New York and London: Routledge.
Cohen, Margaret. 1993. *Profane Illumination: Walter Benjamin and the Paris of Surrealist Revolution*. Berkeley, Los Angeles and London: University of California Press.
Compagnon, Antoine. 1997. "Marcel Proust's *Remembrance of Things Past*." In *Realms of Memory: The Construction of the French Past* II: *Traditions*, directed by Pierre Nora, edited by Lawrence D. Kritzman, translated by Arthur Goldhammer. 211–47. New York: Columbia University Press.
Eells, Emily. 2020. "Proust's Ruskin: From Illustration to Illumination." *Cahiers victoriens et édouardiens* 91 (Printemps) https://doi.org/10.4000/cve.6886.
Eiland, Howard and Michael W. Jennings. 2014. *Walter Benjamin: A Critical Life*. Cambridge, MA and London: The Belknap Press of Harvard University Press.
Ellison, David R. 1988. "Proust's 'Venice': The Reinscription of Textual Sources." *Style* 22, no. 3 (Fall): 432–49.
Ernaux, Annie. 1993. *Journal du dehors*. Paris: Gallimard.
Fussell, Paul. 1980. *Abroad: British Literary Traveling Between the Wars*. New York and Oxford: Oxford University Press.
Hayner, Norman S. 1928. "Hotel Life and Personality." *American Journal of Sociology* 33, no. 5 (March): 784–95.
Hirsch, Marianne. 2008. "The Generation of Postmemory." *Poetics Today* 29, no. 1 (Spring): 103–28.
Huyssen, Andreas. 2003. *Present Pasts: Urban Palimpsests and the Politics of Memory*. Stanford, CA: Stanford University Press.
Jameson, Fredric. 2022. *The Benjamin Files*. London: Verso.
Jennings, Michael W. 1987. *Dialectical Images*. Ithaca: Cornell University Press.
Koestenbaum, Wayne. 2007. *Hotel Theory*. New York: Soft Skull Press.
Leslie, Esther. 2007. *Walter Benjamin*. London: Reaktion Books.
Mahon, Alyce. 2013. "La Feminité triomphante: Surrealism, Leonor Fini, and the Sphinx." *Dada/Surrealism* 19, no. 1: 1–20.
Malt, Johanna. 2011. *Obscure Objects of Desire: Surrealism, Fetishism, and Politics*. Oxford: Oxford University Press.
Nora, Pierre. 1989. "Between Memory and History: *Les lieux de mémoire*." Translated by Marc Roudebush. *Representations* 26 (Spring): 7–24.
Prager, Brad. 2005. "The Good German as Narrator: On W. G. Sebald and the Risks of Holocaust Writing." *New German Critique* 96 (Fall): 75–102.
Prendergast, Christopher. 2013. *Mirages and Mad Beliefs: Proust the Skeptic*. Princeton and Oxford: Princeton University Press.
Proust, Marcel. [1918] 2003a. *In Search of Lost Time. Volume 2: In the Shadow of Young Girls in Flower*. Translated by James Grieve. London: Penguin Classics.
Proust, Marcel. [1921–22] 2003b. *In Search of Lost Time. Volume 4: Sodom and Gomorrah*. Translated by John Sturrock. London: Penguin Classics.
Proust, Marcel. [1923] 2003c. *In Search of Lost Time. Volume 5: The Prisoner/The Fugitive*. Translated by Carol Clark and Peter Collier. London: Penguin Classics.

Proust, Marcel. 2008. *Days of Reading*. Translated by John Sturrock. London etc: The Penguin Group.
Regier, Willis Goth. 2004. *Book of the Sphinx*. Lincoln: University of Nebraska Press.
Rosemont, Penelope, ed. 1998. *Surrealist Women: An International Anthology*. London: The Athlone Press.
Roth, Joseph. [1929] 2015. "The *Patron*." In *The Hotel Years: Wanderings in Europe Between the Wars*, edited and translated by Michael Hoffmann. 180–84. London: Granta.
Ruskin, John. 1853. *The Stones of Venice. Volume the Third: The Fall*. London: Smith, Elder, and Co.
Sebald, W. G. [1990] 2002. *Vertigo*. Translated by Michael Hulse. London: Vintage Books.
Sebald, W. G. 2003. *On the Natural History of Destruction*. Translated by Anthea Bell. London: Hamish Hamilton.
Simon, Daniel. 2001. "Translating Ruskin: Marcel Proust's Orient of Devotion." *Comparative Literature Studies* 38, no. 2: 142–16.
Sontag, Susan. 1979. "Introduction." In Walter Benjamin, *One-Way Street and Other Writings*, translated by Edmund Jephcott and Kingsley Shorter, 7–28. London: NLB.
Sontag, Susan. 1981. "Mind as Passion." In *Under the Sign of Saturn*, 181–204. New York: Vintage Books.
Soupault, Philippe. [1923] 2016. "My Strange Friend Marcel Proust." *The Paris Review*, translated by Alan Bernheimer (October 26) https://www.theparisreview.org/blog/2016/10/26/strange-friend-marcel-proust/
Spiteri, Raymond. 2003. "Surrealism and the Political Physiognomy of the Marvellous." In *Surrealism, Politics and Culture*, edited by Raymond Spiteri and Donald LaCoss, 52–72. Aldershot: Ashgate.
Spurr, David. 2012. *Architecture and Modern Literature*. Ann Arbor: The University of Michigan Press.
Tadié, Jean-Yves. 2000. *Marcel Proust: A Life*. Translated by Euan Cameron. London: Penguin Books.
Tiedemann, Rolf. 1999. "Dialectics at a Standstill: Approaches to the *Passagen-Werk*." In Walter Benjamin, *The Arcades Project*, translated by Howard Eiland and Kevin McLaughlin, 929–45. Cambridge, MA and London: The Belknap Press of Harvard University Press.
Ward, Simon. 2006. "Responsible Ruins? W. G. Sebald and the Responsibility of the German Writer." *Forum for Modern Language Studies* 42, no. 2: 183–99.
Wilson, Elizabeth. 1991. *The Sphinx in the City: Urban Life, the Control of Disorder, and Women*. Berkeley, Los Angeles and Oxford: University of California Press.

Hospitalities, Communities

2 "Blank, blond horror"
The Hotel as Medical Facility

Robbie Moore

Hotels by necessity are concerned with public health. As spaces that bring together crowds of transient strangers in close confinement—spaces where people dine and lounge *en masse*, and where the intimacies of beds and bathrooms are repeated along endless corridors on countless floors—hotels have always been anxious sites where infections, real and imagined, take place. During celebrations in 1857 for the inauguration of the US President James Buchanan at the National Hotel, Washington D.C., hundreds of hotel guests became sick from a dysentery-like infection, including the new President himself. Dozens died, including members of Congress and the President's nephew. Doctors at the time, dampening press speculation about poison and conspiracy, suspected the disease was caused by sewer miasmas emanating from beneath the hotel. The symbolically potent outbreak in the nation's capital further fuelled suspicion of these "crowded, hybrid" spaces (Reichard 2016, 179). Needing to appease an increasingly germ-conscious public, and understanding the potentially ruinous implications of an outbreak, "hotels were among the first commercial institutions to show the marks of the growing concern about infectious disease" (Tomes 1998, 172). American hoteliers were historically ahead of the curve in implementing sanitary techniques and equipment, from modern plumbing, water filtration, and germicide toilet devices in the 1870s, to roller towels, soap dispensers, vacuum cleaners, and sanitary dishwashers (Tomes 1998, 172–74). Led by the Swiss example, European hotels would follow (Bollery 2013, 11). The ability to wipe away any trace of a previous guest, and to make a room appear blank and new, was fundamental to the reputation of a fine hotel at the turn of the twentieth century. As the physician and sanitary reformer George Vivian Poore wrote in 1897, "Hotels are like hospitals in this respect, that guests know nothing of the previous occupants of their room, and it must often be that such ignorance is blissful" (1897, 22–23). In 1909, the Austrian architecture critic Joseph Lux dreamed of a clinical futurist hotel that would be "a synthesis of hospitals, wagon-lifts and machinery" (Heynickx 2013, 112). The idea was not fantastical: the turn-of-the-century grand hotel was already becoming hospital-like in structural, aesthetic, and administrative terms.

DOI: 10.4324/9781003213079-4

This hospital-like quality was partly due to the nature of hotel surfaces. Hard, bare, shiny, white surfaces—the kind idealized by sanitary reformers as more hygienic than dark, thickly-upholstered Victorian interiors—were becoming part of the emerging grand hotel aesthetic (Moore 2021, 66–69). César Ritz's brief for the Hôtel Ritz Paris asked for a "hygienic" and "efficient" building, free from "germ-collecting" wallpaper, ornaments, and heavy, unwashable upholstery. César's wife, Marie-Louise Ritz, claimed that "Ritz was one of the greatest civilising influences of his time as regards this point of hygiene and sanitation," raising the standards of commercial and domestic structures alike (Ritz 1938, 75–76).

The spiritual forebearer of the Ritz style can be found in Florence Nightingale's *Notes on Nursing*, which advocated for hygienic hospital wards made with "pure white non-absorbent cement or glass, or glazed tiles" (1860, 90), with highly polished furniture that "may be wiped with a damp cloth" (89), and without "Heavy, thick, dark window or bed curtains" (86). Like César Ritz, Nightingale demanded surfaces that were not only stain-resistant, but also "pure white": "A light white curtain at the head of the bed is [...] all that is necessary" (86). By the turn of the century, "white paint, white tile, white furniture, white uniforms, and white linens" were standard in hospitals, as Jeanne Kisacky notes, because these surfaces and materials made impurities visible, and therefore "promoted hygienic vigilance" (2012, 118). The most prestigious turn-of-the-century hospitals "installed expensive white marble everywhere—walls, doors, floors, ceilings, and trim" (Kisacky 2012, 118), to signify their respectability and success as well as their cleanliness.

It is not surprising, then, that one reviewer of the newly opened Ritz Paris in 1898 saw its resemblance to a hospital: "Were I afraid of catching tuberculosis—the most contagious of diseases—I should go to the Hôtel Ritz":

> There are no bed curtains. The window-curtains are of white muslin, so as to be often washed. The white walls would show the least speck of dust; so would the highly polished furniture. I cannot think of where a microbe could take refuge, unless in the carpets. [...] The bath is marble, and the walls are faced with Dutch tiles. The whole room might be "scalded" with steam.
>
> (Ritz 1938, 77)

The plain white bathroom is the exemplar of César Ritz's vision: a space in which the stripping back of ornament is most radically achieved, and where style and surface are most strongly determined by the practicalities of hygiene (see Figure 2.1). The bathroom, argue Ellen Lupton and J. Abbott Miller, was a "laboratory" and "aesthetic model" for *fin de siècle* modernism: "an instance of what design would look like unburdened by

Figure 2.1 A bathroom in the Ritz Hotel, London, 1910. Chronicle/Alamy Stock Photo.

historical precedents and styles" that was "poised to influence all areas of domestic life" (1992, 25–26).

The shared aesthetic and hygienic concerns of hotels and hospitals made them uncanny twins in late-nineteenth and early-twentieth-century culture. Each institution could easily mimic the other. Some sub-categories of hotels, like spa hotels, which offered hydrotherapy, and the so-called "hygienic hotels," which offered vegetarian "pure food" regimens ("Hygienic Hotels" 1874, 293), took on some of the appearance of health facilities, while some health facilities, like sanatoria, resembled hotels. Though a hotel visit is likely voluntary and not motivated by an existential threat to the guest's health, the purgatorial dailyness of hotel and hospital life is similar. The hotel guest and the hospital patient share the experience of restless stasis, of empty time beyond the regimens of work, of living in a transient community, and of depleted agency while giving oneself over to the care of strangers. "In a hotel, as in a hospital, I am not at home," writes Joanna Walsh. "I am required to do no home work. Ordinary things are done for me: cooking, shining shoes. I am rendered helpless. I have rendered myself helpless" (2015, 146).

This chapter is interested in the ambiguities of the hospital-hotel, the meanings that attach to (and slip off) its bare surfaces, and the experience of selfhood inside these spaces. It considers two instances when late-nineteenth and early-twentieth-century hotels were literally transformed into medical facilities: the use of Dutch hotels in screening the health of

American immigrants, and the use of hotels as military hospitals in First World War Belgium, as described by British author May Sinclair. Both of these examples show the interchangeability of the hospital and hotel forms in terms of design and organization, as well as the experience of their guests or patients. And in both examples, the facilities are subject to conflicting interpretive frames. The Dutch emigrant hotels are read as both austere and generous, controlling and freeing, to suit divergent political imperatives. In a Belgian military hospital, Sinclair formulates a metaphysics of the bare wall, reading the space simultaneously as the death of all movement and desire, and as a gateway to possibility and transcendence. Both examples display the constellation of affects experienced in modern spaces that uneasily combine care and control.

Waiters and Guards

In the *fin de siècle*, European hotels were co-opted as gatekeepers of trans-Atlantic immigration. The United States Immigration Act of 1891 excluded "persons suffering from a loathsome or a dangerous contagious disease" from entering America, and instituted health screenings for emigrants before they departed from foreign ports. The Act effectively privatized and exported the policing of American borders (Markel and Stern 2003, 761). Steamship companies were financially incentivized to undertake this task: unwell or suspect passengers arriving in America could be hospitalized or detained, or refused entry and returned to their port, all at the company's expense. Fines for transporting ill passengers were subsequently introduced (Feys 2016, 251–52). In response, the steamship companies began to hire specialized medical staff, and to construct or requisition large-scale emigrant hotels in European ports.

One of the most sophisticated facilities was the NASM emigrant hotel in Rotterdam, built in 1893 by the Nederlandsche-Amerikaansche Stoomvaart Maatschappij (known as the Holland-America Line). In the political and cultural imaginary, the NASM Hotel had a double life. In reassuring despatches back to officials in Washington, American consular representatives described the NASM as an efficient medical site for the management of migrant bodies. Emphasizing that the hotel was built "across the river from Rotterdam proper, far removed from the residence part of the city, and quite isolated" (Marine Hospital Service 1895, 73), officials underlined its usefulness as a privately run quarantine zone and a "place of otherness" beyond the city, where suspicious non-citizens could be contained and surveilled (Van de Laar 2016, 296 and 305). As the American Vice Consul approvingly commented in 1903, "[T]he hotel has been constructed in such a manner that, should the need at any time arise, it would be possible to quarantine 800 passengers within its walls as effectually as though they were on shipboard" (Peirce 1903, 35). In Dutch local newspapers, however, the site was very much imagined as a hotel, generously offering hospitality, and even pleasurable touristic experiences, to its guests. This doubleness is encapsulated by the Vice Consul, who acknowledged the prominent local narrative about the NASM Hotel:

> The company's claim that it is furnishing good lodging and board for emigrants at a low figure and at the same time protecting them against low boarding-house runners and sharpers, who would fleece them, is correct, and the Holland-American Line is entitled to a great deal of credit for the humane manner in which it treats and cares for its emigrants.
> (Peirce 1903, 35)

However, the Consul added,

> [W]hat is of more importance [...] from a United States point of view, is the facilities furnished the examining physician at the NASM Hotel for inspecting the emigrants as well as the arrangements for cleaning, bathing, and disinfecting.
> (35)

As Claudio Minca and Chin-Ee Ong argue in relation to the Royal Dutch Lloyd shipping company's emigrant hotel in Amsterdam, these facilities were imagined as combining "care and control, hospitality and intensive biopolitical inspection" (2016, 38).

At the NASM, migrants were first ushered into an observation shed where they were medically inspected and bathed in antiseptic baths. Their clothes and luggage were disinfected, and the hair of men and boys was cropped while the hair of women was combed, before they entered the hotel itself (Feys 2016, 269–70; Brown 2013, 41). American reports, focusing most intently on the hotel's "excellent plumbing" and ventilation systems (Marine Hospital Service 1895, 73), describe a site governed by cleansing circulations. The American Vice Consul sees an interior that foregrounds the imperative to wash, noting the hotel's "spacious wash and bath rooms, with modern appointments [...] located on the vestibules conveniently close to each dormitory" (Peirce 1903, 34). The report does not elaborate on the materials used, but an equivalent emigrant hotel on the Liverpool docks was reported to be equipped with "strictly sanitary" bathrooms and toilets with "every part of them [...] marble and tile lined" (Immigration Commission 1911, 86) in the manner of modern bathroom design. The Holland-America line also ran a "well-maintained and disinfected" emigrant hotel in Leipzig at this time, featuring "toilets that automatically flushed when opening the door" (Feys 2016, 268). In Antwerp, according to an American report, emigrant hotel surfaces were regularly disinfected with sulphur dioxide and chloride of lime (Marine Hospital Service 1895, 170). In the eyes of the Vice Consul, the plain, hygienic bathroom aesthetic extended to the aesthetic of the NASM's social spaces: he notes that "the dining rooms and coffee or conversation rooms are [...] necessarily somewhat sober in appearance in order to insure cleanliness" (Peirce 1903, 34). The moral rightness of this hygienic austerity is signalled by the word "sober," aligned with the hotel's policy of temperance.

Yet despite its appearance as a machine for washing bodies, the NASM still reads as a hotel in several contemporary accounts, because the bathroom aesthetic was not antithetical to (and was in fact constitutive of) the modern hotel paradigm. The modernity of the NASM's surface treatments and technologies, seen by officialdom as clinical and efficient, could alternatively be read as comfortable and convenient in the manner of an ordinary hotel. Dutch newspaper accounts for local readers do mention the hotel's quarantine function, but linger on intimations of care and hospitality, talking up the hotel as a site of touristic pleasure. We are told that neither expense nor effort has been spared to create the hotel ("Het 'Nasm-hotel'" 1893, 1); that the location is convenient (rather than isolated) for transiting passengers ("Het 'Nasm-hotel'" 1893, 1); that the coffee room is cheerful (not sober), with wonderful views of the Maas River ("Het 'Nasm-hotel'" 1893, 1); that the hotel serves healthy and abundant food at a fair price ("Holland-Amerika Lijn" 1902, 1); that it has a tastefully decorated room for business meetings ("Nederlandsche Amerikaansche" 1898, 2); that the hotel is equipped with electric lights, an elevator and a garden ("Binnenland" 1893, 2); and that the emigrants will have a great time here ("Binnenland" 1893, 2). According to an American newspaper, the NASM contains "all the modern conveniences of a first-class hostelry, with an experienced steward, assisted by waiters and guards" ("The Gates are Open Again" 1893, 1), pointing to its double life as a site of service and control.

Likewise, the emigrant hotel built in 1921 by the Royal Dutch Lloyd shipping company, Amsterdam's Lloyd Hotel, could be seen as both a leisure experience and a quarantine apparatus, with a disinfection facility and sick ward as well as a recreational hall that screened Eastern European movies. Enabling the migrant guests to be relaxed and comfortable benefited the shipping companies, argue Ong, Minca, and Felder, but leisure was always carefully stage managed within the bounds of the hotel's control. Strolls down the Amsterdam docks were allowed if accompanied by a Lloyd Hotel employee, an activity which both cultivated and controlled the emigrants' touristic gaze (Ong, Minca, and Felder 2014, 1334). The hotel thereby amplified the ambiguously pleasurable and unsettling experience of being "rendered helpless" (Walsh 2015, 146) by the apparatus that is taking care of you. These ambiguous affects can be read in the faces of the emigrant guests who appear in a contemporaneous documentary film about the facility. In scenes of washing and eating, while being subjected to the gazes of the hotel administration and the documentary team itself, the guests display a mix of emotions from hopefulness, amusement, and contentedness to uncertainty and apprehension (Ong, Minca, and Felder 2014, 1332–34).

A local Amsterdam newspaper claimed that the emigrants undoubtedly had an excellent time, with good food, a good location, and free medical care—as long as they submitted to the rules ("Een Goed Landverhuizersverblijf" 1922, 5). The simultaneous insistence on generosity and authority in accounts of these facilities can be understood with reference to Derrida's argument (written during another *fin de siècle* moment consumed by the politics of borders) that hospitality can be a gesture of power, a gesture that reinscribes the relationship between being-at-home and the alien:

> It does not seem to me that I am able to open up or offer hospitality, however generous, even in order to be generous, without reaffirming: this is mine, I am at home, you are welcome in my home, without any implication of 'make yourself at home' but on condition that you observe the rules of hospitality by respecting the being-at-home of my home [...].
>
> (Derrida 2000, 14)

The migrant trade was lucrative for Rotterdam, but it also generated racist anxieties about disease, with some local magazines labelling the transiting migrants as "unsavoury people" (Van de Laar 2016, 296). Nonetheless, the ascendant liberal narrative about the Dutch temperament asserted the nation's cosmopolitan generosity towards the Other. Debates about the Dutch legacy of colonial expropriation in Indonesia led to the institution of the Ethical Policy in 1901, reimagining colonialism as a moral project of guardianship and uplift—a posture critiqued by Dutch socialists as a diversionary tactic to maintain the empire while assuaging the consciences of the ruling liberal elite (Gouda 2008, 23–26). In a similar manner, the doubleness of the NASM and Lloyd hotels would have reassured Dutch liberals: the hotels stood as monuments to Dutch hospitality, even while carefully controlling and secluding the Other away from sight.[1]

For the guests themselves, emigrant hotels were formative in their interpellation as emigrant subjects: not only through the symbolic laundering of their possessions and the tabulation of their identities, but also through the architecture of the facilities themselves, with their rationalized grid of dormitories and bathrooms, and their effacement of markers of locality in favour of modern functionalism. The migrants' old identities were stripped away in these blank and anonymous spaces. If the bareness of these hotels signalled the emigrants' loss of agency and identity inside a bureaucratic sorting mechanism, the blank and wipeable surfaces also suggested a space which would not retain the marks of inhabitation, rendering it a space of transitoriness, mobility, and possibility—a line of flight away from the embeddedness of place. The emigrant hotel's aesthetic was a negation that was at once disorienting and liberating.

The Hotel Stripped Bare

The machinery developed in response to the mass migrations of the *fin de siècle* provided a foundation for the widespread hotel requisitions that occurred during the First World War. From Ireland to India, hotels were requisitioned as military headquarters, barracks, and storage depots, as internment facilities (especially in Switzerland), and as military hospitals and convalescent homes. As Kevin J. James argues in a discussion of the hotel's role in twentieth-century conflicts, wartime dramatically reveals the hotel's investment in surveillance and biopolitical administration, which are still present though less visible during peacetime (2018, 102–10).

The British author and public intellectual May Sinclair presents a rich and unsettling account of living and working inside a military hotel-hospital. Sinclair's account, in her first-person *Journal of Impressions in Belgium* (1915), registers the effects of the hotel-hospital on consciousness and the body. Sinclair was attached as a "Secretary and Reporter" to a volunteer ambulance corps sponsored by the Belgian Red Cross and led by Dr Hector Munro, a psychotherapist at the Medico-Psychological Clinic of London. Sinclair, independently wealthy from the sale of her books, had helped to establish the Clinic with a £500 donation. Some critics speculate that since Sinclair did not have the practical skills that the ambulance corps required—she had no medical training, no journalistic or accounting experience, and couldn't drive—she may have gained her place in the team by financially backing the expedition (Raitt 2000, 151–55; Jones 2018, 69). Sinclair's ambulance corps arrived at their base of operations in Ghent on 26 September 1914, as Belgian refugees poured into the city to escape the German advance. The corps operated out of Ghent's Flandria Palace Hotel, which had transformed into "Hôpital Militaire No. II" (see Figure 2.2). There was nothing for Sinclair to do the day after her arrival, so she sat and contemplated the hotel:

> this place grows incredible and fantastic. Now it is an hotel and now it is a military hospital; its two aspects shift and merge into each other with a dream-like effect. It is a huge building of extravagant design, wearing its turrets, its balconies, its very roofs, like so much decoration. The gilded legend, "Flandria Palace Hotel," glitters across the immense white façade. But the Red Cross flag flies from the front and from the corners of the turrets and from the balconies of the long flank facing south. [...] The great hall of the hotel has been stripped bare. All draperies and ornaments have disappeared. The proprietor

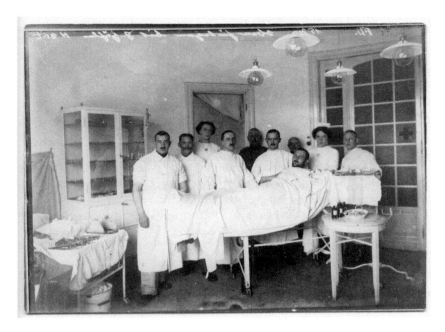

Figure 2.2 An operating theatre in the requisitioned Flandria Palace Hotel, Ghent, during the German occupation, c. 1915–16. Photo: Kommandantur Gent, Photographische Abteilung. Collectie Archief Gent.

has disappeared, or goes about disguised as a Red Cross officer. The grey mosaic of floors and stairs is cleared of rugs and carpeting; the reading-room is now a secretarial bureau; the billiard-room is an operating theatre; the great dining-hall and the reception-rooms and the bedrooms are wards. The army of waiters and valets and chambermaids has gone, and everywhere there are surgeons, ambulance men, hospital orderlies and the Belgian nurses with their white overalls and red crosses. And in every corridor and on every staircase and in every room there is a mixed odour, bitter and sweet and penetrating, of antiseptics and of ether.

(1915a, 19–20)

Two elements stand out in this passage. The first is its representation of hotel labour. The original set of uniformed workers—an "army of waiters and valets and chambermaids"—has been replaced by another army of uniformed personnel. Such military metaphors were already common in the language of hotel managerialism during peacetime: *The Practical Hotel Steward* invokes "the fundamental principles of military organisation" to describe the hierarchical power structure of hotel staff (Tellman 1913, 17), while *The Steward's Handbook and Guide to Party Catering* talks of mustering and inspecting waiters "in line like soldiers," each with a number and a rank (Whitehead 1903, 192). Large hotels strived to offer "uniform service" (Tellman 1913, 222) through a uniformed workforce. Sinclair's comparison of the peacetime and wartime hotel staff therefore reminds us that hotel labour was always-already militarized through the hierarchical discipline of hotel corporations.

The second element is the image of the hotel "stripped bare," its draperies and ornaments removed. Every room in the hotel appears to be similarly stripped; everywhere we find a deathly, vacant whiteness. The ambulance corps are billeted in what was

> once the sitting-room of a fine suite. [...] A pale blond light from the south fills the room. Its walls are bare except for a map of Belgium, faced by a print from one of the illustrated papers representing the King and Queen of the Belgians. Of its original furnishings only a few cane chairs and a settee remain.
>
> (Sinclair 1915a, 24–25)

Sinclair also attends to an injured man "lying in one of the officers' wards, a small room, with bare walls and a blond light, looking south" (180). Later she writes of being "shut in between the blond walls with the wounded man" (251). The repeated use of "blond" attaches a human characteristic to the space and aligns the room's bare whiteness with the stripped and implicitly racialized body of the soldier. Bareness and nakedness, and clothing and stripping, accrue dense figural meaning in the text. These pale rooms represent, on one level, the architecture of the afterlife. The Flandria Palace is seen as if through an X-ray, revealing it as a site for the administration of death. To be inside the white hotel-hospital is, for Sinclair, to be dead. Time stops in these spaces: Sinclair feels like "months of nights" (220) have passed sitting with the patient in the blond room after only two nights have lapsed. It recalls the infinite non-time of the purgatorial hotel in Sinclair's ghost story "Where Their Fire Is Not Quenched," in which the spirit of Harriet Leigh wanders endlessly down a "long, ash-grey, foreign corridor lit by a dull window at one end" (Sinclair 1923, 27–28). Borrowing Joan Copjec's description of the abandoned warehouses, empty corridors, and blank hotel rooms of film noir, these are "spaces that have been emptied of desire" (1994, 192).

Bareness is used in Sinclair's *Journal* to describe several kinds of displaced, diminished, and purgatorial conditions. The thousands of Belgian refugees crowded into a nearby exhibition hall seeking food and shelter have also been "stripped bare." Sinclair helps lay out slices of white bread for the refugees on "Bare wooden tables, one after another, more tables than you can count." As the refugees rest in piles of straw, Sinclair describes them as being reduced to bare life, or a kind of living death:

> This place is terribly still. [...] On all these thousands of faces there is a mortal apathy. Their ruin is complete. They have been stripped

bare of the means of life and of all likeness to living things. They do
not speak. They do not think. They do not, for the moment, feel.
(Sinclair 1915a, 55)

But in a text that, as Suzanne Raitt argues, repeatedly refuses political engagement to focus on the experiences of the self (1997, 66), Sinclair mainly deploys purgatorial bareness as a way of figuring her own feelings of thwarted mobility. Despite having potentially brought the ambulance corps into being with her own money, Sinclair is repeatedly sidelined by her male colleagues in Belgium. She tries to involve herself in hotel care work and in ambulance missions to the front and is continually rebuffed. So Sinclair increasingly spends time "sit[ting] in a hateful inactivity, and a disgusting, an intolerable safety" (1915a, 88) in deserted hotel rooms. She comes to hate the "blank, blond horror of the empty mess-room" (88) and refers to herself as "a prisoner in an Hotel-Hospital" (94).

The language of disgust and horror that Sinclair uses to describe the building and her situation seems to radiate outward from her own perception of herself as abject—as surplus matter discarded by the social body. In the same rolling, page-long, paratactical sentence in which Sinclair recoils at the "blank, blond horror of the empty mess-room," she recounts her habit of sitting "before a marble-topped table with a bad pen, never enough paper and hardly any ink, and nothing at all to write about," while also describing "the man with the bullet wound in his mouth" and other "maimed and crippled men trailing and hobbling about the hall" with their "blood oozing through the bandages" (Sinclair 1915a, 88). The logic of her sentence creates subconscious congruities between the horror of her own abject superfluity and the wounded men's aimless hobbling; between the inkless pen, her inability to write, and the man's inability to speak; and the excess of her own feelings, her own page-long sentence, and the men's oozing fluids. This is a text, Raitt argues, that works through Sinclair's feelings of shame at her own superfluity within a patriarchal regime at war (1997, 65–66). Sinclair, drawn to and repulsed by the horror of the refugees and the wounded, identifies with their experience of empty time and depleted agency. The imprisoning architecture of institutional spaces links them all together. Bare white spaces, argues Kathleen Connellan, can project an image of spatial order and uniformity, throwing into relief that which is non-normative or disordered. In such spaces, "nothing goes unseen," and this hypervisibility generates a fixation on the removal of dirt and disorder (Connellan 2013, 1545). Sinclair's feeling of abjection in the hotel is therefore closely related to the "blank, blond horror" of the ordered and uniformed space she inhabits. The normativity imposed by these spaces makes them carceral and claustrophobic for the non-normative subject.

And yet bareness is also, paradoxically, a state of possibility in the *Journal*. This is signalled by an extraordinary passage after Sinclair and her female colleagues have been "left behind" at the Flandria Palace for the first time by the men of the ambulance corps, and are "hanging about in gloom, disgusted with their fate" (1915a, 36). Sinclair, alone in the empty mess-hall, decides to trail behind an orderly into a huge hotel space that has been stripped bare and transformed into a sick ward:

> I don't want to describe that ward, or the effect of those rows upon rows of beds, those rows upon rows of bound and bandaged bodies, the intensity of physical anguish suggested by sheer force of multiplication, by the diminishing perspective of the beds, by the clear light and nakedness of the great hall that sets these repeated units of torture in a world apart, a world of insufferable space and agonizing time, ruled by some inhuman mathematics and given over to pure transcendent pain. [...] But the one true thing about this impression is its transcendence. [...] From the moment that the doors have closed behind you, you are in another world, and under its strange impact you are given new senses and a new soul. If there is horror here you are not aware of it as horror. Before these multiplied forms of anguish what you feel—if there be anything of you left to feel—is not pity, because it is so near to adoration.
>
> (40–41)

The "nakedness" of the hotel hall means that nothing is concealed or dressed up; looking inside, Sinclair is presented with what she perceives as the bare experience of human pain. With its rows of half-stripped male bodies regarded by Sinclair with something approaching adoration, the scene is a passion play rendered in the language of transcendence. Mystic transcendence in Sinclair's fiction and philosophical writing, drawing on her interest in idealism and early psychoanalysis, is expressed as a detachment from the self: when the self is stripped bare (Raitt 2017, 29; Phillips 2001, 56–57). "If you are tired of the burden and malady of self," Sinclair writes, "go into one of these great wards and you will find instant release" (1915a, 41). The ward fulfils her wish that her "irrelevant former self, with all that it has desired or done" will "cease (perhaps irrevocably) to exist" (23–24). This moment also gifts her with a heightened state of awareness. Sinclair believes she has been equipped with "new senses and a new soul" that allow her to see and feel reality in all its bareness and intensity. These feelings emerge in the *Journal* when gazing upon wounded men, Charlotte Jones argues, because they allow Sinclair to apprehend the body's vulnerability to annihilation: "Sinclair transforms this awareness of acute corporeality so that the potential disintegration of the body entails a dissolution of the walls of consciousness, a commensurately heightened ability to detect the inherent unity of Reality" (2018, 76). This fetishization of the war wounded in Sinclair's text draws an unsettling connection between the blasted body, the stripped hotel, and the transcended self, foregrounding the violence implicit in the process of stripping back.

The adoration of the wounded resonates with an article published by Sinclair in *The Bookman* in 1915, in which she explains her enthusiasm not only for joining the war effort but also for war itself as a social force. Sinclair writes that "Most of us" before the war "were ceasing to live with any intensity [...] and to feel with any strength and sincerity." War would return us to what she calls "naked, shining, intense Reality" (1915b, 10). Reality is closely associated with nakedness (in the *Journal*, Sinclair writes of the "pure and naked surrender to Reality") because the elaborate wardrobe of human manners and culture obscures the "primitive instincts"—love, violence, mysticism—that Sinclair associates with the Real. The nineteenth century, she claims,

> did its best to pretend that Reality was not there, to build up between us and the vision of it, the whole obstructive apparatus of material things. And at last, by means of the cruellest, the ugliest, the most brutally material of material things we are "hacking our way through." We cannot possibly come out of the War as unseeing as we went in.
> (1915b, 10)

In other words, war would cut through fussy Victorian inauthenticity, the wasteful stuff that gets in between us and the Real—war would pull down the drapes, so to speak. The stripped-back grand hotel, therefore, does not only signify bare life and death in the *Journal*; its very deathliness vibrates with possibility as a gateway to naked reality.

The emigrant hotels of the *fin de siècle* and the hotel-hospitals of the First World War were prosaically bureaucratic sites administering routines and events that were heavy with symbolic significance: places for ritualized cleaning, thresholds for crossing over (to a new land or into death), places of purgatory, sanctuary or detention. As Sinclair's *Journal* makes plain, both the disenchanted functionalism and the magical, atavistic, and fetishistic energies of these facilities were contained in their blank white surfaces. These surfaces imposed a claustrophobic bureaucratic normativity within these spaces, and symbolized a disciplinary regime fixated on cleanliness, but they also induced a delirious feeling of placelessness which might lead to death, to transcendence, or to a new world. The stripped-back subjects we see inside these stripped-back emigrant and hospital-hotels lose some of their agency and identity. This is a loss which Sinclair celebrates in her quest to join the world of uniforms and uniformity, hoping to be incorporated into something larger than herself. Sinclair's *Journal* imagines that war, bureaucracy, and the hotel will together obliterate the bourgeois subject; in her reverie in the ward, the Hôpital Militaire No. II stands at the portal of a new, aggressively stripped-back age.

Note

1 This is a dynamic discussed by Gibson (2006, 693–98) in relation to British border politics and refugee hotels.

Works Cited

"Binnenland." 1893. *Ons Zuiden*. February 8, 1893. https://resolver.kb.nl/resolve?urn=MMCC01:048286036:mpeg21:p00002

Bollery, Franziska. 2013. "Beyond the Lobby: Setting the Stage for Modernity—The Cosmos of the Hotel." In *Hotel Lobbies and Lounges: The Architecture of Professional Hospitality*, edited by Tom Avermaete and Anne Massey, 3–48. London: Routledge.

Brown, Kevin. 2013. *Passage to the World: The Emigrant Experience, 1807–1940*. Barnsley: Seaforth Publishing.

Connellan, Kathleen. 2013. "The Psychic Life of White: Power and Space." *Organization Studies* 34 (10): 1529–49.

Copjec, Joan. 1994. *Read My Desire: Lacan against the Historicists*. Cambridge, MA: MIT Press.

Derrida, Jacques. 2000. "Hostipitality." Translated by Barry Stocker and Forbes Morlock. *Angelaki: Journal of Theoretical Humanities* 5 (3): 3–18.

"Een Goed Landverhuizersverblijf." 1922. *De Courant*, October 27, 1922. https://resolver.kb.nl/resolve?urn=MMKB19:003538100:mpeg21:p00005

Feys, Torsten. 2016. "Steamshipping Companies and Transmigration Patterns: The Use of European Cities as Hubs during the Era of Mass Migration to the US." *Journal of Migration History* 2 (2): 247–74.

Gibson, Sarah. 2006. "Border Politics and Hospitable Spaces in Stephen Frears's *Dirty Pretty Things*." *Third Text* 20 (6): 693–701. doi:10.1080/09528820601069631

Gouda, Frances. 2008. *Dutch Culture Overseas: Colonial Practice in the Netherlands Indies, 1900–1942*. Jakarta: Equinox.

"Het 'Nasm-hotel.'" 1893. *Rotterdamsch Nieuwsblad*, February 6, 1893. https://resolver.kb.nl/resolve?urn=ddd:010166551:mpeg21:p005

Heynickx, Rajesh. 2013. "Tracing Tracks: Illusion and Reality at Work in the Lobby." In *Hotel Lobbies and Lounges: The Architecture of Professional Hospitality*, edited by Tom Avermaete and Anne Massey, 103–88. London: Routledge.

"Holland-Amerika Lijn." 1902. *Scheepvaart*, November 12, 1902. https://resolver.kb.nl/resolve?urn=MMKB19:000705278:mpeg21:p00001

"Hygienic Hotels." 1874. *The Health Reformer* 9 (10): 293.

Immigration Commission. 1911. *Emigration Conditions in Europe*. Washington, D.C.: Government Printing Office.

James, Kevin J. 2018. *Histories, Meanings and Representations of the Modern Hotel*. Bristol: Channel View Publications.

Jones, Charlotte. 2018. "Impressions of Modernity: May Sinclair, Ford Madox Ford and the First World War." In *Beyond the Victorian/Modernist Divide: Remapping the Turn-of-the-Century Break in Literature, Culture and the Visual Arts*, edited by Anne-Florence Gillard-Estrada and Anne Besnault-Levita, 69–81. London: Routledge.

Kisacky, Jeanne. 2012. "Blood Red, Soothing Green, and Pure White: What Color Is Your Operating Room?" In *Color and Design*, edited by Marilyn DeLong and Barbara Martinson, 118–24. London: Berg.

Lupton, Ellen, and J. Abbott Miller. 1992. *The Bathroom, the Kitchen, and the Aesthetics of Waste: A Process of Elimination*. New York: Princeton Architectural Press.

Marine Hospital Service. 1895. *Annual Report of the Supervising Surgeon General of the Marine Hospital Service of the United States for the Fiscal Year 1893: Volume II*. Washington, D.C.: Government Printing Office.

Markel, Howard, and Alexandra Minna Stern. 2002. "The Foreignness of Germs: The Persistent Association of Immigrants and Disease in American Society." *The Milbank Quarterly* 80 (4): 757–88. doi:10.1111/1468-0009.00030

Minca, Claudio, and Chin-Ee Ong. 2016. "The Power of Space: The Biopolitics of Custody and Care at the Lloyd Hotel, Amsterdam." *Political Geography* 52: 34–46.

Moore, Robbie. 2021. *Hotel Modernity: Corporate Space in Literature and Film*. Edinburgh: Edinburgh University Press.

"Nederlandsche Amerikaansche Stoomvaart-Maatschappij." 1898. *Scheepvaart*. April 9, 1898. https://resolver.kb.nl/resolve?urn=MMKB19:000704165:mpeg21:p00002

Nightingale, Florence. 1860. *Notes on Nursing: What It Is, and What It Is Not*. New York: D. Appleton and Company.

Ong, Chin-Ee, Claudio Minca, and Martijn Felder. 2014. "Disciplined Mobility and the Emotional Subject in Royal Dutch Lloyd's Early Twentieth Century Passenger Shipping Network." *Antipode* 46 (5): 1323–45.

Peirce, Henry Davis. 1903. *Report to the Honorable John Hay, Secretary of State, Upon a Tour of Consular Inspection in Europe*. Washington, DC: Government Printing Office.

Phillips, Terry. 2001. "The Self in Conflict: May Sinclair and the Great War." *The Literature of the Great War Reconsidered: Beyond Modern Memory*, edited by Patrick J. Quinn and Steven Trout, 55–66. Houndmills: Palgrave.

Poore, George Vivian. 1897. *The Dwelling House*. New York and Bombay: Longmans.

Raitt, Suzanne. 1997. "'Contagious Ecstasy': May Sinclair's War Journals." In *Women's Fiction and the Great War*, edited by Suzanne Raitt and Trudi Tate, 65–84. Oxford: Clarendon Press.

Raitt, Suzanne. 2000. *May Sinclair: A Modern Victorian*. Oxford: Oxford University Press.

Raitt, Suzanne. 2017. "'Dying to Live': Remembering and Forgetting May Sinclair." In *May Sinclair Re-Thinking Bodies and Minds*, edited by Rebecca Bowler, 21–38. Edinburgh: Edinburgh University Press.

Reichard, Ruth D. 2016. "A 'National Distemper': The National Hotel Sickness of 1857, Public Health and Sanitation, and the Limits of Rationality." *Journal of Planning History* 15, no. 3 (August): 175–90. https://doi.org/10.1177/1538513215607718.

Ritz, Marie-Louise. 1938. *César Ritz: Host to the World*. London: George G. Harrap.

Sinclair, May. 1915a. *A Journal of Impressions in Belgium*. New York: MacMillan.

Sinclair, May. 1915b. "Life and Literature—After the War." *The Bookman* 48, no. 283 (April): 10–14.

Sinclair, May. 1923. *Uncanny Stories*. London: Hutchinson, 9–38.

Tellman, John. 1913. *The Practical Hotel Steward*. Chicago: The Hotel Monthly.

"The Gates are Open Again." 1893. *The Indianapolis Journal*, March 13, 1893. https://chroniclingamerica.loc.gov/lccn/sn82015679/1893-03-13/ed-1/seq-1/

Tomes, Nancy. 1998. *The Gospel of Germs: Men, Women, and the Microbe in American Life*. Cambridge, MA: Harvard University Press.

Van de Laar, Paul Thomas. 2016. "Bremen, Liverpool, Marseille and Rotterdam: Port Cities, Migration and the Transformation of Urban Space in the Long Nineteenth Century." *Journal of Migration History* 2 (2): 275–306. https://doi.org/10.1163/23519924-00202004

Walsh, Joanna. 2015. *Hotel: Object Lessons*. London: Bloomsbury.

Whitehead, Jessup. 1903. *The Steward's Handbook and Guide to Party Catering*. Chicago: Jessup Whitehead and Co.

3 Hotel Performance and Its Remains
Jean Cocteau and Mary Butts at the Welcome

Joel Hawkes

Rondeau; or, Welcome to the Hotel

The Hotel Welcome, located harbourside in Villefranche, is more famous than the town itself, and today something of a shrine to the town's past guests, with the many photographs that hang on its walls a homage to the artists, writers, and performers who gathered, worked, and partied here during the late 1920s. The Hotel's website makes much of this era and in particular Jean Cocteau who found a second home at the Welcome in 1924. Cocteau was at the centre of the community of international modernists who assembled here. Visitors to the town included Cedric Morris, Francis Rose, Alec Waugh, Douglas Goldring, and Man Ray. Those who collaborated with Cocteau, like Stravinsky, Picasso, and Isadora Duncan, would visit him in his corner room at the Hotel, along with others like the British artist Christopher Wood and author Mary Butts, whom Cocteau would mentor.

Serge Diaghilev's Ballets Russes production of *Le Train Bleu* (1924) nicely illustrates the kind of collaborations that came out of such interactions at the Hotel Welcome, but also helps position Cocteau and Ballets Russes collaborators as important players in this social and artistic scene, giving shape to the more loosely affiliated modernist communities that moved between Paris and the French Riviera—and, importantly, through the Welcome. *Le Train Bleu* is based on a scenario by Cocteau, with choreography by Bronislava Nijinska, and costumes by Coco Chanel. Henri Laurens designed a cubist beach scene, Darius Milhaud composed the music, and Picasso reproduced his *Deux femmes courant sur la plage (La course)* for the curtain. The ballet is set on the French Riviera, where it and others like it were imagined, sketched, and created. Diaghilev employed other notable composers for his company, such as Georges Auric (one of the informal group of artists known as *Les Six* associated with Jean Cocteau). Stravinsky composed music for works including *Mavra* (1922) and *Les Noces* (1923), both choreographed by Nijinska, a dancer who went on to choreograph many productions, and all six of the company's 1924 performances, notable among them *Les*

DOI: 10.4324/9781003213079-5

Biches (literally "The Does," or "The Hinds") and *Le Train Bleu*. These figures would come and go from the Hotel Welcome, while Cocteau completed his stage play *Orphée* (Steegmuller 1970, 354). Butts corrected an English translation of *Orphée* while staying at the hotel, and scenes from Cocteau's 1960 film *The Testament of Orpheus* (the third in The Orphic Trilogy, following *The Blood of a Poet* [1930] and *Orphée* [1950]) would eventually be shot on the streets behind the Hotel. During the late 1920s, wild parties, ritualized opium smoking, and performances such as those by Isadora Duncan and her dance group from Nice (Steegmuller 1970, 372) added to a frenetic sense of theatre playing out at the Hotel. Cocteau later recalled that the hotel rooms "became [. . .] stage-boxes" (Cocteau 1966, 74), and Butts re-imagines the Hotel scene in "The House Party," a short story named after the English title of Nijinska's 1924 *Les Biches* refashioned as *The House Party* for its London debut in 1925. Like *Le Train Bleu* and other Ballets Russes productions, the Hotel Welcome housed an avant-garde collaboration of writers, dancers, choreographers, musicians, painters, and designers.

Chanson Dansée; or, the Argument and Performance

While the Welcome might be read as both a workshop and stage for the artists who congregated there, I want to propose a re-reading of the hotel as performance art. We might call this artwork *Hotel Welcome, 1925–27*, acknowledging the period in which other artists begin to join Cocteau at the site,[1] with Cocteau himself emerging as a directorial figure, or as Olga Taxidou puts it, an "emblematic [figure] of modernity" on whom "every creative aspect of theatre is seen to converge" (Taxidou 2007, 43). Comparisons might be made between the Hotel Welcome gatherings and the Futurist *serate* (soirées) looking to construct new notions of theatre, and with the "First International Dada Fair" (Berlin 1 July to 25 August 1920), which combined text, art, and performance (Taxidou 2007, 186–91). We see in this period, and through Dada more specifically, the emergence of what we understand today as performance art. Under the guidance, then, of Cocteau, another production plays out not just *at* the Hotel but *of* the Hotel. That is, I read the embodied practices in and around the site as practices of place. Framing the Hotel Welcome as a Lefebvrean "production of space," we see Cocteau, Butts, Glenway Wescott, Christopher Wood, and others read the hotel and town as theatrical performance, helping to construct what Lefebvre would call "representational space"—space as "*lived* through its associated images and symbols" (1991, 39). Cocteau saw "stage boxes" but also emphasized the practices of residents who "drew, created, visited each other from room to room" (Cocteau 1966, 74). The visiting is just as important as the art produced in this performance of place. De Certeau expands upon this idea of practice: "a street is transformed into space by walkers" in the same way a page is practised by readers (1988, 117). The hotel is practised, and, with conscious practitioners and audience, becomes a performance.

In what follows, I read Mary Butts's short story "The House Party" as part of this embodied multimedia performance of the Hotel and use it to track the performance of the Welcome. The story reveals Butts as conscious of the site as performance, and the story can then be read as the *remains* of a performance, or, as Rebecca Schneider would suggest, "as performative act, and as a site of performance" in its own right (2001, 105). The uncertain, shifting, nature of this short story highlights a multiplicity of hotel performativities: tourism, conscious embodied movement around and within the site, artistic production in many forms, and ritual action. Ritual, which informs much of Butts's work,[2] is a structuring principle in the story, acknowledged in art, party, and movement at the site. At the intersection of these exists a queer performativity and sense of a queered space—performed by and encompassing queer performers, along with a space of creativity, dissonance, difference, and blurred boundaries (Sedgwick 1993; Ahmed 2006). This queer space in some ways allows the performance and results from the performance—a queer performance that Penny Farfan suggests is "integral to and productive of modernism" (Farfan 2017, 1). To acknowledge Butts's ballet-influenced short story, and in the playful spirit of both story and ballet, this chapter's section headings follow the movements of Nijinska's *Les Biches/The House Party*.

Adagietto; or, Ghosting Past Performances

Many tourists and artists visit the hotel Welcome today to experience something of the Welcome's modernist, 1920s aura. Their presence, like any visit to a tourist site, is a physical practice of place, and nicely extends and conflates the ritual associated with the creation and aura of the art object with the ritual of the tourist pilgrimage, or a journey, which in Dean MacCannell's terms is undertaken to attach "one's own marker to a sight already marked by others," thereby reaffirming its worth, through participation in a "collective ritual" (1976, 137). The site is again physically practised, and in the self-awareness of tourists, who become an audience of themselves and others, practice again becomes performance, inflected with a peculiar sense of ghosting, as Marvin Carlson has understood it in theatrical performances on stage: the "present experience is always ghosted by previous experiences and associations while these ghosts are simultaneously shifted and modified by the processes of recycling and recollection" (2001, 2, 7). As you enter the hotel, you (the tourist) become both audience and performer, of past and present—here, now, to see the remains of past performances in the hope of glimpsing the "ghost" of performances past, something of its lingering "aura," and channelling, indeed re-performing, those previous practitioners. As with Carlson's reading of the stage, an uncanny effect is produced when past performance is bent to new purpose and form by player and audience. We might complicate our reading of the hotel further, as an archive of performance that holds remains securely, or as a "configuration," a series of "practices"—a performance, in Julie Louise Bacon's elaboration of the concept of the archive (2013, 73).

This reading of the tourist experience is not unique to Villefranche and the Hotel Welcome, but it is important in demonstrating a lineage of performance at this site—a site shaped throughout by tourist practices. An English 1885 guide to the Riviera by the Rev. Hugh Macmillan establishes the town's importance to this stretch of coast by placing the image "Bay of Villefranche" as the book's frontispiece; offered as the apotheosis of the guidebook's subject, the Riviera, we are told, "combines a greater variety of charms and interests" than any other region of Europe (xi). A 1924 travel guide compounds this sense of watching, movement and ghosting, again noting the "beautiful, natural harbour [as] one of the finest in Europe," but also as part of a landscape that might open up to the motorist—"villages hidden away, and quiet corners" revealed to the "public gaze" (Waters 1924, 115, vi). Cocteau, around a year later, would become an object of this tourist gaze himself. If tourists visit the Hotel today because of the 1920s residents, many also headed there for the same reason during the 1920s, to see famous, or indeed notorious, artists and writers. Art historian Georges Isarlo records driving from Monte Carlo to Villefranche "in search of atmosphere and finding Cocteau beating a drum with a sailor's jazz band in the Welcome bar" (Steegmuller 1970, 372). Conscious of being watched, Cocteau in turn observes the comings and goings of others, such as sailors from American navy ships. Cocteau recalls their part in the performance in journals years later (1957, 214), while a contemporary letter from Glenway Wescott (an American poet and novelist who spent much of the 1920s in France) notes Cocteau watching the sailors (cited in Steegmuller 1970, 359). Cocteau also observed the performance of tourists—"those invisible people who come when they will and keep an eye on us, were filling the hotel" (1966, 74)—along with other artists, writers, and hangers-on. Cocteau seems to acknowledge the tourist experience again as he recalls and establishes the scene with a guidebook-like sketch:

> Nice was effectively there on the left, Monte-Carlo on the right, with their shifty architectures. But the Welcome Hotel was simply charming and seemed to have nothing to fear. Its rooms had an enamel paint. A coat of yellow paint had been applied on the Italian style *trompe-l'œil* of its frontage. The gulf sheltered the squadrons. Fishermen were repairing the nets and sleeping in the sun.
>
> (1966, 73)

The scene is idyllic, but is prefaced with an acknowledgment of the spectral nature of the location and its visitors:

> One haunted hotel was the hotel Welcome at Villefranche. True it was us who haunted it, because nothing predisposed it to be so. There was of course the shaded street. There were of course the Vauban ramparts and the barracks which, at night, evoke the absurd magnificence of dreams.
>
> (73)

Originally published in 1947, Cocteau's reflection picks up on the spectral qualities of reminiscence, and perhaps that of fleeting parties and opium- and drink-fuelled gatherings, but also of the poetry of these. Indeed, something of a muted guidebook-poetic begins to come through, inviting readers to this site, to the memory and ghost of the past. Cocteau is conscious of future visitors, warning of the Hotel, "But let travellers beware. It is haunted" (74). They would, of course, come, and still do, to see those very ghosts and the remains of a performance.

Butts's short story "The House Party" captures something of this haunted tourist-practised scene. Butts arrived in Villefranche in November 1925, befriended Cocteau in January 1926, with the two collaborating, partying, and smoking opium together until Butts left France in 1930 after a physical and mental breakdown, partly induced by her cocaine and opium use (Blondel 2001, 253). Butts wrote much of her modernist masterpiece *Armed with Madness* while in Villefranche in 1925–26. The novel, a modern grail quest embarked upon by a group of "Bright young things" brought together by art, ritual, house party, and a queer sexuality, offers a group not that dissimilar to her imaginary gatherings sketched in "The House Party." Butts wrote the short story while staying with Peggy Guggenheim at Pramousquier in July 1927, a coastal location that held similarities to Villefranche. The protagonist, Paul, a troubled American is invited by Vincent, an older Englishman, to a "harmonious mischievous house party," ten miles along the coast from the "Casino of the great town"—a trip from Monte Carlo to Villefranche, though they are never named (Butts 2014, 203). Vincent will "present" him to the "Great André," a Frenchman who is like "lightning and Mozart," a critic/philosopher/spiritual guide at the centre of a homo-social/sexual scene cast in a classical mould. Clearly a homage to Cocteau (to whom Butts dedicates the story), André is known by reputation to Paul, who plans on "observing" the "great" man and his "crowd of lads" (205). Butts makes use of a guide book description and tone, similar to Cocteau's, to allow Paul, and the reader, to quickly take in the scene, alive with the everyday movements of sea, port, and fishing, elevated to the "eternal," or mythic, which the story takes in through Paul's failed spiritual quest for redemption and purity:

> [T]he open bay looked as if it were divided by a wall, pierced with round holes, blazing with circular light, behind which could be heard voices and music; the space between the wall and the quay shot across by launches turning and tearing, ripping the water's green back; and little ceremonies of recommitment to land or sea took place on the quay, as the commander of the battleship welcomed or was welcomed.
>
> (209)

The sense of movement quickens in this verb-driven scene of parties and boats, which are presented as if on a stage, and as something transcendent. The acknowledgement of "ceremonies" (209) offers another sense of performance, while the repeated pun, "welcome," gestures to the hotel's name and the movement that takes place around and towards it. Paul goes on to consider the theatre he witnesses between sailors on leave—a "spectacle" for many, but for Paul, who has been one of them, "a play of which Paul had seen the rehearsals. Might at any moment run off behind the scenes" (210). Butts not only sets the stage for her troubled protagonist, who must negotiate both a closed queer community and a spectral figure called the "Pimp" who threatens to ruin him (a story of operatic qualities), but looks to introduce something of the queer and avant-garde performance she observed in the community around Cocteau at the Welcome, in which everyone played a part.

Jeu; or, Reading and Watching Movement and Performance

Recalling a 1926 party at the Hotel Welcome, Cocteau records in miniature something of the various practices in performance. He is worth quoting at length:

> It all began with Francis Rose. His mother was a clairvoyant. In the dining-room she would get up from the table, approach some gentleman or lady and foretell their future. She wore linen dresses on which Francis used to paint flowers. He was nearly seventeen. Everything dates from the dinner party given for his seventeenth birthday. [...] Lady Rose had only invited some English officers and their wives. About eight o'clock a strange procession appeared at the bottom of the slopes which led from town to the harbour. Crowned with roses Francis Rose gave his arm to Madame Isadora Duncan in a Greek tunic. She was very fat, a little drunk, escorted by an American woman, a pianist and few people picked up *en route*. The stupefaction of Lady Rose's guests, her anger, the entry of the procession, the fishermen flattening their noses against the window panes, Isadora kissing me, Francis very proud of his crown, that is how this birthday dinner began. A deathly silence turned the guests to stone. Isadora kept laughing, sprawling against Francis. She even rose and

led him into a window recess. It was just then that Captain Williams, a friend of the Roses, came on the scene. He had a habit of bringing pigeons and rabbits out of his sweater and sleeves. He drank a lot. I supposed he had drunk a lot. He was holding a stick. He crossed the room, approached the window, and crying out in a loud voice "Hi, you old hag, let go of that child!" he brought his stick down on the head of the dancer. She fainted. Everything dates from that blow with the stick. Our rooms became, as in *Le Sang d'un Poète* ["*The Blood of a Poet*," 1930], stage-boxes from which henceforth we witnessed the battles between the sailors of the French, English and American ships. Christian Bérard, Georges Hugnet, Glenway Westcott, Mary Butts, Monroe Wheeler, Philippe Lassel lived in the hotel. We drew, we invented, we visited each other from one room to another. A mythology was born of which *Orphée* sums up the style.

(1966, 74)

If Cocteau's memory of Francis Rose's age is correct, the party dates to September 1926. Cocteau's rendition of the clairvoyant mother lends a mystical bent to proceedings, and from here multiple performances, theatrical, operatic, ritualistic, and of dance and party spill out, blending in a classical and modern spectacle. Artists, military men, and everyday folk (fishermen and stuffy relatives) collide; they are performance and audience, watching and watched, with faces against windows or staring out from "stage-boxes." Performances blur as the military man, Captain Williams is described as a magician, before his drunken assault on the dancer, Isadora Duncan, dressed in her iconic Greek tunic. The Captain resists a Dionysian scene but initiates another rite and transformation, ushering in an awareness of the performance they enact. Invoking *Orphée*, Cocteau casts this hotel performance in the mode of the classical mythic quest into the underworld, but also a "supernatural" and surrealist experience, like his play—a demanding modern performance that challenges conceptions of art.

One of Cocteau's main "performers" in this scene, Butts also perceives a classical theatre playing out at the hotel, the town having "been there since the curtain was rung up on the [M]editerranean scene" (quoted in Blondel 2001, 153). The language of the stage privileges a classical historicity, as Butts places the 1920s moment in a lineage of "Greeks and Phoenicians," "Moors and Genoese," exploring and fighting, "cut[ting] each other's throats" on the "stones" of the town (153)—high historical drama, in other words. In her poem "Juan-les-Pins," the Riviera coast reminds her of Crete; again aligning her experience with Greek antiquity, the poem's speaker "prays," "Set your stage and terrify them." More immediate observations of dawn at Villefranche produce a feeling of "holy calm" (quoted in Blondel 2001, 154), suggesting a typically Buttsian sense of spiritual experience sought through rites of nature and classical heritage. Butts, like Cocteau, then, positions herself in Villefranche in an ongoing historical and ritual drama, while her short story "The House Party" brings her vision of a "ritual re-enactment" that focuses on the "collective" (Garrity 2003, 207) even closer to Cocteau's "myth," also offering an underworld adventure in the back streets of the town.

Rag Mazurka; or, Movement

Another of the Hotel Welcome community, Glenway Wescott, also notes the ritual and theatre of the Hotel, where life was "not a series of parties, but one constant long party," with "impromptu dressing-up, processions, fireworks" (Steegmuller 1970, 372). As Arthur King Peters points out, Wescott's description of town and Hotel is like the description of an "opera set" (1987, 96):

> Washing on strings from window to window, worn out banners and ragged flags of underwear, with glimpses of dishevelled beds, and shapeless females leaning out of upper stories with thin dresses slipping off their shoulders, and all the ground floors breathing forth an odor of the salvia of a large beast.
> (Wescott, quoted in Peters 1987, 96)

Wescott also draws attention to the importance of the party, as do Cocteau and Butts. We might follow Kate McLoughlin's lead and read the modernist party as "performance, as display" (2013, 6), which is what Cocteau also reads in the extract quoted above.

Embodied movement is key here, and between 1925 and 1927, the Hotel Welcome was alive with movement. Butts notes this energy: "Villefranche is at its best: one roaring, sucking, mixed riot" (2002, 287). Francis Rose too, in his autobiography *Saying Life*, recalls the comings and goings, with Nina Hamnett arriving "perfectly dressed by Chanel" alongside the "untidy dramatic Mary Butts" (1961, 58). Butts records another train journey between Cannes and Villefranche, during which Wescott and Butts discussed whether or not they really were "a lost generation," while anticipating future readers of their work and the "necessity to be novelists [. . .] So much more to tell than Pepys" (2002, 246). In likening the performance at the Welcome to his play *Orphée*, and clearly aware of the ritual implications, Cocteau looks to explain the intersecting practices he observes.

Butts's story similarly seeks to house the performances of the hotel. Also conscious of the ritual implications of what she sees, her text pulses with movement. Hotel, town, and story flow in constant motion, the remains of a performance managing to capture that sense of "riot" she witnessed around the hotel. The opening line of the story anticipates movement, the performance to come, while simultaneously recalling something of the stillness of a painted scene:

> He wanted to go and stay with them, in the sea-washed, fly-brown, scorched hotel, along the coast, whose walls were washed primrose above the blue lapping water where one mounted to bed by plaster stair outside above the shifting sea, under the stars shaken out in handfuls.
>
> (Butts 2014, 202)

Movement is textually performed here: the verb-filled first sentence articulates the desire to go stay at the town, skitters through something like a jazz rhythm that often runs through Butts's writing. The two spondees and possibly a molossus, in the irregular but suggestively iambic syntax of "sea-washed, fly-brown, scorched hotel," the alliteration, sibilance, and hint of rhyme, and the added movement of prepositions, lead to the final image of a "hand" shaking out stars in an embodied moment/ movement that symbolically drives the whole sentence. This sense of movement propels Paul, the story's protagonist, towards Vincent who has invited him to Villefranche. And yet it is here Paul might come to rest, "under Vincent's wing," Vincent "cajoling, hypnotising away certain objections" (202). What might be read as a loss of will takes him to a land of "lotus eaters." The sense of a painted scene suitably frames this anticipation, but no rest is found, but rather, a performance enacted around André, its symbolic and ritual centre. Another oscillating movement between performance and "painting," a technique we find in Butts's other works (see Hawkes 2017), adds to the rhythm of the scene, an experience Butts describes in another performative landscape (her *Armed with Madness* [1928]) as "for ever moving, for ever at rest" (1992, 92). In this we may also glimpse the performance of the Hotel Welcome but also its remains on the printed page.

Andantino; or, Ballet and the Intersecting Arts

The art created at and about the Hotel Welcome is a documentation of that space and time, but also a practice of it. This is a collective performance. With good reason, Butts acknowledges Nijinska's ballet in the title of her short story: "The House Party" can be read as a kind of dance, an assemblage of various performative practices that she witnessed at the Hotel. The preface to the published score of Nijinska's ballet helps set the scene:

> The action passes in a large, white drawing room with just one piece of furniture, an immense blue sofa. It is a warm summer afternoon and three young men are enjoying the company of sixteen lovely women. Just as in 18th-century prints, their play is innocent in appearance only.
>
> (Poulenc 1948)

Butts's short story explores the interactions of those at a "house party" where, similarly, innocent appearances give way to an exploration of sexuality, or indeed ambiguous and deviant sexualities. In Nijinska's ballet, a ballerina dressed in a boy's blue velvet costume and the interactions of two other ballerinas help establish a repressed homoeroticism. Butts's story focuses on the homosocial and homosexual interactions of a group of men assembled around André (Cocteau). André might be seen to take the place of the ballet's "hostess," and perhaps something of Nijinska, who originally danced the part, survives in that figure as well. Butts's movement-focused, rhythmic diction and syntax compound this sense of dance, as do the mapping movements of characters in and out of the hotel and along the streets and waterfront of the town. This sense of multiple movements (of phrase, narrative, character, and intertext) recalls the collaborative multiplicity of *The House Party*: Nijinska choreographed the ballet, Francis Poulenc wrote the score, and avant-garde painter Marie Laurencin designed costumes and scenery.

The various movements around André in Butts's story point to a distinctly performative space. In 1925, Cocteau's hotel room became a central point—a place of pilgrimage, meeting, and collaboration. Collections of art objects in his room, made from "pipe cleaners and plaster," transformed the room into a kind of gallery space—pieces ready for the 1926 exhibition in Paris entitled "*Poesie Plastique— Objects, Dessins*," seen as adaptations of collages by Picasso and others (Steegmuller 1970, 334). In 1924, Cocteau spent many hours staring at himself in the wardrobe mirror in his corner room—a meditation on the self which saw him draw himself over and over again, picking up on repetitions and conflation of practice, art, and ritual. Christopher Wood's pencil and watercolour *The Hotel Welcome, Villefranche* (1925) offers a technique that recalls his *Romeo and Juliet*, Scene design (1926), created but not used for Diaghilev's surrealist ballet *Roméo et Juliette* (1926). The painting pictures a woman leaning over the Hotel Welcome balcony, with sea, boats, and sailors spread out below—a sense of the stage again, and with similarities to Cocteau's description of the hotel scene, quoted above. In 1926, painter Jean Dufy, known for his Fauvist and impressionist paintings of stages, circuses, and orchestras, painted Villefranche and the Hotel Welcome over and over again in bright oil paints. His brother Raoul Dufy likewise painted scenes of the town and hotel. The strong Fauvist colours of both brothers' paintings highlight their artistic process and perhaps that of the Hotel as well.

Chanson Dansée; or, Ritual, Mysticism, and Anthropological Observation

In watching and recording events they were involved in at the Hotel Welcome, Cocteau, Butts, Wescott, and others take on something of the blended role of artist, anthropologist, and ritual practitioner, mixing the "reproduction" of "performance art" and the "capturing" of events of the ethnographer (Auslander 2012, 54–55). In particular, observations record the ritual and occult interests of the period. While Alec Waugh, another performer of the Hotel party scene, writes more broadly of the "enchanted coast that has never lost its magic for me" (1962, 187), Butts activates more specific ritual and classical associations. Jane Ellen Harrison's claim that art comes out of religion and is linked by a "bridge" that is "ritual" (1925, 84) is illuminating when reading Butts's work. Butts ponders such ritual survivals in a journal entry written as she travelled to Villefranche for the last time in 1928: "The best art keeps forgotten ritual in." Tellingly, she gives the ballets *The Midnight Sun* and *Le Train Bleu* as examples (2002, 283). Something of this ritual consciousness plays out in Cocteau's description of Rose's birthday parade or ceremony, and his "clairvoyant" mother adds mystical colour to the scene. Cocteau might be seen to share medium-like skills here, as they too channel past practices of the hotel into their work. We return to a sense of ghosting, but this time on the page. Something of a classical "ghosting" is also embodied in Isadora's Duncan's presence in Villefranche, dressed in her Greek tunic; her dance, an attempted reanimation of Greek art, suggests a further ritualized action playing out in her performances in the town.

A further and more discreet part of the performance of the hotel plays out through opium and is also of ritual significance. Steegmuller writes that opium fumes filled the hotel corridors (1970, 389). They were sought and expected by visitors in the know. Cocteau was an addict, and a second hotel room was used for communal smoking away from his main room and any curious parties, though spectacles around the drug would play out more openly at times, observed by onlookers as something of the continued performance at the Welcome. Fellow practitioners of these opium rites included Wood, Butts ("Nuit de Pavot" she entitled her 3 March 1926 journal entry), Cocteau's friend and frequent collaborator Auric, and Christian Bérard (an artist who worked as a fashion illustrator for Chanel and would later design costumes for Cocteau's 1946 film *La Belle et la Bête*). These opium nights are not only tied to the collaborative artistic interactions at the hotel, but also add a sense of ritual and mystery to proceedings. Butts notes something of this in her journal from January 1926:

REMEMBER: Cocteau, the night I had a touch of fever. That he had found life a burden always. Then de Q[uincey]. Then the want. Then the religion, because art could not be for its own sake or the people's, but for "God's" [. . .] Spoke of invisible world, ghosts pushing in & frightening us, like a disease. Of Stravinsky, of Picasso.

(Butts 2002, 223)

Art, ritual, and a kind of anthropological observation blend in Butts's recording of events. The mysticism finds an uncanny reflection in an ink sketch of a figure (likely of Butts) held in the Butts archive at the Beinecke. The sketch is another repetition and collaboration, carrying the names of Butts and Cocteau—a surreal, gothic image of a reclining woman, drawn in black ink, with numerous opium pipes protruding from her body. The figure seems to emerge alongside Cocteau's collection of poems, *Opéra* (published in 1927), which he describes as showing "the celebrated deformations due to opium" (quoted in Steegmuller 1970, 373). The underworld image, the surreal and gothic tones of Cocteau's play *Orphée*, again position the hotel on the stage, or *as* stage, here read through the myth of adventure into the underworld, and through the opium fumes from which revelation might come.

Butts's short story picks up on this sense of ritual and revelation. We might even interpret aspects of the tale as a fevered opium dream. Acolytes assemble around the "Great André" in ritual fashion ("Worship carefully disguised" [2014, 202])—this production is a ceremony (209), and the troubled outsider, Paul, is suggested as "scapegoat" (206) and linked to T. S. Eliot's *The Waste Land* (204), for which healing is traditionally sought through the rites of the Grail quest. Picking up on Grail symbolism of the lance that pierced Christ, André is described as "the lance-point of the boy's world" (202), though the sexual innuendo also points to the role of Paul as virgin sacrifice (making use of his "virgin energy" [202]). The evocation of this mythical energy leads us to the opening of *The Waste Land* in its quest for rejuvenation or returns us to the "The House Party"'s Nijinska intertexts and the sense of sacrifice through a woman's duty to marry explored in *Les Noces* or the loss of innocence in *The House Party*. While Paul is linked to the *Waste Land*, André, his circle, and surrounding nature are connected to the rites of Pan. Paul is "corrupt" (215), fallen, unclean, associated with "disease" (220, 221). Sea, town, and André are clean (221). A further sense of movement develops as the story oscillates between a language of dirt, infection and brightness, "crystal" (206), cure, and rebirth. Paul seeks rebirth but cannot resist a shadowy figure known only as "the Pimp," who haunts the docks and leads Paul away from a pure form of art and homosexuality towards a diseased heterosexuality opened up by the Pimp in dirty backstreet rooms of prostitutes. The Pimp might be a ghost which then haunts this story, but Paul sees him as a devil (217). Read through an allegorical lens, the Pimp, "a spectre of [Paul's] imprisonment" might be an emanation of Paul himself, or his doppelgänger. In that sense, Paul mirrors William Blake's dancing youth in the poem "The Crystal Cabinet," to which Butts alludes repeatedly in the story. Pulled from the wilds, imprisoned in a "Crystal Cabinet"—a place of divine possibilities but also restrictive—he falls from innocence into experience. For Blake, the progression is necessary: imaginative, sexual, and spiritual development might be attained, but ruin is also risked. Paul departs, with the story suggesting that what has been experienced will likely not save the story's damaged protagonist, but ceremony, a performance has involved and brought together the group around André—a dark reflection of Cocteau, his acolytes, opium, ritual, and art at the Welcome.

Final; or, Queer Intersections

From Butts's ritual theatre, we approach the last "movement" in the performance of the Hotel Welcome. Butts's story is in part inspired by Cocteau and the young men who gathered around him. Finding myth and beauty in this group, Butts referred to them as the "Achilles set" (Blondel 2001, 159). This positions Cocteau as demigod, though the phrase also observes a vulnerability in a group of predominantly gay men. As commentators and Butts's own works suggest, she was fascinated by gay men (Foy 2000, 79; Rives 2010), and something of that fascination emerges in her short story, as does a binary of homo/ heterosexualities— another binary motif alongside that of purity/impurity, innocence/experience. Though focus is on gay men (and there are no important female characters in this story), the story is more broadly a reflection (or the remains) of queer performance at the Hotel that moves beyond simple binaries, becoming a "mixed riot" (Butts 2002, 287) of sexualities and artistic practices, in which boundaries blur.

Butts's allusion to Blake's dancing youth in "The Crystal Cabinet" is telling in that sense too, returning us to performance through dance— a young figure, of unstated gender, dancing happily in the wilds (we might imagine him naked, like many of Blake's painted figures), then caught in the cabinet. The cabinet might be a woman's sex—a sexual and heteronormative formative encounter, but the experience also offers a threefold vision—multiple possibilities and realities are suggested in the cabinet (anticipating, at least symbolically, the "closet"). Blake's dancing youth compares nicely to Butts's homoerotic image of Achilles and manifests in Paul and perhaps André/Cocteau as well, but also suggests multiplicity in her short story, and a more expansive sense of "queer." This more broadly queer space and community, an "open mesh of possibilities, gaps, overlaps, dissonance and resonances, lapses and excesses" (to borrow Eve Kosofsky Sedgwick's definition [1993, 8]) that emerges from the Hotel performance offers a space that queer bodies can inhabit. The young queer male body, though, is central to this performance, physically and symbolically. Cocteau, of course, observed these queer bodies. "In Villefranche," he writes, "I once watched American sailors for whom the exercise of love presented no precise form, and who adjusted to anyone for any kind of practice" (1957, 214). Other young queer bodies thronged the beach. It is tempting to read the beach as a kind of catwalk—early iterations of which evolved through the work of Coco Chanel in 1920s Paris. Chanel, like Cocteau, likely watched the beach scene unfolding: young gay men, relaxed, tanned under the hot sun, playing, arguing, strolling the bay—there, in part, to be seen—a performance. Photographs by American photographer George Platt Lynes, known for his images of gay writers and artists, captured something of this. Photographs record Cocteau with opium pipe, the hotel, harbourside and fishing nets, but also the young men, including Wheeler and Wescott, in speedos, bronzed under the Mediterranean sun—the apotheosis of queer youth and beauty.

In "The House Party," Blake's dancing youth, Butts's Achilles, and the young Paul represent something of this queer performance. Butts also explores this sense of ideal beauty and queer identity in a journal entry for March 1926. Noting conversation between Cocteau, Wheeler, Wescott, and Auric, on such subjects as fairy tales, goddesses, the Surrealists, and the ballet *Parade* (1917; scenario by Cocteau), Butts then records what "Cedric [Morris] said: on being 'queer'": "They start out a perambulating poem, & nature gives them several more years of boy's beauty than she gives a 'normal' man" (2002, 228–30). This leisurely movement of beautiful youths must, Morris goes on to suggest (according to Butts), be cultivated and developed carefully into maturity if it is not to go wrong (320).

Yet, in spite of the text's open queerness, a sense of an uncanny return of the repressed does emerge in "The House Party," as Butts presents her queer community tucked away in a small enclave between two cities, hidden in some ways from a disapproving French culture. The Hotel Welcome at this time was famous to some—those "in the know"—but it was also a little notorious, and for this reason, something to be seen. We return to Cocteau in room 22 of the hotel. He watches, directs, and records the hotel performance, but appears, as Wescott describes him, "like a dancer, with extraordinarily elegant movements, particularly in the cutting gestures of his long energetic hands" (quoted in Pohorilenko and Crump 1998, 35)—a figure in Butts "Crystal Cabinet," leading the performance of the Hotel Welcome.

Notes

1 While the beginning of the performance of the Hotel Welcome can be easily located in 1925 when other artists and visitors (following Cocteau's 1924 arrival) began to congregate in Villefranche, the end of the performance is less certain. But we might suggest that on or about May 1927 the performance ends. Returning to Villefranche in early 1927, Butts acknowledges the busy scene, meeting friends and "up and down the coast half the world" (cited in Blondel 2001, 180). A symbolic end, and a climax of sorts in collaboration, might be marked with Villefranche residents travelling to Paris to see the premiere of Stravinsky's (and Cocteau's) *Oedipus Rex* on 30 May 1927. On her final visit to Villefranche, in early 1928, though Butts still sees the town "at its best" (2002: 287), she records a sense of looking back in her journal, noting her suggestion to Cocteau that he writes a novel about the place. He replies that only poetry or a memoir would do.

2 Butts was a voracious reader and student of both occult and anthropological works; she even studied briefly under notorious occultist Aleister Crowley in 1921 in Italy. But one of the biggest influences on her writing is feminist classical scholar Jane Ellen Harrison. Roslyn Reso Foy (2000), Jane Garrity (2003), and Andrew Radford (2014) explore ritual in Butts's work and Harrison's importance.

Works Cited

Ahmed, Sara. 2006. "Orientations: Toward a Queer Phenomenology." *A Journal of Lesbian and Gay Studies* 12 (4): 543–74.

Auslander, Philip. 2012. "The Performativity of Performance Documentation." In *Perform, Repeat, Record: Live Art in History*, edited by Amelia Jones and Adrian Heathfield, 47–58. Bristol: Intellect Books.

Bacon, Julie Louise. 2013. "'Unstable Archives: Languages and Myths of the Visible." In *Performing Archives/Archives of Performance*, edited by Gunhild Borggreen and Rune Gade, 73–93. Copenhagen: Museum Tusculanum Press.

Blondel, Nathalie. 2001. *Mary Butts: Scenes from the Life*. Kingston: McPherson & Company.

Butts, Mary. 1992. *The Taverner Novels: Armed with Madness and Death of Felicity Taverner*. Kingston: McPherson & Company.

Butts, Mary. 2002. *The Journals of Mary Butts*. New Haven: Yale University Press.

Butts, Mary. 2014. *Complete Short Stories*. Kingston: McPherson & Company.

Carlson, Marvin. 2001. *The Haunted Stage: The Theatre as Memory Machine*. Ann Arbor: University of Michigan Press.

Cocteau, Jean. 1957. *The Journals of Jean Cocteau*, edited and translated by Wallace Fowlie. London: Museum Press.

Cocteau, Jean. 1966. *The Difficulty of Being*. Translated by Elizabeth Sprigge. London: Peter Owen.

De Certeau, Michel. 1988. *The Practice of Everyday Life*. Translated by Steven Rendall. Berkeley: University of California Press.

Farfan, Penny. 2017. *Performing Queer Modernism*. Oxford: Oxford University Press.

Foy, Roslyn Reso. 2000. *Ritual, Myth, and Mysticism in the Work of Mary Butts*. Fayetteville: The University of Arkansas Press.

Garrity, Jane. 2003. *Step-Daughters of England: British Women Modernists and the National Imaginary*. Manchester: Manchester University Press.

Harrison, Jane Ellen. 1925. *Reminiscences of a Student's Life*. London: Hogarth Press.

Hawkes, Joel. 2017. "Primitive Modern Practices of Place: Mary Butts and Christopher Wood in Paris and Cornwall." In *Beyond Given Knowledge: Investigation, Quest and Exploration in Modernism and the Avant-Gardes*, edited by Harri Veivo, Jean-Pierre Montier, Françoise Nicol, David Ayers, Benedikt Hjartarson, and Sascha Bru, 315–30. Berlin: De Gruyter.

Lefebvre, Henri. 1991. *The Production of Space*, translated by Donald Nicholson-Smith. Oxford: Blackwell.

MacCannell, Dean. 1976. *The Tourist: A New Theory of the Leisure Class*. London: Macmillan.

Macmillan, Rev. Hugh. 1885. *The Riviera*. London: J. S. Virtue & Co.

McLoughlin, Kate, ed. 2013. *The Modernist Party*. Edinburgh: Edinburgh University Press.
Peters, Arthur King. 1987. *Jean Cocteau and His World: An Illustrated Biography*. London: Thames and Hudson.
Pohorilenko, Anatole, and James Crum. 1925. *When We Were Three: Travel Albums of George Platt Lynes, Monroe Wheeler and Glenway Wescott 1925–1935*. San Francisco: Arena Editions.
Poulenc, Francis. 1948. *Les biches: suite d'orchestre*. Paris: Heugel.
Radford, Andrew. 2014. *Mary Butts and British Neo-Romanticism: The Enchantment of Place*. London: Bloomsbury.
Rives, Rochelle. 2010. "A Straight Eye for the Queer Guy: Mary Butts's 'Fag Hag' and the Modernist Group." In *Modernist Group Dynamics: The Politics and Poetry of Friendship*, edited by Fabio A. Durao and Dominic Williams, 95–118. Newcastle: Cambridge Scholars Press.
Rose, Francis. 1961. *Saying Life: The Memoirs of Francis Rose*. London: Cassell.
Schneider, Rebecca. 2001. "Performance Remains." *Performance Research* 6 (2): 100–08.
Sedgwick, Eve Kosofsky. 1993. "Queer and Now." In *Tendencies.*, 1–20. Durham: Duke University Press.
Steegmuller, Francis. 1970. *Cocteau: A Biography*. Boston: Little, Brown and Company.
Taxidou, Olga. 2007. *Modernism and Performance: Jarry to Brecht*. Basingstoke: Palgrave Macmillan.
Waters, Helena L. 1924. *The French and Italian Rivieras*. London: Methuen & Co.
Waugh, Alec. 1962. *The Early Years of Alec Waugh*. London: Cassell.

4 Performing Belonging in Early Twentieth-Century Literary Hotels and the Case of Rich Americans

Bettina Matthias

In "Death in Venice" (1912), Thomas Mann's description of the hotel society and atmosphere in Venice's "Grand Hôtel des Bains" where his ill-fated protagonist Gustav von Aschenbach spends the final chapter of his life is famous:

> he arrived a little early in the hall, where he found a considerable number of the hotel guests assembled, unacquainted with each other and affecting a studied mutual indifference, yet all united in expectancy by the prospect of their evening meal. [. . .] Discreetly muted, the sounds of the major world languages mingled. Evening dress, that internationally accepted uniform of civilization, imparted a decent outward semblance of unity to the wide variations of mankind here represented.
>
> (1999, 115, 116)

Built in 1900, the real Grand Hôtel des Bains on Venice's Lido attracted a wealthy international clientele, amongst them Thomas Mann himself who spent his summer vacation there in 1911, and in letters and diary entries, documented in detail the influence of this space on his writing of the novella. More broadly speaking, though, both socially and architecturally, Mann's Venetian grand hotel can be considered an excellent representative of the many elegant resorts that we encounter in early twentieth-century European literature, and it suggests a first set of parameters that helps us to understand the social dynamics in which authors such as Arthur Schnitzler, Stefan Zweig, Franz Werfel, Thomas Mann, Henry James, and many more set their stories.

Three main questions will guide this exploration of the literary hotel and leisure class in early twentieth-century Europe, as exemplified in Mann's "Death in Venice," Stefan Zweig's novel *The Post Office Girl* (*Rausch der Verwandlung*, publ. posthumously in 1981), and several additional hotel stories from the period. First, I will examine the representation of general behavioural premises governing social interactions amongst "unacquainted" guests whose only shared value is the fact that they all have the means to stay at this elegant hotel at the same time.

DOI: 10.4324/9781003213079-6

Second, as the focus of this essay is on literary hotels that are destinations in and of themselves instead of urban sociocultural settings, I will consider the ways in which their guests interact with each other for substantial amounts of time, in close quarters, examining how the general behavioural framework works in action and what social activities might affirm belonging in these literary spaces. This analysis will lead to the last question, namely whether a wealthy international leisure class engaged in codified performances of belonging overrides the concept of national or ancestral culture and allegiances and instead embraces a form of cosmopolitanism in these stories. The case of rich Americans in European literary hotels is an interesting lens through which authors model such a transnational concept at a time when capitalism and American cultural influences shaped much of Europe's pre- and interwar society.

As the introductory brief passage from Mann's "Death in Venice" suggests, social interaction in literary grand hotels from the early twentieth century is generally characterized by a sense of reserve and discretion, polite anonymity, and adherence to a visual code that expresses itself most prominently in the "[e]vening dress, that internationally accepted uniform of civilization" (Mann 1999, 116). Gathered in the hall, a space that is neither private nor public, engaged in waiting, guests recognize each other's legitimacy through self-effacement: lowered voices, outward conformity to the aesthetics of the place, and "affecting studied mutual indifference" are expected manifestations of self (115). National differences, discernible through the sounds of various languages, are only relevant insofar as their aural effects contribute to the overall international atmosphere. Neither curiosity nor tolerance seems to be challenged in this elegant international setting. It is a social space whose main characteristic is its immanence, as Siegfried Kracauer explains poignantly in his 1927 essay "The Hotel Lobby": "The person sitting around idly is overcome by a disinterested satisfaction in the contemplation of a world creating itself, whose purposiveness is felt without being associated with any representation of a purpose" (1997, 54). If people in earlier times had gathered in the cathedral to reach the transcendental as a community, modern man and woman have lost their ability to congregate and engage in the quest of a higher purpose.[1] The hotel lobby, according to Kracauer, encapsulates this loss of community and shows people in their modern existential state that no longer points to anything but itself. In fact, Kracauer's astute description of this immanence echoes what Mann suggests more subtly in the above-quoted paragraph. Kracauer writes: "The visitors in the hotel lobby who allow the individual to disappear behind the peripheral equality of social masks,[2] correspond to the exhausted terms that coerce differences out of the uniformity of the zero" (1997, 56). Politeness, distance, and indifference characterize the behaviour of these "social masks." Confirming belonging in this space is an aesthetic rather than an ethical task, to the point where one's substance gets lost entirely. As Kracauer remarks, "[A]s pure exterior, [the visitors] escape themselves and express their non-being through the false aesthetic affirmation of the estrangement that has been installed between them" (1997, 58).

A precondition for residence and any social interaction in the literary grand hotel is the assumption that everyone assembled there shares a similar cultural and socio-economic background. In other words, everyone must appear to be legitimate in this social sphere by following the above-described behavioural conventions, a code that requires significant capital and experience. In fact, hotels themselves actively support aestheticized surface interactions to camouflage what Martin Katz, using Gilles Deleuze, describes as capital's "power to radically deterritorialize" (1999, 148). Deleuze's ideas develop views proposed by Georg Simmel in "The Metropolis and Mental Life" (1903), where he writes:

> To the extent that money, with its colourlessness and its indifferent quality, can become a common denominator of all values, it becomes the frightful leveller—it hollows out the core of things, their peculiarities, their specific values and their uniqueness and incomparability in a way which is beyond repair.
>
> (1997, 73)

As Martin Katz argues, unable to fully acknowledge its capitalist foundations, that is its "hollow[ness]," the elegant hotel invents and reinforces "various forms of place making" (1999, 148), ranging from domestically inspired interior design to said interactional codes that allow guests to acknowledge and simultaneously ignore each other elegantly. Whether it is Mann's "Grand Hôtel des Bains," the "St. James and Albany" in his novel *Confessions of Felix Krull* (1954), Arthur Schnitzler's "Hotel Fratazza" in his interior monologue "Fräulein Else" (1924), the unnamed expensive resort in Franz Werfel's short story "The Staircase" (1927) or the elegant grand hotel in the Swiss town of Pontresina where Stefan Zweig's "post office girl" Christine Hoflehner gets to vacation with rich relatives, all of these hotels feature a similarly distanced social atmosphere in which interest in and connection with fellow guests can only go as far as the interactional codes established in each hotel allow, engaged enough to camouflage the sobering "colourlessness" of the hotel business's foundations, but distanced enough to maintain the integrity of the "social mask." It is no wonder, then, that many protagonists of these stories, especially women, experience major crises when they are faced with existential decisions for which they can neither rely on substantial personal support from peers in the hotel nor a moral value system to which this hybrid space would point.[3] Michel Foucault later pushes this idea further when he examines the hotel as a "crisis heterotopia" in his lecture "Des Espaces Autres. Hétérotopies" (1967, publ. 1984).

While Mann's portrayal of proper hotel behaviour in the semi-public space that is the hall reveals some of the most defining structural and ideological underpinnings of interactions amongst the leisured international hotel society, many of the German-language texts set in exclusive hotels, especially countryside hotels, feature a wider range of interactions between guests that seem to contradict the main interactive mode described so far. Guests play sports, cards, and roulette together, they go on outings and hikes, they dine and dance together well into the night. There are lively conversations and jokes amongst guests, and, of course, there is a lot of sexual tension and actual sex happening in these stories. All of this seems to run counter to the idea that proper hotel behaviour entails keeping one's distance from other guests and "studied mutual indifference" (Mann 1999, 115) towards their three-dimensional existence in this shared space.

However, a closer look at the nature of more time-consuming and direct interactions between guests in the (literary) grand hotel reveals their striking structural similarities to the more aloof demeanour expected in the hall. With the help of Norwegian-American sociologist Thorstein Veblen and his *Theory of the Leisure Class* (1899), it is easy to see how even seemingly intimate interactions are depicted as deeply steeped in a capitalist semiotic system of performing and securing membership to the moneyed class, a system whose success depends on keeping a careful and calculated personal distance from others. It is also a system that seems to have originated in American society and its foundational premise that monetary success would lead to social success, and further ways of social distinction would need to be implemented as soon as the upper class would be established. As the child of Norwegian immigrants in the United States, Veblen might have been especially perceptive about such stratification mechanisms in early twentieth-century American society.

Since the basis for legitimacy as a guest in an elegant hotel is one's belonging to the class that can afford a stay, all activities and expressions of self are under the mandate of proving this status. To do so, the leisure class developed a whole range of strategies to demonstrate their financial might, both explicitly and implicitly, in order to flaunt one's privilege as "conspicuous[ly exempt] from all useful employment" (Veblen 1994, 26). Veblen writes: "Conspicuous abstention from labour therefore becomes the conventional mark of superior pecuniary achievement and the conventional index of reputability" (25). Staying at an expensive hotel, preferably for a significant amount of time, is already an ideal way to display and prove one's abstention from labour, these stories signal. With enough additional money to waste on "useless" objects of consumption such as perfume, alcohol and other narcotics, luxury foods, ever-changing fashionable outfits, cars etc., and the affordance of spare time to waste on acquiring "useless" knowledge such as foreign languages, fashionable sports, the latest dances, or gossip, the member of the leisure class is then constantly engaged in producing and boasting conspicuous waste, material and immaterial. The elegant hotel, with its many halls, salons, lounges, tennis courts, and grounds, provides the perfect stage for an effective display of such affluence, and authors explore these qualities extensively. Schnitzler's "Fräulein Else" starts on the hotel's tennis court where the protagonist, in her fashionable red sweater, has just finished her highly visible match with her cousin. The hotel's hall becomes a catwalk where Else can model her beautiful black dress, and the music salon serves as the setting for a fellow guest to display her skills as a pianist (and of course as the stage where Else's scandalous and suicidal striptease rips open the assembled hotel society's smooth façade). Similarly, Werfel's Francine performs belonging to the leisure class as a participant in evening dances where, dancing the fashionable Slow Boston, she gives in to the sexual advances of a fellow guest. As a liftboy in the "St. James and Albany," Thomas Mann's Felix Krull observes the newly rich Mrs Twentyman during mealtimes and in the salon when she flaunts her jewellery and expensive high fashion. And poor Christine Hoflehner in Zweig's novel *The Post Office Girl* is only accepted as a full member of the leisure class when she appears in the right outfit in the hall and participates in the public consumption of expensive foods and in social dances. It is an intricate semiotic code that members of the leisure class must master, meant to constantly distinguish the upper from the lower classes who do not have the means and the time to keep up with "conspicuous leisure" and "conspicuous consumption," as Veblen calls it (1994, 23 ff. and 43 ff.).

What is missing from all of these performances of affluence is substantial engagement with the other. Scripted behaviour, predetermined movement, be it on the dance floor or, following the hotel's dining schedule, within the hotel, and stock-conversations that should never scratch the surface of a guest's "social mask" can guarantee endless engagement with other guests without ever challenging them to drop their façade and expose that there is nothing behind that mask. Fittingly, Werfel's Francine, recognizing the hollowness of hotel interactions after having slept with fellow guest Guido, keeps referring to him as the "jointed doll" (1937, 426). And Felix Krull, himself profiting greatly from the fact that belonging to the leisure class is based on mastering and flaunting symbols of wealth, observes:

> There was, for example, an idea that occasionally preoccupied me when for a few leisure moments I stood in the lobby or dining hall. [...] It was the idea of *interchangeability*. With a change of clothes and make-up, the servitors might often just as well have been the masters, and many of those who lounged in the deep wicker chairs, smoking their cigarettes, might have played the waiter. It was pure accident that the reverse was the fact, an accident of wealth; for an aristocracy of money is an accidental, an interchangeable aristocracy.
> (Mann 1955, 224, emphasis in the original)

There is nothing intrinsically superior about the leisure class in these literary grand hotels; social distinction and privilege are ultimately based on that most quality-free kind of asset, money. Wealth inserts itself into all interactions while members of the leisure class constantly worry about preserving their status and warding off unwanted "intrusion" from the lower classes. In fact, it is exactly this intrusion that leads to Christine Hoflehner's demise in the "Grand Hotel Pontresina" in Zweig's *The Post-Office Girl*. Jealous of Christine's success with the hotel society in general and with a dashing German engineer in particular, a young woman from Mannheim embarks on mercilessly taking down Christine as a fraud when she notices some gaps in her mastery of leisure class culture:

> Unwittingly, Christine revealed the gaps in her worldliness. She didn't know that polo was played on horse-back, wasn't familiar with common perfumes like Coty and Houbigant, didn't have a grasp of the price range of cars; she'd never been to the races. Ten or twenty gaucheries like that and it was clear she was poorly versed in the lore of chic. [. . .] No secondary schooling, no languages.
> (Zweig 2008, 106)

As if taking his motifs from Veblen's list of activities and material signs that exemplify effective proofs of belonging to the leisure class, Zweig shows the predatory nature and effects of a system that has abandoned a more Kantian definition of social superiority. In his lecture entitled "The Sociology of Sociability" (1910), Simmel describes this alternative social superiority as an "art or play form of association" (1949, 254) with "no ulterior end" (255) where "[r]iches and social position, learning and fame, exceptional capacities and merits of the individual have no role" (256). There is a recognition of and trust in an *a priori* equality amongst members of this circle, a substantial equality that stands in stark contrast to Kracauer's "peripheral equality of social masks" (1997, 56) and especially to Veblen's depiction of an almost Darwinian fight for social superiority in which only those behind the capitalist-consumerist supply chain are the real winners. Hotel literature from the earlier twentieth century seems to share Kracauer's and Veblen's assessment of the dynamics governing social interactions in the upper echelons of society.

A leisure class that distinguishes itself through conspicuous leisure, wealth, and consumption is thus a phenomenon steeped in consumerism and a product of a society that ultimately assesses a person's social worth in monetary value, explicitly or implicitly. Such a quantitative approach to social standing is vulnerable to corruption, as Christine Hoflehner's example shows. But it is also one that allows for social mobility when belonging can be learnt and trained with the right amount of wealth at one's disposal, and when the stages needed for the performance of belonging are accessible. If the aristocratic upper classes of earlier centuries had gathered in members' private estates, and lineage and connections determined access to these spaces, Felix Krull's new "aristocracy of money" gathers in elegant hotels to which their wealth guarantees access and in which one's mere physical presence is the first proof of belonging.

European hotel owners seized the opportunity to monetize this sociocultural shift, trying to attract rich American travellers especially to stay at their hotels and emulating the many accommodations that American grand hotels had first introduced to respond to their guests' needs for opportunities to flaunt their status. As an example, after an initial ban on expansions and new constructions of American-style grand hotels in Switzerland between 1915 and 1925, Swiss hoteliers sought to outdo their competition by offering the most luxurious accommodations to appeal to "well-heeled American visitors" (Williams 2019, 448), who were looking for places to play luxury sports, race their expensive cars, and dance to fashionable live music at night while consuming expensive foods and drinks. This new international "aristocracy of money" seemed to take over leisure-class life in Europe's favourite destinations, possibly indicating major changes to the way in which the European upper classes defined belonging and allowed a geosocial broadening of their circles.

And indeed, many of the hotel stories discussed so far feature a very international clientele: Russians, Britons, French people, Italians, Czechs, Poles, Germans, Austrians, and Americans vacation together at elegant resorts and spas and mingle as performing members of their hotels' societies. As long as everyone performs well, internationalism seems to trump nationalism—though interestingly, many stories discussed here suggest that adult guests still prefer to stay within their own linguistic peer groups,[4] a first sign that they subscribe to a much less cosmopolitan spirit than the hotels in which they stay. And even though American guests should be depicted as most suitable and successful participants in these European hotels' leisure class, considering that the ideas of conspicuous wealth and consumption might have their roots in American society, their status in many of the stories is complex.

This motif is central in Stefan Zweig's *The Post Office Girl*, Swiss author Meinrad Inglin's *Hotel Excelsior* (1928), but also, much earlier already, in Henry James's "Daisy Miller" (1878). James, an American himself but highly critical of his fellow country people's behaviour and demeanour in Europe, has little patience for Felix Krull's "aristocracy of money" that buys itself access to Europe's most elegant and distinguished places, and he admonishes his fellow countrymen and women for their lack of refinement and delicacy—both qualities that do not factor into Veblen's performances of upper-class belonging. Take, for example, the first pages of "Daisy Miller," in which American-turned-European Frederick Winterbourne describes the Swiss town of Vevey with its grand hotel "Trois Couronnes" in the month of June:

> Vevey assumes at this period some of the characteristics of an American watering place. There are sights and sounds which evoke a vision, an echo, of Newport and Saratoga. There is a flitting hither

and thither of "stylish" young girls, a rustling of muslin flounces, a rattle of dance music in the morning hours, a sound of high-pitched voices at all times. You receive an impression of these things at the excellent inn of the "Trois Couronnes" and are transported in fancy to the Ocean House or to Congress Hall. But at the "Trois Couronnes," it must be added, there are other features that are much at variance with these suggestions: neat German waiters, who look like secretaries of legation; Russian princesses sitting in the garden; little Polish boys walking about held by the hand, with their governors; a view of the sunny crest of the Dent du Midi and the picturesque towers of the Castle of Chillon.

(James 1963, 135)

The American presence in this town and hotel imposes upon the serenity of Switzerland's landscape and the discreet and "decent outward semblance of unity" (Mann 1999, 116) of European hotel guests. Style is now "stylishness," the traditional acoustical routine in a hotel is turned upside down (dance music is for evening hours), "high pitched voices" cut through the air and disturb the conventional subdued volume of elegant togetherness in upscale hotels. For these rich American guests, knowing how to engage in performances of belonging clearly does not mean doing so within the broader framework of discretion and being elegantly disengaged. Pierre Bourdieu's idea of "taste" comes to mind as a marker that "defines and marks off the high from the low [. . .] and the 'legitimate' from the 'illegitimate' " (Allen and Anderson 1994, 70), suggesting that even within the leisure class, there are internal and unbridgeable fissures that set European guests apart from their American counterparts. And though James softens his critique by choosing the nine-year-old Randolph Miller, an "unrefined" child, as the first American hotel guest to speak in the opening pages, the contrast between European and American approaches to being a guest in an upscale hotel could not be starker. Unabashed, this boy brags about his father being "rich, you bet!" (James 1963, 141), and he dismisses European candy, hotels, and men as inferior to their American counterparts: " 'American men are the best!,' he declared" (138). Loud, indiscreet, and chauvinist, this representative of the next generation of Americans announces the refusal of the new upper class to play by the rules established in European upscale circles. And even if judging a group of guests by their youngest and least protocol-abiding member might be pushing things, Winterbourne's interactions with Randolph's older sister, Daisy, still reveal James's apparent conviction that American approaches to social interactions are incompatible with "upper-class European moral codes" (Despotopoulou 2018, 508). Declaring that "[European] hotels [are] very good, when once you got used to their ways" (James 1963, 143), Daisy pretends to have adapted to European hotel culture. But her interactions with Winterbourne suggest that she knows these "ways" in name only and that the (presumably) less sophisticated Vevey accommodates her untraditional behaviour more leniently than the international metropolis nearby would:

> In Geneva, as [Winterbourne] had been perfectly aware, a young man was not at liberty to speak to a young unmarried woman except under certain rarely occurring conditions; but here at Vevey, what conditions could be better than these? [. . .] He was ceasing to be embarrassed, for he had begun to perceive that she was not the least embarrassed herself.
>
> (139–40)

Not abiding by the dictate of seductive reserve for young women, Daisy is clearly not compatible with this high society's rules of engagement and its demure nature, and it comes as no surprise when she complains:

> The only thing I don't like [. . .] is the society. There isn't any society; or, if there is, I don't know where it keeps itself. Do you? [. . .] I'm very fond of society, and I have always had a great deal of it.
>
> (143)

Obviously, Daisy's unconventional conduct in Switzerland is a critique of "an American expatriate society that has developed and adapted upper-class European moral codes, applying them in an almost puritanical way to new American invaders" (Despotopoulou 2018, 508). Indeed, one could argue that ultimately, James's depiction of his fellow Americans' demeanour in European hotels doubles as a critique of stuffy European moral and behavioural codes and a "[reduction] of all social interaction to well rehearsed performance" (Despotopoulou 2018, 508). Still, James seems to admit that transgressive behaviour such as Daisy's can only be told with empathy as long as she does not survive the novella's end, contributing to the (European) literary trope of the "interesting transgressive female" whose sad and predictable demise allows stories such as Alexandre Dumas's *La Dame aux Camélias*, Stéphane Mallarmé's *Carmen*, but also Schnitzler's "Fräulein Else" and so many more to be told, and with pleasure. Metaphorically sentenced to death by her creator, Daisy succumbs to an illness contracted during a "scandalous" outing with an Italian admirer—the result of not just her stereotypical innocence or frivolity, but also her engagement with a member of the leisure class from a different linguistic and cultural background. Again, we see the idea(l) of a cosmopolitan leisure class in and around Europe's grand hotels subtly undermined by the story's development.

Interestingly, Americans seem to have been aware of the possible pitfalls that moving within European upper-class circles could present. Maureen E. Montgomery discusses several American etiquette manuals, published between 1864 and 1918, that sought to advise members of the upper bourgeoisie on how to avoid giving the impression of being either nouveau riche or boorish. In Daphne Dale's *Our Manners and Social Customs. A Practical Guide to Deportment, Easy Manners, and Social Etiquette* (1892), for example, an entire chapter is devoted solely to the deportment in a hotel. In it, the interested reader finds:

> advice to gentlemen regarding demeanor, table manners and against staring at others.
> The rest of the chapter is devoted to ladies to save them from "embarrassment" and "insult" in the public space of the hotel. This includes advice on how to arrive at a hotel, how to traverse public space, what to do on seeing acquaintances, how to take one's place in the dining room, how to order food, how to interact with other diners, what not to do in public parlors, how to deal with valuables and baggage, and how to deal with servants who are "negligent or disrespectful."
> (Montgomery 2018, 159)

The advice given in this manual seeks to prime members of the leisure class for proper behaviour in upscale American hotels. But it seems even more relevant for these guests as they travelled to Europe where leisure-class behaviour was expected to materialize within the framework of reserve and quasi-self-effacement and respectability. Daisy Miller was likely not amongst the readers of such advice books.

However, even those literary American hotel guests who respect European sensibilities and "envelop [themselves] [. . .] in a wrapping of personal dignity" (Montgomery 2018, 160), while being fully fluent in the semiotic code of leisure-class performances, still face general resistance. In Swiss author Meinrad Inglin's novel *Hotel Excelsior* (1928), the plot's main conflict between brothers Eugen and Peter Sigwart, both heirs to their father's Swiss lakeside hotel, revolves around the role that Americans, as financiers and as clientele, should play in their hotel's makeup and future. Quite obviously a sympathizer with Switzerland's conservative opposition to the commercial development of the country's beautiful countryside, afraid of the impact that such development could have on its beauty, culture, and essence, the younger Peter frequently clashes with Eugen over the latter's plans to expand the business and appeal to American guests. Though many of the novel's European hotel guests behave in much the same way as the stereotypical American *parvenu*, it is the abstract prospect of welcoming a "stream of Americans" (Inglin 1988, 107) that constitutes the end of what Peter deems noble and moral. Contemplating the possibility of his brother expanding the family's hotel into an American-style grand hotel with over 200 beds and all the comforts and entertainments known from American resort hotels, Peter muses:

> Only this is certain: if a God-like visage appeared right now, the Western world would not hold its own in front of him, it would

be adamantly rejected. Yes, who knows, maybe it has already been rejected and is doomed beyond repair, maybe that is this world's real destiny.

(Inglin 1988, 83, translation mine)

The novel's most prominent American guest, a gentleman with the speaking name of Mr Barker who is well versed in American business practice and European leisure class etiquette, cannot redeem his fellow rich countrymen from being deemed the nemesis of the Sigwart family, their hotel, and the region, if not the nation. The fact that Eugen fails as a hotel owner whose offerings always come up short of what Americans expect seems to prove Peter right in his warnings not to surrender to the new, American-influenced hotel culture. If James portrays American hotel guests as indiscreet and lacking the personal distinction that European guests command, Inglin takes his protagonist's criticism further: the Americanization of Swiss hotel culture is tantamount to a veritable cultural apocalypse. The novel's end—Mr Barker dies and the "Hotel Excelsior" burns down to the ground—is a fitting fulfilment of this vision. But it is also not the novel's final verdict. Having insured the hotel extremely well, Eugen will be able to build a much bigger and more "American" hotel, like "the gigantic hotel palace with 600 beds in Atlantic City" (Inglin 1988, 243, translation mine):

> He will build a very efficient gigantic hotel with its own electric power plant, with self- propelled lifts, magnificent social halls and hundreds of bedrooms, offering cold and warm water, private telephones and wireless radios, with bathrooms, places to play and famous dance bands, offering every possible modern indulgence and the most sophisticated degrees of comfort. Guests will not have to forego anything and will not wish for anything, it will be a paradise for forward-looking people where the international lifestyle of those who count in society can unfold in the most dazzling manner; no troubled spirit, however, will disturb this peace and spoil the fun, no Peter will enjoy its hospitality here any longer, unless as a fool.
> (Inglin 1988, 299, translation mine)

Hotel culture, in this dystopian scenario, will no longer be a matter of behaviour or social codes but instead be determined by material overkill. The real and psychological noise of such a space will leave no need for guests to prove themselves compatible with traditional European sensibilities.

Yet, the most interesting and maybe most subtle literary example of the European leisure class's rejection of rich Americans as equals can be found in Stefan Zweig's novel *The Post Office Girl*, a story set in summer 1926. Its initial premise suggests that the American upper class has established itself firmly in European good society when Christine, a poor young woman from Austria's countryside, gets invited to join her rich American aunt and uncle in a Swiss resort hotel. These relatives, the van Boolens, seem to have found full admission into European good society. Her aunt's scandalous past—as a young woman, she had to emigrate from Vienna to the United States due to a sexual scandal—has been forgotten thanks to her Dutch-American husband's millions. Known and embraced by many European upper-class hotel guests, participating successfully in the many performances that affirm belonging, the van Boolens enjoy their standing so much that they can afford to invite a poor and potentially compromising relative to join them and partake in their social status. However, even though Christine's transformation from penniless country bumpkin to social butterfly succeeds at first thanks to the dresses, jewellery and other accessories that the van Boolens shower upon Christine, and due to her quick grasp of this hotel society's semiotic code, it becomes clear very quickly that the assembled hotel society is not interested in welcoming a "rags to riches" kind of person into their midst. Adopting her aunt's last name "van Boolen" might be enough for Christine to feel like a new person, but fellow guests prefer to misunderstand her last name and refer to her as "von Boolen," turning the non-aristocratic Dutch "van" into a low-level German aristocratic title. Christine herself, asked about her first name, assumes that "'Christine' [. . .] [doesn't] seem impressive enough for the borrowed title" and renames herself "Christiane" (Zweig 2008, 82). And when Christine is found out as a "fraud," her uncle Anthony argues in vain in front of his panicked wife and the assembled hotel society when he insists:

> Why is [Christine's background] a disgrace? All Americans have poor relatives. I wouldn't want to look too closely at the nephews of the Guggenheims, or the Roskys [. . .] I don't see why it's a disgrace that we dressed her up respectably [. . .] I didn't borrow a penny from anyone here and I couldn't care less if they think we're classy or not. (118, 119)

To which his wife responds: "But I care. I care" (119). Shunned by her aristocratic European acquaintances like the von Trenkwitzes who feel duped, and afraid to lose fellow guest Lord Elkins as a friend, Christine's aunt drops her niece as soon as she, Claire van Boolen, appears as nothing but newly rich and disrespectful of older and less material laws of social distinction ("classiness"), despite her own mastery of expected displays of belonging. Christine gets chased away from Pontresina, leaving a hotel society for whom the mastery of the leisure class's performative code is a necessary but not complete precondition for admission to their ranks.

As American millionaires invade the gathering places of Europe's upper class, old aristocratic and tribal attitudes provide a last defensive bulwark against the Americanization of good society. Gathering in places whose architecture tries to seamlessly connect old aristocratic aesthetics and values with the modern capitalist leisure class, living at a time when American millions save old Europe's postwar economies from complete collapse, good society cannot (yet) fully acknowledge its own preconditions for survival and fails to realize the vision of truly transnational or cosmopolitan social interaction. The newly rich American misfit in European grand hotels will remain a trope that even post-World War II narratives like Alfred Hitchcock's movie *To Catch a Thief* (1955) will successfully explore.

Notes

1 See also Zitzlsperger's analysis of hotels as "Cathedrals of Modernity" in chapter 11.
2 For example, Mann's evening dress.
3 My monograph *The Hotel as a Setting in Early 20th-Century German and Austrian Literature* examines in detail the literary topic of the personal crisis in the semi-anonymous space of the hotel.
4 In "Death in Venice," for example, Mann has the hotel's adult Polish-speaking guests stay strictly with their linguistic peers. Their children do mingle with children from other linguistic communities at the beach at first, but a fight towards the end of the story abruptly ends this multilingual community, leaving little doubt that this is the spirit that will lead to the gruesome Great War just three years later.

Works Cited

Allen, Douglas E., and Paul F. Anderson. 1994. "Consumption and Social Stratification: Bourdieu's Distinction." *NA – Advances in Consumer Research* 21: 70–74. www.acrwebsite.org/volumes/7565/volumes/v21/NA

Bourdieu, Pierre. 1984. *Distinction: A Social Critique of the Judgement of Taste*. Translated by Richard Nice. Cambridge: Harvard University Press.

Dale, Daphne. 1892. *Our Manners and Social Customs: A Practical Guide to Deportment, Easy Manners, and Social Etiquette*. Chicago and Philadelphia: Elliott and Beezley.

Despotopoulou, Anna. 2018. "Monuments of an Artless Age: Hotels and Women's Mobility in the Work of Henry James." *Studies in the Novel* 50 (4) (Winter): 501–22.

Foucault, Michel. 1984. "Des Espaces Autres. Hétérotopies." *Architecture, Mouvement, Continuité* 5: 46–49.

Inglin, Meinrad. 1988. *Grand Hotel Excelsior*. Zürich: Ammann Verlag.

James, Henry. 1963. "Daisy Miller." In *Daisy Miller and Other Stories*, edited by Michael Swan, 135–92. Harmondsworth: Penguin Books.

Katz, Martin. 1999. "The Hotel Kracauer." *Differences: A Journal of Feminist Cultural Studies* 11 (2): 134–52.

Kracauer, Siegfried. 1997. "The Hotel Lobby." In *Rethinking Architecture: A Reader in Cultural Theory*. Translated by Thomas Levin, edited by Neil Leach, 53–59. London: Routledge.

Levenstein, Harvey. 1998. *Seductive Journey: American Tourists in France from Jefferson to the Jazz Age*. Chicago: The University of Chicago Press.
Mann, Thomas. 1955. *Confessions of Felix Krull, Confidence Man: The Early Years*. Translated by Denver Lindley. New York: Alfred Knopf.
Mann, Thomas. 1999. "Death in Venice." In *Death in Venice, Tonio Kröger, and Other Writings*. Translated by David Luke, edited by Frederick A. Lubich, 95–161. New York: Continuum Publishing Company.
Matthias, Bettina. 2006. *The Hotel as Setting in Early 20th-Century German and Austrian Literature*. Rochester: Camden House.
Montgomery, Maureen E. 2018. "Henry James and 'The Testimony of the Hotel' to Transatlantic Encounters." In *Anglo-American Travelers and the Hotel Experience in Nineteenth Century Literature: Nation, Hospitality, Travel Writing*, edited by Monika Elbert and Susanne Schmid. 149–66. New York: Routledge.
Schnitzler, Arthur. 2003. "Fräulein Else." In *Desire and Delusion*. Translated by Margret Schäfer, 192–264. Chicago: Ivan Dee.
Simmel, Georg. 1949. "The Sociology of Sociability." Translated by Everett C. Hughes. *American Journal of Sociology* 55 (3): 254–61.
Simmel, Georg. 1997. "The Metropolis and Mental Life." In *Rethinking Architecture: A Reader in Cultural Theory*. Translated by Edward Shils, edited by Neil Leach, 69–79. London: Routledge.
Steward. Jill. 2004. "Tourism in Late Imperial Austria." In *Being Elsewhere: Tourism, Consumer Culture, and Identity in Modern Europe and North America*, edited by Shelley Baranowski and Ellen Furlough. 108–36. Ann Arbor: University of Michigan Press.
Veblen, Thorstein. 1994. *The Theory of the Leisure Class*. New York: Dover Thrift.
Werfel, Franz. 1937. "The Staircase." In *Twilight of the World*. Translated by Helen Tracy Lower-Porter, 421–38. New York: Viking.
Williams, Seán. 2019. "Home Truths and Uncomfortable Spaces: Swiss Hotels and Literature of the 1920s." *Forum for Modern Language Studies* 55 (4): 444–65.
Zweig, Stefan. 2008. *The Post Office Girl*. Translated by Joel Rotenberg. New York: New York Review Books.

5 "No longer a hotel"
Colonial Decadence in Lawrence Durrell's *The Alexandria Quartet*

Athanasios Dimakis

In his introduction to the 1982 edition of E. M. Forster's *Alexandria: A History and Guide*, Lawrence Durrell describes his own view of a room at the Cecil Hotel, Alexandria, while also comparing it to his first impressions of the hotel, in the autumn of 1942, when he had stayed in the very same room overlooking the city's Eastern Harbour, the famed Corniche. Several years after his first occupancy of that room, in his introduction to the Forster book, Durrell ponders his exilic condition which seems irrevocably tied to the hotel setting:

> I spent a week there in the old familiar room at the Cecil, now stripped of all its finery and echoing like a barn with the seawind sweeping under doors and through the windows; I reflected on exile in general and my own in particular. When I came here there was no reason to suppose that the war would ever end, that I should ever leave Egypt. It was lucky that I was rootless by background and inheritance—a colonial.
>
> (Durrell 2014, xv–xvi)

Identifying himself as a "colonial," forever immersed in a state of exilic rootlessness, Durrell distances himself from Forster's account of the British colonial enterprise in Alexandria, maintaining that it is "remarkable" that the modernist author "should have responded to his own exile in such positive fashion, putting down new roots in this unfamiliar soil" (2014, xvi). Durrell discerns a celebratory tone in Forster's accounts of the empire, whose British members emerge as "the gainers"; instead, Durrell foregrounds the peculiar mix of complicity and indulgence that he grudgingly embodies and which he sees enacted within the microcosm of the colonial hotel (xvi). Colonial hotels often housed the political, military, and administrative apparatus of imperial powers—for example, the Cecil housed the British Secret Intelligence Service Headquarters (Siegelbaum 2015, n.p.)—but Durrell seems to propose a more ambivalent understanding of the hotel that reflects his torn identity and double allegiance rather than reassuring hegemonic schemata. In his short introduction as well as in *The Alexandria Quartet*, he turns the war years in

DOI: 10.4324/9781003213079-7

Egypt into a parable about the British empire through a vision of the hotel in slow decay, "now stripped of all its finery and echoing like a barn" (Durrell 2014, xv).[1] Durrell's conflicted view of colonial hotels is also suggested by George Seferis in a letter to Henry Miller, where he describes the discontents of Durrell's hotel life in Egypt. The letter seems to anticipate Durrell's later reading of the hotel as a symptom of the disintegration taking place in war-ridden Egypt. In Seferis's anecdote, Durrell, who first arrived in Cairo in 1941, having fled Nazi-occupied Greece, humorously renamed his first lodging, the Cairo Luna Park Hotel, opting for an alternative that combined colonial hotels with the fate of empire as well as with the insanity of World War II: the Luna Park hotel became for Durrell the "Lunatic Park" (quoted in Haag 2004, 192).

In his discussion of colonial hotels, Maurizio Peleggi traces the ways in which such hotels accommodate "the ideological nexus between colonial morality and colonial authority" through the polarities that they set up between colonized and colonizers, Orientals and Occidentals (2012, 139). Peleggi proposes that the Shepheard's Hotel in Cairo was the colonial hotel *par excellence*, being the ostentatious, cosmopolitan playground of the elite wielding the influence of foreign powers.[2] In "Other Spaces of the Empire: A Colonial Hotel," Tijana Parezanović underscores the charged emotive potential of hotel literature within the context of postcolonial writing, arguing that colonial hotels can also offer "a spatial contextualization of the historical downfall of the British Empire" and can serve to "question the sustainability of the imperial project of colonialism" (2016, 53). This is also the thread in Tarek Ibrahim's reading of the paradigm of the Cairo Shepheard's, where it is suggested that, while the hotel initially reflects the waxing power of empire through its civilizing mission and peculiar immanence, it also inevitably showcases the empire's precarious fate and progressive waning (2019). While the colonial hotels of Egypt function as an offshoot of the pervasive spirit of British imperialism reflecting its grandeur, the irony of the impermanence that they simultaneously signify as transitory spaces suggests a double bind and an irredeemable tension. Durrell's hotels become metonymic of the imperial apparatus and its slow disintegration.

This oxymoron of the colonial hotel is the thematic heart of Durrell's *The Alexandria Quartet* (1957–1960, 1962), the sensuous tetralogy consisting of *Justine* (1957), *Balthazar* and *Mountolive* (1958), and *Clea* (1960). The flowery, ornate language and maximalist plot largely highlight the pathos and the challenged position of the colonizers, rather than the colonized. There is no Egyptian Muslim amongst the main characters, an omission that underlines Durrell's imaginative construction of Alexandria as a colonial cosmopolis. The narrative unfolds from several, often conflicting, viewpoints against the backdrop of hotels, tracing the interrelated stories of a group of characters that include the British ambassador to Egypt (Sir David Mountolive), an eccentric English novelist and British propaganda officer, a low-ranking French diplomat, and a cross-dressing police officer and spy. The amorous adventures of Justine Hosnani, in love with the novelist Ludwig Pursewarden and marrying an Egyptian Copt (Nessim Hosnani), merge with interludes of political suspense and diplomatic intrigues, often narrated by L. G. Darley (an alias of Lawrence George Durrell).

The first three volumes describe a series of events in Alexandria before World War II; the fourth carries the story forward into the war years. The leap from the temporal stasis of the first three books to the later war years helps Durrell's saga better articulate material decay in tandem with the disintegration of the imperial hold over Egypt. The experimental nature of *The Alexandria Quartet* and its convoluted prose are suggested in Durrell's "Note" in *Balthazar* where he explains that the first three parts of the tetralogy "are to be deployed spatially" and are "not linked in a serial form," with their time "stayed" and the fourth part alone being "a true sequel" (1958, 7). The sequence of events is linked spatially through the foregrounding of Alexandria and, to a lesser extent, Cairo or, as Forster aptly puts it in his chapter on the aesthetic principles of continental modernity, through the city's hotels and clubs as localizers of the modern spirit (1962, 59). Thus, the *Quartet* lays emphasis on the ambivalent position of the Cairo Shepheard's Hotel, the Alexandria Cecil Hotel, as well as the fictional Alexandrian accommodations of a British secret intelligence service agent lodged in an unnamed hotel appositely nicknamed "the Mount Vulture Hotel" (Durrell 2012a, 519).

The hotels of Alexandria and Cairo in the *Quartet* become fluid spaces where colonial binaries can be easily played out. Durrell often accentuates the materiality of space in order to trace the grand oriental hotels' inevitable trajectory from imperial glory to progressive destabilization, crisis, and decline. For example, the sequence featuring Justine and Nessim Hosnani seated in the elaborate lounge of Shepheard's hotel foregrounds the luxurious materiality that discloses the imperial superstructure of the colonial hotel. The hotel's thick, plush sofas and chairs, the Britishness of the towering clock, the implied orientalizing in Justine's "untouched Turkish coffee before her," Nessim's graceful choreography as he passes through the "swing doors" of the hotel lobby forever admitting and/or excluding individuals based on their rank and privilege, as well as Justine's account of her encounter with the British ambassador, Sir Mountolive, escorted by "bankers or something" (Durrell 2012a, 608–09), all call attention to the status of the hotel as a materially constituted space that evokes an immaterial (cultural and political) ideology.

However, the aura of self-assured complacency within the hotel recreational areas is unexpectedly challenged. The hotel concomitantly hosts what reads as a colonial dialectic on the muddled state of Levantine affairs which are mirrored in the intertwined subplots of the *Quartet*. A sardonic plot twist involves Nessim and Justine both supporting a Zionist organization of underground fighters in Haifa and Jerusalem, which aims at establishing an independent Jewish state and conspires against the British presence in the region: "[t]he sort of pressure the British are bringing is based upon those files of correspondence they captured in Palestine. The Haifa office told Capodistria so" (2012a, 609). The colonial hotel then houses a conspiracy that serves to undo its very foundations orchestrated by individuals above suspicion. The irony of plotting against the British within the hospitable premises of the (British) colonial hotel brings forth the susceptibility of hotels to geopolitical machinations and their inherently precarious position.

The ensuing cinematic scene transports Justine and Nessim from Shepheard's Hotel, the metaphorical heart of Britishness in Cairo, to the literal edifice preoccupied with the advancement of British interests in the region, the British embassy, where they enjoy the nocturnal, spectral spectacle of the "barefooted," "sleepless Ambassador"; a somnambulist evidently done with his "big dinner" at the hotel (2012a, 608–10). Holding a cigarette and a telegram, Mountolive anxiously roams "the brilliantly lighted gardens of the British Embassy" (608–10). As Anne Zahlan notes, Mountolive is consistently portrayed as a doomed imperial expatriate, a "frustrated Englishman all too painfully aware of the deprivation of self" prompted by the "decline of his country's Empire" (1986, 11). In fact, the British embassy, like the hotel lobby, becomes the second, unsettling, colonial space. The contrast between the glittering façade in the hotel lobby and the embassy gardens and the hints about the fall of empire serves to highlight the suspense and the socio-political tension manifest in the vexation and angst of the ghostly ambassador himself. Hotel and embassy thus function interchangeably in *Mountolive,* and gradually the complicity between these spaces and colonial rule is challenged.

Durrell's protagonists filter the late-colonial reality of Egypt through the hotel. In the opening part of the *Quartet*, the narrator merges long quotations from *Moeurs*, the autobiographical book of Justine's first husband Jacob Arnauti, with his own summary of events. Enjoying the screen of palms framing the Alexandrian horizon, he also encounters Justine's refracted image. Yet, the consistently negative register, the "gaunt" and "moribund" hotel premises, as well as the "motionless" surroundings evoke sterility and a sense of *vanitas* through the overarching theme of spectrality, lifelessness, and old age (Durrell 2012a, 58):

> They met, where I had first seen her, in the gaunt vestibule of the Cecil, in a mirror. "In the vestibule of this moribund hotel the palms splinter and refract their motionless fronds in the gilt-edged mirrors. Only the rich can afford to stay permanently—those who live on in the guilt-edged security of a pensionable old age."
>
> (58)

The "gilt-edged mirrors" refract not the expected grandeur, but an image of decay, and the literal senescence of a "guilt-edged" complacency and civility (58). Most importantly, the cultivation of extravagant mannerisms and affectations in the hotel lounge evokes an ideology of excess, artificiality, and hedonistic aestheticism:

> In the lobby tonight a small circle of Syrians, heavy in their dark suits, and yellow in their scarlet *tarbushes*, solemnly sit. Their hippopotamus-like womenfolk, lightly moustached, have jingled off to bed in their jewellery. The men's curious soft oval faces and effeminate voices are busy upon jewel-boxes—for each of these brokers carries his choicest jewels with him in a casket; and after dinner the talk has turned to male jewellery. [...] They croon like eunuchs over the jewels, turning them this way and that in the light to appraise them. They flash their sweet white teeth in little feminine smiles. They sigh. A white-robed waiter with a polished ebony face brings coffee. A silver hinge flies open upon heavy white (like the thighs of Egyptian women) cigarettes each with its few flecks of *hashish*.
> (58–59)

The Cecil hotel lobby accommodates a plethora of decadent traits—disregard for personal health, promiscuity, complete surrender to materiality, excessive indulgence in pleasure or luxury. The self-indulgence of the *Belle Époque* of Alexandria finds expression in the extravagant hedonism of Georges-Gaston Pombal's "gaunt bedroom" in *Justine* (141). The realization that the private chamber of the lewd French consular official is "vaguely *fin de siècle*" is followed by a reference to Oscar Wilde (141). The tetralogy summons a neo-decadent aura, connected both with orientalist perspectives and the demise of the British colonial project in Egypt. Durrell's decadent aesthetics, with which his hotels are imbued, become, in other words, the index of colonial decline. While the author zooms into the interior spaces of the decadent hotel, the overt exoticization, misogyny, and homophobic demonization of Arab homosociality in the previous excerpt expose the consistent framing of Alexandrians as immured in narcissistic ridiculousness by the western, colonial gaze. The intoxicating, hallucinatory effect of hashish—the Egyptian import most favoured by continental decadents—is also suggestive of this version of oriental decadence and the lingering presence of decadent traits in Durrell's tetralogy.

My reading of Durrell's decadent tropes is in line with recent repositionings of literary representations of Egypt within an expanded decadent canon.[3] Colonial Egypt brought forth a transnational and transcultural formulation of decadence marked by, according to Dennis Denisoff, the "common turn by Westerners to non-European aesthetics and scenarios to evoke a sexualized exoticism," thus contributing to the "globalism of decadence" (2021, 137). David Fieni's *Decadent Orientalisms* (2020) also posits Orientalism and decadence as joint discursive modes that subvert the binary of Orientalism or counter-Orientalism. Fieni's premise that the debate on decadentism must be situated within the triangle of "decadence, Orientalism, and colonial modernity" and that the Orient is constituted by its internal decay and regression (2020, 5) finds clear application in the *Quartet*. Yet Durrell is conspicuously absent from this critical discussion. In an earlier essay, George Steiner mentions that Durrell's graceful prose admittedly saves the *Quartet* from purely resembling a "decadent show-off," concluding that the tetralogy's maximalist abundance and "bitchy camaraderie, verbal sophistication, and erotic coolness" would, rather, connect it with the legacy of the "Camp and the dandyism of the Edwardians" (1986, 284, 285). While Steiner connects Durrell's style with a presumed a-political stance (1986, 285), this essay argues that through decadence the tetralogy displays a high degree of awareness of the socio-political realities of Alexandria and the empire. In fact, the overwhelming displays of colonial hotel decadence coupled with the theme of the exilic rootlessness of colonizers torn between complicity and guilt construct the political vision of the *Quartet*.

The exploration of Durrell's decadent hotel rooms suggests a fresh way of engaging with an author that has not been considered part of the decadent canon. While separating the characters from the city, at the same time, the hotel rooms enable incursions from the outer to the inner and vice versa, figuratively facilitated by the "cracked and peeling ceilings" of inaccessible, private, "shuttered rooms" that remain nevertheless visible (Durrell 2012a, 700). The zooming in on the private rooms evokes C. P. Cavafy, whose confinement of Alexandria and the Alexandrians to small, ephemeral rooms and interiors in his poems presents the contrast between the interior and the exterior, always to the detriment of the latter.[4] The presence of six Cavafy poems freely translated by Durrell in the *Quartet*—including "The Afternoon Sun" which posits a "familiar," "shabby," "little room" as the cornerstone in Cavafy's poetic universe casting an erotic glow on the most mundane and trivial things—suggests an affinity between the two writers (2012a, 882). Durrell's hotel rooms also radiate, but with the blaze of depravity of wanton Alexandrians, who, sequestered in "a hotel," seem to spend an inexcusably long time "in bed" (288). Looking at their city from afar, they seem to visualize Alexandria from the microscopic promontories of hotel rooms.

The decadent extensions of Durrell's objectified, fallen, seductive, demi-monde world are manifested in the climactic revulsion at the city that has eventually come to resemble a purgatory: "Alexandria, princess and whore. The royal city and the *anus mundi*" (2012a, 700).[5] The reference to Alexandria as "anus mundi" (the world's anus), in accordance with the definition of Auschwitz by its SS staff member Dr Heinz Thilo, imposes a haunting holocaust metaphor on the setting and atmosphere of the *Quartet* (700). The hotels of Alexandria partake in the "mere saturnalia of a war" (668).

A characteristic example of the exaggerated appropriation of the decadent mode within the colonial hotels of Alexandria is the disintegration of the "gaunt" Mount Vulture Hotel and its aura of moral decline reflected in its material decay:

> Justine raced ahead of me up the staircases of the gaunt hotel which he had loved so much (indeed, he had christened it Mount Vulture Hotel—I presume from the swarm of whores who fluttered about in the street outside it, like vultures).
> (2012a, 311–12)

The dilapidation suggests that the promise of grandeur within the colonial hotel is an illusion. The decline of the empire encroaches upon the hotel which is presented as "rotting," falling literally to pieces, becoming dark and uncanny: "The old dirty lift, its seats trimmed with dusty brown braid and its mirrors with rotting lace curtains, jerked them slowly upwards into the cobwebbed gloom" (528). Groping for the bed-lamp, Pursewarden finds that it does not work (529). Immersed in the total darkness of his hotel room, the British expatriate writer and member of the diplomatic corps begins to realize that, at least in this narrow corner of the British empire, the sun has finally set and that there is nothing to illuminate the darkness of Britain's terminal imperial deterioration. His humorously rendered predicament caused by "[t]he irregularities in the water system of the Mount Vulture Hotel" (519) which obstruct his showers and shaving rituals points to the impossibility of leading any kind of decent, coherent, or even clean life in the hotel premises: "How typical of the Mount Vulture Hotel, to have hot bathwater at such an hour and at no other" (534). Things soon take an even darker twist.

The suicide of Pursewarden in the Mount Vulture Hotel becomes one of Durrell's most potent formulations of hotel decadence. Before lying down "on that stale earthly" hotel bed for the last time, the head of the British cultural mission in Egypt leaves secret messages "on the mirror of that shabby hotel-room" and then kills himself (2012a, 565). Having been a permanent hotel guest and undercover agent in Alexandria, serving the Diplomatic Service in intelligence and propaganda, Pursewarden wryly inscribes his will on the hotel mirrors with a wet shaving stick. Nessim frantically tries to conceal his involvement in the conspiracy against the British in Palestine: "'There must be nothing for the Egyptian police to find.' [...] Every mirror bore a soap-inscription. Nessim had partly obliterated one. I could only make out the letters OHEN... PALESTINE...." (312). The narcissism implied in the use of the mirror image couples in a twisted way with the decadent symbol of sterility and despair, Pursewarden's suicide. The first account of Pursewarden's hotel suicide in *Balthazar* is followed by a different viewpoint on the same scene in *Mountolive*. The later instalment also emphasizes the "shabby," dilapidated, ramshackle setting of the hotel drama: "On the mirror of that shabby hotel-room, [...] he found the following words written in capitals with a wet shaving-stick: NESSIM. COHEN PALESTINE ETC. ALL DISCOVERED AND REPORTED" (565–66).

These British intelligence messages constitute a vain attempt at safeguarding the sustainability of the empire that is radically questioned. Pursewarden—the doomed British novelist in exile willingly deconstructing the myth of empire via the infecundity of his hotel life and death—certainly reads as a literary foil to Durrell. The empire projects onto the colonial hotel its expectations of stateliness, stability, and continuity; yet the hotel itself disproves them as mere illusions, with the hotel suicide functioning as the most poignant expression of this disillusionment. Charting the demise of an old order that will bring about no renewal at all, as the death motif clearly suggests, the *Quartet* is often posited as "the British Empire's last gasp" (Seymour 1998, n.p.). Against the backdrop of Alexandria and the hotel as places of perpetual unrest, Durrell's decadence conveys a different type of modernist restlessness, a "typical Alexandrian animation" (Durrell 2012a, 183) placed "at the decadent tail-end of this *Belle Époque*" and literary Orientalism (Diboll 2000, 155). Degeneration, disease, the propagation of a cult of death and suicide—the signifiers of decadence and, perhaps, the other side of the spectrum, the corollary of the Dionysian erotica of the *Quartet*—underscore the novels' decadent hotel modernity.

Pursewarden's suicide is never adequately explained and is variously attributed to imperial politics, incest, or ennui. The correspondence of Pursewarden with James Joyce and D. H. Lawrence positions the novel and its themes within a modernist setting, combining it, nevertheless with decadence. The excerpt on Pursewarden's suitably salacious correspondence with these authors is decadently charged:

> I have seen him so moved in describing Joyce's encroaching blindness and D. H. Lawrence's illness that his hand shook and he turned pale. He showed me once a letter from the latter in which Lawrence had written: "*In you I feel a sort of profanity—almost a hate for the tender growing quick in things, the dark Gods....*" He chuckled. He deeply loved Lawrence but had no hesitation in replying on a postcard: "*My dear DHL. This side idolatry—I am simply trying not to copy your habit of building a Taj Mahal around anything as simple as a good f——k.*"
>
> (Durrell 2012a, 284; emphasis in original)

Joyce's "blindness," Lawrence's "illness," Pursewarden's paleness, malady, and degeneration, coupled with the obsession with "profanity," the presence of "the dark Gods," and copulation, are symptomatic of a modernist climate favouring more visceral responses to socio-political crisis and revelling in physical decay; physical weakness is conflated with moral deviance.

The same need drives Justine whose wail over Pursewarden's corpse echoes through Mount Vulture hotel. The bodily suffering of Pursewarden is followed by Justine's pathologized breakdown when she begins to urinate over the hotel room carpet. Her grotesque ritual —an assault on public decency and sure sign of a colonial sense of entitlement within the hotel space—seems to recall what Arthur Symons in an 1893 article on "The Decadent Movement in Literature" called the *"maladie fin de siècle,"* a sickness associated with a "spiritual and moral perversity" (1893, 865, 859). Justine's sexualized, uninhibited urinating stands out as an indication of world sickness, disgust, and aberration:

> Then she put her palms to the top of her head and let out a long pure wail like an Arab woman—a sound abruptly shut off, confiscated by the night in that hot airless little room. Then she began to urinate in little squirts all over the carpet. I caught her and pushed her into the bathroom.
>
> (Durrell 2012a, 312)

Manifestations of the excremental and the urinary abound in a regressive sequence of disintegrative forces with Alexandria having become a "great public urinal" (732). The perverse ennui of the *Quartet*, its "mental saturnalia" (732), highlights social disintegration. The grotesque imagery creates a total impression of decay that echoes the atmosphere of moral and cultural decline of the 1890s. Memlik, the police chief, is an unapologetic sadist. Scobie is a disreputable transvestite with paederastic fantasies who firstly cooperates with the Egyptian police and then becomes head of the British secret service in Alexandria. This violently transgressive character is "battered to death," while cross-dressing, in an ugly fashion by his compatriot seafarers, "the ratings of H. M. S. *Milton*" (329–30). The locals raid Scobie's lodgings and drink his alcohol. The ensuing *arak* poisonings surreally lead to the canonization of Scobie as El Scob. Justine is consistently portrayed as a nymphomaniac. The "barbaric adult figure" of a French sailor who stands in the centre of a house of child prostitutes, amidst a dozen girls not "much above ten years of age," including a child "horribly shrunk" "on a rotting sofa" in a posture that "suggested death," evokes extreme sexual degradation and brutalized degeneracy (42). Similarly, the less indulgent British ambassador Mountolive is lured into an edifice that resembles an abandoned hotel turned into a brothel. The reference to the "worm-eaten staircases," "the abandoned upper floors," the "long corridor" of rotten woodwork, the orientalizing "imprint of dark palms" and rotten tapestries on the high walls of rooms, and the overall scale of the edifice bring forth a poignant hotel-brothel formulation. Within this decadent universe, desiccated child prostitutes repulsively swarm upon him like "defeated angels" (627–28).

The fallen hotel turned brothel motif is revisited in *Clea*. The decadent plot finds culmination in a love story that concerns a brother–sister incestuous affair set in a filthy hotel room fermenting in libidinal frenzy. Pursewarden's blind sister Liza reveals their consensual incest while visiting the hotel room where her brother committed suicide. Liza's sightlessness, the grotesque simile of her being "like an eyeless rabbit in a poultry shop" while groping in the dark next to an old prostitute asleep on her brother's hotel bed, emphasizes their moral blindness (2012a, 825). Pursewarden's suicide, his sacrifice, marks the first step in the transformation of the Mount Vulture hotel into a metaphorical slaughterhouse. The hotel as "poultry shop" becomes a place of repulsion where human stench lingers and wasted bodies become available for sale: it is "no longer a hotel" (825). The revelation of the incestuous affair—a taboo at the heart of decadence—is followed by a sensuous rendition of a Dionysian, wine-soaked crowd of soldiers and prostitutes roaming the former hotel corridors and ramshackling rooms:

> She wanted me to take her to her brother's room in the Mount Vulture Hotel. [...] But I did not know then that the Mount Vulture was no longer a hotel. It had been turned into a brothel for the troops. We were half-way up the stairs before the truth dawned on me. All these naked girls, and half-dressed sweating soldiers with their hairy bodies; their crucifixes tinkling against their identity discs. And the smell of sweat and rum and cheap scent. I said we must get out, for the place had changed hands, but she stamped her foot and insisted with sudden anger. Well, we climbed the stairs. Doors were open on every landing, you could see everything. I was glad she was blind. At last we came to his room. It was dark. On his bed there lay an old woman asleep with a hashish pipe beside her. It smelt of drains. [...] "This is a house of ill fame now, Liza, I keep telling you."
> (Durrell 2012a, 825)

No longer a playground for the colonial elite, the hotel has become a brothel for the troops. At the onset of World War II, the cosmopolitan colonial hotels of Alexandria end up as waste spaces of the empire exposing, with their smell of sewage, its irrevocable decline. The voyeurism of the scene suggests that the characters are both attracted and repelled by the fornication in the open rooms which defy the assumption of privacy that the hotel embodies. They are morally affronted by it but also share in the decline and deterioration it symbolizes. The fact that the Alexandria Claridge, an important colonial hotel, had, indeed, been transformed into the Fleet Club where sailors on leave could indulge in sensual pleasures adds veracity to Durrell's "no longer a hotel" schema (825).[6] The scene registers the inevitable end of the colonial grand hotels and, by extension, the end of the empire, the end of an era.

The theme of decadence also features in Durrell's hotel novel *The Black Book* (1938). Herbert "Death" Gregory, a former hotel resident, is the author of the black book found by Lawrence Lucifer in a room of the Edwardian Hotel Regina. Entombed within his seedy London hotel room, the diary entries of the now deceased Gregory ooze morbidity. A by-product of Durrell's eclectic affinities with decadent art and the Parisian Villa Seurat network,[7] the novel fictionalizes the long period the Durrells spent at Queen's hotel in London in the early 1930s. In his Preface to the 1959 edition of *The Black Book*, a year before the *Quartet*'s final instalment was published, Durrell admitted to "the crudity and savagery of the book" (2012b, 10), suggesting that its lurid pictures and aura of black despair read as an effort to "try and break the mummy wrappings—the cultural swaddling clothes which I symbolized here as 'the English Death'" (2012b, 9). Ann-Catherine Nabholz maintains that the trope of "the English Death," whose "connotative power can range widely from corporeal damage to culture decay," enables Durrell to "intensify and dramatise the signs of decadence and the exhaustion of modern life" (2014, 306). Moreover, the phrase "mummy wrappings," with its Egyptian associations, may indeed allude to the numbing influence the empire had on its own English subjects. The opening sequence of *The Black Book* points to its shared thematic with the hotel decadence of the *Quartet* and the "English death" it signifies there, albeit from a colonial perspective: "I am dying again the little death which broods forever in the Regina Hotel: along the mouldering corridors, the geological strata of potted ferns, the mouse-chawed wainscoting which the deathwatch ticks" (Durrell 2012b, 21). Both novels foreground a late modernist vision of national crisis, sickness, and death within the hotel premises.

The hotel, therefore, rather than being a mere backdrop, becomes a participant in the struggles and stories that eventually converge in its destruction. The colonial historical context corroborates the plot of the *Quartet*. The turbulent life of the Cairo Shepheard's, for example, ends on 26 January 1952, during the anti-British protests. The rioters set Cairo ablaze, with Shepheard's hotel being one of the arsonists' primary targets: "in 1841, [...] the hotel started its diffusion into the East in parallel to imperialist advance (a linkage that proved eventually fatal to the Shepheard's, burnt to the grounds in the 1952 riots that precipitated the end of British rule)" (Peleggi 2012, 125; see also James 2018, 103–04). After the 1952 *coup d'état*, the British agreed to withdraw their troops, and by June 1956 had done so only to return during the Suez crisis. The burning of the colonial hotel and the ensuing departure of the British troops almost coincide with the publication of the *Quartet*. In the first three parts of the tetralogy, then, Alexandria is the city of the decadent phase of slow colonial decline. The Alexandria of the final volume of the *Quartet* becomes a considerably darker and more cynical place given the fact that, as Diboll notes, "as the tetralogy was being written Nassertie mobs tore down Khedive Ismail's African Paris" (2000, 155).

In *The Alexandria Quartet*, Durrell showcases how the fallen colonial hotels and clubs of Egypt become dens of debauchery, exposing the impermanence of empire. His hotel rooms become symbolic extensions as much of the socio-political failure he witnessed as of an esoteric, queer, lush, and louche apocalypticism. The prevalent decadent tropes become the means of registering this transformation of Alexandria from a prewar colonial cosmopolis to a postwar, decolonized, largely monophonic and monocultural city. In 1962, Anthony Burgess bitterly dismissed the *Quartet* as "sadistic-sentimental exotic escapism [...] in a rather old-fashioned fin de siècle way, suggesting languor and satiety after elaborate self-indulgence" (1967, 96–97). It could be argued, however, that Durrell uses a stale, sentimental, old-fashioned, decadent set of images to portray something profoundly of its time. Out of the decaying fragments of Alexandria coalescing in the "musty hotel-room[s]" (Durrell 2012a, 305), Durrell constructs his own troubled version of a postwar, postcolonial, Britishness in crisis.

Acknowledgements

This essay is part of a research project entitled "Hotels and the Modern Subject: 1890–1940," supported by the Hellenic Foundation for Research and Innovation (H.F.R.I.) under the "First Call for H.F.R.I. Research Projects to support Faculty members and Researchers and the procurement of high-cost research equipment grant" (Project Number: 1653).

Notes

1 The Alexandria Cecil hotel also figures in Naguib Mahfouz's 1967 (hotel) novel *Miramar*, in which a fallen aristocrat similarly experiences the discontents of exilic life within the hotel, which does not stand up to its promise of exclusivity. The excerpt has a distinct Durrellian resonance manifest in the use of the hotel room as an in-hospitable space that simultaneously accommodates the paradox of old (colonial) privilege and present (republican) ennui:

> My room has a formal air, like our family house in Tanta. It bores me. [...] "How bored I am in this grand hotel of yours!" I say to Muhammad, the Nubian waiter, as he serves me breakfast in my room. [...] The only reason I've come to the Cecil is old habit—and, let's face it, ineradicable pride.
> (1992, 53–54)

2 Anthony Trollope's short story "An Unprotected Female at the Pyramids" (1859) and Amelia Edwards's travelogue *A Thousand Miles up the Nile* (1877) display the Shepheard's Hotel relevance to the colonial agenda. The grand hotel, in both works, attracts the high-ranking and distinguished officials, the *crème de la crème* of the empire, and both authors present the rudiments of the British imaginative intercourse with the colonial hotels of Egypt at the time of their establishment glorifying them as mirrors of the imperial sentence through fits of colonial pride. According to Kevin J. James, Shepheard's Hotel in Cairo had become by the 1890s a popular winter destination for European travellers, related to the appeal of "the city's disorienting, cosmopolitan character" (2018, 91).

3 The increasing critical *corpus* on decadent modernisms includes Kate Hext and Alex Murray's *Decadence in the Age of Modernism* (2019), which engages with the "blushingly denied" modernist decadent canon (2019, 3). The volume traces how modernism evolved out of the decadent movement offering a revisionary history of modernism while drawing attention to decadent thinking in F. Scott Fitzgerald, D. H. Lawrence, James Joyce, and H. D. among others.
4 See Jeffreys (2016) for an analysis of Cavafy's decadent hues.
5 See Christophe Ippolito who has traced the allegorical feminization of Alexandria in Anatole France's *Thaïs* and Pierre Louÿs's *Aphrodite* (2000, 125–33). The consistent "feminization" of Alexandria as princess and whore, its "odalisque-like quality," also points to the reanimation of decadent dialectics (Halim 2013, 20–21).
6 Durrell's retrospective observation in "Alexandria, Cairo and Upper Egypt, 1977" also humorously points to this:

> And troops always, you know, make an awful mess of countries and towns when they move in. All the hotels had been taken over and become HQs. You were likely to get caught in the swing doors of Shepheard's Hotel, because General de Gaulle used to enter at such a rate that if you were light you would get swept round and round.
>
> (2019, 412)

7 In *Personal Modernisms*, James Gifford discusses the Villa Seurat group as a critical nexus of intellectual activity and *avant-garde* authors who shared common surrealist interests largely developed out of Henry Miller's works and associations. Excerpts from Durrell's *The Black Book* were amongst the very first works published in the network periodical (2014, 61–67).

Works Cited

Burgess, Anthony. 1967. *The Novel Now: A Guide to Contemporary Fiction*. London: Norton.
Denisoff, Dennis. 2021. "Feminist Global Decadence." *Feminist Modernist Studies* 4 (2): 137–45.
Diboll, Mike. 2000. "'A Disciple Has Crossed Over by Water': An Analysis of Lawrence Durrell's *Alexandria Quartet* in its Egyptian Historical and Intellectual Contexts." PhD Thesis. University of Leicester.
Durrell, Lawrence. 1958. *Balthazar*. London: Faber & Faber.
Durrell, Lawrence. 2012a. *The Alexandria Quartet*. London: Faber & Faber.
Durrell, Lawrence. 2012b. *The Black Book*. London: Faber & Faber.
Durrell, Lawrence. 2014. "Introduction." In *Alexandria: A History and Guide*, edited by E. M. Forster, xv–xx. London and New York: Tauris Parke Paperbacks.
Durrell, Lawrence. 2019. "Alexandria, Cairo and Upper Egypt, 1977." In *Lawrence Durrell's Endpapers and Inklings 1933–1988, Volume I: Autobiographies, Fictions, Spirit of Place*, edited by Richard Pine, 407–17. Newcastle: Cambridge Scholars Publishing.
Edwards, Amelia B. 1891. *A Thousand Miles up the Nile*. London: George Routledge & Sons.
Fieni, David. 2020. *Decadent Orientalisms: The Decay of Colonial Modernity*. New York: Fordham University Press.

Forster, E. M. 1962. *Pharos and Pharillon: A Novelist's Sketchbook of Alexandria Through the Ages*. New York: Alfred. A Knopf.
Forster, E. M. 2014. *Alexandria: A History and Guide*. London and New York: Tauris Parke Paperbacks.
Gifford, James. 2014. *Personal Modernisms: Anarchist Networks and the Later Avant-Gardes*. Edmonton: University of Alberta Press.
Haag, Michael. 2004. *Alexandria: City of Memory*. New London: Yale University Press.
Halim, Hala. 2013. *Alexandrian Cosmopolitanism: An Archive*. New York: Fordham University Press.
Hext, Kate, and Alex Murray, eds. 2019. *Decadence in the Age of Modernism*. Baltimore: Johns Hopkins University Press.
Ibrahim, Tarek. 2019. *Shepheard's of Cairo: The Birth of the Oriental Grand Hotel*. Wiesbaden: Reichert Verlag.
Ippolito, Christophe. 2000. "Paris, 1890: La Décadence Au Miroir Alexandrin." *Romance Studies* 18 (2): 125–33.
James, Kevin J. 2018. *Histories, Meanings and Representations of the Modern Hotel*. Bristol: Channel View Publications.
Jeffreys, Peter. 2016. *Reframing Decadence: C. P. Cavafy's Imaginary Portraits*. Ithaca: Cornell University Press.
Mahfouz, Naguib. 1992. *Miramar*. New York: Anchor Books.
Nabholz, Ann-Catherine. 2014. "Discourse of Pathology and the Vitalistic Desire for Unity in Lawrence Durrell's *The Black Book*." In *Decadences: Morality and Aesthetics in British Literature*, 2nd edn., edited by Paul Fox, 303–26. Stuttgart: Ibidem.
Parezanović, Tijana. 2016. "Other Spaces of the Empire: A Colonial Hotel in J. G. Farrell's *Troubles*." *Prague Journal of English Studies* 5 (1): 53–70.
Peleggi, Maurizio. 2012. "The Social and Material Life of Colonial Hotels: Comfort Zones as Contact Zones in British Colombo and Singapore, ca. 1870–1930." *Journal of Social History* 46 (1): 124–53.
Seymour, Miranda. 1998. "Sensuous Empire: A Life of Lawrence Durrell, Author of the Alexandria Quartet." *New York Times*. September 13, 1998.
Siegelbaum, Max. 2015. "The Pencil Is Mightier." *Foreign Policy*, April 23, 2015. https://foreignpolicy.com/slideshow/the-pencil-is-mightier-historic-buildings-alexandria-egypt/
Steiner, George. 1986. "Lawrence Durrell and the Baroque Novel." In *Language and Silence: Essays on Language, Literature, and the Inhuman*, 280–86. New York: Athenaeum.
Stilling, Robert. 2021. "Claiming Modernity in Egypt: Decadent Orientalism and Mayy Ziyādah's *Fleurs de Rêve*." *Feminist Modernist Studies*, 4 (2): 182–202.
Symons, Arthur. 1893. "The Decadent Movement in Literature." *Harper's New Monthly Magazine*, 87 (522): 558–67.
Trollope, Anthony. 1867. "An Unprotected Female at the Pyramids." In *Tales of All Countries*, 140–66. London: Chapman and Hall.
Zahlan, Anne Ricketson. 1986. "The Destruction of the Imperial Self in Lawrence Durrell's *The Alexandria Quartet*." In *Self and Other: Perspectives on Contemporary Literature XII*, 3–12. Lexington: University of Kentucky Press.

Rooms, Views

6 Landslide at the Pension Bertolini

Anti-tourism versus Groundless Transculturalism in E. M. Forster's *A Room with a View*

Shawna Ross

In the tornado of modern travel, a hotel is the eye of the storm. Stilling the whirlwind of mobility, a hotel provides the security and repose of home, wondrously stripped of its routine obligations and unvarying environs. But for some guests—including Lucy Honeychurch, the sheltered heroine of E. M. Forster's *A Room with a View* (1908), who chafes against the claustrophobic conventionality of her bourgeois milieu—even this is too homelike. When Lucy checks in to the Pension Bertolini, she and her cousin, Miss Bartlett, have been allocated rooms without the view promised by its lamentably English proprietor: "'And a Cockney besides!' said Lucy, who had been further saddened by the Signora's unexpected accent. 'It might be London. [...] I can hardly believe that all kinds of other things are just outside'" (2018, 3). It fails to mollify her when a fellow guest declares, "here you are as safe as in England" (10). Her disenchantment deepens in the pension's lounge, "which attempted to rival the solid comfort of a Bloomsbury boarding-house," prompting her to protest, "Was this really Italy?" (7). Like Dorothy Gale's farmhouse in *The Wizard of Oz*, the boarding-house is whirled up and plunked down *in toto* far away—not by a literal tornado but by modern travel infrastructures that, ironically, threaten to de-differentiate Italy from the country Lucy lately departed. "Just fancy how small the world is," she remarks, lukewarmly pronouncing it "specially funny" that another guest happens to be the new incumbent in her home parish (6). Trailed to Florence by her local clergyman, her prudish cousin, and a Cockney matron, can Lucy ever, truly, leave home?

It would be tempting to answer in the negative and blame it on the pension's obstinate insularity. Certainly, its viewless rooms and middle-class English clientele create an aggressively provincial atmosphere. By contrast, the hotels served a wide market, including foreign and domestic tourists, businessmen, salesmen, colonial administrators, and permanent hotel residents. And grand hotels, though somewhat standardized (stocked by a rotating set of international architects with similar amenities, public rooms, grand staircases, and French chefs), were not self-contained or homogeneous. Their numerous, diverse employees surpassed

DOI: 10.4324/9781003213079-9

Lucy's Cockney Signora, and locals flowed through to rendezvous with guests or use their eating and meeting facilities. The grand hotel, perhaps, afforded a greater scope for transcultural exchange. What Forster's pension offers instead is a uniquely clear articulation of a tension that underlies all hotels: the tension between movement and stillness arising from travellers' need for the advantages of homes they have deliberately relinquished. A key component in a sprawling network of transportation infrastructures, the hotel's primary responsibility is to facilitate movement elsewhere—yet it must cultivate the impression of a sanctuary. The hotel must be outward-facing (open, accessible, well-connected) *and* inward-facing (private, secure, predictable). In Forster's novel, the guests' ceaseless chatter foregrounds both functions; they applaud the pension's faithful reproduction of familiar domesticity while acknowledging its bare utility as an architectural convenience optimized for interfacing with Italy's tourist industry. This double vision causes an obsession with the trappings of travel, not its destinations, resolving into a discourse of anti-tourism that acknowledges the limits of modern mobility for encouraging transcultural experiences.

Yet the Bertolini does transform Lucy. To recover how this happens, this chapter analyses Forster's image of a generously fenestrated Florentine suite. But it also maps a broader geography by sorting *A Room with a View*'s judgments on modern mobility into quarters. Each quarter transposes the elements of the novel's titular formula: a room without a view, a room with a view, viewless without a room, and a view without a room. First up is a room without a view—the unideal hotel that overrates its inward-facing function, exemplified by the Bertolini and by tourists who privilege safety over novelty. Next, the room with a view manifests physically in transculturally auspicious hotels that balance their inward and outward functions and morally in characters who use mobility to seek new perspectives and grow in compassion. Then I consider the featureless quarter that boasts neither room nor view, populated by those who forgo the corporeal comforts of rooms and the cognitive stability of fixed perspectives. Dramatic falls await them, for their cultural explorations expose them to unanticipated bodily dangers and desires. Finally, in the view-without-a-room, I link the novel's considerations on authorship and war with a 1958 essay in which Forster speculates on Lucy's eventual fate.

Redistributed as a quarter of room-and-view permutations, *A Room with a View* is an exhortation to reject insularity in all its forms: the intimately corporeal, the abstractly philosophical, and the overtly sociopolitical. Uniting these forms is spatiality, the power of individual places to reinforce or undermine Forster's cherished liberal humanism.[1] Because the hotel brings together guests and employees of different national, political, ethnic, and socio-economic backgrounds into contact, while simultaneously providing visual and physical access to a foreign space, it offers a textual mechanism that encompasses the figurative meaning of "view" (an anti-judgemental openness that respects other perspectives and recognizes one's own situatedness) *and* its literal meaning (an orientation of the senses within a particular body towards a particular space). Residence at a hotel, under Forster's treatment, unearths the sensory dimensions of phenomena that otherwise appear intellectual, ultimately exposing the intimate connections among the characters' bodies, the rooms they inhabit, and the sociopolitical views they espouse.

Forster and the Transcultural

For Lucy and her eventual husband, erstwhile nihilist George Emerson, these connections are malleable and fertile. Yet the novel's persistent anti-tourism undermines their triumph, suggesting that the hotel poses a limit case for transculturalism, the theory of cultural mixing that stresses the boundaryless condition of identity in a highly mobile, globalized world. Transculturalism has been embraced in literary criticism because of its affinity with hybridity; when Bill Ashcroft, Gareth Griffiths, and Helen Tiffin named hybridity a "key concept" of postcolonialism, they defined it as "the creation of new transcultural forms within the contact zone produced by colonization" (2007, 108). New forms can be represented *in* literature or produced *by* it, as Arianna Dagnino implicitly acknowledges while cataloguing writers "who do not belong in one place or one culture—and usually not even one language—and who write between cultures and are interested in the complex dynamics of cultural encounters and negotiations" (2015, 14). The founders of *Transtext(e)s Transcultures* 跨文本跨文化 also identified scholars themselves as transcultural theorists when they explained that this journal was intended to transcend the "entrenched isolationism of most academic disciplines that even now are still anchored in nineteenth-century ideologies" and "facilitate exchanges among those who already think in boundless ways beyond boundaries" (Lee 2007, 5, 6).

Like-minded attempts to "think in boundless ways" fill modernist studies, where the rise of transnational criticism followed Arjun Appadurai's entreaty to "think ourselves beyond the nation" (1993, 411). In 1999, Douglas Mao and Rebecca Walkowitz observed the fluorescence of

> scholarship that widens the modernist archive by arguing for the inclusion of a variety of alternative traditions [...], scholarship that argues for the centrality of transnational circulation and translation in the production of modernist art [...], [and] scholarship that examines how modernists responded to imperialism, engaged in projects of anticolonialism, and designed new models of transnational community.
>
> (2008, 739)

I argue elsewhere that hotels hold special significance for modernism because they were an essential means through which transnational modernity developed (Ross 2011). Here, I contend that the hotel's material support of the dislocations behind new cultural forms makes it ideal for transcultural analysis. Additionally, given that modernists also theorized the consequences of modernity's enhanced mobilities (Chalk 2014; Short 2019), and given that modernism and early transculturalism arose simultaneously, we might explore how the two developed interdependently.

I begin with Forster. Transcultural theory originated in the work of Caribbean and South American political thinkers like Fernando Ortiz Fernández (1881–1969), Gilberto Freyre (1900–1987), and José Julián Martí Pérez (1853–1895), contemporaries of Forster (1879–1970). All four wrote in a wide number of genres to diagnose liberal democracy's limitations, with Forster calling himself "a liberal who has found liberalism crumbling beneath him" (1966, 76). All four analyse cultural changes in countries structured by empire and globalization. Forster wrote prolifically about cultural geopolitics in novels, essays, and radio broadcasts that defined liberalism, critiqued fascism, and brought Indian and English authors into conversation.[2] For Ortiz, the Cuban anthropologist who coined "transculturation" in 1940 to describe the Caribbean's mixture of African, European, and indigenous cultures, transculturation denotes the creation of new cultural forms from the convergence of ethnic groups within a nation-state. The appearance of these forms amid violent conflict and cultural losses surfaces in Forster's *A Passage to India* (1924), where Adela Quested's insincere wish to see the "real" India leads to an unfounded allegation that sets into vicious motion the British Raj's juridical system, though its injustices horrify her. In *Howards End* (1910), the rich, conservative Wilcoxes attempt to suppress the cultural influence of the liberal, Germanic Schlegels, exemplifying how resistance against transculturation develops among elites whose supposed racial purity rationalizes their privilege.

Forster's travel writing, promotion of Indian writers, and pleas for cross-cultural understanding are popular subjects for transnational scholarship (McNaugher 2014; Snaith 2019). Daniel Ryan Morse argues that Forster's inclusive, iconoclastic broadcasts "turned what was supposed to be a source of imperial propaganda into an unlikely but vivacious cauldron of artistic experimentation and transnational exchange" (2020, 77–78). Forster appears in transcultural criticism about the works of Zadie Smith, who identifies his liberal humanism as a major inspiration (Moraru 2011; Saloman 2021), and in Gabriel Hankins's recentering of liberalism in transnational modernism, which situates Forster within the "queer modernist origins of interwar liberal order" (2019, 24). Critics explicitly figuring *A Passage to India* as transcultural include Narugopal Mukherjee, who concludes that "Forster's primary concern [...] is to create a transcultural space" (2017, 166). Nadia Butt (2020) and Irina Stanover (2021) concur that its commitment to inclusivity is a transcultural theme, while Richard Rathwell (2014) finds that the failure of its dissonant voices to effect political harmony prefigures post-1940s debates over the efficacy of transcultural encounters.

A Room with a View is more subtly transcultural. It represents neither novel cultural forms nor profound Briton-Italian exchanges. The one character who deliberately assumes a transcultural identity—deeming himself an "Inglese Italianato" after "a quiet winter in Rome with his mother"— is ridiculed for "affect[ing] a cosmopolitan naughtiness which he was far from possessing" (Forster 2018, 91). The novel's genuine transcultural affinities mirror Jessica Berman's meditation on the prefix *trans*, which "functions as a critical optic, practice, or critique of the discursive categories of nationalism, rather than describing a new internationalism or global canon" and "shares the oppositional valence of the prefix in such words as 'transgress' and 'transform'" (2017, 220). *A Room with a View* invokes this critical register of transculturalism by using the hotel to consider how particular spaces assist individuals to think beyond the nation and test its moral frameworks. Forster's all-encompassing conceit of the room persists even after Lucy's repatriation, iterating kaleidoscopically until what comes into focus is the corporeal and moral dizziness overtaking characters when excursions threaten to question national norms. The transcultural forces of modern mobility collide with Edwardian attitudes towards the body, whose pleasures and vulnerabilities are dangerously amplified every time Lucy advances towards a view.

A Room without a View

Before Forster proposes a cure for this transcultural malaise, he diagnoses its symptoms: a series of viewless spaces whose disappointments provoke characters into censuring modern tourism's perverse parochialism. As Forster realized while touring Italy, "what a viewpoint is the English hotel or Pension! Our life is where we sleep and eat, and the glimpses of Italy that I get are only accidents" (1985, 52). In the novel, while Lucy is complaining about her allotted chamber, she occupies a windowless dining room:

> She looked at the two rows of English people who were sitting at the table; at the row of white bottles of water and red bottles of wine that ran between the English people; at the portraits of the late Queen and the late Poet Laureate that hung behind the English people, heavily framed; at the notice of the English church (Rev. Cuthbert Eager, M.A. Oxon.), that was the only other decoration of the wall.
> (Forster 2018, 3)

Unrelieved by the dynamism of a riverfront view, the room's austere, rectilinear geometry becomes oppressively domestic with the incantation "English people." This repetition, which grammatically recapitulates the

Bloomsbury boarding house's physical replication, structures the novel's opening: "'The Signora had no business to do it,' said Miss Bartlett, 'no business at all. She promised us south rooms with a view close together, instead of which here are north rooms, looking into a courtyard, and a long way apart'" (3). This courtyard view, giving upon nothing but the pension itself, typifies its occupants' self-reflexive focus on the instruments of travel. Intensive conversations comparing hotels, museums, and guidebooks endlessly defer their contemplation of destinations. Italians become mere mechanisms of transit, extensions of the tourist industry, as when, during a drive to view Florence from Fiesole, the pensioners complain that the driver behaves "as if we were a party of Cook's tourists" (57) and ignore Mr Emerson's admonition, "He has bargained to drive. [...] We have no rights over his soul" (58). While disparaging electric trams, Reverend Eager denounces their less-privileged passengers, "hot, dusty, unintelligent tourists who are going to 'do' Fiesole in an hour in order. [...] I think—I think—I think how little they think what lies so near them" (56). Eager's tripled "I think" softens the hypocrisy of the pensioners' insularity while sonically recapitulating the rhythmic clangour of modern transit. For all its convenience and speed, it feels like bleak repetition.

Once Italy becomes a collection of amenities rated for convenience, tourists in turn become object-like, "handed about like a parcel of goods [...], living herded together in pensions and hotels" (Forster 2018, 56). With "their noses [...] as red as their Baedekers," they metamorphose into the guidebooks they vigilantly clutch (19). Trapped by vendors who "bind [...] their hands together by a long glossy ribbon of churches, pictures, and views," they gaze intently at "hideous presents and mementoes" that "would have cost less in London" (48, 49). This debasement of esoteric, hallowed views into ubiquitous, hackneyed reproductions is syntactically encoded by the repetition in the Emersons' offer to cede their rooms-with-views. Miss Bartlett's fastidious refusal causes uncouth Mr Emerson to repeat, "I have a view, I have a view," until she responds, as if distracted, "A view? Oh, a view! How delightful a view is!" (4). Lucy's ingenuous wish to appreciate the Arno is devalued not only by this feigned indifference, but also by the absurd repetition of "view," which drains its allure. A "perplexed" Lucy dimly perceives that the conflict "dealt, not with rooms and views, but with—well, with something quite different, whose existence she had not realized before" (5). Subsumed into a graceless social scuffle, the view becomes a commodity whose allocation is—contrary to Miss Bartlett's entitled complaint—*precisely* the Signora's business.

Remarkably, the pensioners understand that their obsession with amenities does not promote transcultural experiences. A powerful antitourist rhetoric circulates in the Bertolini. Self-proclaimed "real Radical" Miss Lavish proclaims, "The narrowness and superficiality of the Anglo-Saxon tourist is nothing less than a menace," and announces that her next novel will "be unmerciful to the British tourist" (Forster 1018, 16, 56, 45). Every character, regardless of political and moral orientation, concurs. Traditionalists like Miss Bartlett and the Miss Alans fleetingly criticize their own national norms and agree with the sardonic Reverend Beebe and the socialist Emersons. They do not so much tour a foreign *place* as an unaccustomed mindset. Once Miss Bartlett uncharacteristically espouses feminism, she is asked about George's unchecked amorous attentions, and "her recent liberalism oozed at the question" (47). Sheer intent to experience Italy authentically is powerless to correct the problem. Consider Miss Lavish, who pledges to "emancipate [Lucy] from Baedeker. He does but touch the surface of things. As to the true Italy—he does not even dream of it" (15). In practice, she dispenses tepid advice and offensive stereotypes. She tells Lucy that showing "a little civility to your inferiors" is "the true democracy," before exclaiming, "Look at that adorable wine-cart! How the driver stares at us, dear, simple soul!" (16).

Preposterous as Miss Lavish is, this futile romanticism saturates antitourism rhetoric. Lucy's guileless admission, "I am here as a tourist," dismays them; they would rather she be "a student of art" or "a student of human nature" (Forster 2018, 55), especially since curiously familiar references to former guests "Teresa and Miss Pole" (33) suggest that sets of sheltered maidens and prim cousins are, like Baedekers, standard-issue pension furnishings. The Miss Alans deprecate mere rooms-with-views: they "want a pension with magic windows opening on the foam of perilous seas in fairylands forlorn! No ordinary view will content the Miss Alans. They want the Pension Keats" (166). Their unfulfilled desires are projected onto Florence's expatriate colony, which is presumed to possess that "intimate knowledge, or rather perception, of Florence which is denied to all who carry in their pockets the coupons of Cook" (46). But their villas, hidden in "perfect seclusion" behind "thick hedges" they are "very proud of," reject views altogether (56). If the blinkered antiquarianism of the colony's reclusive writers cannot give Lucy a view, neither do the photographers' "vulgar views" (48). For Lucy to experience "anything that is outside Baedeker" (56), she must combine literal and figurative views.

A Room with a View

Lucy's desire for a conduit to Florence inside her room serves as a corrective to the Bertolini's overinvestment in its inward function. Ensconced in her room, she immediately opens her window, which dissipates the "fog" of Miss Bartlett's "protecting embrace" and lets her "breath[e] in the clear night air, thinking of the kind old man who had enabled her to see the lights dancing in the Arno [...] and the foothills of the Apennines, black against the rising moon" (Forster 2018, 12). The view promotes empathic open-mindedness, for Lucy appreciates the pension's pariah and apprehends movement in what could have seemed static, reducing

Italy itself to yet another art gallery. Inversely, England becomes a still life when letters from home conjure images that "hung before her bright and distinct, but pathetic as the pictures in a gallery to which, after much experience, a traveller returns" (52). At her window, Lucy savours the tumult of everyday life while locals and foreigners intersect:

> Over the river men were at work with spades and sieves on the sandy foreshore, and on the river was a boat, also diligently employed for some mysterious end. An electric tram came rushing underneath the window. No one was inside it, except one tourist; but its platforms were overflowing with Italians [...]. Over such trivialities as these many a valuable hour may slip away, and the traveller who has gone to study the tactile values of Giotto [...] may return remembering nothing but the blue sky and the men and women who live under it.
> (14)

This ironic understatement champions Lucy's refusal to ignore, romanticize, or intellectualize Italians. What her view achieves is this novel's version of Forster's famous dictum "only connect" (*Howards End*'s call for empathy, which is Forster's *sine qua non* for liberal humanism) and "come, come" (*A Passage to India*'s chant, which specifies the essential precondition for transculturation).

Lucy's viewing, coming, and connecting are constrained because her sex cannot roam Florence freely. She protests, "Why are most big things unladylike?" (Forster 2018, 37). As Reverend Beebe notes, "she had found wings" (87). Back home, she demands "equality beside the man she loves" and dismisses her controlling fiancé: "I will choose for myself what is ladylike and right" (103, 160). It is brave to do so in Sussex, where "the Honeychurch habit of sitting in the dark to save the furniture" shutters stunning views of the Weald, and feminism means "shar[ing] a flat with another girl" and becoming "thin as a lath with the bad food" (81, 181). Like Lucy's reassessed feminism, her naïve liberalism matures "in Italy, where anyone who chooses may warm himself in equality, as in the sun" (102–03). Mr Emerson, Forster's liberal-humanist avatar, considers such simple goodwill the foundation of social justice. Rejecting the pensioners' judgementalism, he lectures, "I do believe in those who make their fellow creatures happy. There is no scheme in the universe—" (21), stopping short before becoming doctrinaire. This resistance to rigid moralism undergirds Lucy's new politics, and "the water-tight compartments in her [...] break down," making her "heroically good, heroically bad— too heroic, perhaps, to be good or bad" (86). Moving beyond good and evil, Lucy overcomes her training to meet sexual advances with missish outrage: "George would seem to have behaved like a cad throughout [...]. At present she neither acquitted nor condemned him; she did not pass judgment" (72). In the process of acquiring scenic views, Lucy unintentionally collects moral ones as well, so that the novel productively conflates literal and figurative views to suspend judgement within tolerant empathy.

Working against empathy is the pension's obsession with privacy. Miss Alan complains about hearing Lucy's music through the wall: "No one has the least idea of privacy in this country. And one catches it from another" (32). The guests surrender to this infectious openness in chapter 6, titled "The Reverend Arthur Beebe, the Reverend Cuthbert Eager, Mr Emerson, Mr George Emerson, Miss Eleanor Lavish, Miss Charlotte Bartlett, and Miss Lucy Honeychurch Drive Out in Carriages to See a View." Finding views becomes a common project. But it is potentially temporary: Beebe asserts that "pension joys, pension sorrows, are flimsy things" (35), and Lucy professes, "How quickly [...] one returns to the old life!" (42). Still, the misogynist fiancé, Cecil, learns to reject "silly notions of what a woman should be" (161), and Beebe concedes, "We of that pension, who seemed such a fortuitous collection, have been working into one another's lives [...]. We really must give the Signora a testimonial" (172). What remains obscure is how Forster's doubled view effects lasting change. Lucy develops a theory that "magic" Florence is able "to evoke passions, good and bad, and to bring them speedily to fulfilment" (51)—perhaps, given Forster's difficulty in completing the novel, a reflection of the author's own wishes to create a passionate tale with a speedy fulfilment. But her theory evaporates in an overwrought scene punctured by asides like, "unless we believe in a presiding genius of places" (53). This aside typifies Forster's Greek gods motif, invariably ironized because a deterministic Fate—the deity George and Lucy initially blame for their romantic indiscretions (55, 170)—would inhibit the individual freedoms that predicate liberalism. Lasting conversions occur when individuals own the choices they made when faced with accidents or contingencies. Insisting she was "not to blame" for kissing George, Lucy self-corrects, "I am a little to blame. I had silly thoughts [...]. For a moment he looked like someone in a book [...] Heroes—gods—the nonsense of schoolgirls" (67). Another correction remains: she must admit she loves George. To marshal her courage, she must "recall" how she prudishly "refused the room with a view" (188). This feat is so daunting that, once accomplished, she confesses, "I remember on how little it all hangs" (194). George's serene rejoinder, "I acted the truth—the only thing I did do—and you came back to me" (194), explains that pension joys lose their flimsiness, without *genii loci*, when empathy and openness replace domination and privacy.

Roomless without a View

The novel's transcultural emphasis on empathy (on understanding people radically different from oneself) and on openness (on changing one's mind) undermines the fixity of Lucy's accustomed parochialism, which dissolves under her (moral) feet in the same way that the Italian ground slips out from under her (literal) feet. Indeed, Forster constantly erodes the ground characters stand on, creating a motif of topographical instability that reinforces the pension's own aura of mobility, ephemerality, and transience. Reconsider Lucy's morning view, where "men were at work with spades and sieves on the sandy foreshore" (Forster 2018, 14). This earthworks scene depicts efforts to dredge the Arno and control its shifting riverbank. Rains destabilize the river, "rising in flood, washing away the traces of the little carts" (31), and disrupt tourists' effortless mobility, as when waterlogged Miss Bartlett lurches back to the pension with her "pulpy Baedeker" reverting to its original form (30). Forster uses this image of decaying organic matter to link ethics and unstable earth: Miss Alan's habit of "being charitable against her better judgment [...] perfumed her disconnected remarks, giving them unexpected beauty, just as in the decaying autumn woods there sometimes rise odours reminiscent of spring" (33), and "strong" emotion overcomes Lucy on a late summer evening that "brought her odours of decay, the more pathetic because they were reminiscent of spring" (156). Earthly decay softens Miss Alan and restores Lucy's suppressed memories of her Italian spring. Through seasonality, the past persists in the present—not because the former overdetermines the latter, but because unresolved problems, like fallen leaves, linger. Thus, when the Emersons move near Lucy, Miss Bartlett's enmity resurfaces: "It was the Pension Bertolini again, the dining-table with the decanters of water and wine. It was the old, old battle of the room with the view" (142). Though Lucy has transformed, her family has not, severely limiting the influence of her travels. Forster's solution is more movement, the constant promulgation of new perspectives by ironizing all judgements and indefinitely prolonging Lucy's displacement in a whirl of transit.

Moving ceaselessly across unstable ground, Lucy passes into the quarter with nothing *but* mobility. When characters lacking the grounding reassurance of fixed rooms and clear views tread on ground that proves shaky, slippery, or porous, they fall. This risk is endemic to modern mobility; lean into the view too far, you will find yourself *in* the Arno. Driving in charioted comfort to Fiesole, Reverend Eager indicates Lady Laverstock's villa but warns, "you can only see it if you stand—no, do not stand; you will fall" (Forster 2018, 56). Their return occasions a brush with death when a tramline support beam and its live wire fall yards away (66). Such incidents occur in other pieces of travel fiction by Forster—including Mr Lucas's near-miss from death via a falling tree at a Greek inn in "The Road from Colonus" and the fear-inducing visitation of the god Pan among English travellers, followed by two perilous falls (one of which results in death), in "The Story of a Panic"—creating a firm link between unstable ground, corporeal risk, and personal transformation. In *A Room with a View*, these proliferating falls refute any simple equation of travel with transculturation. When travel is too easy, it provokes not growth but comfort in amenities; when it is difficult, it

Landslide at the Pension Bertolini 105

may provoke self-reflexive meditations on national mores. Forster accordingly disrupts characters' effortless mobility with a series of falls, faints, and landslides, from the Amalfi grotto that "fell roaring onto the beach" and swallowed up Miss Lavish's manuscript (33) to a toddler whose self-imposed injuries at Santa Croce remind Lucy of nihilist George, "who ought to have been playing" (25). Lucy flops down onto tennis courts to end gameplay, faints after witnessing a murder, and tumbles when her Fiesole perch crumbles underfoot. The latter two deliver her into the arms of George, himself dumped into a pond whose spongy bank collapses. Falls push Forster's view metaphorics to its logical limit. Although the transcendental suspension of a foreign view can destabilize national mores, a view's work is incomplete until a violent re-grounding strips away the buffer of tourist conveniences. Mobility accelerates until the traveller, out of control, finally falls—forced into stillness, intimate with grounds they tried gliding over in cabs and trams and scenic overlooks.

With its harsh physicality, a fall emphasizes the corporeality of political realignment. The bodily dangers endured by toppling tourists make the possibility of permanent transformation inescapably palpable (like the suggestion, in "The Story of a Panic," that the death-defying Englishman galvanized by Pan will permanently adopt Italian social and sexual mores). Lucy's post-murder faint makes her "cross...some spiritual boundary" (Forster 2018, 40). Waking, she finds the "world [...] pale and void of its original meaning" (39) and "the joys of life [...] grouping themselves anew" (49). The swoon's corporeal effects seem temporary—"strong physically, she soon overcame the horror of blood" (40)—but Lucy's fleshly fortitude matters inside a pension scandalized by Mr Emerson saying "stomach" and Miss Lavish's mildly smutty novels (32). When George and Lucy assume the same posture while discussing the murder, this corporeal mirroring, to which Forster attributes the "magic in identity of position," is so powerful that the unbaptized nihilist decides, "I shall want to live" (41). His own fall occurs while he hesitates to bathe in an inviting pond. Intellectualizing its attractions, he taxonomizes various water-plants until "the bank broke away, and he fell into the pool" (120). As he frolics uninhibitedly, this "call to the blood" becomes a "passing benediction whose influence did not pass" (123)—a belated baptism celebrating his conversion to his father's conviction "that by the side of the everlasting Why there is a Yes" (26). Paradoxically, these involuntary falls rouse Lucy and George to take control over their lives and enjoy their bodies. This is because falling interrupts the passive spectatorship of view appreciation. Take the Fiesole outing: other pensioners take great pains to locate the precise view that "caught the fancy of Alessio Baldovinetti nearly five hundred years before [...] with an eye to business" (59). Motionless, they re-enact a clichéd view, reproductions of which had predetermined what Florence would mean to them. Rambling unpremeditatedly, Lucy plummets into an "open terrace [...] covered in violets from end to end." Encountering nothing less than the "primal source whence beauty gushed out to water the earth," Lucy feels "radiant joy" and is kissed, awakening her dormant sexuality (63).

A View without a Room

Through Lucy's political and sexual awakenings, Forster exposes the narrowness of viewless rooms, espouses the liberality of viewed rooms, and peels away the layers of cultural insulation furnished by commercialized tourism. Forster takes modern mobility to the extreme to plumb its corporeal and political potential, while using irony to temper his most fanciful hypotheses. Lucy, after all, nearly chooses righteousness over happiness and extends her democratic values only to fellow Britons. When she savours her Weald view—"The hills stood out above its radiance, as Fiesole stands above the Tuscan Plain, and the South Downs, if one chose, were the mountains of Carrara"—the transcultural potential of seeing Italy inside England is unrealized because this "new game with the view" is confined within her imagination (Forster 2018, 145). The novel turns these critiques upon itself metafictionally via Miss Bartlett's trite teatime chatter, "Could literature influence life?" (175), Cecil's claim, "All modern books are bad" (147), and Miss Lavish's novelettes. The Amalfi landslide performs its own judgement on her first manuscript, and she devalues her second by admitting, "We literary hacks are shameless creatures" (45).

The flaws of Miss Lavish's fiction, with its sensationalism and objectification of Italian characters, rebound upon *A Room with a View* because Forster arguably makes similar decisions. Miss Lavish fixates on romance, provides an "absurd account of a view" (Forster 2018, 148), and uses one trip to Florence and a "few calculations in realism" to generate "local colour" and "humorous characters" (44). When Cecil unwittingly paves the way for Lucy to leave him by bringing the Emersons to her neighbourhood, he believes it "a great victory for the Comic Muse" (108), a devastatingly precise but self-incriminating insight. Cecil's Pyrrhic victory becomes Forster's own when his tortured, six-year process of composition produced a novel he called "slight, unambitious, and uninteresting" and his publisher "not sufficiently compelling for a transatlantic audience" (1985, 91). Its bipartite structure divides an "Italian half" from an "English half," further estranging cultures that might have mixed. Although Lucy's egalitarian, sensuous marriage neatly compensates for commercial tourism's stubborn parochialism on the individual level, *A Room with a View* hesitates to propose a more comprehensive solution to this transcultural conundrum.

Forster rectified this oversight in 1958, when he revisited the pension on which he based the Bertolini. In an essay about the trip, "A View without a Room: Old Friends Fifty Years Later," Forster muses on the fate of Florence, Lucy, and George after World War II. Happily married with children and grandchildren, they suffered the financial and social costs of being conscientious objectors during World War I but became active anti-fascists in World War II, with George taken prisoner of war in Mussolini's Italy and Lucy surviving her home's destruction in the Blitz. Forster projects onto George both his own political shifts and his own nostalgic trek. Both men find the pension's neighbourhood intact but "renumbered and remodelled and, as it were, remelted [...], so that it is impossible to decide which room was romantic half a century ago":

> George had therefore to report to Lucy that the View was still there and that the Room must be there, too, but could not be found. She was glad of the news, although at that moment she was homeless. It was something to have retained a View, and, secure in it and in their love as long as they have one another to love, George and Lucy await World War III—the one that would end war and everything else, too.
>
> (1988, 233)

Lucy and George have entered the final quarter: the view without a room. Their liberal-humanist openness persists, allowing their political views to evolve in response to historical shifts that (both literally and figuratively) moved them around with far less comfort than modern tourism. Forster's postscript unsettles the finality of the novel's original ending by insisting on the couple's continued growth and puts their romance in perspective against the background of perpetual war. Lucy's homelessness and the Bertolini's "remelting" clarify Mr Emerson's enigmatic claim that "there is only one perfect view—the view of the sky straight over our heads, and that all these views on earth are but bungled copies of it" (Forster 2018, 157). A room with a view, however coveted, lends a false sense of stability in a world where pensions melt, grottoes crumble, and Baedekers deliquesce. Tourists may search for timeless monuments to sidestep modernity's ephemerality, but for Forster, mobility is, in itself, the only perspective with lasting value.

Notes

1 Forster outlined the key features of his secular democracy, which foregrounds personal connection and tolerance, protects individuality, deemphasizes nationalist patriotism, and denounces totalitarianism, in his anti-fascist essay of 1939, "What I Believe" (Forster 1966). Analyses of liberal humanism have been a cornerstone of Forster criticism (Cox 1963; Trilling 1943) and, since the 1990s, increasingly acknowledge how Forster ironized his own views and understood the limits of liberal humanism (Armstrong 1992; May 1997; Medalie 2002). Recently, postcolonial scholars regard Forster's liberal humanism as the reason for his continued relevance to global Anglophone literature (Shaheen 2004), while queer scholars have taken advantage of the posthumous publication of Forster's homoerotic texts to dimensionalize his liberal humanism as a queered form of nationalism (Goodlad 2006).

2 Forster's most trenchant essays on cultural geopolitics and anti-fascism (originally published in progressive periodicals like the self-consciously leftist *The New Statesman*, the radical *Reynold's Weekly*, and the anti-fascist literary magazines *Horizon* and *New Writing*) and radio broadcasts (some originally broadcast on the BBC Eastern Service) are collected in *Two Cheers for Democracy* (1966). His critiques of the British empire and English parochialism are collected in *Abinger Harvest* (1936), while his notes from his experiences in India in 1912–1913 and 1945, along with some radio broadcast scripts and journal entries related to India are collected in *The Hill of Devi and Other Indian Writings* (1983). For more on Forster's engagement with Indian writers, see Moffat (2010), Singh (2006), Snaith (2019), and Stanova (2021), as well as celebrated Indian writer Mulk Raj Anand's own account of his relationship with Forster (Anand 1983). For more on Forster's BBC broadcasts, and their radical redefinition of Anglo-Indian literary and political relations, see Morse (2020).

Works Cited

Anand, Mulk Raj. 1983. "E. M. Forster: A Personal Recollection." *The Journal of Commonwealth Literature* 18 (1) (March): 80–83.

Appadurai, Arjun. 1993. "Patriotism and its Futures." *Public Culture* 5: 411–29.

Armstrong, Paul B. 1992. "Reading India: E. M. Forster and the Politics of Interpretation." *Twentieth-Century Literature* 38 (4): 365–85.

Ashcroft, Bill, Gareth Griffiths, and Helen Tiffin. 2007. *Post-Colonial Studies: The Key Concepts*. London: Routledge.

Berman, Jessica. 2017. "Is the Trans in Transnational the Trans in Transgender?" *Modernism/Modernity* 24 (2): 217–44.

Butt, Nadia. 2020. "Travel and Transformations: The Transcultural Predicament of Female Travelers in E. M. Forster's *A Passage to India*." *Language and Literary Studies of Warsaw* 119 (October): 141–61.

Chalk, Bridget. 2014. *Modernism and Mobility*. Basingstoke: Palgrave.

Cox, C. B. 1963. *The Free Spirit: A Study of Liberal Humanism in the Novels of George Eliot, Henry James, E. M. Forster, Virginia Woolf and Angus Wilson*. London: Oxford University Press.

Dagnino, Arianna. 2015. *Transcultural Writers and Novels in the Age of Global Mobility*. West Lafayette, Indiana: Purdue University Press.

Forster, E. M. 1936. *Abinger Harvest*. New York: Harcourt Brace.

Forster, E. M. 1966. *Two Cheers for Democracy*. New York: Harcourt Brace.

Forster, E. M. 1983. *The Hill of Devi and Other Indian Writings*. London: Arnold.

Forster, E. M. 1985. *Selected Letters of E. M. Forster, Vol. 1: 1879–1920*. London: Arena.

Forster, E. M. 1988. "A View without a Room: Old Friends Fifty Years Later." In *A Room with a View*, edited by Oliver Stallybrass, 231–33. New York: Penguin.

Forster, E. M. 2018. *A Room with a View*. New York: Penguin.

Goodlad, Lauren M. E. 2006. "Where Liberals Fear to Tread: E. M. Forster's Queer Internationalism and the Ethics of Care." *NOVEL: A Forum on Fiction* 39 (3): 307–36.

Hankins, Gabriel. 2019. *Interwar Modernism and the Liberal World Order*. Cambridge: Cambridge UP.
Lee, Gregory B. 2006. "Editorial." *Transtext(e)s Transcultures* 跨文本跨文化 1: 5–7.
Mao, Douglas, and Rebecca L. Walkowitz. 2008. "The New Modernist Studies." *PMLA* 123 (3): 737–48.
May, Brian. 1997. *The Modernist as Pragmatist: E. M. Forster and the Fate of Liberalism*. Columbia and London: University of Missouri Press.
McNaugher, Heather. 2014. "'She Sought a Spiritual Heir': Cosmopolitanism and the Pre-Suburban in *Howards End*." In *Literary Cartographies*, edited by Robert T. Tally, 75–87. Basingstoke: Palgrave Macmillan.
Medalie, David. 2002. *E. M. Forster's Modernism*. Basingstoke: Palgrave Macmillan.
Moffat, Wendy. 2010. *E. M. Forster: A New Life*. London: Bloomsbury.
Moraru, Christian. 2011. "The Forster Connection or, Cosmopolitanism Redux: Zadie Smith's *On Beauty*, *Howards End*, and the Schlegels," *The Comparatist* 35 (1): 135.
Morse, Daniel Ryan. 2020. *Radio Empire*. New York: Columbia University Press.
Mukherjee, Narugopal. 2017. "Joseph Conrad and E. M. Forster in Search of a Transcultural Space." *Yearbook of Conrad Studies* 12: 159–72.
Rathwell, Richard. 2014. "The Architecture of Transculture." In *Building Barriers and Bridges*, edited by Jonathan Gourlay and Gabriele Strohschen, 131–44. Leiden: Brill.
Ross, Shawna. 2011. "Spaces of Play: Inventing the Modern Leisure Space in British Fiction and Culture, 1860–1960." PhD diss., The Pennsylvania State University.
Saloman, Randi. 2021. "'The Battle against Sameness': Zadie Smith's Rewriting of E. M. Forster's Liberalism." *Textual Practice* 35, no. 4 (April): 687–705.
Shaheen, Mohammad. 2004. *E. M. Forster and the Politics of Imperialism*. Basingstoke: Palgrave Macmillan.
Short, Emma. 2019. *Mobility and the Hotel in Modern Literature*. Basingstoke: Palgrave Macmillan.
Singh, Amardeep. 2006. "The Lifting and the Lifted: Prefaces to Colonial Modernist Texts." *Wasafiri* 21 (1) (March): 1–3.
Snaith, Anna. 2019. "Introducing Mulk Raj Anand: The Colonial Politics of Collaboration." *Literature & History* 28 (1) (May): 10–26.
Stanova, Irina. 2021. "The Creation of Transcultural Space in E. M. Forster's *A Passage to India* and its Film Adaptation." International E. M. Forster Society Conference, University of Warsaw. 7 June 2021.
Trilling, Lionel. 1943. *E. M. Forster*. New York: New Directions.

7 H.D.'s Hotel Visions

Polly Hember

Hotels occupy a curious space in H.D.'s autobiographical writing and fiction. She spent a significant amount of time staying in hotels, both in her travels and as a semi-permanent resident in her later life, yet the presence of hotels within her writing has yet to be explored. H.D.'s keen sense of other places and settings has inspired many brilliant investigations: from the presence of the sea in *Palimpsest* (Kloepfer 1986); the liminal shores in her short stories (Richardson 2019); the restorative Cornish coast in *Madrigal* and *Asphodel* (Friedman 1990, 183); *Paint It To-Day*'s Greek cliffs and Californian highlands (Friedman 1990, 194); the wild pastoral imagery in "Sea Garden" (Gregory 1986) and its craggy terrains that echo the American landscapes of H.D.'s youth (Debo 2004); and, finally, the later war trauma of London's fractured buildings in *Trilogy* (Graham 2007). Adding to this body of work, this essay identifies a palimpsestic patterning of hotel spaces within H.D.'s writing, which are connected to profound moments of spiritual revelation. I draw connections between two of H.D.'s autobiographical visionary experiences that took place during hotel stays in 1919 and 1920, and a less discussed but nonetheless significant otherworldly vision depicted in the semi-autobiographical short story "Mira-Mare" ([1934] 1996), in which H.D.'s protagonist Alex undergoes a spiritual awakening in a nameless hotel bedroom in Monte Carlo.

H.D. experienced and wrote about her first psychic vision—her "jellyfish" experience (1982, 19)—while staying at Tregarthen's Hotel on St. Mary's in the Scilly Isles with her partner Bryher (McCabe 2022, 95). These reflections formed the essay *Notes on Thought and Vision* (1982). In the following spring, while sitting with Bryher in a bedroom at the Grand Hôtel d'Angleterre et Belle Venise on the Greek island of Corfu, H.D. had what she describes as her "writing-on-the-wall" vision, later recounted in *Tribute to Freud* ([1956]1985, 30). Both visions were crucial to H.D.'s personal, spiritual, and poetic philosophies. She revisited them repeatedly throughout her work, reflecting that the "writing-on-the-wall" was "in part, the theme of a novel that I could never finish" (1986, 190). Indeed, H.D.'s work is full of dreams, divination, mysticism, mythology, and Moravian spirituality (see Morris 1984; Anderson 2013; Hobson

DOI: 10.4324/9781003213079-10

2011; Ostriker 1983; Gregory 1997). However, the presence of the hotel space and its significance in "Mira-Mare" has yet to be considered. Alex's hotel vision in "Mira-Mare" reveals the poetic site of the hotel to be a conduit for otherworldly experiences, where time and space are "broke[n]," "another planet" is glimpsed, and Alex's deep "mythopoeic sense of her[self]" is awakened (1934, 93).

Hotels in H.D.'s Life and Work

Hotels act as peripheral but persistent markers that situate H.D. within various places and periods of her life, from profound visions to quotidian experiences. Hotel names are scattered throughout H.D.'s biography: from her argument in London's Hotel Littoral with her husband Richard Aldington that prompted their separation in 1919 (Silverstein 1990, 37), to the celebration with Bryher of the thirtieth anniversary of their meeting in the Swiss Minerva Hotel in 1948 (Souhami 2020, 204). Writing about H.D. and Bryher in the 1920s, Diana Souhami characterizes them as "writers on the move" (152), tracing their travels through Italy (where they stayed at the Hotel Europe in Brindisi and the Grand Hotel in Rome), Cornwall (in the Mullion Cove Hotel), Egypt (at the Hotel Luxor and the Winter Palace Hotel), Capri (staying at the Hotel Quisisana with Nancy Cunard), London (the Hotel Washington), and Paris (where Sylvia Beach reserved rooms for them at The Foyot on the Left Bank) (153; Guest 1984, 160). H.D. had no permanent residence between 1946 and 1955. Instead, she alternated between the Hôtel de la Paix in Lausanne and the Minerva Hotel in Lugano (Silverstein 1990, 43; Souhami 2020, 204). As her health worsened, H.D. chose not to reside in Bryher's Swiss villa Kenwin, opting instead for the nearby Alexandra Hotel, before moving to a clinic which Barbara Guest describes as "a comfortable mixture of hotel, rest home and hospital" (1984, 306), and then to the Hotel Sonnenberg in Zürich in May 1961, where she stayed until her death a few months later (Souhami 2020, 203; Silverstein 1990, 45). Hotels also act as spatial anchors in H.D.'s own autobiographical writing. She often roots texts within specific hotels: *The Mystery* is tethered to "1949, Hotel Croce Bianca – in Lugano; it was done in two halves, the second half was written in 1951, Hotel Bristol" (2012, 134; underlining in the original). Similarly, H.D. begins *Tribute to Freud* with the dates and name of the hotel she stayed at throughout her sessions with Sigmund Freud: "It was Vienna, 1933–1934. I had a room in the Hotel Regina, Freiheitsplatz" (1985, 3).

Within H.D.'s fiction, hotel spaces are interwoven in a number of different ways. For example, the Hotel Danieli in Venice, where H.D. stayed in 1928 with Bryher and her lover Kenneth Macpherson on their "un-official honey-moon à trois" (H.D. 2012, 134), manifests itself in the character Daniel, who appears repeatedly throughout H.D.'s Dijon series.[1] She describes Daniel as "a Kenneth fantasy" (2012,

128), encapsulating the intertwined presence of the Hotel Danieli and Macpherson within his name. The Danieli surfaces again in the POOL group's film *Foothills* (1929), which starred H.D. and was directed by Macpherson.[2] Although *Foothills* is lost, the synopsis maps a romantic drama that culminates with Jess (played by H.D.) abandoning her fiancé for the "young peasant" Jean, and cryptically recalls the hotel in its final line: the "camera pans upward to a label on [her] suitcase. Hotel Danieli, Venice" ("Synopsis of Foothills" n.d.). When placed in dialogue with its biographical significance, the Hotel Danieli becomes a shared affective code that links H.D., Bryher, and Macpherson to one another. The Hotel Danieli is thus bound to the POOL group's private lives, covertly rippling throughout H.D.'s short stories and *Foothills*. POOL's feature-length film *Borderline* (1930) utilizes the space of the hotel in a different manner, as an indeterminate site of convergence for its guests, who are described by H.D. as "borderline social cases, not out of life, not in life" ("Borderline Pamphlet"). Affairs and murders are concealed in different hotel bedrooms, and *Borderline*'s "cheap hotel-café" ("Borderline Pamphlet") acts as a transgressive queer space for the pianist (Robert Herring) to gaze longingly at a picture of Pete (Paul Robeson), and for the manager (Bryher) and the barmaid (Charlotte Arthur) to hang from each other's arms. While *Borderline*'s hotel operates at an intersection, bridging the borderline states that the film explores, the hotel space in H.D.'s novel *Palimpsest* offers a simulacrum: the destabilizing Winter Palace Hotel "seemed an unreality made up of paper cardboard" (1968, 188). Different hotel spaces surface throughout H.D.'s writing and film works in various capacities: as loaded biographical markers, as liminal hosts to borderline states, as an alienating "unreality" (H.D. 1968, 188), or acting as sites for otherworldly visions, as I will explore in my reading of "Mira-Mare."

It is perhaps unsurprising that H.D. spent so much time staying in hotels, or that they should play such an integral part in her literary imagination. Hotels are uncanny iterations of home comforts, yet they can offer guests a transient space devoid of everyday domestic responsibilities. H.D. highlights the creative possibilities that hotels can offer, reflecting on her stay at the Hotel Bristol in Lugano in the early 1950s:

> I had a seven o'clock [breakfast] tray, then after putting the tray in the hall, outside my door, I would go back to bed, and propped up on the pillows, dream in a warm half-light for another hour. I loved this waking dream, in the half-stupor of the early morning; I was perhaps inclined to over-do this waking-dream state, then.
>
> (2012, 136)

This introspective "waking-dream state" (136) is made possible by the unseen and unmentioned systems of labour, of the hotel staff that prepare and clean breakfast trays from hotel corridors. The in-between state of consciousness of H.D.'s "waking-dream" (136) also speaks to the hotel's inherent liminality. Hotels present multiple contradictions, offering a place of shelter and respite, yet often defined by transience and rootlessness. As Emma Short shows, hotels exist on the cusp of both private and public spheres, yet they resist both (2019, 17). Charlotte Bates also notes the difficulty with defining hotels, describing them as a building but "also a state of mind and a resonant metaphor for modern life" (2003, 71). Indeed, the proliferation of hotel spaces within late nineteenth and early twentieth-century literature is tethered to the culture of modernity, which saw the rapid growth of the hotel and travel industries, railway networks, and urbanization (Short 2019, 11–15). The intrinsically modern site of the hotel, then, is a liminal space that not only welcomes but may actively awaken alternate states of being.

Tregarthen's Hotel, Grand Hôtel d'Angleterre et Belle Venise, and the Two Hotels in "Mira-Mare"

It is the galvanization of new modes of experience within H.D.'s writing that occur in hotel settings that interests me, from her curious "waking-dream state" (2012, 136) in the Hotel Bristol, to her visionary experiences in Tregarthen's Hotel, the Grand Hôtel d'Angleterre et Belle Venise, and as set out in "Mira-Mare." H.D. experienced her first vision during an intense time of personal upheaval and recovery. Following the birth of her daughter Perdita, Bryher had brought H.D. to the Scilly Isles to rest and, as Albert Gelpi writes, to "rise again from the wreckage of the previous five years" (Gelpi 1982, 7).[3] It was on this trip that H.D. formulated the concept of the "over-mind" (H.D. 1982, 17), which re-inscribes the psyche to form a new psychological, poetic, and spiritual model. H.D. describes the over-mind through several metaphors: she visualizes it as a watery "cap of consciousness over my head" that affects her sight, "as if seen under water" (18); or "like a closed sea-plant, jelly-fish or anemone" that is "like water, transparent, fluid yet with definite body" (18–19). This jelly-fish over-mind sits over her head and within her womb, the "love-region" (20), both with "jelly-fish feelers" that "reached down and through the body" (19). H.D. envisions consciousness as crucially connected to the world outside of the subject; she describes how, within the fluid jelly-fish model, "thoughts pass and are visible like fish swimming under clear water" (19). It is through this fluid space, outside and within the body, that a new or greater engagement with the other states can be reached: they are, H.D. explains, like lenses that when "properly adjusted, focused, they bring the world of vision into consciousness" (23).

Vision is also key to H.D.'s experience in Corfu's Hôtel d'Angleterre et Belle Venise, the "picture-writing on the wall of a hotel bedroom" (H.D. 1985, 44), in which H.D. saw a series of dreamy images, "a silhouette cut of light, not shadow" (45), projected onto a wall as if by a "*moving finger*" (52; emphasis in the original). She reflects on this vision and the meaning behind the hieroglyphic symbols in her analysis with Freud, who interpreted them as a "dangerous symptom" (51) of megalomania. However, H.D. felt her visionary "picture-writing" to be a mystical "inspiration" instead of illness:

> this writing-on-the-wall is merely an extension of the artist's mind, a *picture* or an illustrated poem, taken out of the actual dream or daydream content and projected from within (though apparently from outside), really a high-powered *idea,* simply over-stressed, *over-thought,* you might say.
>
> (51; emphasis in the original)

The phrasing of "*over-thought*" and its formation from both "within" and "outside" of the body resonates with H.D.'s over-mind model (51). The visions in Corfu and the Scilly Isles outline a poetic and spiritual method of accessing new knowledge and ways of being. They were understood by H.D. as "a sort of halfway state between ordinary dream and the vision of those who, for lack of a more definite term, we must call psychics or clairvoyants" (1985, 41). H.D. was fascinated by the possibility of an entry point into alternate modes of existence and, as Adalaide Morris writes, these visions "marked and measured the rest of her life" (1984, 411).

Indeed, the ideas sparked by these experiences surface repeatedly throughout H.D.'s work: the impact of the two visions has been explored in *Trilogy* (Faubion 2004; DuPlessis 1986; Anderson 2013); her cinema work (Emerson 2020); *Helen in Egypt* (Hirsh 1990; Edmunds, 1994; DuPlessis 1986); in *Palimpsest,* through Helen's vision and Raymonde Ransome's connection with an ancient past (Kloepfer 1986); in *Majic Ring,* where the poet is described as "a projector casting her memories and visions" (Sword 1995, 358; Anderson 2013); in the oceanic feelings of "Kora and Ka" (Richardson 2019); within her relationship to religion and spirituality (Anderson 2013; Hobson 2011; DuPlessis and Friedman 1981); and her position as a "visionary poet" (Ostriker 1983, 8). The setting, shape, and forms of H.D.'s visions vary across her fiction. As Elizabeth Anderson notes, H.D.'s "strange psychic phenomena" (2013, 2) evade straightforward definition. Some are more visual, others more embodied, and some more emotionally charged. Despite their idiosyncrasies, they are united through the notion of her "visionary consciousness" as a spiritual and artistic "quest for transformation" (Anderson 2013, 3). The visionary consciousness in "Mira-Mare" is closely bound to multiple hotel spaces. Understood as part of H.D.'s spiritual quest, "Mira-Mare" expands on the ideas set out in *Notes and Thought on Vision* and *Tribute to Freud,* where the poetic space of the hotel actively awakens Alex's spiritual transformation.

"Mira-Mare" is a short story set on the coast of Monte Carlo and is split into three fragments spanning the last 24 hours of Alex's and

Christian's holiday. The day begins with Alex's discovery of the text's eponymous Mira-Mare hotel, writing and retracing the name of the hotel in her pocket diary, with the intention to return the following day before their departure. Alex does not visit the Mira-Mare again; yet its presence persists throughout the text: Alex repeats its name like "a charm" (1996, 91). Instead, "Mira-Mare" documents Alex's trip to the beach and the mounting tension between her and her companion Christian, before detailing Alex's restless night in her unnamed hotel bedroom. It is in this hotel that Alex experiences a profound awakening, where she feels external sounds in her blood, and perceives a clock strike from "another planet" (73), which starts her "mythopoeic heart" beating (94). "Mira-Mare" is a story that occupies an elusive in-between space, hovering at multiple thresholds. It ends with an ambivalent acknowledgement that something in Alex has changed: pondering on an old memory, Alex and Christian reflect that the "moth having seen the light- [...] never returns to the darkness" (102).

From the moth's turn from darkness to blinding light, to Alex's spiritual awakening, "Mira-Mare" hinges on the idea of transition and the bridging of opposing states. This is accentuated by H.D.'s liminal settings. As Short has shown, hotels are often defined by flux, of a coming and going (2019, 5), which H.D. draws upon through her play with different hotel spaces in "Mira-Mare." More broadly, the text hangs between the urban excitement of Monte Carlo's casinos and the natural coastal imagery. H.D. draws attention to this meeting point between land and sea: looking out from the beach, Alex is fascinated by "the slippery 'last' rock" (1996, 70) on the horizon, and swims out to it. The sense of transit is intensified by the fact that the text narrates the last day of Alex and Christian's holiday, anxiously anticipating a departure that the text never delivers. Even its length, at 47 pages long, sits somewhere between a short story and a novella, with H.D. labelling it as one of her "long-short stories" (1986, 219). The long-short story also resists easy categorization as either autobiography or fictional writing. "Mira-Mare" draws inspiration from a trip to Monte Carlo that H.D. and Macpherson took in July 1930 ("Autobiographical notes"), with H.D. describing the text as part of a collection of tales that "enshrined Kenneth" (2012, 132). H.D.'s and Macpherson's romantic relationship ended shortly after their visit to Monte Carlo, and criticism on "Mira-Mare" often interprets it as an autobiographical sketch of the dissolution of their affair, with Susan Stanford Friedman describing it as a "mood piece attached to Macpherson's desertion, which it never narrates" (1990, 264), and Robert Spoo mapping a similar affective tapestry, noting its happy "watercolour scenes" laced with a "jazz-age ennui and brittleness" (1996, xii), as if ready to crack. "Mira-Mare" shows many such fracture lines. These become generative openings through which we can read the space in-between that anticipates a further opening of the self to "another world" (1996, 93) in Alex's vision.

Sub-Aqueous Spaces and Sounds: Alex's Vision in "Mira-Mare"

Not only is Alex's vision located in a hotel, but H.D. makes the hotel Mira-Mare the catalyzing force behind it. The vision begins as Alex lies in bed listening to the festivities outside as Monte Carlo celebrates Bastille Day, wondering whether Christian will say goodnight when he returns. As she waits in her nameless hotel bedroom, another hotel space appears within her mind: "Mira-Mare. She said Mira-Mare. It was a charm. It held her up, supported her, so that she could sit erect, her feet stretched sideways, out from the bed, wrapped round in the cool sheet" (1996, 91). The Mira-Mare is the building that Alex discovers at the start of her day and the hotel that lends the story its title. The hotel's name is repeated like an incantation, signalling the Mira-Mare as integral to Alex's revelation. It acts like a conduit and also embodies a number of preoccupations that underline visionary consciousness. Firstly, the Mira-Mare establishes a tension: a concern with opposing or separate states that is accompanied by a yearning for unison. Although Alex's mind recalls the Mira-Mare multiple times throughout the day, in conversation with Christian and at night as her private "charm" (91), the text evades its physical presence. Alex does not set foot in the Mira-Mare again, despite her intention to return. Alex's fixation with the hotel Mira-Mare contrasts sharply with her disinterest towards the hotel in which her vision takes place. Her unnamed hotel is most likely based on the Hotel Reserve, which is where H.D. stayed during other trips to Monaco she took with Robert Herring in the early 1930s ("Autobiographical Notes"). However, in "Mira-Mare," H.D. describes Alex's nameless hotel as "a large doll-house" with "tiny rooms" and "interminable hallway[s]" (96). The dissonance between the named yet intangible Mira-Mare and the unnamed but palpable "doll-house" allows Alex to exist both inside and outside; split between two hotel spaces, she occupies both the material and the metaphysical. This is compounded by Mira-Mare's metatextual presence, hanging quietly over the entire text. Despite Alex's departure from the hotel Mira-Mare at the beginning of the day, it persists within the story's title; so, in a sense, H.D. never allows Alex to leave the Mira-Mare.

H.D.'s layering of hotel spaces within "Mira-Mare" encapsulates the impetus behind her visionary consciousness. It sets up a complicated duality and desire for cohesion that runs throughout the text before it is realized in Alex's vision. This is set out in the text's first syllables: "Mira. Mare. Miramare. A pencil traced words in a pocket diary" (1996, 57). Full stops physically split the hotel's name on the page, outlining a sense of separation and subsequent reconciliation as the two distinct words fuse together to create one, "Miramare" (57). However, H.D. does not allow Miramare to be whole for long. It is broken up and splintered throughout the text, emerging with a hyphen splitting it into half, "Mira-Mare" (59), or further still, as "M-i-r-a she spelt […] M-a-r-e" (59). The hyphens fragment the words but also reach out to one another across the page, acting as a bond that is also a threshold. The melding of separate states is then experienced within Alex's body, where boundaries between self and other are temporarily dissolved in her vision, mirroring the syntactical play that the first three words anticipate. A sound outside catches Alex's attention, reminding her of a previous disagreement with Christian:

> Now there was shrill continual trembling, like (Christian said) "wind in telegraph wires." They were, she was certain, tree-toads [...] She said, "I'm sure they're tree-toads." The shrill persistent song of the far insects thrilled in her, like her own blood. The cry beat in her, was her. She was beating with it, was it, wrapped in the cool sheet.
> (92)

The external "shrill" converges inwards, dissolving corporeal boundaries until the sound beats in Alex's blood, transforming her in a moment of profound connection between human and non-human until she "was it" (92). The repetition of "shrill" alongside the echoing slant rhyme of "thrilled" accentuates the sense of diffusion, mirroring the flux occurring as part of Alex's vision (92). Blurring the boundaries between self and world, the vision in "Mira-Mare" allows access to a new mode of being. This process carries traces of H.D.'s previous visions: in her writing-on-the-wall experience, H.D. perceives the "pictorial buzzing" (1985, 48) of images that are "projected [outside] from within" (1985, 51); she feels the jelly-fish as outer "cap of consciousness over my head" (1982, 18), questioning the borders between body and world, just as the sonic vibration in "Mira-Mare" exists both outside the hotel and within Alex's veins.

As Alex's revelation develops, more similarities between H.D.'s previous visions in the Scillies and Corfu come into focus. Alex feels the "shrill" sound within her as "antennae under water," as "defined yet motivated, like sea-tentacles" (1996, 92–93). The oceanic imagery recalls the floating tentacles of the over-mind, the "closed sea-plant" (1982, 19), and a sense of being underwater, as H.D. asks of her vision in Tregarthen's Hotel: "[d]id I (sub-aqueous) in the Scilly Isles, put out a feeler?" (1985, 133). The word *sub-aqueous* sits curiously in parentheses, aligning the feeling of being underwater with visionary consciousness, as H.D. writes in *Tribute to Freud*: "[m]y psychic experiences were sub-aqueous" (1985, 133). The word (1996, 71, 79, 101) resurfaces throughout "Mira-Mare," too, where H.D. directly conflates it with the subconscious mind. Alex corrects Christian's suggestion that cacti are "sub-conscious plant life." Instead, she ponders: "She had said, 'sub-aqueous.' The things, she thought, were under the water" (1996, 71). "Mira-Mare" aligns the sub-aqueous with inaccessible aspects of consciousness that emerge through psychic vision—a concept that H.D. first puts forward in *Notes on Thought and Vision*: a sub-aqueous or "sub-conscious dream may become an over-conscious [over-mind] dream at the moment of waking" (1982, 49). Alex teeters on the edge of a drowning dream world, as her vision overflows with watery imagery, from submerged sub-aqueous spaces to sounds that move like sea-tentacles.

H.D.'s visions in the Scillies, Corfu, and in "Mira-Mare" are all accompanied by the feeling of being submerged in water. Drowning, diving, or dreaming underwater are all motifs that H.D. uses to access her visionary consciousness. Of her jelly-fish vision, she writes: "Sometimes when I am in that state of consciousness, things about me appear slightly blurred as if seen under water" (1982, 18). Similarly, H.D. recounts that as she saw the writing-on-the-wall:

> I have the feeling of holding my breath under water. As if I were searching under water for some priceless treasure [...] So I, though seated upright, am in a sense diving, head-down underwater [...] already half-drowned to the ordinary dimensions of space and time [...] I must drown completely and come out on the other side.
> (1985, 53–54)

H.D. uses watery imagery to interrogate a process of psychic pearl diving. Alex's vision is no different: from sound that moves like sea-tentacles, pools of being, and sub-aqueous imagery, the text follows a similar underwater voyage in pursuit of "some priceless treasure" (1985, 53). This extends to the Mira-Mare itself: H.D. emphasizes the hotel's name, as Alex explains to Christian: "what do you think its name is? It's called Mira-Mare; Mira, the Wonderful, and Mare, the Sea, obviously" (1996, 88). The wordplay around her translation allows the hotel space to encompass a sense of the sublime and watery depths for Alex to dive into.

It is within these psychic waters that Alex feels another sound. Unlike the "shrill" vibrations, which collapse the human and non-human into a transformative "beat" (1996, 92), this new sound shatters stable concepts of time and space:

> A clock far, far, far, far, struck one. It dropped *one* into a pool of being. [...] *One*. Far, far, far *one* sounded. [...] *One* came from another world, the human element was alien. [...] *One* broke the charm, yet still was part of that charm. *One* recalled space, time, broke like a careless hand through paper scenery.
> (92–93; emphasis in the original)

The otherworldly clock strike overwhelms both Alex's stream of consciousness and the narrative. The repetitions unravel the sentence structure as well as the borders between different planetary dimensions, as Alex perceives a sensation sent from "another world" (92), and temporal states. "*One*" echoes throughout the passage not only through its many repetitions, but also within the single-syllable words proceeding and trailing after the strike. The chimes of "far, far, far, far" (92) come before "one" (92), reversing the linearity of the clock's chime and its reverberations through H.D.'s syntactical play, anticipating the "recall[ing]" (93) of chronological time. Instead, time and space are experienced as crumpled "paper scenery" (93), its lines folded and furled, creating new points of contact and structures that bring the past, present, and future together in new formations.

H.D. uses the hotel space to further the notion of alternate conceptions of space and time. Not only does Alex's vision contort space by bringing the two different hotels—Alex's hotel and the Mira-Mare—into contact with one another, but by repeating "Mira-Mare" like a "charm" (1996, 91) throughout the text, it acts like a temporal tidal pull back to the start of Alex's day. Past and present are pressed together in non-chronological formations, which are further drawn out through H.D.'s presentation of the hotel Mira-Mare's historical presence through time. Alex is taken with the "brand-new building" (87) she discovers, which, a hotel employee informs her, is the "Miramar, Bd. Des Moulins from 13,000 francs" (59). Alex rejects the modern title—Miramar—and identifies instead with the hotel's past iteration. She notices a stone engraving that offers a different spelling: "Alex turned to stare at them. M-i-r-a she spelt, to make certain; the Wonderful. She ran her fingers, Braille fashion round the letters. The Wonderful; she read M-a-r-e. [...] Miramar didn't mean anything, it must be Mira-Mare" (59).

The dissonance between the hotel's different names draws attention to the passage of time, where meaning can only be attained by Alex's haptic touch reaching back to feel the old stone letters. The play between long stretches of time is accompanied and contrasted by the sense of everyday movement that the hotel space entails, its temporal rhythms largely constituted by the coming and going of guests. Mira-Mare thus embodies the bridged and unstable states that Alex's vision seeks to reveal.

New "alien" spaces are exposed as Alex hears the strike "*One*" from "another world," and alternate modes of time are accessed by the persistent presence of hotel Mira-Mare and the echoes of the mystical clock chime (1996, 93). However, Alex's vision uncovers a further revelation, which again demonstrates key aspects of her psychic experiences. H.D.'s visions, despite their variances, broadly seek out new spiritual registers, insights, and forms of knowledge. As H.D. explains of her writing-on-the-wall experience, visionary consciousness is her route to accessing "a new set of values, my treasure dredged from the depth. I must be born again or break utterly" (1985, 54). As Anderson (2013) notes, H.D. pursues her visions, which are often precarious, taxing, and dangerous. This is true for "Mira-Mare," too. Alex feels something shatter in her vision: "*One* broke the charm, yet still was part of that charm" (1996, 93). The Mira-Mare hotel becomes fragmented through her vision yet remains, somehow, tethered to the hotel's connotations of bridged states, of liminality and distortions of time and space. Alex is then "born again" (1985, 54) as she remarks: "their lives had shaped to two lives, their separate abstract mythopoeic life and the personal concrete hotel life" (1996, 95). Just like the charm, something has split inside Alex to form something new: she is still grounded in the "concrete" (95) reality of the hotel, but her vision has awakened something else, a life propelled by Alex's "mythopoeic heart, that she had almost forgotten" (94). Mythopoeia—a term derived from the Greek *mythos*, meaning "myth," and *poieîn*, meaning "to make"—is the "treasure" (1985, 54) that Alex uncovers in her vision. It revives her spiritual poesis, allowing connection to other temporal planes and forms of ancient knowledge, while also centring the importance of creation, craft, and storytelling.

"Mira-Mare" unravels the mystic skein of H.D.'s previous autobiographical experiences, presenting a subtle sketch of her own trip to Monte Carlo in 1930. Although the forms and shapes of the visions vary, the underlying currents are the same: they share the sub-aqueous imagery of water and drowning; they all play with and undermine boundaries between opposing states, focusing on liminality and flux; and each have a mythopoeic goal awaiting beneath the surface that, for H.D., galvanizes new inspiration. Whether Alex's vision is a fictional dive into psychic waters, or whether the semi-autobiographical "Mira-Mare" offers an account of a revelation that H.D. had herself while staying at the Hotel Reserve, is unclear and largely inconsequential. What is certain, however, is H.D.'s continued captivation with her gift—her ability to access visionary consciousness—and how this fascination manifests throughout her work. Although the occult, for H.D., is in no way bound exclusively to hotel spaces, the overwhelming presence of the titular hotel in "Mira-Mare" and the common thread that weaves her experiences in Tregarthen's Hotel and the Grand Hôtel d'Angleterre et Belle Venise all signal the hotel as a crucial space within H.D.'s literary and spiritual register. Hotels were familiar spaces in H.D.'s personal life, scattered throughout her writing in a number of ways. "Mira-Mare" forms a dialogue with H.D.'s previous visions, of which the paralleled liminal settings are a part of, to create a third hotel vision. Hotels are perfect environments to catalyse and contain H.D.'s "waking-dream state" (2012, 136), a site of modernity that operates on transience and flux, acting in "Mira-Mare" as a totemic charm, and a conduit that allows Alex to hear otherworldly sounds and bring two lives into being.

Notes

1 Bryher and Macpherson were wedded in September 1927 in a marriage of convenience, creating an unconventional, intimate family dynamic that also underpinned the creative formation of the POOL group. H.D. defines her Dijon cycle in her essay "Compassionate Friendship" (2012) as the seven-year period between 1927 and 1934, which includes "Narthex," first published in the journal *The Second American Caravan* in 1928, and the three pamphlets which were printed and privately distributed by the Dijon printer, Maurice

Darantière, and funded by Bryher. These are: *The Usual Star* (1934) (which included "The Usual Star" and "Two Americans"), *Kora and Ka* (1934) (which included "Kora and Ka" and "Mira-Mare"), the *Nights* (1935). It may have also included a short story "Low Tide" that was also based on H.D. and Macpherson's trip to Monte Carlo, which H.D. destroyed but alludes to in "Autobiographical Notes." The character Daniel appears in "Narthex," "The Usual Star," and "Two Americans."

2 For more information on the POOL group, see Donald, Friedberg, and Marcus (1998); Schlun (2017); and Townsend (2019).

3 These five years saw the declaration of World War I in 1914; the stillbirth of her first daughter in 1915, which led in part to the dissolution of her marriage with Aldington; surviving double pneumonia contracted during her second pregnancy; the death of her father and brother in 1919; and the rejection of both Aldington and the father of Perdita, Cecil Gray.

Works Cited

Anderson, Elizabeth. 2013. *H.D. and Modernist Religious Imagination: Mysticism and Writing*. London and New York: Bloomsbury.

Bates, Charlotte. 2003. "Hotel Histories: Modern Tourists, Modern Nomads and the Culture of Hotel-Consciousness." *Literature & History*, 12 (2): 62–75.

Borderline Pamphlet, n.d. Bryher Papers. General Collection, Beinecke Rare Book and Manuscript Library, GEN MSS 97, Box 168, Folder 5637.

Debo, Annette. 2004. "H.D.'s American Landscape: The Power and Permanence of Place." *South Atlantic Review*, 69 (3/4) (Fall): 1–22.

Donald, James, Anne Friedberg and Laura Marcus, eds. 1998. *Close Up, 1927–1933: Cinema and Modernism*. Princeton: Cassel.

DuPlessis, Rachel Blau. 1986. *H.D.: The Career of that Struggle*. Bloomington: Indiana University Press.

DuPlessis, Rachel Blau, and Friedman, Susan Stanford. 1981. "'Woman Is Perfect': H.D.'s Debate with Freud." *Feminist Studies*, 7 (3) (Autumn): 417–30.

Edmunds, Susan. 1994. *Out of Line: History, Psychoanalysis, Montage in H.D.'s Long Poems*. Stanford: Stanford University Press.

Emerson, Kent. 2020. "H.D.'s Interfaces." *Modernism/modernity Print+*. Accessed May 5 2021. https://modernismmodernity.org/articles/emerson-hds-interfaces

Faubion, René. 2004. "'This Is No Rune Nor Symbol': The Sensual in H.D.'s Feminized Sublime." *Paideuma: Modern and Contemporary Poetry and Poetics*, 33 (2, 3) (Fall/Winter): 111–30.

Friedman, Susan Stanford. 1990. *Penelope's Web: Gender, Modernity, H.D.'s Fiction*. Cambridge: Cambridge University Press.

Gelpi, Albert. 1982. "Introduction: The Thistle and the Serpent." *In Notes on Thought and Vision & The Wise Sappho*, edited by Albert Gelpi, 7–16. San Francisco: City Lights.

Graham, Sarah. 2007. "Falling Walls: Trauma and Testimony in H.D.'s *Trilogy*." *English*, 56 (216): 299–319.

Gregory, Eileen. 1986. "Rose Cut in Rock: Sappho and H.D.'s 'Sea Garden.'" *Contemporary Literature*, 27 (4) (Winter): 525–52.

Gregory, Eileen. 1997. *H.D. and Hellenism: Classic Lines*. Cambridge: Cambridge University Press.

Guest, Barbara. 1984. *The Poet H.D. and Her World*. New York: Doubleday.
H.D. n.d. Yale Collection of American Literature, Beinecke Rare Book and Manuscript Library, Autobiographical Notes, YCAL MSS 24, Series III, Box 47, Folder 1181.
H.D. 1928. "Narthex." In *The Second American Caravan: A Yearbook of American Literature*, edited by Alfred Kreymborg, Lewis Mumford and Paul Rosenfeld, 225–83. New York: Macaulay Company.
H.D. 1934. *The Usual Star*. Dijon: Imprimerie Darantière.
H.D. 1935. *Nights*. Dijon: Imprimerie Darantière.
H.D. 1968. "Secret Name: Excavator's Egypt (*circa* A.D. 1925)." *Palimpsest*, 173–240. Carbondale: Southern Illinois University Press.
H.D. 1982. "Notes and Thought on Vision." *Notes and Thought on Vision & The Wise Sappho*, edited by Albert Gelpi, 17-56. San Francisco: City Lights Books.
H.D. [1956]1985. *Tribute to Freud*. Manchester: Carcanet.
H.D. 1986. "H.D. by Delia Alton." *The Iowa Review*, 16 (3) (Fall): 180–221.
H.D. [1934] 1996. "Mira-Mare." In *Kora and Ka*, edited by Robert Spoo, 55–102. New York: New Directions.
H.D. 2012. *Magic Mirror, Compassionate Friendship, Thorn Thicket: A Tribute to Erich Heydt*, edited by Nephie K. Christodoulides. Victoria: ELS Editions.
Hirsh, Elizabeth A. 1990. "Imaginary Images: 'H.D.,' Modernism, and the Psychoanalysis of Seeing." In *Signets: Reading H.D.*, edited by Susan Stanford Friedman and Rachel Blau DuPlessis, 430–54. Madison: University of Wisconsin Press.
Hobson, Suzanne. 2011. *Angels of Modernism: Religion, Culture, Aesthetics 1910–1960*. London: Palgrave Macmillan.
Kloepfer, Deborah Kelly. 1986. "Fishing the Murex up: Sense and Resonance in H.D.'s Palimpsest." *Contemporary Literature*, 27 (4): 553–73.
McCabe, Susan. 2022. *H.D. and Bryher: An Untold Love Story of Modernism*. Oxford: Oxford University Press.
Morris, Adalaide. 1984. "The Concept of Projection: H.D.'s Visionary Powers." *Contemporary Literature*, 25 (4): 411–36.
Ostriker, Alicia. 1983. *Writing Like a Woman*. Ann Arbor: University of Michigan Press.
Richardson, Séan. 2019. "A Queer Orientation: The Sexual Geographies of Modernism 1913-1939." Unpublished doctoral thesis. Nottingham Trent University.
Schlun, Betsy van. 2017. *The Pool Group and the Quest for Anthropological Universality*. Berlin: Walter de Gruyter.
Short, Emma. 2019. *Mobility and the Hotel in Modern Literature: Passing Through*. London: Palgrave Macmillan.
Silverstein, Louis H. 1990. "Herself Delineated: Chronological Highlights of H.D." In *Signets: Reading H.D.*, edited by Susan Stanford Friedman and Rachel Blau DuPlessis, 32–45. Madison: University of Wisconsin Press.
Souhami, Diana. 2020. *No Modernism without Lesbians*. London: Head of Zeus.
Spoo, Robert. 1996. "Introduction." In *Kora and Ka*, edited by Robert Spoo, v–xv. New York: New Directions.
Sword, Helen. 1995. "H.D.'s *Majic Ring*." *Tulsa Studies in Women's Literature*, 14 (2) (Autumn): 347–62.

Synopsis of Foothills, n.d. Bryher Papers. General Collection, Beinecke Rare Book and Manuscript Library, GEN MSS 97, Series VIII, Box 170, Folder 5674.

Townsend, Christopher. 2019. "A Deeper, Wider POOL: Reading *Close Up* through the Archives of Its Contributors." *Papers on Language and Literature*, 55 (1): 51–76.

8 Carnivorous Flowers and Poisoned Webs

Surrealist Experimentation in Djuna Barnes's *Nightwood* and Anaïs Nin's *House of Incest*

Josie Cray

In early twentieth-century literature, the hotel becomes a setting for women to renegotiate familial, social, and domestic expectations. More specifically, the hotel bedroom is often a literary site where modernist women writers experiment with style and form. Emma Short notes how in the works of Jean Rhys, Elizabeth Bowen, and May Sinclair, "the hotel as setting offers a unique opportunity for women writers to fully interrogate the subjectivities of their female protagonists, and to comment on the lives of women" (2019, 22). While the hotel has been examined in relation to women's relationship with the home (Bates 2003; Matthias 2004; Mandell 2019) and as a space of both refuge and threat (Short 2019, 133), in this chapter I explore the hotel bedroom as an experimental literary space. I turn to two experimental modernist texts by women writers, Djuna Barnes's *Nightwood* (1936) and Anaïs Nin's *House of Incest* (1936), and argue that both writers redeploy surrealist aesthetics and imagery through the hotel bedroom to explore violence, sexuality, otherness, and transgression. Although Barnes and Nin are not counted as part of André Breton's close circle of Surrealists, their time in Paris during the interwar period suggests the movement influenced both women's literary experimentation.[1]

Shari Benstock documents the time both writers spent in Paris, with Barnes arriving in 1921 as an expatriate, and Nin returning to her place of birth in 1932. According to Benstock,

> [t]he living and writing patterns of Barnes, […] and Nin reveal complex reactions *against* the call to social and political involvement in the period. In a political climate that demanded social relevance in literature, these women writers experienced difficulties in finding a reading public because their fictions seemed to exploit an entirely private, even secret, female experience.
>
> ([1986] 2008, 424)

DOI: 10.4324/9781003213079-11

Surrealist Experimentation in Djuna Barnes and Anaïs Nin   125

Surrealism in this period had developed and separated from Dada and was building its own following amongst artists and writers. Part of the attraction to the movement was its challenge against postwar bourgeois ideals. Amy Lyford notes that "[a]fter the formation of a conservative coalition government in November 1919, social and economic programs promoting a return to traditional values—particularly in the family—became familiar topics of discourse" (2007, 4).[2] These programmes which promoted a return to stricter, heteronormative structures, Lyford argues, informed "the surrealist approach to cultural criticism [and] carried an implicit critique of the bourgeois sex-gender system in France, which surrealists despised as an oppressive system of social and economic convention" (2007, 5). Both *Nightwood* and *House of Incest* use the hotel as a setting to explore the experiences of queer characters who are excluded from government policies and domestic spaces,[3] and develop unique styles that suggest an engagement with surrealist aesthetics and ideologies.

Taking the hotel bedroom as my starting point, I examine how each text is shaped by its interaction with surrealist aesthetics. A site of literary experimentation, the hotel bedroom in both texts inflects the protagonists' ventures and the formal style and structure of the narrative. In *Nightwood*, Barnes critiques the figure of the hysterical woman, passive and at the mercy of the male gaze. By hinting at the danger hidden in Robin Vote, Barnes complicates surrealist ideas of female sexuality through images of hybridity and transformation, which break down social limits leading to Robin's progressively transgressive behaviours. Similarly, in *House of Incest* Nin reconsiders the relationship between psychoanalysis and Surrealism, drawing them closer together in her literary methodology. Violent images of castration, death, and rebirth are given new meaning as the nameless narrator navigates a purely psychological landscape, disconnected from reality. Both Barnes and Nin utilize the space of the hotel bedroom to engage with Surrealism in novel form, redeploying certain aesthetic choices and images to examine sexuality, otherness, and identity, leading to the texts' innovative form.

Carnivorous Rooms and Hybrid Women in *Nightwood*

In his introduction to *Nightwood*, T. S. Eliot struggles to describe what the text is: "To say that *Nightwood* will appeal primarily to readers of poetry does not mean that it is not a novel, but that it is so good a novel that only sensibilities trained on poetry can wholly appreciate it" ([1936] 2007, xviii). In dense prose, the *Nightwood* probes the novel form through its poetic style, experimenting with what Ina Danzer describes as "certain surrealist tenets like, for instance, an interest in the mentally deranged and the primary importance of the unconscious" (1998, 240). *Nightwood*, Eliot suggests, is "not simply a collection of individual portraits; the characters are all knotted together, as people are in real life [...]. [I]t is the whole pattern that they form, rather than any individual constituent, that is the focus of interest" ([1936] 2007, xx). Barnes's time in Paris as an expatriate is shaped by her lesbian relationships, coming to the fore in *Nightwood*. Benstock describes Barnes's routine, "propp[ing] herself in bed in the mornings at the Hôtel Angleterre, balancing a writing pad on her knees" ([1986] 2008, 231). The hotel becomes an important site in the novel, then, that allows Barnes to explore themes of sexuality and agency.

In *Nightwood*, the hotel shares some characteristics with the surrealist street, notably as a site for chance encounters. *Le hasard objectif*, or objective chance was seen by the Surrealists as a way of accessing the unconscious, destabilizing the boundary between the rational and irrational, surreality and reality. In "Surrealism," Mary Ann Caws writes, "[w]hat was of the highest importance was [...] a continuous state of expectancy: an openness to chance" (2006, 190). Chance was found outside of the domestic realm, the space shaped by bourgeois and patriarchal ideals of family structure. Robin's hotel is described as "one of those middle-class hostelries which can be found in almost any corner of Paris, neither good nor bad, but so typical that it might have been moved every night and not have been out of place" (Barnes [1936] 2007, 30). Its ability to be found on "every street corner" suggests an openness to possibilities or chance encounters through the hotel's ubiquitous nature. With its blurring of public and private, and its mixing of guests from different socio-economic backgrounds, the hotel is loaded with potential chance encounters and becomes a space for Barnes to experiment with the unconscious and its effect on Robin.

The hotel bedroom complicates the boundary between conscious and unconscious, the rational and irrational. Through the lack of privacy afforded to the sleeping Robin, which provides the "openness to chance" (Caws 2006, 190), Matthew and Felix gain access to the unconscious space. As they arrive at Robin's room, the pair find the "door standing open, exposing a red carpeted floor, and at the further end two narrow windows overlooking the square" (Barnes 2007, 30). The room is no longer separated from the communal corridor and so loses its element of privacy as the door stands open. The use of "expose" here suggests that something more than just the red carpeted floor is being revealed. Similarly, the attention given to the windows which "overlook" the square highlights the voyeuristic character of the hotel bedroom and draws attention to the porous boundary between interior and exterior, private and public; the "two narrow windows" resemble eyes looking out, connecting the unconscious site of the bedroom with the square, a symbol of rationality and social interaction. Matthew and Felix access the unconscious space in part through Robin drawing a connection to the surrealist notion of "woman" as passive conduit to the unconscious, laying the foundation for a surrealist reading of Robin.

Barnes's visual style creates a bedroom that is dense and overcrowded. Moving through the room, the images of plant and animal life create a feeling of unnaturalness as Matthew and Felix find Robin passed out:

> On the bed, surrounded by a confusion of potted plants, exotic palms and cut flowers, faintly oversung by the notes of unseen birds, which seemed to have been forgotten—left without the usual silencing cover, which, like cloaks on funeral urns, are cast over their cages at night by good housewives—half flung off the support of the cushions from which, in a moment of threatened consciousness she had turned her head, lay the young woman, heavy and dishevelled.
> (Barnes 2007, 30–31)

Contradiction arises in the image of the "confusion" of plants populating the room. For Caws, "all the chosen images of Surrealism are, as it were, double-jointed: a swinging door, communicating vessels, the convergence of things previously separate or/and contradictory, such as day and night, life and death, and so on" (2006, 190). The plants suggest a return to nature and the natural, a state idolized especially by male Surrealists. However, these plants are "potted" and "cut" or removed from their "exotic" locations, highlighting an unnaturalness about the hotel room; the flowers are both living yet contained, unable to grow out of control. Barnes's inclusion of sensory images of songs by "unseen birds" adds another dimension to the unconscious space created in the hotel bedroom. The birds remain contained in their birdcages, "forgotten," again suggesting something unnatural about this simulacrum of nature. In Surrealist women's work, as Georgiana M. M. Colvile puts it, the birdcage "acquire[s] a political irony in works by certain women" (2009, 67), where birds denote freedom and cages represent the limitations placed on women artists of the movement. In Robin's room, the birds remain caged but "left without the usual silencing cover" (Barnes 2007, 30–31), which, if the birds are read as symbolic of Robin, suggests a subversion of the limits placed on women; the birds remain singing, even if they have been forgotten.

The hotel bedroom's transformation into a surrealist jungle is further emphasized through its comparison to Henri Rousseau's painting, *The Dream* (1910). Barnes describes the space, with all its exotic plants, as "[l]ike a painting by the *douanier* Rousseau" (2007, 31), with Robin lying "in a jungle trapped in a drawing room (in apprehension of which walls have made their escape), thrown among the carnivorous flowers as their ration" (31). Rousseau's paintings were revered by Surrealists for their "primitive" style. *The Dream* depicts a nude woman reclining on a divan looking at a dense confusion of jungle plants with birds, fruit, and a lurking tiger. The hotel bedroom becomes an unconscious space through its transformation into a jungle. The rational, symbolized by the domestic drawing room walls, no longer has control over the irrational.

The unconscious as a feminine space is emphasized through Felix's position as voyeur in the hotel room; Robin has become the conduit for him to access this space through her immobile position. The privacy of her hotel bedroom is breached, and Felix, although "out of delicacy, stepped behind the palms" (31), still watches Robin; his gaze places her as the spectacular subject. In her comparison to Rousseau's reclining woman, Robin is initially made passive through her construction as art, as something to be gazed upon. However, even though the room undergoes a surrealist transformation, its unnaturalness and staged qualities work against the marvellous image; Barnes roots her subversion of masculine surrealist aesthetics in this unnaturalness.

Like the staged room around her, Robin is found posed on the bed, a posture suggesting an unnaturalness to her state. Hutchison argues that Barnes's use of Rousseau's image critiques "the association of women and the primitive in art generally" (2003, 219). I suggest that Barnes, by positioning Robin in a hotel bedroom that recalls the surrealist jungle, adds to this critique, subverting the masculine surrealist figure of the hysteric. In her "pose of annihilation" (Barnes 2007, 32), Robin is not too dissimilar to the photographs of women under the treatment of Jean-Martin Charcot, reprinted in surrealist magazines with her hands "either side of her face" (31). Hysteria informed early surrealist aesthetics of desire, positioned, as David Lomas suggests, "a convulsive force to be pitted against the despised status quo of bourgeois, patriarchal society and religion" (2001, 55). Yet Barnes transforms the surrealist image of the hysteric, while simultaneously subverting notions of passivity and lack of agency tied to the figure of woman: Robin becomes a queer force who exists against the "status quo."

Though presented as the passive figure of hysteria, Robin becomes dangerous through this pose. Barnes writes, "The woman who presents herself to the spectator as a 'picture' forever arranged, is, for the contemplative mind, the chiefest danger" (2007, 33). The first glimpse of Robin is through Felix, who sees her lying on the bed: "[h]er legs, in white flannel trousers, were spread as in a dance, the thick lacquered pumps looking too lively for the arrested step" (31). Robin's positioning suggests she has been caught mid-movement, with the description of her legs and shoes suggesting some sense of activity in the pose. Although initially viewed as the passive object in the unconscious space, the hint of movement in Robin's pose suggests she gains power in a space often viewed as for men's use. Perceived as the centre of the spectacle, Robin becomes loaded with subversive power. Felix, unable to comprehend the "danger" posed by Robin, attempts to contain her by comparing her to other pieces of art: after Robin wakes, "he felt that he was looking upon a figurehead in a museum" (34), and later he compares her to "an old statue in a garden" (37). He tries to reposition her as the passive object he set eyes upon when entering the room. By undermining notions of power and agency connected to the figure of the passive hysteric, Barnes casts Robin as a transgressive figure.

Transgression in *Nightwood* comes in the form of transformation. Barnes's use of shape-shifting, connected to images of nature and hybridity, draws parallels with the work of women Surrealist artists, such as Remedios Varo and Leonor Fini. The use of bodily transformation in Surrealist women's work challenges the masculinist connection between woman, nature, and the primitive. Colvile notes how "[i]n order to find herself, the surrealist woman artist was not appropriating nature as divorced from culture, but retracing her steps back to matriarchy and Goddess cult, to the prehuman world of animals" (1991, 161). After seeing Robin awake, Felix recalls how "[s]ometimes one meets a woman who is beast turning human" (Barnes 2007, 33); Robin appears before him in a state of transformation, although after leaving the hotel room, it is difficult to see Robin "turning human." Earlier in the passage, as Felix watches Robin passed out on the bed, she is described through images of nature and decay: "[t]he perfume that her body exhaled was of the quality of that earth-flesh, fungi, which smells of captured dampness and yet is so dry" (31); "[h]er flesh was the texture of plant life, and beneath it one sensed a frame, broad, porous and sleep-worn, as if sleep were a decay fishing her beneath the visible surface" (31). Robin's body appears mid-transformation, hovering between states of life and death. Barnes's depiction of Robin shares similarities with Leonor Fini's images of sphinxes, which Colvile reads as sitting on the boundary between the living and the dead (1991, 176).[4] Robin's between-state is emphasized by Barnes's description of her having "the troubling structure of the born somnambule, who lives in two worlds" (31).

Robin's hybrid transformation remains evident after the events in the hotel bedroom. When Felix meets her again, he finds that "[r]emoved from her setting—the plants that had surrounded her, the melancholy red velvet of the chairs and curtains, the sounds, weak and nocturnal, of the birds—she yet carried the quality of the 'way back' as animals do" (36). Her transformation from beast to human remains unfinished, and instead Robin appears even more at odds with the world around her. She rejects her own child, rejects the homemaking practices of her lovers, Nora and Jenny, and engages in even more transgressive sexual behaviours. Hutchison argues that Robin's "active role in indulging in the full range of transgressive sexual behaviours [...] discreetly repudiates the one-dimensional image of female sexuality as it is portrayed in the figure of the hysteric" (2003, 224). Barnes's experimentation with surrealist aesthetics to depict Robin's sexual explorations ultimately sees Barnes undermine masculine surrealist portrayals of passive female sexuality. Robin's behaviour culminates in a final sexually transgressive act which underscores her transformational hybridity, as she begins "to bark also, crawling after him [Nora's dog]—barking in a fit of laughter obscene

130 *Josie Cray*

and touching" (Barnes 2007, 153). Through this act of bestiality, Barnes deploys the surrealist tool of shocking spectacle in a way that asserts a queer sexual agency. Robin's arrival at this scene, though shocking, is anticipated by the transformative scenes in the hotel bedroom.

Scissor-Arched Ceilings and Immobile Fishes in *House of Incest*

In comparison to Barnes's subtle invocation, Anaïs Nin's *House of Incest* is much more overt in its surrealist lineage. Nin's interest in Surrealism began in the 1920s after reading work by André Breton. The Surrealists' focus on the unconscious and the dream, influenced by psychoanalysis, became the core of Nin's experimental style. While the Surrealists moved away from psychoanalysis after becoming disenchanted with Freud, Nin sought to bring the two together, arguing that together they would form the foundation of the novel's evolution. Writing in *The Novel of the Future* (1968), Nin parallels the roles of psychoanalyst and writer, suggesting that psychoanalysis

> proved that dreams were the only key to our subconscious life. What the psychoanalysts stress, the relation between dream and our conscious acts, is what the poets already know. The poets walk this bridge with ease, from conscious to unconscious, physical reality to psychological reality.
>
> ([1968] 2014, 5)

Nin's aim in her writing was to "find reality by discarding realism" ([1968] 2014, 3). This discarding of realism would help form the literary techniques for the novel of the future, which Nin suggests is a "poetic novel" ([1968] 2014, 3), much like Eliot's description of *Nightwood*. One of her more experimental texts, *House of Incest*, was described by Nin as "what it is to be trapped in the dream, unable to relate it to life, unable to reach 'daylight'" ([1968] 2014, 18). Like Barnes, Nin struggled to find publishers for her work, leading to the first edition of *House of Incest* being published by Siana Press, Nin's own press (Benstock [1986] 2008, 430).

Nin's experimental methodology of merging surrealist and psychoanalytic techniques allows her to emphasize the threatening aspects of the modern hotel bedroom. Already in an unconscious landscape, *House of Incest*'s "room number 35" (Nin [1936] 1979, 18) is constructed through violent surrealist imagery which points to the nameless narrator's struggle to choose between rebirth and death. Prior to her arrival at the unnamed hotel, the narrator engages in an all-consuming relationship with Sabina, a woman who "was an idol in Byzance" (9) with "[a] voice that had traversed centuries" (8). Like Robin Vote, Sabina appears timeless and fleeting to the nameless narrator. However, unlike Robin, who wanders away from her lovers, Nora and Jenny, Sabina and the nameless narrator become "inextricably woven" (14); the narrator loses herself *in* Sabina as the two lovers merge. The narrator dissolves into Sabina and becomes "THE OTHER FACE OF YOU" (14), a phrase underlining Nin's distorted meaning of incest: the incest here is finding one's self or resemblance in another and falling in love, to the point of obsession, with that resemblance. This obsession leads to a point of self-destruction and erasure: Sabina's overwhelming beauty "drowns the core" (12) of the narrator; the boundary between self and other has been washed away. When the relationship breaks down, the narrator experiences a moment of dislocation:

> I see two women in me freakishly bound together, like circus twins. I see them tearing away from each other. I can hear the tearing, the anger and love, passion and pity. When the act of dislocation suddenly ceases—or when I cease to be aware of the sound—then the silence is more terrible because there is nothing but insanity around me, the insanity of things pulling, pulling within oneself, the roots tearing at each other to grow separately, the strain made to achieve unity.
>
> (16)

The image of the two women "freakishly bound together" echoes the work of German artist Hans Bellmer and his dolls. Bellmer's *poupées* resemble the dismembered bodies of women, with missing legs and arms, articulated in uncomfortable and erotic poses. His *La Poupée* (1938) shows four legs, each with white sock and black shoe, jutting from a central stomach at odd angles. Inspired by automata and *The Tales of Hoffmann* (1881), Bellmer's dolls are for Hal Foster an exploration of "a destructive impulse that is also self-destructive. In this way the dolls may go inside sadistic mastery to the point where the subject confronts its greatest fear: its own fragmentation and disintegration" (2001, 208). Foster's reading illuminates the scene above. Nin's narrator experiences a double loss in the violent tearing away of Sabina: the loss of the other and, simultaneously, the loss of self she found in Sabina. The narrator is now confronted with her own fragmentation as "the roots tearing at each other [...] strain [...] to achieve unity" (Nin 1979, 16); the "soldering" together of narrator and Sabina, and subsequent tearing apart, is both destructive and self-destructive, and the narrator is left alone to deal with this dislocation. As a homosexual, fragmented figure, unable to find sanctuary in the domestic spaces she is excluded from, the narrator finds refuge in a hotel bedroom.

The narrator finds herself in "room number 35," a room loaded with violent, surrealist symbols, opening up the complexity of the hotel bedroom as a dwelling space. The narrator stares at "a ceiling threatening [her] like a pair of open scissors" (17), recalling images where Surrealists played with various symbols to represent Freud's castration complex, including women's legs mimicking scissors. Foster explains that in Surrealism's aim to liberate desire, women became "*sites* of desire more than [...] *subjects* of desire; women were asked to represent it more than inhabit it" (2001, 203). Foster reads the images of women's bodies manipulated into phallic symbols as representative of the "anxiety [which] derives from a threat that is specifically associated with woman, with the 'castration' that her body is said to signify to the boy/man" (2001, 203).[5] In *House of Incest*, Nin redeploys the scissor-castration image with the hotel room, rather than a woman's body, becoming the signifier. In doing so, Nin opens up the idea of castration, turning it into a broader image of severance, of being cut off from desire. As an unconscious space, the hotel room in *House of Incest* reflects the psychological turmoil of the narrator, with the image of the scissors here evoking the violent separation she has experienced from her lover. Building upon the possible loss of desire, the scissors represent the possibility of the narrator being forcibly cut off from the psychological landscape she wishes to inhabit. Through the scissor's ability to sever the narrator from the unconscious space, it is the threat of forcible rebirth that hangs over her in the hotel bedroom.

Lying on the "bed of gravel" (Nin 1979, 17), the narrator feels "[a]ll connections breaking. Slowly [she] parts from each being [she] love[s], slowly, carefully, completely" (17). The room around her continues the theme of severance suggested by the scissor imagery. The narrator feels the room closing around her: "this room growing around me like a poisoned web, seizing my imagination, gnawing into my memory so that in seven moments I will forget who I am and whom I have loved" (18). Feelings of fragmentation and dislocation are further experienced by the narrator as she describes "d[ying] in a small scissor-arched room, dispossessed of [her] loves and [her] belongings, not even registered in the hotel book" (17). Severance leads to the potential for rebirth, with the whole bedroom exhibiting the qualities of the scissor-arched ceiling. The narrator realizes that the room becomes a way of leaving the dreamscape: "if I stayed in this room a few days an entirely new life could begin—like the soldering of human flesh after an operation" (17–18). The violent image of "soldering of human flesh" recalls the "two women [...] freakishly bound together" (16), yet draws attention to the isolation the narrator faces at possibly living life alone. "It is this terror of this new life," the narrator says, "more than the terror of dying, which arouses me" (18), leading to her exiting the hotel room. Through the violent imagery of severance and rebirth which constructs the hotel bedroom, the narrator makes her choice to reject reality and continue following the path she is on, one which allows her to keep her memories at the cost of entering a state of personal stasis. Leaving hotel "room number 35," the narrator begins a journey which takes her through a number of spaces that offer her the option of rebirth until she finds herself at the titular house of incest.

Nin's construction of the house of incest echoes elements of the hotel with a twist. As the narrator enters, she finds "[t]he rooms were chained together by steps—no room was on a level with another—and all the steps were deeply worn" (Nin 1979, 33). Although rejecting the organized structure of the hotel with no room sharing a level with another, the house of incest draws on the labyrinthine aspects of hotels with possibilities behind every door. The rooms trouble notions of privacy as the narrator describes "windows between the rooms, little spying-eyed windows, so that one might talk in the dark from room to room, without seeing each other's face" (33). While images of confessional boxes become apparent here, I suggest the permeable boundaries between the rooms be compared to the hotel corridor where the sounds of private discussions and activities can be heard; much like Robin's hotel bedroom, the rooms in the house of incest do not offer the inhabitant robust privacy, drawing attention to the unrestrained space of the unconscious. In this dreamscape the boundaries set up by society in reality become destabilized.

Nin draws on the hotel's repetitive quality and pushes it to the extreme through nightmarish sensory illusions. The rooms of the house of incest are

> filled with the rhythmic heaving of the sea coming from many sea-shells. The windows gave out on a static sea, where immobile fishes had been glued to painted backgrounds. Everything had been made to stand still in the house of incest, because they all had such a fear of movement and warmth, such a fear that all love and all life should flow out of reach and be lost!
>
> (Nin 1979, 33–34)

Repeated images of imitation and stagnation construct the space. It is not the sea which creates the "rhythmic heaving," but rather the "many sea-shells" found in the room. The "immobile fish" and "painted backgrounds" complete the illusion of the seaside and emphasize the danger of remaining in the dreamscape too long: without engaging with reality the inhabitants are suspended in a state of inert imitation. Unlike the hotel where repetition is connected to change and movement, as guests change and rooms are made, in the house of incest repetition forms the basis of stagnation. Much like the earlier hotel bedroom which reflected the narrator's psychological turmoil, the rooms in the house of incest reproduce the inhabitants' fear of movement, shared by the narrator who is unable to "bear the passing of all things. All flowing, all passing, all movement" (51). Paired with the anonymity it offers, repetition in the house of incest leads to a point of annihilation through stasis. Nin takes characteristics of the hotel and the hotel room and redeploys them through unsettling surrealist imagery to underline the surrealist goal of connecting the unconscious with the conscious, reality with the dream. Rejecting one in favour of the other leads to an annihilation of the self.

The final image that confronts the narrator is one of departure. Even if guests stay in hotels for months, or even years in the case of some expatriates in Paris, the inevitability of departing the space is present. Again, Nin deploys this sense of departure in the extreme in *House of Incest* through the final image of the tunnel that all inhabitants inevitably face. This tunnel "led from the house into the world on the other side of the walls, [...] where there was daylight and joy" (Nin 1979, 48). Benstock argues that "the only escape [from the house of incest] is death" ([1986] 2008, 430). In Nin's engagement and experimentation with surrealist aesthetics the tunnel holds multiple meanings. The text itself opens with a birth scene into the unconscious landscape the narrator moves through, and Nin repeatedly uses images of rebirth to point to the inevitable departure from the dreamscape. Unlike the scissor-arched ceiling in the first hotel, which suggests a violent removal from this space, the tunnel is a non-violent image. Rather than as a threat, Nin uses the tunnel as a means for the narrator to realize the position she is in: to remain in the house of incest and lose all sense of self, or leave the unconscious landscape behind and confront reality. She is unable to make the journey through the tunnel at the end of *House of Incest*, but there is a sense of open-endedness in the final moments of the prose poem. Nin uses the surrealist interest in contradiction to experiment with her idea of "no-end" which rejects the "booming climax" of standard literary forms (Nin [1968] 2014, 28). The tunnel remains an option for the narrator unlike the earlier hotel space, which required urgent decision. In this final image Nin exposes the complexity of the hotel as both a sanctuary and threat. In its configuration as an unconscious space, it reflects the narrator's psychological state. By drawing upon characteristics of the hotel and deploying them in extreme ways through surrealist imagery, Nin produces a highly experimental text where the hotel both shapes and reflects the experience of the narrator.

After *Nightwood* and *House of Incest* both writers continued to experiment with literary themes and form. In 1958, Barnes's verse play, *The Antiphon*, was published. Later, she published *Creatures in an Alphabet* (1982), a collection of rhyming poems. Nin continued to write and release novels, novelettes, and short stories after *House of Incest* up until the 1970s. In 1939, "The Voice" was published as part of *Winter of Artifice*, another text that uses the hotel as an experimental space where Nin combines surrealist aesthetics and psychoanalytic practices. She would continue experimenting with Surrealism and psychoanalysis throughout her literary career.

Notes

1 It is important to distinguish here between those artists considered Surrealist and others, such as Barnes and Nin, who have experimented with surrealist

aesthetics and have been read through a surrealist lens. Penelope Rosemont makes this distinction, referring to Nin specifically:

> Many are the writers who at some point in the course of their careers have expressed themselves in a surrealist voice—to cite only a few examples: [...] the French-born U.S. eroticist Anaïs Nin, [...]. But that is not the same as actually *participating in the surrealist movement.*
> (1998, xxxvi–xxxvii)

2 Lyford explains: "[t]he French government gave economic incentives to families who bore multiple children, while the increasingly sophisticated advertising industry encouraged robust industrial growth" (2007, 4).
3 Surrealism as a movement has shown a complex, and at times contradictory, engagement with gender and sexuality. Natalya Lusty notes how "Breton's reputation for the public support and promotion of women within the movement, particularly throughout the 1930s, stood in stark contrast to his more traditional and conservative expectations of the women he became personally involved with" (2007, 25). For scholarship that interrogates Surrealism's treatment of gender and sexuality, see Caws, Kuenzli, and Raaberg, *Surrealism and Women* (1991); Conley, *Automatic Woman* (1996); and Allmer, *Intersections* (2016).
4 On surrealist sphinxes and hotels, see Kolocotroni, Chapter 1 in this volume.
5 For example, see Lee Miller's *Nude Bent Forward* (1931), Brassaï's *Nude* (1931–1932), and Man Ray's *Anatomies* (1929).

Works Cited

Almer, Patricia. 2016. *Intersections: Women Artists/Surrealism/Modernism*. Manchester: Manchester University Press.
Barnes, Djuna. [1936] 2007. *Nightwood*. London: Faber & Faber.
Barnes, Djuna. 1958. *The Antiphon*. London: Faber & Faber.
Barnes, Djuna. 1982. *Creatures in an Alphabet*. New York: Dial Press.
Bates, Charlotte. 2003. "Hotel Histories: Modern Tourists, Modern Nomads and the Culture of Hotel-Consciousness." *Literature & History* 12 (2): 62–75. https://doi-org.abc.cardiff.ac.uk/10.7227/LH.12.2.5
Benstock, Shari. [1986] 2008. *Women of the Left Bank: Paris, 1900–1940*. Austin: University of Texas Press.
Caws, Mary Ann. 2006. "Surrealism." In *A Companion to Modernist Literature and Culture*, edited by David Bradshaw and Kevin J. H. Dettmar, 189–97. Oxford: Blackwell.
Caws, Mary Ann, Rudolf E. Kuenzli, and Gwen Raaberg, eds. 1991. *Surrealism and Women*. Cambridge: MIT Press.
Colvile, Georgiana M. M. 1991. "Beauty and/Is the Beast: Animal Symbology in the Work of Leonora Carrington, Remedios Varo and Leonor Fin." In *Surrealism and Women*, edited by Rudolf Kuenzli, Gwen Raaberg, and Mary Ann Caws, 159–81. Cambridge and London: MIT Press.
Colvile, Georgiana M. M. 2009. "Women Artists, Surrealism and Animal Representation." In *Angels of Anarchy: Women Artists and Surrealism*, edited by Patricia Allmer, 64–73. Munich, Berlin, London and New York: Prestel.

Conley, Katharine. 1996. *Automatic Woman: The Representation of Woman in Surrealism*. Lincoln: University of Nebraska Press.

Danzer, Ina. 1998. "Between Decadence and Surrealism: The Other Modernism of Djuna Barnes." *AAA: Arbeiten aus Anglistik und Amerikanistik*, 23 (2): 239–57.

Foster, Hal. 2001. "Violation and Veiling in Surrealist Photography: Woman as Fetish, as Shattered Object, as Phallus." In *Surrealism: Desire Unbound*, edited by Jennifer Mundy, 203–26. London: Tate Publishing.

Hutchison, Sharla. 2003. "Convulsive Beauty: Images of Hysteria and Transgressive Sexuality in Claude Cahun and Djuna Barnes." *symplokē* 11 (1/2): 212–26.

Lomas, David. 2001. "The Omnipotence of Desire: Surrealism, Psychoanalysis and Hysteria." In *Surrealism: Desire Unbound*, edited by Jennifer Mundy, 55–70. London: Tate Publishing.

Lusty, Natalya. 2007. *Surrealism, Feminism, Psychoanalysis*. Aldershot: Ashgate.

Lyford, Amy. 2007. *Surrealism Masculinities: Gender Anxiety and the Aesthetics of Post-World War I Reconstruction in France*. Los Angeles and London: University of California Press.

Mandell, Nikki. 2019. "A Hotel of Her Own: Building by and for the New Woman, 1900–1930." *Journal of Urban History* 45 (3): 517–41. https://doi-org.abc.cardiff.ac.uk/10.1177/0096144218762631

Matthias, Bettina. 2004. "A Home Away from Home? The Hotel as Space of Emancipation in Early Twentieth Century Austrian Bourgeois Literature." *German Studies Review* 27 (2): 325–40. https://doi.org/10.2307/1433085

Nin, Anaïs. [1936] 1979. *House of Incest*. Athens: Swallow Press/Ohio University Press.

Nin, Anaïs. [1939] 2016. "The Voice." In Winter of Artifice: Three Novelettes, 82–128. Athens: Swallow Press/Ohio University Press.

Nin, Anaïs. [1968] 2014. *The Novel of the Future*. Athens: Swallow Press/Ohio University Press.

Rosemont, Penelope. 1998. *Surrealist Women: An International Anthology*. London: The Athlone Press.

Short, Emma. 2019. *Mobility and the Hotel in Modern Literature: Passing through*. London and New York: Palgrave Macmillan.

9 "Found his anxiety frothing"
Denton Welch's *In Youth Is Pleasure* and the Hotel as Camp Allegory

Allan Pero

Denton Welch is something of a nonesuch, enjoying as he does a minor, but unwavering place in late British modernism. He can count figures like Edith Sitwell, Vita Sackville-West, W. H. Auden, William S. Burroughs, and John Waters among his admirers. Born in Shanghai in 1915, Welch was both an artist and a writer, having studied art at the then Goldsmith School of Art (now the School of Art and Design in Goldsmith's College, University of London). At the age of twenty, Welch was knocked down by a car while cycling from his flat in Greenwich to visit relatives in Surrey. He was for a time paralyzed, and then struggled with kidney ailments and spinal tuberculosis until his death at 33 in 1948 (De-la-Noy 1984). His determination to continue working as an artist and writer, coupled with the isolation he felt as a disabled gay man, prompted him to turn inward, focusing his imaginative powers almost exclusively on the past.

In Youth Is Pleasure (1945), Welch's second novel, tells the story of an adolescent boy's summer holiday at a sumptuous hotel in Surrey on Thames with his father and brothers. Welch based his setting on Oatlands Palace, built by Henry VIII from the stones of Chertsey Abbey, which had fallen into ruin with the dissolution of the monasteries. Oatlands Palace was used with some regularity by the monarchs Elizabeth I, James I, and Charles I. It had extensive gardens; Charles I engaged the baroque gardener John Tradescant the Elder to execute them for Queen Henrietta. It passed through several hands, its gardens having been extended and rendered more formal by the Duke of Newcastle, Henry Clinton. The mansion near the palace burned down in 1794, and was quickly rebuilt, in the emerging Neo-Gothic style of the period (*Oatlands Park Hotel* 2021). It included a grotto that also appears in Welch's novel. Oatlands Mansion became a hotel in 1856, and still exists, but its grotto, having been declared dangerous, was demolished in 1948 (*Oatlands Grotto Weybridge* n.d.).

Virtually everything Welch wrote was autobiographical, or, as Max Saunders has suggested, is better described as "autobiografiction" (2010, 7). It is thus no surprise that he had been a guest of the hotel with his father and brothers some years after his mother's untimely death in 1927. In the novel, Welch's counterpart Orvil Pym has recently recovered from food

DOI: 10.4324/9781003213079-12

poisoning at his school, and has spent some time in a sanatorium, before being fetched by his father to join his brothers at the hotel. The liminal age of adolescence is uncannily mirrored in the spaces through which he passes, school, sanatorium, and hotel alike. One of the interesting elements of Welch's novel is that it takes place exclusively in liminal spaces. Home is never mentioned, except as something lost or out of reach. Of course, Oatlands Palace itself was never intended as a permanent home, but was instead a royal hunting lodge. And Outlands Hotel is a site for rest and amusement, but one's stay is perforce meant to be brief. Pym is boarded at a private school (Welch went to Repton), and sanatoria are not places where one wants to be permanently ensconced. As we know, schools and sanatoria are also sites of violence and abjection. Although liminal spaces can be sources of excitement, recovery, and growth, their existence is predicated on places of normalcy or permanence outside them. The novel considers the question: what does it mean to live a life that seems utterly liminal, utterly provisional?

Before we turn to the hotel, we must look first at Pym's experience in the sanatorium. During his illness, he is seized by a delirium that makes him proclaim that he has been transformed, as "he hopped on all fours round his bed, croaking, 'I'm a frog, I'm a frog, a huge white frog'" (Welch 2014, 3). A fellow patient calls for the nurse: "come quickly; Pym has gone queer and is hopping round the floor saying he's a frog" (3). Here, the boy's "amphibiousness" points to the ambivalence and doubt that plagues him. When the nurse appears, she clasps and calms him, and proceeds to give him a sponge bath to cool his fever. As is typical of Welch's peculiar phenomenology, the experience is marked by sensory confusion; his bath is simultaneously embarrassing, pleasurable, erotic, and chilling. Finally, the nurse prepares to take her leave:

> Once more she tried to comb her fingers through his hair, but she gave it up, laughing. "It's like a terrier dog's coat, or the best thatch, guaranteed to keep the rain out for a hundred years." Then she added more softly, "Good night, lad," and left him. "'Lad' is queer," Orvil thought; "it's full of sex." And he went on thinking of words and the different feelings they gave him, until at last he fell asleep.
>
> (4)

Within a few pages, the term "queer" appears once again; its meaning as ambiguous and perplexing—strange and sensual—as Pym's relationship to his body. Matthew Clarke rightly argues that this peculiarity makes the novel part company with the usual emplotments of the *Bildungsroman*, and that Welch's own "attraction to perverse pleasures and sensations could not easily be assimilated into a normative model of adolescent development" (2020, 4). As a writer, Welch is particularly adept at capturing the confusions of sensation; in phenomenological terms, the affective dimensions of the body's contact with the world of objects cannot be organized neatly or simply by perception. As Maurice Merleau-Ponty reminds us, a phenomenological relationship to the world runs counter to the notion that we encounter "objects purged of all ambiguity, pure and absolute" (2005, 13). While Pym is being washed, the panoply of sensations collides as the points of contact between nurse and patient, water, wet cloth, and skin, shift and turn. Welch narrates the perception in a way that does not simply signal confusion or juxtaposition. In effect, words are not inherently stable or neutral. Instead, he shows us how words produce feelings, how they shape perception. That is, we use language to construct and organize spaces of feeling.

Welch is particularly interested in the problem of orientation. In somatic terms, orientation is obviously spatial, but it is also a question of desire. If one cannot rely upon the paths set out by heteronormativity, how does one orient oneself, one's desire? (2006, 543). Questions like this tend to be explored in the realm of Camp. In their queerness, such moments in *In Youth Is Pleasure* defy the organizational quality generally assigned to attention, to the body's capacity to comprehend and absorb what it experiences when being touched. As he is being bathed, the shifting points of touch resist what Merleau-Ponty calls "the invariable factor" of precise touch that can only be comprehended aesthetically once the subject "has stepped back from the changes of appearance" (2005, 34). In short, attention is something that must be shaped and framed in the galleries of memory, as an act of creation.

This impulse, which one finds persistently in Welch's work, is a crucial dimension of his aesthetic relationship to imagination and the past; somatic experiences require, indeed demand, the architecture of language, of narration and reflection, to make sense of them. Otherwise, the pressure of phenomenological experience is simply too intense, too variegated; more pointedly, Welch's injured body contributes to the depth of his fevered relationship to objects. As Steve Finbow notes in his introduction to the novel, Welch is condemned to "focus his mind on emotions recollected, not so much in tranquillity, but in pathology" (Welch 2014, iii). As a disabled person, Welch calls upon the spatial logic of Camp to make sense of the body's relation to the world. But why Camp? As we know, Camp is often characterized as the stuff of excess; it is not simply that Camp characters are too archly theatrical, or "too much," it is that the worlds of Camp are spatially and aesthetically overwhelming.

In Camp, perception is fraught with exception and deception. Welch's phenomenology is Camp in the sense that the world of objects is often a disorienting one; in his work, aesthetic experience is supersaturated, resistant to appraisal, and is ultimately more the stuff of transcription than decipherment. As Merleau-Ponty puts it, experiences of the sort Pym has at the sanatorium generate "not only the intellectual experience of disorder, but the vital experience of giddiness and nausea, which is the awareness of our contingency, and the horror with which it fills us" (2005, 296). Reading Welch is a study in the disorientation of *jouissance*;

the intensity of the pleasures Pym encounters suggests a Freudian "beyond the pleasure principle," one that Lacan characterizes as a form of transgressive suffering (1981, 184). In Welch's novel, the pleasures of youth are neither simple nor sentimental; they are instead evocative of a horror or sickness that lurks behind the world of objects, a melancholy that taints not just their contingency, but also brings to the fore the fragility and vertigo that inform the contingent nature of the body's mortality.

The Camp body seeks out sensation and pleasure but is constantly threatened by the possibility of being engulfed by the nothingness "beyond" or "behind" the object of its desire, leaving the subject caught between the giddiness of jouissance and the vertigo of allegory. In this sense, the novel's hotel setting is a theatrical one, staging the painful pleasures of youth. This is one of the ways in which Camp and the baroque have an affective kinship. Walter Benjamin describes this experience as constitutive of allegory:

> Precisely this is the essence of melancholy immersion: that its ultimate objects, in which it thinks to assure itself most fully of what is debased, abruptly change into allegories, and that these allegories fulfill and revoke the nothingness in which they present themselves.
> (2019, 254)

In short, Pym's melancholy is not simply aesthetic nor is it a pose. For him, the nothingness of death and loss are real. He cannot discuss the loss of his mother with his father, whom he rarely sees, for

> if he even so much as mentioned her, his father's face would freeze and harden, and his voice become abrupt and cruel and contemptuous. She was never to be thought of or considered again—because she had been loved so much. It was disgusting to show that you knew such a woman had ever existed.
> (Welch 2014, 4)

Melancholy coupled with the vicissitudes of adolescence produces, at moments, a self-consciousness tipping towards crippling anxiety. Since his desire cannot be expressed except through prevarication and circumlocution, Pym has nothing to shield him from the shame and humiliation he experiences at virtually every turn. His older brothers are handsome and muscular. They mock and bully him, using their size and more confident masculinities to pin him down with their bodies, in the kind of pubescent psycho-sexual antics that masquerade both as teasing and camaraderie. For Pym, the hotel would seem to promise a respite from the agonies of British public school, but the freedom he feels is utterly provisional, and anxiety and humiliation threaten to break in at any moment.

The hotel itself, a site of transit and transience, becomes an allegorical one, as Pym is variously engaged in a psychic battle for control, in overcoming his grief over the death of his mother, and a battle for his future. In the way that allegory tends to become ensnared in *allegoresis*, that is, in a struggle over allegorical interpretation, so too does Pym periodically fall into a despair born of adolescent awkwardness, even as he chafes against the constraints of school and family that give his life structure. Following Fredric Jameson's contention that, in imagining a contemporary form of allegory, the spectre of *allegoresis* (in late capitalism) makes its erstwhile aesthetic and political freedom difficult, one can argue too that in psychic terms, allegoresis "dramatizes the lack of autonomy of any individual work in a social field now saturated by the aesthetic in general in all its forms" (Jameson 2020, 351). In spatial terms, the aesthetic beauties of the hotel, with its various riches, would seem to offer Pym a way of organizing his relationship with the world, but his supersaturated perceptions can only make his social interactions things more to be endured than relished.

Since this is a Camp novel, Pym does not simply endure; he is engaged in a process of inurement, of reformation. In effect, the novel is a story of plasticity in the form of Camp allegory. Following the work of Catherine Malabou, I shall argue that Camp is very much interested in the question of being, in deploying a kind of plasticity that does not simply privilege form over content, but instead reveals the ways in which Camp form—both material and intellectual—opens possibilities for metamorphosis. Camp and plasticity converge in liminal spaces; this is yet another reason why the hotel is crucial to Pym's fraught struggle to become what he is meant to be. One of the reasons why certain people are drawn to Modernist Camp is that, in its plasticity, it seems to hold out the possibility of alleviating suffering—the consequences of isolation, loneliness, alienation, and ostracism. Camp invites, with a nod to Eve Kosofsky Sedgwick, reparative reading, but is regrettably often subject to paranoid reading (2003, 128). As a site for a reading of this sort, the hotel is particularly suited because it offers opportunities for rest, reflection upon one's life. In sum, the hotel is a place for re-orientation. On the other hand, one may not necessarily be in command of what one reflects upon.

But for now, we should ask: what would a reparative reading entail? One of the issues I must first address is the difference between the plastic and plasticity, which requires some historicization. The idea of the plastic arts was taken up by different thinkers in the Rococo and Romantic periods—Lessing, Schelling, Schlegel, and Hegel among them; generally, the term "plastic" is used to describe those arts which involves the spatial alteration of material—clay, ceramics, marble, bronze, and so on—but to a particular end. Even as Lessing, in *Laocoon*, wished to distinguish between plastic arts as spatial and narrative, musical, or poetic arts as temporal, it was Schelling in his published lecture "On the Relation of the Plastic Arts to Nature" who recognized that art, including plastic art, is not utterly divorced from nature, nor is it its lesser other; rather, for Schelling, plastic art functions as a form of freedom and resistance (freedom in its capturing the universal in the particular, resistant in its form) such that it functions as the "vital synthesis" of art and nature. "Plastic," Schelling tells us,

> scorns to give its object space; it contains it in itself. But even this forbids its further extension; indeed, it is forced to display the beauty of the universe almost in one point. It must thus immediately strive after the highest, and can only arrive at maniformity separately, and by the most severe distinction of antitheses.
>
> (1845, 16)

In other words, the plastic arts have a more severe task than arts like painting; "For, in plastic, the highest seems necessarily (in that it manifests its ideas by corporeal things) to consist in the perfect equipoise between the soul and matter"—that is to say, the soul as potentially universal and matter as the perforce particular—"if it gives to the latter the preponderance, it sinks beneath its own idea; but quite impossible does it seem to elevate the soul at the cost of matter, since thereby it must overpass itself" (Schelling 1845, 24). This overpassing of the soul implies transcendence, of course, but it also implies something like a freedom that lies beyond nature (or the species of freedom nature provides), and to which art grants us access.

The vital synthesis of plastic art offers a window into the potential for the identity of the intuitive dimension of artistic practice and its object—that is, art can be the embodiment of a universal ideal, one that overcomes the unconsciousness of nature and the moral approximations of practical reason. The infinite plasticity of forms manifests itself in the artwork as finite form. It is the work of productive imagination, bringing together intellectual and aesthetic intuition to effect what Devin Zane Shaw calls "the informing of the infinite into the finite" (2011, 91).

Here we encounter a gap—there is no guarantee that the artist (or the observer, for that matter) can create or duly appreciate the shaping, the plasticity of the infinite into a finite form. This gap is the site of the creative act, of imagination. Yet the problem is twofold: the imagination itself also has a gap or split (Schelling acknowledges this, as does Kant in the *Third Critique* 1987, 186). This is not merely a matter of training or intuition; the relationship of infinite to finite (or the plastic artwork as intuitive reflection of the absolute) is such that another spectre "re-splits" it, as it were. But the question is—re-splits it into what? Camp knows the answer: the desire generated by objects and a fascination with danger and death. Camp writers like Welch turn our attention to how many of their characters exhibit an uncanny cathexis to objects. One does not simply "like" a particular object or find it beautiful. Rather, Camp objects provide a peculiar affective support; in Camp novels, objects of this sort immerse us in spaces of dazzling colour framing us in the rococo

The Hotel as Camp Allegory   143

escutcheon surrounding mirrors, spaces that speak of desire's longing to give shape to the death drive.

But if enjoyment is one of the effects of the fascination with danger, we also discover that enjoyment and abjection are, in Welch's world, intimately linked. For example, the pleasure he takes in eating creamed spinach in the hotel's dining room evokes a Proustian memory of stepping in cow shit, after "his foot [...] had broken through the hardened outer crust. It lay in a trough lined with darkest richest green [...] just like velvet or jade, or creamed spinach" (Welch 2014, 7). Benjamin tells us that "The scent is the inaccessible refuge of the *mémoire involontaire*. It is unlikely that it will associate itself with a visual image; of all sensual impressions it will ally itself only with the same scent" (2007, 184). In this Camp inversion, colour supplants odour. The enjoyment evoked by the colour is just as quickly transformed into the fascination, even hunger for abjection: "Now, as the waiter put the soft spoonfuls on his plate, the image was with him again. 'I'm eating cow-pat, I'm eating cow-pat!' he said to himself as he dug his fork in" (Welch 2014, 7). In this Camp aesthetic, the enjoyment comes from the Baudelairean *correspondance* he has found between the pleasure of the memory of stepping in the cow pat, discovering its colour, and how it now informs the aesthetic experience of the spinach he is eating. This kind of inversion is endemic to a Camp aesthetic; one does not repair to an aesthetic ideal to "escape" the horrors of reality. Instead, the hotel opens the possibility to use abjection and horror as aesthetic tools to charge one's experiences with a phenomenological vividness, one that can be transformed into the work we are now reading.

However, the hotel is itself a site of ambivalence. On the one hand, it offers the pleasures of service and luxury; on the other, it is a place demanding propriety and decorum. When Pym loses his way back to his room, he is thrilled by a chambermaid offering help and calling him "sir," even as "it made him feel" suddenly "ashamed." He knows she is being perfectly friendly, but his awkwardness threatens to become something worse:

> "This old place is a proper Chinese puzzle, isn't it!" she laughed. It seemed a very smart, gay sentence to Orvil. He had never heard the expression "a Chinese puzzle" before [...] Then suddenly he saw the hotel as a terrifying labyrinth, with the Minotaur waiting for him somewhere in the dark.
>
> (Welch 2014, 13)

In summary, the perspective from which Pym encounters this liminal world is a Camp one. Here, dark enjoyments are promised in the well-maintained grounds, in the hotel's grotto and even the violent grotesquerie that informs his experience of the hotel and its surroundings. The hotel's sumptuousness, meant to encourage relaxation and the pleasure of being served, only seems to occasion up spaces of contemplation for what and whom Pym has lost. He dreams again of his dead mother, whose makeup he so skilfully helped her apply; she appears before him

> in a tousled peach nightgown, her eyes were shut, her golden toast-coloured hair matted and pressed down with earth. The earth crumbled out of her eye-sockets; Orvil saw a piece roll down and disappear between her breasts. Her nose had rotted away!
>
> (14)

Upon waking, he tries to console himself with the bitter knowledge that she had been cremated, and thus could not be rotting away, but even this victory over his anxiety is Pyrrhic. The image of decomposition is deposed by that of her screaming, burning corpse. In identifying with her pain, he is seized by yet another memory, one of her angrily chasing him round the house, repeatedly striking him with a hairbrush, stinging and marking his body.

The next day, in the hotel chemist's, Pym finds himself shoplifting a lipstick. Later, alone in his room, he takes it out, noting its colour, its sweet, cheap scent. "Look[ing] at it carefully [...] [he] saw that it had 'Sang de Rose' written on it in very peculiar lettering, which reminded him of nothing so much as white worms wriggling in and out of angular lattice-work" (Welch 2014, 88). In the seclusion of his hotel room, the images and scents collide with his melancholy in a synaesthetic riot. The lipstick case evokes a corpse riddled with devouring worms, the makeup's rather grisly name the blood of a rose; together, they are juxtaposed with its ostensive function: to improve one's looks. Looking in the mirror, Pym proceeds to paint his lips, cheeks, and nose, and then his body—covering his nipples, fingertips, and torso in gashes of cerise red, finally twisting his body into a bizarre erotic fandango and feigned horse riding that is suddenly interrupted by his brother knocking furiously at the door.

Interestingly, this expression of private "identity" occurs in front of a hotel room mirror—which ostensibly confers on the subject a sense of coherence—that we can see our faces and bodies before us in a way that is otherwise denied to us. The hotel room initially evokes the fantasy of a greater freedom, "with adult rights fully protected; with a little money, a little room, and work he loved to do" (2014, 14), but this reverie elicits something transgressive, theatrical. There is something ritualistic about this mirrored performance. He uses the lipstick to anoint himself, as he once did his mother, but in a grotesque parody of dawning eroticism. In its grotesquerie, Pym's dance would also seem to be a way of re-enacting the scene of being beaten, replete with lipstick welts, of reconciling both with his mother and with her death. The goal would seem to be the freedom of enjoying one's body, a body free from shame and guilt.

At one point, Pym tries to leap onto the mantelpiece above the mirror, as if to get a better view of himself, as if hoping to become a bauble or gewgaw one might find on a mantelpiece. The image points to the materiality and plasticity of bodies that I alluded to earlier. Pym is engaged in an act of orientation—to objects, to history, and to forms of feeling. But the enjoyment of this act of orientation is grounded in opposition. Malabou, in her reading of Hegel, speaks of the kinds of determinants, historical and accidental alike, that make up the spirit. Together, they create a "reciprocal tension" in a "space-between" that is bound not by confrontation but by a "difference-within-continuity" (Malabou 2005, 165). In their combinations, the reciprocities are both mobile and multiple, producing a kind of mirroring

> that is no longer the work of individual consciousness and no longer depends on a single centre. It is a composition of perspectives, allowing the determinate moments to be connected to each other even while they are in opposition, rather than simply being opposed. (Malabou 2005, 166)

What are the implications of this reciprocity to Pym's orientation? His resistance to the repressive and oppressive elements of his upbringing is staged in the mirror of Camp. That said, it is just as indebted to a polymorphous perversity that informs the mobile and multiple versions of his body which pose and caper in front of it. This is one of the liberties that the "space-between" of the hotel provides. Pym's lipsticked dance offers a confrontation with the mirror that is polymorphously perverse in the sense that, in typical Camp style, the figure derives enjoyment or *jouissance* from the mirror's framing the image of the body, even as it metaphorically evokes the multiple poses and reflections of enjoyment itself.

The bizarre dance we witness here is described as a possibility for traversing a fantasy, sensual and absurd, one whose meaning "communicates before it is understood." In its theatricality, it is a dance of comic, absurd distortion, grotesque, erotic, and utterly private in its intensity. But this too is what hotels also invite; one is not simply a guest of the hotel, one can explore the liminal space or gap of imagination, of re-imagining oneself.

As these scenes show, Welch is especially adept in capturing both the way the hotel encourages fantasy, liminality, possibility, even as he limns the absurdity and danger lurking in fantasy: the danger of discovery. Self-discovery, and being discovered persistently, embarrassingly overlap. Pym's tarrying with danger is intrinsic to his Camp aesthetic, one that is melancholic, but not ultimately despairing. Since this is a Camp novel, decay and beauty, sex and the absurd are messily, even histrionically linked. In a Proustian sense, these collisions of difference within continuity are one of the effects of involuntary memory, giving a psychic weight to the simultaneity of affect and experience, of history and its plastic potential. For example, one evening Pym decides to explore the grotto connected to a cottage orné on the hotel's grounds. He steals a knife from the hotel and "felt delightfully like a criminal" (Welch 2014, 94). He manages to prize open one of the rotting stained glass windows. Once he enters,

> Everything was in terrible decay. The elaborate Gothic paper hung down from the walls in weeping strips. Orvil saw that it was made to imitate stone arcades filled with cinquefoil tracery. On the ceiling, patches of naked laths showed through the broken plaster. [...] There was a terrible smell of death and decay. Orvil could not understand it until he went up to the grotesque little fireplace, shaped like a hooded shrine with pinnacles. There on its hearthstone lay a large dead bird with crooked wings. Half its breast was eaten away, and the small downy feathers were caked and stuck together round the black decaying hole.
>
> (94)

One would expect this scene to produce nothing but horror or disgust, but Pym sees it as a site of possibility—a particularly Camp attitude. Why? Because camp allegory is not only marked by a tendency towards theatricality and saucy brittleness, but it is also a space that finds consolation and intrigue in decay. Camp allegory is an affective carnival that, no matter how colourful, extravagant, or artificial, attracts and prepares its participants for the real of death. In Lacanian terms, art and artifice shape themselves around the hole of the real that is death. The hearth of this refuge houses nothing but the remains of life, nevertheless reminding him that decay is also a form of progress. The "hooded shrine" does not repulse him; for Pym, the hotel has provided another opportunity for fantasy on the darkened path to self-knowledge.

So, what is the first step? Plan a renovation. He begins to re-imagine this space as a melancholic site of redemption—that he could become master of the grotto and reclaim it: "he would make it: the beams receiled, the floors scrubbed and polished, the leaded windows mended, the ivy torn away, and the fantastic Gothic paper repaired and patched as carefully as possible" (2014, 95). If the hotel room furnishes the chance to re-imagine his relationship with grief and his body, the hotel's grotto suggests how he might furnish a more permanent home. Decay is ultimately another form of plasticity. The hotel's grotto is another space, a chance to re-imagine one's life. In this regard, the grotesque is merely the origin of the beautiful.

But the reverie is broken by the sound of people outside; it drives him out of the cottage orné proper farther into the grotto:

> What he saw amazed him. All the walls of the cave were lined with giant shells, feldspars, quartzes, stalactites and fossils. In one place, a thin trickle of water dripped from pink lip to pink lip of beautiful and enormous scallop-shells. In the centre of the cave stood a

> monumental stone table and stools carved like dolphins with their tails in the air. King George IV had once been entertained to dinner here by the son of the duke who made the grotto, but Orvil knew nothing of this. He loved the grotto for itself alone as something beautiful and strange.
>
> (Welch 2014, 95)

In a word, Pym has struck a Camp Motherlode. Camp, charged as it is with forgotten culture, with the erstwhile exoteric, with the glittering arcane, grants to objects an orienting and ontological status. Essentially, objects, in their capacity to orient, open the possibility of a reciprocity that, though crackling with tension, is both mobile and multiple. Camp objects are not simply pretty things; they evoke strangely erotic relationships forged in the name of daring self-discovery, or in the case of the grotto, indulging in building a particular fantasy of self.

But Pym discovers that the hotel has a labyrinth after all. His fantasy crumbles as he continues his exploration of the grotto, following a "narrow tunnel," down which he "walk[ed] [...] as delicately as if great danger waited for him at the other end" (Welch 2014, 95). At its end, he encounters a parody of a Freudian primal scene: Pym shines his flashlight on one of his brothers, his mouth on the exposed breast of another guest of the hotel, a young woman whom Pym also fancies. Horrified, he retreats, filled with confusion and lust, hoping to avoid capture. As he reconstructs the scene, Pym imagines it akin to a baby suckling its mother: "Once having imagined this, Orvil could not rid his mind of the grotesque picture. It hung before his eyes, growing and fading, and growing again" (96). The grotesque returns, but in a different form. Grotesque comes from "grotto"—which is often fashioned as a pleasant retreat. But what makes it "pleasant"? Because "grotto" is a Latin derivation of the Greek "*kruptos*" which means "hidden." Yet this grotto, this space of Camp pleasure, of potential homeliness, has become uncanny. What was meant to have remained hidden has come to light. Despite his attempts to drive the image from his mind, "The frightening vignette, like something seen through a keyhole, still hung in the air." He tries to shift the fact of his brother's being an object of desire for the young woman into one of Madonna and child, but this form of fetishistic disavowal does not provide any consolation.

On the last day of the vacation, Pym's father takes him for an elaborate lunch at The Ritz. Pym gloomily fantasizes about becoming a hermit, of escaping the clutches of school and the awkwardness of adolescence, but the journey into hermitage, like his fantasy of restoring the cottage orné, is a Camp one:

> A barge would be waiting there for him. It would be like Cleopatra's barge, all golden, with feather fans and music. And he would swim out to this barge and they would draw up the anchor at once and sail

with him thousands of miles, until at last they came to an extraordinary island of ruined temples. There they would put him on shore, and he would build a hermitage in a corner of one of the ruined temples.

(Welch 2014, 149)

But he does just return to school. For now. Pym constantly imagines or experiences forms of humiliation, shame, abjection—including being chased and wrestled to the ground by an older man, as if he were about to be raped, having his long eyelashes mockingly trimmed by a school bully, provoking a shattering scream from Pym that marks a line that would not be crossed—experiences turned into forms of sacrifice, of *kenosis*, not in its theological sense, but rather as a form of plasticity. Kenosis refers, theologically, to an emptying out. When one thinks about it, hotels are essentially filled with empty spaces, encouraging us to give up a particular version of ourselves. However briefly, we are invited to empty ourselves of stress and anxiety. As we have seen, the problem is that the sojourn from the everyday gives us time to think more largely about our lives, and what troubles us. So, what can this Camp novel teach us about anxiety and its discontent? Despite assertions to the contrary, Camp is not empty. Rather, Camp is a devotee of kenosis, to an emptying out. Camp is a form of kenosis, but with a twist. Another way of thinking about it is that Christ, in his sacrifice, is saying farewell to Christ for his sacrifice to do its work: to renew the world. In Catholic terms, kenosis is part and parcel of Christ's incarnation, a dimension of his becoming a state of exception (humiliation) so that he may experience a state of exaltation, of his becoming-sacrificial, as it were (Malabou 2005, 94).

Pym has a similar episode, one of virtual dissociation, as he attempts to detach himself from the fact of returning to school:

He tried to soar higher and higher, until he was perching on the pinnacle of a church steeple and looking down at the whole panorama of his life and seeing it lightly, as nothing. There was no pain or pleasure, only nothing.

(Welch 2014, 149)

If kenosis is divine alienation, then Camp is an alienation that is simply divine. The distance required in saying goodbye to a particular version of oneself—one that puts one in the uncomfortable position of having to slowly say farewell to a version of oneself. To say goodbye to a version of oneself that may be a site of pain, embarrassment, even humiliation is to occupy precisely the kind of liminal space that Camp explores. But Camp knows that the distance between what one is, and what one is becoming, "posit[s] a beyond that remains inaccessible" (Malabou 2005, 103). Desire is condemned, in its repetition, to pursue its future, but in order to preserve itself, it must always find that future somehow wanting. This is the melancholy inherent to desire. On the other hand, Camp knows that the death drive promises a sublime enjoyment or *jouissance* that, in cancelling out desire, it will bring one's future to an end. Desire ultimately fails. Seriously.

The seriousness of a "failed" future haunts all of Welch's work. As Clarke has shown, Welch has repeatedly been held up as an example of failed potential, or as an exemplar of a writer who has failed to develop. Yet Clarke parries such dismissals with the poignancy of Welch's larger project: "Against the demands of growth and formation, Welch makes the case for the various pleasures that can be sustained by not maturing, not growing up, and not coming to an end" (2020, 2027). In a Paterian sense, Welch's *oeuvre* is haunted less by failure and more by the knowledge that, because of the chronic injuries sustained in the traffic accident, he does not have the luxury of time. He must burn with a "hard gem-like flame, to maintain this ecstasy" (Pater 1919, 197) because he knows he will not live into old age.

As a result, Welch must take a different approach to the question of what constitutes "serious" art. From a Camp perspective, seriousness, as an aesthetic principle, is a failure precisely because it sets up a limit, an earnestness we dare not cross. With the hotel as a site of Camp allegory, Welch *stages* kenosis, the alienation of oneself from oneself. Another way of putting it is that the hotel is a theatre, enacting the distance between being and becoming. This space is an absurd one—it can be confusing, amusing, humiliating, and alienating. To be a spectator of this process—this process of self-dispossession—can at first blush look like mere narcissism. Given Camp's propensity for the histrionic, this reaction is understandable, but misguided. Camp is profoundly external, profoundly resinous, and only superficially internal. Internality is, for Camp, boringly, a question of empty knowledge, not of its representation; internality is there to be, slowly, painfully, even ridiculously, emptied out. By contrast, externality is, in its theatricality, a question of being, of being-for-itself, of life itself. What I am driving at is that Welch's setting his novel in a hotel does not merely show us "the man behind the curtain"; rather, it invites us into a kind of witnessing of the process of staging the sacrifice of the self into its presentation.

More bluntly, the ruination of the self is the business of Camp. Again, it can be mistaken for mere narcissistic enjoyment of one's own suffering. We must keep in mind a crucial difference between divine kenosis and that attempted by Pym. In response to his anxiety about returning to school, he engages in one last fantasy of seizing control of his destiny, of becoming consecrated in apotheosis:

> He would suddenly feel holy, sanctified, consecrated to God, a noble martyr about to face some terrible ordeal calmly. He thought of the Colosseum at Rome, lit by the torches of burning human beings strapped to flower-garlanded posts. He thought of the lions lapping

up the sticky pools of blood that stained the sanded stage of the amphitheatre. He smelt the sour cat smell of the lions [...].
(Welch 2014, 151)

In terms of Camp allegory, kenosis is the movement through which Pym, in theatricalizing his self-alienation, reaches for a fulfilment that will always remain alien, beyond, *becoming an accident in search of its predicate*. This is an awkward position to be in, and that position is often made even more awkward for its observer. Malabou views "the essence of modern subjectivity as *kenosis*," denoting a shift from its theological to its more philosophical meaning (2005, 111). Kenosis becomes a model for self-determination—of the dialectical shift from substance (being-in-itself) to subject (being-for-itself). In short, it is a question of transition. In aesthetic as well as subjective terms, this transition has implications for Camp.

The affective confusions of Camp require us to think about Camp's uncanny temporality. In his journal, Welch once wrote that even if his latest book were a failure and his pictures remain unsold, "Working is stepping into the dark and making each tiny happening into a sign" (1986, 344). Welch's hotel novel subverts the logic of plasticity as a form of anticipatory agency, plumping instead for the fashioning of small events into intimations or signs. Pym's destined becoming and contingency work together to create a future to be seen *in advance*. Why? Because Camp recognizes the ways in which, coming as it does from the margins, that futurity, like a hotel, has the appearance of a luxurious possibility, one enjoyed by those who can live as if they were always already enjoying the fruits of what they have become—as if they were embodiments of plastic art in subjective form. What *In Youth Is Pleasure* invites us to witness is Pym's protean, repeated attempts to overcome the anxieties and agonies of waiting to become what he knows he was born to be.

That is, the locus of the hotel permits Pym, this Camp subject, to dare to stage the shattering of his ego in order to imagine other possibilities for love of another, one that occupies the threshold—one of shame—between desire and death, between knowledge and enjoyment. The hotel suggests that maybe Camp, so often chastised for its failure to be reality, for its theatricality, its artificiality, offers us the chance to see how the glittering, viciously defended borders between ego and other, between idea and accident can be fashioned into an impersonal, but nevertheless loving, relation based upon kenosis; that Camp should not be viewed as failure, but as allegories of redemption or warning for what seriousness has itself failed to provide. From a Camp perspective, *In Youth Is Pleasure* shows the struggle of making one's future possible and the ways in which theatricality and excess inform the enjoyment of the froth of that struggle. This novel, in its Camp evocation of the confusions and anxieties of youth, exploits the space of the hotel to help us love our shame—the shame of failure, of mortality, of loss, and ruin—for the sake of a future to come, a future that Denton Welch was denied, but his work was not.

Works Cited

Ahmed, Sara. 2006. "Orientations: Toward a Queer Phenomenology." *GLQ: A Journal of Lesbian and Gay Studies* 12 (4): 543–74.
Benjamin, Walter. 2007. "On Some Motifs in Baudelaire." In *Illuminations: Essays and Reflections*. Translated by Harry Zohn. New York: Schocken Books.
Benjamin, Walter. 2019. *Origin of the German Trauerspiel*. Translated by Howard Eiland. Cambridge: Harvard University Press.
Clarke, Matthew. 2020. "Beyond Gay: Denton Welch's *In Youth Is Pleasure.*" *Textual Practice*, 34 (12): 2021–36.
De-la-Noy, Michael. *Denton Welch: The Making of a Writer*. Harmondsworth and New York: Viking, 1984.
Jameson, Fredric. 2020. *Allegory and Ideology*. London: Verso.
Kant, Immanuel. 1987. *Critique of Judgment*. Translated by Werner S. Pluhar. Indianapolis: Hackett Publishing.
Lacan, Jacques. 1981. *The Seminar of Jacques Lacan, Book XI, The Four Fundamental Concepts of Psychoanalysis*. Translated by A. Sheridan. New York: W. W. Norton and Company.
Malabou, Catherine. 2005. *The Future of Hegel: Plasticity, Temporality and Dialectic*. Translated by Lisabeth During. London: Routledge.
Merleau-Ponty, Maurice. 2005. *The Phenomenology of Perception*. London: Routledge.
Oatlands Grotto Weybridge, n.d. http://osborne.house/profilego.asp?ref=284237
Oatlands Park Hotel, 2021. www.oatlandsparkhotel.com/history/
Pater, Walter. [1873] 1919. *The Renaissance*. New York: The Modern Library.
Saunders, Max. 2010. *Self Impression: Life-Writing, Autobiografiction, and the Forms of Modern Literature*. Oxford: Oxford University Press.
Schelling, F. W. J. 1845. *The Philosophy of Art: An Oration on the Relation of the Plastic Arts to Nature*. Translated by A. Johnson. London: John Chapman.
Sedgwick, Eve Kosofsky. 2003. *Touching Feeling: Affect, Pedagogy, Performativity*. Durham and London: Duke University Press.
Shaw, David Zane. 2011. *Freedom and Nature in Schelling's Philosophy of Art*. London: Continuum.
Welch, Denton. 1986. *The Journals of Denton Welch*, edited by Michael De-la-Noy. New York: E. P. Dutton.
Welch, Denton. 2014. *In Youth Is Pleasure*. Norwich: Galley Beggar Press.

Labour, Love

10 "The hotel story he made up"
Hotel Life, Death, and Work in James Joyce's *Ulysses*

Emma Short

Critics have long been drawn to deciphering the topography of James Joyce's *Ulysses* (1922), particularly in the wake of the author's own admission that one of his main aims when writing the novel had been "to give a picture of Dublin so complete that if the city one day suddenly disappeared from the earth it could be reconstructed out of my book" (quoted in Budgen 2004, 262). Yet while there has been a considerable amount of critical debate devoted to mapping the routes and locations of *Ulysses*,[1] anything beyond a cursory mention of the hotel—a key space of modernity—has been strikingly absent from this work, and the novel has also thus far been largely overlooked in emerging criticism on the hotel in modernism. This is despite the centrality of the hotel within *Ulysses* itself—the "Sirens" episode, which takes place at the novel's literal epicentre, is set almost entirely in the bar of the Ormond Hotel—and despite the fact that there are no fewer than fourteen named hotels in the novel (along with several unnamed). This chapter addresses this critical lacuna and repositions the hotel as a vital part of the intricate fabric of everyday existence woven by Joyce. In doing so, I make clear the need for a renewed critical approach to *Ulysses*, one that is more closely attuned to its individual spaces, in line with the recent spatial turn in modernist studies (Parsons 2000; Berman 2001; Thacker 2003, 2020; Beaumont 2017). Taking as my primary focus the Ormond Hotel and the City Arms Hotel—two of the novel's most prominent establishments—I consider how Joyce not only situates the hotel as a vital space of life (birth) and death, but also how he employs the hotel to interrogate the intersections of work, class, sexuality, and morality. Crucially, through this analysis I demonstrate the ways in which the hotel effectively engenders the various forms of power enacted by and upon the characters of Joyce's novel.

"Wouldn't mind being a waiter in a swell hotel": Sex, Power, and Hotel Work

Throughout *Ulysses*, the hotel takes on a number of different functions, and this multiplicity of signification is by no means unique to Joyce's

DOI: 10.4324/9781003213079-14

novel. Indeed, as I argue in *Mobility and the Hotel in Modern Literature*, the space of the hotel is characterized by impermanence, in the relentless stream of guest departures and arrivals, and yet also structured by the rigidly routine work of its staff. As such, "it is a space that at once exemplifies the flux and chaos of modernity in the early twentieth century, as well as the rationalisation of space that was taking place during the same period" (Short 2019, 1). *Ulysses* is thoroughly engaged with these conflicting notions of order and chaos that are so central to conceptions of modernity. In the hotel, several of the novel's central themes—sex, food, work, class, exile, surveillance, and death—all come to intersect in varying ways. The Grosvenor Hotel at 5 Westland Row, Dublin, for example, is one of the first hotels to appear in the novel, and it is outside this establishment that Bloom, standing across the road, "gaze[s] at" a woman leaving the hotel about to board a jaunting car. The hotel itself is small, but notably upmarket, a fact reaffirmed by Bloom's reflections on both the quality of the woman's clothing—"Stylish kind of coat with that roll collar, warm for a day like this, looks like blanketcloth"—and her relaxed stance, which betrays her privilege: "Careless stand of her hands in those patch pockets. Like that haughty creature at the polo match" (Joyce 2008, 70–71). These reflections quickly and seamlessly evolve into sexual fantasies, which themselves are firmly rooted in the class distinction between this woman and Bloom. As Bloom considers the idea that "Women all for caste till you touch the spot," his thoughts increasingly turn to his own sexual domination: "Reserved about to yield. […] Possess her once take the starch out of her" (71). Such fantasies are reinforced in the observation of her "Proud: rich: silk stockings," and culminate in Bloom's desperation to "Watch! Watch! Silk flash rich stockings white. Watch!", a climactic visualization that is ultimately frustrated by "A heavy tramcar," that "honking its gong slewed between" (71). Crucially, it is the Grosvenor Hotel itself, and Bloom's awareness that this woman has been a guest here, that immediately denotes her higher socio-economic status, and which triggers his class-based sexual fantasies.

When the same woman is again briefly recalled later by Bloom in "Lestrygonians," the memory leads him to reminisce, and ultimately fantasize, about another upper-class woman in yet another upmarket hotel, this time the grand Shelbourne Hotel on St Stephen's Green:

> That one at the Grosvenor this morning. Up with her on the car: wishwish. […] Who is this she was like? O yes? Mrs Miriam Dandrade that sold me her old wraps and black underclothes in the Shelbourne hotel. Divorced Spanish American. Didn't take a feather out of her my handling them. As if I was her clotheshorse. Saw her in the viceregal party when Stubbs the park ranger got me in with Whelan of the *Express*. Scavenging what the quality left. High tea. Mayonnaise I poured on the plums thinking it was custard. Her ears ought to have

tingled for a few weeks after. Want to be a bull for her. Born courtesan. No nursery work for her, thanks.

(Joyce 2008, 153)

Here again, Bloom's sexual desires stem from the class hierarchy that clearly separates him from this woman. He unashamedly "scavenges" what she and the other "quality" guests have left of their high tea and derives pleasure from the idea of being "her clotheshorse" in the Shelbourne, the animalistic pun leading to his more overtly carnal desire to "be a bull for her." The hotel again plays a central role in Bloom's erotic fantasies later on in the same episode, in which he imagines working in a grand hotel and the sexual opportunities this might offer him: "Wouldn't mind being a waiter in a swell hotel. Tips, evening dress, halfnaked ladies. May I tempt you to a little more filleted lemon sole, miss Dubedat? Yes, do bedad. And she did bedad" (167). In both of these examples, not only do sex and food seamlessly intersect, feeding into one another in Bloom's apparently insatiable appetite for both, but much of his pleasure is derived from the marked distinction between his own class and that of the upper-class women of his daydreams. The role of the "waiter in the swell hotel" in which he imagines himself is one that both encapsulates this distinction and is intrinsically bound up in the temptation and consumption of food, thereby offering Bloom sexual gratification on numerous levels. As Miriam O'Kane Mara points out, food in *Ulysses* is always politically weighted "because starvation, both willing and unwilling, is a recurring theme in Irish history" (2009, 94). These implications are something that Joyce himself was distinctly aware of. Mara cites Joyce's lecture of 1907, "Ireland, Island of Saints and Sages," in which he argues that "the negligence of the English government left the flower of the people to die of hunger" (quoted in Mara 2009, 94). Joyce's reference to "the flower of the people" here arguably comes to fruition in the character of Leopold *Bloom*, resulting in a reading of Bloom's coalescing fantasies of sex, food, and class as a resistance to a colonial power that attempts to deny the survival and sustenance of Ireland.

Bloom's dream of being a waiter is not, however, the only time that the hotel figures in Bloom's imagination as a potential site of employment or enterprise. In "Ithaca," for example, Bloom daydreams of an opulent country residence—"Bloom Cottage. St Leopold's. Flowerville" (Joyce 2008, 667)—and of the means by which he might acquire the wealth to build or buy such a property. These encompass a number of inventions, industrial proposals, and schemes, including the development of a hotel resort:

> A scheme to enclose the peninsular delta of the North Bull at Dollymount and erect on the space of the foreland, used for golf links and rifle ranges, an asphalted esplanade with casinos, booths, shooting

158   *Emma Short*

> galleries, hotels, boardinghouses, readingrooms, establishments for mixed bathing.
>
> (671)

In "Penelope," Molly Bloom reflects on the various plans and money-making schemes her husband has had over the course of their relationship, one of which was opening a hotel:

> [...] musical academy he was going to make on the first floor drawingroom with a brassplate or Blooms private hotel he suggested go and ruin himself altogether the way his father did down in Ennis like all the things he told father he was going to do and me but I saw through him [...].
>
> (716)

Molly's palpable doubt in her husband aside, given both the number and variety of forms of employment that Bloom has thus far undertaken, and the fact that his late father, Rudolf Virag Bloom, was himself the proprietor of the Queen's Hotel in Ennis, County Clare, it is arguably highly likely that Bloom may yet end up fulfilling his dreams of working in a hotel. Despite these dreams, however, and despite the prominence of the hotel throughout *Ulysses*, it is only in the "Sirens" episode that we are afforded any real insight into the lives and experiences of those who work there. The hotel staff that make an appearance over the course of this episode are the barmaids, Miss Douce and Miss Kennedy, the hotel boots, and Bald Pat, the waiter. I have written elsewhere about the control that Miss Douce and Miss Kennedy exert over the largely masculine space of the hotel bar through their careful and adept management of their feminine sexuality (2019, 100–02). This control is simultaneously reinforced and complicated early on in the episode in the interaction between the hotel boots and Miss Douce. While the exchange between the two characters is undeniably brief, it demonstrates a clear hierarchy between the young male boots and the (presumably slightly older) female barmaids, with the women occupying a position of superiority that was relatively rare in early twentieth-century Ireland. The resentment of the boots towards this superiority is made immediately apparent from the way in which "he banged on the counter his tray of chattering china," an action directly attributable to the barmaids "unheeding him" (Joyce 2008, 247). His attempt to involve himself in their conversation is rendered "unmannerly," an arrogant intrusion rather than a true desire to engage with the women, and his assumption that Miss Douce is spying on her "*beau*" comes across, and is certainly received as, at the very least, a patronising dismissal of their concerns. Despite the brevity of this exchange—taking place over no more than a third of a page—it is nevertheless effective at revealing a working relationship between the boots and the barmaids that is noticeably fraught.

The figure of the barmaid was relatively new to the Ireland of 1904. However, the higher pay and better working conditions than most other forms of employment available to women meant that the number of women engaged in bar work grew rapidly in early twentieth-century Ireland.[2] Women working in the hotel industry was not a new phenomenon, however. As the lowliest member of the hotel staff, the boots would have been fairly well accustomed to women occupying positions of authority over him, from the chambermaids and housekeeper, to, in the case of the Ormond Hotel, the hotel owner (in both fiction and fact), Mrs de Massey. However, the boots' "impertinent insolence" towards Miss Douce and Miss Kennedy, and his demonstrable lack of respect towards them, can be traced to what Katherine Mullin characterizes as "the reactionary abolitionist equation between barmaid and prostitute" (2004, 484). In this sense, the boots' reference to Miss Douce's *beau* is more than a mere dismissive caricature of women's romantic infatuations; rather, it is a scathing and critical summation of the barmaid's assumed sexuality. But it is in its aforementioned brevity that this incident forms part of Joyce's efforts in the episode to make what Mullin reads as not only a "'manifestly political' intervention into debates about gender, sexuality and labour," but also a "creative, playful and energetic resistance to the often reactionary pieties of moral reform" (2004, 476). Despite his scornful and antagonistic behaviour towards his female superiors, and the misogynistic and moralistic attitudes out of which this emerges, the hotel boots is allotted no more than a mere fraction of the episode. Instead, it is the barmaids who sustain the focus of the narrative throughout, and whose sexuality is further complicated by the level of agency it affords them, particularly over the primarily masculine space of the hotel bar. In devoting such attention, and in giving such power to the barmaids over the boots, Joyce makes clear the importance of the hotel in the early twentieth century in providing employment for women, and renders objections to such employment on moral grounds spurious and obsolete.

"Never know whose thoughts you're chewing": Life, Death, and Privacy

The City Arms Hotel, where the Bloom family resided from 1893 to 1894, is one of the other hotels central to the narrative of *Ulysses*. The period in which the Blooms—Leopold, Molly, and their daughter Milly— moved from their residence in Lombard Street West to Raymond Terrace, and then on to the City Arms Hotel, was accompanied by two further life changes for the family. The first was Leopold Bloom's new employment "as an actuary at Laurence Cuffe & Sons' cattle traders," and the second, more significant change, is the birth and then death of their son, Rudy (Crispi 2015, 231). Luca Crispi and Carl Niemeyer have attempted to piece together the precise dates of the Blooms' movements in this period, but have been thwarted by both the scarcity and the inconsistency of the evidence provided by Joyce across the various manuscript versions of *Ulysses* (Crispi 2015, 227; Niemeyer 1976, 182). Of particular interest to this discussion is whether the Blooms moved into the City Arms Hotel before or after the birth—and death eleven days later—of their only son, Rudy. The specific chronology has distinct implications for how the space of the City Arms Hotel is read and interpreted. If, as Joyce suggests in a late August 1921 note,[3] the Blooms' move to the hotel was precipitated by Rudy's death, then the City Arms functions, first and foremost, as a space of grief. In this reading, the transience of the hotel and the lack of any real ownership or belonging of this space are for the Blooms bound up with the process of grieving. Untethered by the premature death of their son, the Blooms are effectively propelled away from the security of their former home into the impermanence of the City Arms Hotel. If, however, the Blooms' move to the City Arms Hotel takes place in late 1893, before Rudy is born, then the hotel takes on a different meaning. Although the Blooms' initial period of mourning will ultimately take place in the City Arms, it is not their grief which drives them into this space. Instead, with the reason for their move being Bloom's new employment at Cuffe's cattle traders, the hotel is associated, for him at least, with work. Equally or even perhaps more importantly, however, if the move takes place while Molly is still pregnant, then this hotel takes on a greater significance as a space of both birth and death, of beginnings and endings.

The City Arms is just one in a series of temporary residences for the Blooms. It is therefore marked by transience, though one that is, of course, by no means unique to this particular establishment. Transience is instead a defining quality of the hotel in general. As I have argued elsewhere, the hotel is, by its very nature, a space of mobility, one which "is brought into being and reified by the movement of people from one place to another, and [which] is typically (though not always) a point on a journey or a destination in itself" (Short 2019, 6). In a novel such as *Ulysses*, however, the transience of the hotel—and of the City Arms Hotel in particular—is inextricably bound up with the novel's central themes of exile and displacement. The very opening pages of the novel "invoke," as Vincent Cheng notes, "a Hebraic history of displacement, diaspora, and struggle for one's homeland and for Home Rule," and what he terms the "racialized, Jewish-Hebraic parallel to the 'Irish Question' " is a key motif throughout (1995, 151). This shared history of dispossession between the Jewish people and the Irish—and in particular, Irish Catholics such as Stephen—is central to the novel. The Blooms' transient lifestyle and their numerous relocations to new accommodation, particularly in the early years of their marriage, echo the formative experiences of Joyce and his future wife, Nora Barnacle, both of whom moved frequently between addresses during their childhood. As Brenda Maddox notes, "[i]n turn-of-the-century Ireland, Catholics had not yet advanced very far towards the status of homeowner. [...] Before Nora left Galway in 1904 her parents had changed address seven times," and in the case of Joyce this number was around twelve or thirteen, largely due to his father's alcoholism and consequent financial troubles (1998, 11). Such a fraught relationship with property ownership was largely due to what Andrew Gibson sees as the "complex and thorny problem" of property law in Ireland up until the early twentieth century (2013, 952). The property laws that governed rural areas of Ireland, which benefited the landlords rather than their tenants, also, as Gibson points out, determined "the conditions of renting in Dublin," meaning that, "like most peasant tenants, most urban ones were on yearly leases and could very promptly be evicted" (955). Consequently, Gibson notes, "[i]n Joyce's Dublin, 'nobody owns' their homes. Joyce's people rent" (955). This distinct lack of property ownership in the novel further contributes to the overwhelming question of homelessness, transience, and class anxiety that pervades it, a question which the impermanence of the hotel is uniquely placed to answer.

However, unlike the various rented accommodations occupied by the Blooms throughout their marriage, the City Arms Hotel is, by necessity, a space shared with multiple occupants. The precise number of guests residing in the City Arms at the same time as the Blooms is never confirmed in the novel, but external photographs of the building suggest that there were somewhere between twenty-five and thirty guest rooms in the hotel. The Blooms stayed in room nine, a room likely situated near the malodorous toilet described by Molly in "Penelope" as "that charming place on the landing always somebody inside praying then leaving all their stinks after them always know who was in there last" (Joyce 2008, 722). The stench recalled by Molly here all too literally preempts Maurice Merleau-Ponty's "atmosphere of humanity," those detectable traces left behind by others. For Merleau-Ponty, "not only do I live in the midst of earth, air and water, I have around me roads, plantations, villages, streets, churches, implements, a bell, a spoon, a pipe" ([1945] 2002, 405). To this list of cultural spaces and objects we might well add the (hotel) bathroom, another space that is, according to Merleau-Ponty, "moulded to the human action which it serves," and which,

> spreads round it an atmosphere of humanity which may be determinate in a low degree, in the case of a few footmarks in the sand, or on the other hand highly determinate, if I go into every room from top to bottom of a house recently evacuated.
>
> (405)

D. J. van Lennep also discusses the "atmosphere," and in particular the "smell" that inhabited spaces can take on, noting that "[i]t is this smell particularly which has an influence on us, and which can give us the feeling of familiarity or of alienation" (1987, 210). The higher the concentration of this "atmosphere of humanity," or the more strongly it is able to be perceived, the lower the likelihood of the space in question being fully habitable. As van Lennep maintains in relation to the hotel bedroom, "[t]here are those which have lost their habitableness" due to the traces of previous occupiers (215). A hotel bedroom should, ideally, bear minimal traces of previous guests if one is to be able to inhabit it fully. The bathroom of the City Arms Hotel is at once alienating and uninhabitable thanks to the "stinks" left behind by the other guests, and yet these same smells also ground this space in the (overly) familiar, in the everyday and the commonplace that the hotel in *Ulysses* so aptly encapsulates. The atmosphere, or rather "stink" of humanity in the hotel bathroom is a constant and unrelenting reminder to the Blooms that this space is not simply one that does not belong to them, but crucially, one that is shared with, and thus bears the traces of, multiple others.

Of course, the palpable presence of these others means that there is also a distinct lack of privacy implicit in the fetid facilities on the hotel landing—if Molly is able to detect "who was in there last" by the smell they leave behind, then, by the same token, any remaining odours left by herself, her husband, or her daughter will be equally discernible to the other guests. In her discussion of hotels in the work of Henry James, Anna Despotopoulou refers to "the permeation of boundaries between public and private enacted by the hotel," and indeed no space within a hotel can ever be truly private (2018, 505). While in its interior design and layout the hotel may attempt to echo the domestic space, it can never fully replicate the privacy of the home. In the communal spaces of the hotel, such as the lobby and dining room, as well as the stairs, landing, and corridors, the presence of other guests and staff is a constant possibility. Yet even in the most private spaces of the bedroom and bathroom, privacy is—as evidenced by the City Arms toilet—by no means guaranteed.

The lack of privacy enjoyed by the Blooms in the City Arms Hotel is most starkly evidenced by the malicious gossip spread by Andrew "Pisser" Burke, which contributes to the personal attacks on Bloom in the "Cyclops" episode. As Crispi observes, "[t]he stories about the Blooms around this time are intrinsically linked with the lack of privacy that they had to endure as residents in the City Arms Hotel" (2015, 231–32). In "Cyclops," the episode's unnamed narrator draws heavily in his account of Bloom's character on rumours passed on to him by Burke:

> Time they were stopping up in the *City Arms* Pisser Burke told me there was an old one there [...] and Bloom trying to get the soft side of her doing the mollycoddle playing bezique to come in for a bit of the wampum in her will.
>
> (Joyce 2008, 293)

Despite the confused and slightly incoherent nature of the anecdote, it nevertheless contains a significant amount of detail concerning Bloom's friendship with another guest at the hotel, Mrs Riordan, and the possibly financial yet ultimately unsuccessful motives of this association. The attacks on Bloom in "Cyclops" increase in severity throughout the

Hotel Life, Death, and Work in Ulysses 163

episode, and his masculinity is called into question through yet another story the narrator has heard from Burke concerning Bloom's behaviour in the City Arms:

> One of those mixed middlings he is. Lying up in the hotel Pisser was telling me once a month with headache like a totty with her courses. Do you know what I'm telling you? It'd be an act of God to take hold of a fellow the like of that and throw him in the bloody sea. Justifiable homicide, so it would.
>
> (323)

That this anecdote refers to Bloom "lying up in the hotel" exemplifies the distinct lack of privacy in the hotel even within those spaces, like the hotel bedroom, that should offer a level of security and refuge from prying eyes. The invasion of privacy here is all the more disturbing given the threat of violence to which it leads, remarks in which murder is deemed "justifiable" based on a wholly negligible non-conformity to norms of Irish masculinity. For the Blooms, and particularly for Leopold, the City Arms Hotel may be a space in which the company of others provides some friendship, but the surveillance enabled by this space equally carries a potential threat to his future safety in Dublin.

Pisser Burke's surveillance of the Blooms in the City Arms Hotel is thus a primary source for the gossip that, Crispi argues, forms one of the three primary modes of storytelling through which the reader gleans information about the family over the course of the novel. While details of the Blooms' lives together are covered through both the individual and shared memories of Leopold and Molly, "[t]he third kind of storytelling is," Crispi argues, "most often presented as (usually malicious male) gossip about Leopold Bloom and Molly Tweedy Bloom, individually and as husband and wife" (2015, 13–14). In particular, the period between 1893 and 1894, which comprises the Blooms' sojourn in the City Arms Hotel, is a period that is relayed primarily through gossip. The semi-public nature of the hotel, and its inherent lack of privacy, renders it an ideal space for the production of gossip.

As a narrative strategy, gossip in *Ulysses* is bound up with questions of morality and power. As Nicholas Martin observes, "[w]hile acts of gossiping are invariably hypocritical and at odds with their implied moral purpose, (the) gossip nevertheless often claims to be acting as both the guardian and the censor of public morals" (2014, 138). There is, in the male gossip concerning Leopold and Molly Bloom, an implicit moral justification in the focus on sexuality—excessive in Molly's case, and potentially deviant in the case of Leopold. Molly herself adds a deviant gloss to her husband's tendency, "since the City arms hotel," "to be pretending to be laid up with a sick voice," convinced that "either it was one of those night women if it was down there he was really and the hotel story he made up a pack of lies to hide it" (Joyce 2008, 691). And in "Sirens,"

Simon Dedalus's remark that "Mrs Marion Bloom has left off clothes of all descriptions," is in keeping with the overtly sexualized, demeaning, and misogynist manner in which she is discussed by the men of Dublin (Joyce 2008, 258); but the judgemental (if jovial) tone here is undercut by the reader's knowledge that the majority of these men are themselves adulterers. Any attempt by these characters to occupy a moral high ground is thus immediately destabilized by Joyce, and it is revealed that their true objective is simply, as Crispi suggests, "to impugn the reputation of one or both of the Blooms" (2015, 232). The motive behind this reveals less about the Blooms and more about the men engaged in this gossip and their own insecurities. Gossip is more often than not entangled in complex networks and hierarchies of power, and can afford the gossiper a sense of control and authority over the person being gossiped about. As Patricia Meyer Spacks maintains, "[k]nowledge is power, knowledge about other people is power over them [...]. The interpretations gossip offers inhere in the stories it tells. The organizer of a narrative controls its meaning, thus takes partial possession of other people's lives" (1982, 30). In gossiping about the Blooms—and, in particular, about Leopold—the men of *Ulysses* attempt to organize and control the narrative surrounding him, and in doing so to assert not only their own superiority, moral or otherwise, but also exert power over him. By providing a primary source for this gossip, the hotel is thus heavily implicated in these endeavours of control.

Gossip is, however, not solely the preserve and pleasure of Leopold Bloom's male adversaries. Any suggestion that Bloom is merely the passive, helpless victim of such attacks is complicated by his own engagement and enjoyment in gossip about others. To return to the restaurant of the Ormond Hotel, Bloom displays not only an awareness of Bald Pat the waiter's deafness, but also a surprisingly detailed knowledge of the number of corns on Pat's feet: "Bald Pat, bothered waiter, waited for drink orders. Power for Richie. And Bloom? Let me see. Not make him walk twice. His corns. Four now" (Joyce 2008, 256). This knowledge might seem to demonstrate a level of familiarity between the two men, and perhaps that Pat himself has at some point regaled Bloom with accounts of these ailments. However, it is also likely that this is yet another example of the seam of male gossip threaded through the novel. Given the central role of gossip in the circulation of information in Joyce's Dublin, it is perhaps more probable that Bloom's knowledge of Pat's ailments has been gained through his own engagement in this process. This idea is further reinforced as the "Sirens" episode progresses, and Bloom's references to Pat become noticeably briefer, increasingly reducing the man to little more than his role as waiter. These references move through a distinctly Bloomian process of wordplay:

> Bloom signed to Pat, bald Pat is a waiter hard of hearing, to set ajar the door of the bar. The door of the bar. So. That will do. Pat, waiter, waited, waiting to hear, for he was hard of hear by the door.
> (262)

A few pages later, having finished his meal and unable to get Pat's attention, Bloom finds this play on the word "waiting" hilarious, dissolving into a fit of giggles:

> Bald Pat who is bothered mitred the napkins. Pat is a waiter hard of his hearing. Pat is a waiter who waits while you wait. Hee hee hee hee. He waits while you wait. Hee hee. A waiter is he. Hee hee hee hee. He waits while you wait. While you wait if you wait he will wait while you wait. Hee hee hee hee. Hoh. Wait while you wait.
>
> (269)

The mildly hysterical tone here might well be attributed to the pint of cider that Bloom has just consumed (as well as the glass of burgundy he drank a few hours earlier in Davy Byrne's Moral Pub). It might also signify Bloom's realisation of how the combination of Pat's role as a hotel waiter and his deafness somehow echo the absurdity of his own situation. "Sirens" is after all, as Andrew Warren points out, above all else "the story of a man in his most painful hour" (2013, 655). It is during this episode that the tryst between Boylan and Molly is scheduled to take place, and the restaurant of the Ormond Hotel is where Bloom chooses to take refuge—to wait out the moment of their meeting, and to attempt to distract himself through the cacophony of sounds that flow through the chapter. But most crucially, Bloom's strategies of self-distraction and self-comfort depend on diminishing another character, who himself is made visible and thus vulnerable to this through his role as a hotel waiter, and his enforced movements within the more public spaces of the hotel restaurant and bar. Reflecting on gossip's more sinister potential, Spacks writes that "gossip may damage others, both by threatening others and by converting people into fictions" (1982, 36). As Bloom's reflections on Pat turn from an initial level of seemingly genuine concern (in not wanting to make him walk over twice) into derogatory, one-dimensional observations, his monologic gossip here reduces Pat to little more than a fiction, a flimsy construct of a hotel waiter as opposed to a character on equal footing with himself. Like the men who take such malicious pleasure in demeaning him, Bloom's own insecurities are implicated in his treatment of Pat.

The hotel in Joyce's *Ulysses*, then, is a multifaceted space. Through it, many of the key themes of the novel—such as the interplay between sex, food, and class, the shifting roles and increased opportunities for women in society, and the peripatetic existence of its central characters—are explored and interrogated. In addition, through the lack of privacy in the hotel, together with the way in which the hotel bar is figured as a space of masculine community, Joyce foregrounds the hotel as both a locus and generator of gossip and reveals its centrality to one of the novel's key narrative strategies. In offering a brief overview of just a few of the many ways in which the hotel takes on significance in Joyce's *Ulysses*, this chapter has demonstrated how the intersection of work, sexuality, morality, and power is so adeptly articulated by Joyce through the complex space of the hotel.

Notes

1 See Hart and Knuth (1975); Seidel (1976); Delaney (1982); Howes (2000); and Hegglund (2003).
2 Katherine Mullin notes that "[t]he 1901 census counted 27,707 barmaids in the United Kingdom and Ireland, yet by 1908 this figure had increased to an estimated 100,000" (2004, 477).
3 Crispi records Joyce's note from late August 1921: "left Lombard street because Rudy † [died]" (2015, 223).

Works Cited

Beaumont, Matthew. 2017. "Modernism and the Urban Imaginary 1: Spectacle and Introspection." In *The Cambridge History of Modernism*, edited by Vincent Sherry, 220–34. Cambridge: Cambridge University Press.
Berman, Jessica. 2001. *Modernist Fiction, Cosmopolitanism, and the Politics of Community*. Cambridge: Cambridge University Press.
Budgen, Frank. 2004. "Conversations with Joyce." In *James Joyce's Ulysses: A Casebook*, edited by Derek Attridge, 257–66. Oxford: Oxford University Press.
Cheng, Vincent. 1995. *Joyce, Race, and Empire*. Cambridge: Cambridge University Press.
Crispi, Luca. 2015. *Joyce's Creative Process and the Construction of Characters in* Ulysses: *Becoming the Blooms*. Oxford: Oxford University Press.
Delaney, Frank. 1982. *James Joyce's Odyssey: A Guide to the Dublin of* Ulysses. New York: Holt.
Despotopoulou, Anna. 2018. "Monuments of an Artless Age: Hotels and Women's Mobility in the Work of Henry James." *Studies in the Novel* 50 (4) (Winter): 501–22.
Gibson, Andrew. 2013. "'Nobody Owns': *Ulysses*, Tenancy, and Property Law." *James Joyce Quarterly* 50 (4): 951–62.
Hart, Clive, and Leo Knuth. 1975. *A Topographical Guide to Ulysses*. Colchester: Wake Newslitter.
Hegglund, Jon. 2003. "'Ulysses' and the Rhetoric of Cartography." *Twentieth Century Literature* 49 (2): 164–92.
Howes, Marjorie. 2000. "Goodbye Ireland I'm Going to Gort: Geography, Scale, and Narrating the Nation." In *Semicolonial Joyce*, edited by Derek Attridge and Marjorie Howes, 58–77. Cambridge: Cambridge University Press.
Joyce, James. 2008. *Ulysses: The 1922 Text*, edited by Jeri Johnson. Oxford: Oxford University Press.
Maddox, Brenda. 1998. *Nora: A Biography of Nora Joyce*. New York: Fawcett Columbine.
Mara, Miriam O'Kane. 2009. "James Joyce and the Politics of Food." *New Hibernia Review* 13 (4) (Winter): 94–110.
Martin, Nicholas. 2014. "Literature and Gossip—An Introduction." *Forum for Modern Language Studies* 50 (2): 135–41.

Merleau-Ponty, Maurice. [1945] 2002. *Phenomenology of Perception*. Translated by Colin Smith. London: Routledge.
Mullin, Katherine. 2004. "'The Essence of Vulgarity': The Barmaid Controversy in the 'Sirens' Episode of James Joyce's *Ulysses*." *Textual Practice* 18 (4): 475–95.
Niemeyer, Carl. 1976. "A *Ulysses* Calendar." *James Joyce Quarterly* 13 (2): 163–93.
Parsons, Deborah. 2000. *Streetwalking the Metropolis: Women, the City, and Modernity*. Oxford: Oxford University Press.
Seidel, Michael. 1976. *Epic Geography: James Joyce's* Ulysses. Princeton: Princeton University Press.
Short, Emma. 2019. *Mobility and the Hotel in Modern Literature: Passing through*. Cham: Palgrave.
Spacks, Patricia Meyer. 1982. "In Praise of Gossip." *The Hudson Review* 35 (1): 19–38.
Thacker, Andrew. 2003. *Moving through Modernity: Space and Geography in Modernism*. Manchester: Manchester University Press.
Thacker, Andrew. 2020. *Modernism, Space, and the City: Outsiders and Affect in Paris, Vienna, Berlin, and London*. Edinburgh: Edinburgh University Press.
van Lennep, D. J. 1987. "The Hotel Room." In *Phenomenological Psychology: The Dutch School*, edited and translated by Joseph J. Kockelmans, 209–15. Dordrecht: Martinus Nijhoff.
Warren, Andrew. 2013. "How to Listen to 'Sirens': Narrative Distraction at the Ormond Hotel." *James Joyce Quarterly* 30 (3) (Spring): 655–73.

11 Life and Work in Interwar "Cathedrals of Modernity"

Ulrike Zitzlsperger

By the late 1920s, German readers of newspapers and novels, and visitors of cinemas and variety shows were familiar with the trope of the "Cathedral of Modernity."[1] Referring to hotels, department stores, and train stations, it reflects, from the last third of the nineteenth century onwards, the growing number of accessible public institutions with an impressive architecture and awe-inspiring interior design. These "Cathedrals of Modernity" became important landmarks in the cityscape, next to and increasingly in competition with the church spires of old. Siegfried Kracauer highlights the parallels and contradictions between churches and their congregations, on the one hand, and the gatherings in hotel lobbies, on the other.[2] In "Die Hotelhalle" ["The Hotel Lobby"], written between 1922 and 1925 as part of a treatise on detective novels, Kracauer's hotel lobby represents a meeting place that allows visitors an escape from daily life (1977a, 161). For him, however, this space is synonymous with mass culture and lacks spiritual meaning. Despite such contemporary reservations, hotels and department stores attracted attention for their technological sensations, such as escalators in department stores, and innovations, such as the American-style bar and running water from taps in hotels. Both are transitory spaces (Knoch 2005, 136; Spiekermann 2005, 213) where the requirements of a real world of mass consumption coincide with the public's imagination. Both aimed to dazzle and positively overwhelm visitors from the middle of the nineteenth century on: "Grand hotels," writes Ben Wilson, "were complemented by *grands magasins*, shimmering new department stores built on a monumental scale" (2020, 241).

In literary and cinematic contexts, hotels (in particular Grand Hotels) and department stores mirror society in miniature. The distinct spatial organization of hotels and department stores is rich in symbolism that structures the experience between arrival and departure. Customers and visitors take centre stage; they are able to rely on the immaculate workings of hotels and department stores. While omnipresent, the employees who maintain these places blend into the background. In contemporary film and literature, employees tend to be nameless facilitators, characterized by their roles within the institution, rather than by their personalities,

DOI: 10.4324/9781003213079-15

Interwar "Cathedrals of Modernity" 169

dedication and loyalty aside. It is their provision of a tightly regulated, at times ritualistic service that, beyond the imposing architecture, triggers the association of hotels and department stores with "Cathedrals of Modernity." Within an institution associated with society's progress, this service has a number of characteristics that determine the lives of those who work there: the need for time keeping, the principle of efficiency, and unquestioning subservience. This chapter seeks to examine the usually neglected literary and cinematic hotel and department store staff of the 1920s to explore the perceived patterns of day-to-day experience of modernity in interwar Germany.[3] For this purpose, two writers who enjoyed popularity in the interwar period are of particular interest: Joseph Roth and Vicki Baum. Well established as writers and journalists by the late 1920s, both frequently referred to hotels and at times to department stores in their writing. The chapter will also discuss the novel *Hotel Amerika* (1930) by left-wing author Maria Leitner[4] and the film *Der letzte Mann / The Last Laugh* (1924) by F. W. Murnau to highlight patterns in the treatment of employees and the hotel as a place of work.

In 1929 Joseph Roth published in the *Münchner Neueste Nachrichten* an article entitled "Das ganz große Warenhaus" ("The Very Large Department-Store") (2002, 95–101), reviewing Berlin's newly opened Karstadt department store at Hermannplatz. He lists the architectural characteristics of the building, among them escalators and a spectacular roof-terrace. In Roth's review, wherever the observer turns, the scale of innovation thwarts human beings. In the same year, Roth published a sequence of *feuilletons* in the *Frankfurter Zeitung* titled "Hotelwelt" ["Hotelworld"] (2016, 142–70).[5] In contrast to the department store, Roth's ideal hotel facilitates a profound sense of belonging: he describes himself as a "hotel citizen, a hotel patriot" with an international outlook (144).[6] Five of the seven contributions to "Hotelworld" are dedicated to individual members of staff who for Roth are prototypes of their trade: "The Chief Receptionist," "The Old Waiter," "The Cook in His Kitchen," "Madame Annette," and "The *Patron*." These pieces are framed by "Arrival in the Hotel" and "Leaving the Hotel," emulating the guests' homecoming and the (temporary) loss of home. The themes of Roth's hotel essays rehearse those explored in his other *feuilletons* and novels with references to hotels, such as *Hotel Savoy* (1924) and *Die Kapuzinergruft* (1938). For Roth, in fact, hotels are part of a wider-reaching context that includes train stations, coffeehouses, and department stores. Together they facilitate a familiar network that reflects his understanding of history and society (Zitzlsperger 2013, 93–104).

Also in 1929, Vicki Baum published her best-selling novel *Menschen im Hotel* (translated in English in 1930 as *Grand Hotel*). Baum intertwines the fate of select guests who reside in one of Berlin's modern flagship hotels, an institution that boasts a variety of novelties such as an illuminated façade, a telephone switchboard, and tea dances for the public. In her memoir, Baum claims that it was the clichés of hotel life that ensured the success of her novel, even though she intended these clichés to be understood ironically (2018, 453). This irony appears to have been lost on the public because the specific types and situations resonated with her readership. In 1939 her *Hotel Shanghai* was to maintain a similar formulaic approach, no longer mirroring one city (Berlin) but a world in crisis. In 1937—Baum by now an émigré from National Socialist Germany—her novel *Der große Ausverkauf (The Big Sell-Off)* appeared. The novel is set in a New York department store and, contrary to the hotel-novels, tells the story of a number of hapless employees. Baum does not develop idealized individuals, but rather distinct types with strengths and flaws, such as dedication and greed, loyalty and superficiality.

In a period characterized by tumultuous change, hotels and department stores were tangible locations. They epitomized some of the characteristics of postwar life, including the particularities of metropolitan culture, the threat and the comfort provided by technology, the challenges of a mobile society, and the unpredictability of the economy. Postwar societies in general and Germany in particular faced a world of juxtapositions between the countryside and the city; tradition and modernity; the emergence of a buoyant popular culture and an established "high" culture. Literary and cinematic hotels and department stores provided ideal settings to explore such concurrent trends—including the contrast between customers and employees. Roth pays close attention to hotel employees because for him they facilitate his longed-for sense of home in an otherwise itinerant life. In her autobiography, Baum remarks upon her own experience as one of Ullstein publishing house's 8,000 employees (2018, 429), and before writing *Grand Hotel* she spent some time working in a hotel. In Germany, employees, white-collar workers, or salesgirls had limited agency: after all, most could count themselves lucky to have work in a society traumatized by World War I, the flu pandemic, and the impact of inflation. In the same decade, the plight of the working classes gained more attention. In *Die Angestellten* [*The Salaried Masses*] ([1930] 2010) Kracauer, for example, provides a phenomenology of white-collar workers; in "Die kleinen Ladenmädchen gehen ins Kino" ["The Little Shopgirls Go to the Movies"] he explores how contemporary film confirmed the emotional disposition of the salesgirls who devoured this kind of entertainment ([1927] 1977b, 280).

The comparison of fictional hotels and department stores, their similarities and differences, and the attention paid to their staff underpin the analysis of the way in which they have come to represent key settings of modernity. Hotels dominate in the literature of the period as they provide more complex timeframes (including night-time) and multiple spaces, and they play a particular role in periods of personal and national crisis. Gertrud Lehnert argues that both locations, hotels and department stores, are characterized by the experience of alienation and loneliness but also of crowds (2011, 151). Although Lehnert focuses on guests and consumers, I argue that these perceptions also affect the experiences of the staff. While workplaces prove all-consuming in terms of dedication and demands, private lives and concerns are sidelined. In terminology reminiscent of Wolfgang Schivelbusch's study of railway stations (2007, 157), Habbo Knoch describes modern Grand Hotels as thresholds revealing changes in society (2016, 28). Knoch lists the ways in which the markers of modernity in hotels mirror urban life: the acceleration of daily life, the importance of economic considerations, technology, and a sense of alienation (12). It is worth noting that these concerns were known well before the postwar period, mainly in the United States, where hotel modernity had made itself felt earlier, eventually setting standards in Europe too.[7] In 1910 Paul Vehling had observed that the average hotel employees, due to their demanding labour, had no home and no end to their working days (2019, 83). In the next sections, I focus on those aspects that determined the working day: the "Cathedral of Modernity" as a workplace; the impact of hierarchies within the workforce; perceptions of the individual's role in the workplace; and the relationship between employees and customers. I suggest that the employees' hotel- and department store modernity, as presented in 1920s novels, *feuilletons*, and films, fosters patterns of perception that to this day serve as stock images of a typical hotel and department store environment.

Workplaces

Grand hotels and major department stores were built to impress at first sight. Fittingly, Wes Anderson's (2014) comedy-drama *The Grand Budapest Hotel*, which combines a nostalgic take on Grand Hotels with a play on the role of the all-knowing concierge, uses the atrium of a former department store in Görlitz (Germany) to capture the grandeur of the hotel lobby. The opulent façades of hotels and department stores correspond with an interior that is both technologically advanced and theatrical in appearance. For patrons this positively overwhelming visual spectacle is one reason they are drawn to such spaces. Meanwhile, the employees who make these places work belong to them only by courtesy of their job description. The juxtaposition of the experiences of customer and staff of the hotel and department-store space mirrors that between leisure and work.

Roth celebrates the hotel from the guests' point of view as a home away from home. By contrast, he criticizes the department store as an overwhelming experience. Karstadt's impressive roof-terrace—offering food, live music, a view over the cityscape—is a case in point. According to Roth, abundance and access for everyone enhance nothing but the circulation of goods; they do not offer personal enjoyment. Once they reach the rooftop, the visitors themselves are only part of the perpetual motion within the building:

Rare delicacies are offered in such profusion and with such insistence that their rarity is lost. And just as, within, the merchandise and the shoppers became modest, so too delicacies on the roof become modest. Everything is within reach of anyone. Everyone may aspire to anything. Therefore the very large department store should not be viewed as a sinful undertaking, as, for example, the Tower of Babel. It is, rather, proof of the inability of the human race of today to be extravagant. It even builds skyscrapers and the consequence this time isn't a great flood, just a shop.

(Roth 2002, 98)

In contrast to department stores, hotel space is more differentiated: the hotel lobby, the restaurant, the corridors, and individual rooms allow for more varied encounters. Guests and employees experience two profoundly different spaces. The guest's arrival affords the check-in and then the allocation of an appropriate room; an opulent dinner necessitates the work of the cook and the waiters; a good night's sleep is followed by the need for the room to be cleaned. At times there are interesting crossovers between staff and customers: Baum's book-keeper Kringelein, in a big city for the first time and keen to experience life in the hotel before he dies, serves as a link between the reality of a hotel and the dream it sells. First provided with a less attractive room ("The furniture [...] was just polished nut-wood. There was furniture like that in Fredersdorf" [Baum 2016, 14]), he acquires the insight of a man who has lived among shabby furniture his whole life: "This is not what I came for" (14). He desires to be deceived by the splendour intended for the paying guests, not to encounter a replica of his working life back home.

The employees' exhaustion in hotels and department stores is a frequent literary and cinematic motif, one underpinning the notion that the façades hide the reality of a place which has to be made to work. The reader's first encounter in Baum's *Grand Hotel* is the exchange between the hall porter Senf, whose wife has gone into labour with their first child, and the busy "operator at the switchboard, earphones over his head and red and green plugs between his fingers" (2016, 3). Despite Senf's anxiety and the operator's desire to be helpful, both are forced to carry on with their allotted tasks. In Maria Leitner's *Hotel Amerika,* the reader is introduced to the appalling quarters for employees that are in stark contrast to the spectacular roof garden of the hotel. Baum's *The Big Sell-Off* begins with a difficult encounter between one of the salesgirls and a potential customer—only then is the "Zentral-Warenhaus" brought into view: its enormous size in the city centre, its massive window displays, its countless goods and bustling atmosphere. In Murnau's *The Last Laugh* we find the porter at work, protecting the guests from the rain and carrying luggage into the hotel. In both literature and film, department stores and hotels are primarily associated with their workforce, not with the customer's impression of grandeur. While Roth's first *feuilleton* in "Hotelworld" adopts the perspective of the visitor, in the next five pieces, the staff take centre stage. The staff, however, function as a complex entity, a society in miniature.

Hierarchies

One key aspect of modernity is social mobility. The main trajectory for employees in the 1920s and 1930s was determined by the threat of dismissal or the loss of a particular place in the internal hierarchy of the hotel or the department store. Literature offers snapshots of personal fates, such as Senf's, Baum's fearful hall-porter. In *The Last Laugh*, Murnau purposefully plays on the spatial experience of hierarchies. The viewer shares the despair of the proud porter who, too old to carry heavy luggage, loses his uniform and with it his standing in society. Demoted, he ends up in the hotel's washrooms. A final scene shows him eating and drinking in the hotel's restaurant, courtesy of an inheritance from a grateful customer. This ending has all the trappings of a fairy tale, one that serves to underpin the reality of the modern workplace: the viewer is forced to acknowledge that the loss of standing within the hotel hierarchy is the more plausible scenario. While hotel guests and department store customers experience emotional and other upheavals (falling in and out of love, pursuing, losing, and gaining important deals, being overwhelmed by goods and the desire to purchase etc.), employees are forced to remain professional. Neither Baum's salesgirls nor the employees of the Grand Hotel are able, if they wish to keep their work, to put their own needs first or to question the order that determines their life at work.

In his hotel essays, Roth takes these hierarchies a step further and aligns the hotel with the structure and the effect of a cathedral. There is the doorman, whose look "welcomes me" with "more than a father's embrace" (2016, 142); the liftboy "takes my suitcases one under each arm. Probably it's the way an angel spreads his wings" (142). The guest leaves the outside world behind him (143); the chief receptionist resides over a spiritual ambience: "When the lobby is quiet and empty and an idyllic golden light floods the reception area, the chief receptionist reminds me of a kind of gold-braid and mobile saint in an iconostasis" (146). If the chief receptionist controls the lobby like the priest his church, the cook is in charge of the crypt: he "dwells in the underworld of the hotel" (155).

Individual employees maintain their distinct niches within the hotel. The lower their position, the less their homelife matters. The person in charge of Roth's hotel is the aforementioned chief receptionist. He controls the strict hierarchies and the efficiency among employees. In his role, he is comparable to the detective in department stores. Contrary to other employees who are familiar with their individual department and the range of duties attached to it, detectives and chief receptionists understand the complexities of the institution and its various spaces without ever escaping them. The consequences prove exhausting: Baum characterizes the porters as sleepless (2016, 268), noiseless and circumspect (265), watchful (211), unfeeling (210), and dutiful (133), and thereby highlights the dehumanizing workings of the modern hotel. Roth's chief receptionist is in charge of the nameless employees who are "all about other people's business as messengers, agents or servants" (2016, 146). Roth observes that while "everyone else here wears the sign of their service and their function, only they have retained the anonymity" (146). The chief receptionist does not simply guarantee the smooth running of the hotel; he is also in charge of the atmosphere. At one point he "exhales a cloud of pure silent anger into the lobby" (148). God-like, he has a gift that enables him to switch "almost instantaneously between fury and graciousness, indifference and curiosity, cool aloofness and anxiety to be of service" (148). He exudes authority and he is also in a position to assess the guests, reading their social standing in an instant. While the paying guest may feel in charge, his social standing is at all times categorized.

Roth's "perfect" employees, meanwhile, defy time. The Old Waiter's [*sic*] name has fallen into disuse (2016, 151). He has joined the ranks of those whose names no longer matter, because they represent a function, not a human being. Indeed, he represents "waiterdom" and age. He is an anachronism, the representative of a bygone era. The old waiter will die in service, his body removed discreetly through the back door (153)—he is part of the furniture. In reality, he is as redundant as the old-fashioned staircase Roth describes at the Hermannplatz department store: once gone, it may be perceived as a loss, but it stands no chance against the shiny new escalator.

If employees are acknowledged only when needed and then solely in their particular function (see Baum 2021, 49, 63), guests, from the perspective of the employees, are merely the trigger of their clocklike routine. Baum narrates these hotel routines: "At ten minutes past nine, a drowsy chambermaid fleetingly swept up the dust in room no. 68, threw away the faded floral tributes, took out the tea tray and finally came back with fresh linen" (2016, 137). The daily rituals performed by hotel staff are, like the revolving door at the entrance of the Grand Hotel in Murnau's film, responsible for the permanent renewal of hotel life.[8] If, as Ueli Mäder argues, daily life is determined by the seemingly banal and repetitive (2017, 1), this is at the heart of what the hotel staff maintain. While their service ensures that a guest's visit is memorable, they also make sure that no traces of visitors are left. The drama that unfolded in "room no. 68," for example, has no bearing on the chambermaid. The hotel guests' unique experiences are meaningless once employees decontextualize the former props of a drama and routinely clear out what remains: old flowers, used cups, and dirty bed linen which, the night before, were tangible signs of admiration, heartbreak, and a promising love story. Similarly, for the shop-girls in the department store, customers have "no face" (Baum 2021, 167).

In each *feuilleton* apparently focusing on the individuality (and peculiarity) of hotel staff, Roth sketches prototypes of institutionalized employees. Few are able to shrug off their work-persona once they leave the building. His idealized hotel employees defy modernity, for the sake of a tradition that takes on transcendental qualities. The members of staff discharge their specific role with pride and confidence; their place in the hierarchy of the hotel is never challenged. The chambermaid Madame Annette, for example, has a history of personal disappointments; she remains unmarried but establishes her standing among the other employees. "She thought it pleasanter in the course of a morning to clean twenty rooms of unknown and constantly changing persons, than eight or ten thoroughly established for all eternity, on whom she depended for bread and keep" (Roth 2016, 160). Roth employs a modern term when he associates her with a white-collar worker: she likes the "cold, *clear objectivity* of a trade, almost of an office" (160; emphasis added). When the hotel guest takes her to the cinema and a restaurant, no one recognizes her outside her usual environment (162). Annette is not taken in by the plot and voices her criticism of the film they watch: the American production does not convince her, as reason prevails over fiction. Roth's portrait of Annette, highlighting her dedication to the profession as a way of life, her complete acceptance of existing hierarchies, ultimately determines her as one of the parts of what in 1920 the Austrian journalist Alfred Polgar termed the "hotel machine" (quoted in Gruber 1994, 74). Hotels and department stores are corporate environments, regulated systems displaying the demands of a modern workplace. Like the design of the buildings, the internal hierarchies sustain a whole system. In contrast to the guests, hotel employees are aware of the repetitive nature of their profession, and, by implication, life.

Cogs in the Machine

The "cog in the machine" is a 1920s trope in German film and literature that reflects the experience of soldiers during World War I: forced to obey orders, easily replaced, free of agency. It also refers to the by now omnipresent role of technology—undermining the role of the individual in postwar society and at the same time providing a topic of profound fascination.[9] In hotels and department stores, where technology ruled in terms of modern achievements, employees are forced to respond to the system of push buttons. In his 1933 essay, "System von Druckknöpfen," the critic Anton Kuh identifies this as key for the workings of the hotels' amenities (quoted in Gruber 1994, 64)—regardless of whether the hotel was explicitly associated with a cathedral of modernity (Roth) or a miniature 1920s Berlin (Baum). The system of push buttons allows guests to exert power, while employees are forced to respond to their demands. Push-buttons are the particular remit of a specific group of employees, the lift-boys. Thomas Mann's striving Felix Krull (*Confessions of Felix*

Krull), Franz Kafka's struggling Karl Rossmann (*Amerika*), and Joseph Roth's lift-boy, an eerie incarnation of death (*Hotel Savoy*), all understand the social implications of the different hotel floors they navigate within the lift cage.

From the employees' perspective, the distinct meaning of spaces in the hotel—such as the entrance hall or the private room—becomes de-mystified: all are, ultimately, workplaces that can be filled by anyone able to perform the repetitive tasks. The daily performance of duties in the hotel or the department store may have no direct bearing on the narrative. It does, however, provide a framework for the employees' interaction with the guests. Furthermore, to be a "cog in the machine" is still the reserve of those in employment. Interwar German literature and film are rich in depictions of those with no income and no home at all: Slatan Dudow's *Kuhle Wampe* (1932), Ernst Haffner's *Blutsbrüder* [*Bloodbrothers*] ([1932] 2013), and Otto Nagel's *Die weiße Taube oder das Nasse Dreieck* ([c. 1928] 2017), to name but a few, foreground poverty and homelessness. Here, the very young and the old are permanently busy finding food and shelter and maintaining their dignity. Only the left-wing politics in *Kuhle Wampe* allow for a degree of perspective. In contrast, hotel and department store staff have, as long as they adapt to the modern age, an income.

In particular, young employees are guided by contemporary ideals. The so-called "New Woman" of the German interwar period was a media construct (Price 2015, 282). Like the American flapper pushing social boundaries, the "New Woman" broke with the traditional norms in terms of fashion, aspirations, and behaviour. In Baum's *Grand Hotel*, Flämmchen officially works as a typist, but she is willing to act as an escort too. In *The Big Sell-Off*, Baum introduces similar protagonists in her portrayal of the shop-girls, the ruthless and ambitious Lilian and the rather innocent but no less determined Nina. Flämmchen understands hotel society intuitively and harbours no illusions, just as the shop-girls see through the workings of the department store without questioning their place. They are all in pursuit of dreams, which, while seemingly personal, are in reality dictated by the media—mostly by the desire to become a film star.

The assessment of Flämmchen's abilities is flattering: "She is very quick and intelligent" (Baum 2016, 64). The first encounter between Flämmchen and her employer takes place in the hotel lobby. She does not lack confidence; indeed, in contrast to the uniform-clad employees, she oozes individuality:

> She was leaning back in an armchair as though she were quite at home in such surroundings; she was swinging one foot in a neat shoe of light blue leather, and looked as if she was out to have a jolly good time.

(68)

Hoping to succeed in the film business, Flämmchen treats her body as a commodity: "I'm very good in the nude, you see. But it's wretchedly paid" (72), she observes. Those without names meanwhile form part of the surrounding workforce she longs to escape: the "dead-tired chambermaid" after midnight (36); the pageboys with the "feverishly bright eyes of children" (36), and "ill-tempered one-armed" men (36, 37) running the elevator. The first scene in the film *Grand Hotel* (directed by Edmund Goulding, 1932), based on Baum's novel, takes the impact of routine at work further. It shows the busy switchboard where employees speedily facilitate the phone calls between different parties. This serves to set the scene for the main characters. The switchboard, which had made considerable technological advances during the 1910s and 1920s, became an integral part of hotel modernity, and yet here it illustrates that even life-changing conversations are ruled by machines. It is no coincidence that during one of these phone calls Senf compares his job with "being in jail" (*Grand Hotel* 1932).

Maria Leitner uses the American hotel setting to detail the growing political awareness of her protagonist, Shirley. Each item and space in the hotel is characterized by its users. Exquisite spaces are reserved for the wealthy, and shabby ones reduce the employees to human machines. Nanny, the hotel's oldest cleaner, remains immobile until the ringing bell calls her back to work. As in the case of the switchboard, the noise of the bell prompts an immediate reaction. Machine-like, she performs her work with amazing agility, only to return to her vegetative state at its end (Leitner 2020, 3–4). The only possible resolution is for Shirley to develop a critical political awareness, leave the hotel, and start afresh. Flämmchen is forced to compromise to pursue her dream; Shirley exchanges an exploitative system for an ideological belief system.

Customer Service

The provision of excellent customer service is at the heart of the success of department stores and hotels. Baum's hotel provides dancing for the guests' entertainment, iced fruit salads for their refreshment, and electric fans for their comfort (Baum 2016, 36). The modern amenities that hotels and department stores boast maximize the experience of their customers: consumption is king. This service has an immediate impact on the role of employees. In *Berlin: Absolute Stadt*, Rolf Lindner suggests that staged events and objects, rather than individuals, determine urban modernity (2016, 69–72). In *The Great Sell-Off* Nina serves as a living mannequin in a shop window. This takes Flämmchen's confident display in the hotel entrance hall a step further, since Nina is here showing her availability on behalf of her employer, who determines her salary. The living mannequin is the promise of an abstract female perfection, one without personal qualities. The scope for autonomy shrinks while the consumers are promised the gratification of all their desires: Nina has turned into yet another available, exquisite commodity. She has a "vague idea" about buying and selling as the foundation of life: "payment and the provision of a service" determine the workings of society (Baum 2021, 167). According to Nina and Lilian, customers believe that the employees are "speaking and lifeless machines, blind, deaf and without feelings" (64). This also holds true for the perception of hotel employees: they may lend proceedings a face, but not a personality. Baum's employees are shaped by market forces. For Roth, the hotel that was perfect in prewar conditions is spoiled by the mechanization of the 1920s; in "The Very Large Department-Store," this mechanization turns staff and customers into parts of the commercial cycle.

Reading and Visualizing 1920s Modernity and Beyond

The interest film directors and writers harbour in the 1920s and 1930s for hotel and department store employees is significant. The extraordinary experiences of the guests are offset by the daily routine of the employees. It is their working life that illuminates the contemporary context—the increase in speed, the mechanization, the social restrictions, the gendered approach to work, the power of consumer culture. Observations about employees in department stores tend to be more candid. Tales of commerce do not need to imitate a sense of home; nor do they, in contrast to literary hotels, need to create lasting myths. Thanks to the repetitive patterns outlined above, the role of the employee in fictional hotels and department stores is embedded in our culture. To this day, glossy brochures and coffee table books visually perpetuate a distinct perception of employees, one that illustrates perfect service and cultivates the customer's sense of being special. The publication *The Hotel Adlon*, for example, covers the history of Berlin's famous hotel. Strikingly, the majority of images in the book show no people at all. The few that do display human beings—a few famous guests aside—show employees at work, fulfilling the duties one would expect: they are porters, waiters and caterers, chefs, and barmen (Demps and Paeschke 2004, ii, 36, 82–83, 125, 137, 188–89). They are an intrinsic part of the success story of the Adlon.

The chapter "Hotel-Stories—Living in a Legend. Employees and Guests Remember" includes a well-known photograph of the writer Thomas Mann and an unknown pageboy announcing one of Mann's visitors (109) (see Figure 11.1). Thomas Mann is placed against the window. There is no eye contact between him and the pageboy and this emphasizes the sense of a professional exchange. In 1929, when the photograph was taken, Mann was on his way to Stockholm to receive the Nobel Prize for Literature. The photograph owes its appeal in part to juxtapositions: the mature writer on his journey to receive the extraordinary prize, and the young pageboy performing a routine service; the famous author, apparently not interested in the person who delivers the note, and the unknown young man taking the encounter in his stride.

Figure 11.1 Thomas Mann at Hotel Adlon, Berlin 1929. © Bundesarchiv, photo 183-H27032. No named photographer, 1929.

In *Hotels: Geschichte in Geschichten,* a range of Grand Hotels are depicted with the help of their histories, incorporating photographs of employees in characteristic scenarios: the portrait of London's Savoy Hotel shows cooks at a buffet, waiters preparing immaculate breakfast tables, and lift-boys delivering roses (Walther 1990, 96–97); the Oriental in Bangkok illustrates its opulence by the stock images of a telephone exchange, a chauffeur and, again, cooks (160). Here, in contrast to the Adlon photo of 1929, customers are not in sight—the service is limited to the very performance of the routine itself. Hotels and department stores celebrate institutional anniversaries with photos that depict all their employees—usually strictly divided by department (see, for instance, 202). To this day, the approach to the profile of hotels remains associated with its employees in typical poses. Since 2017, the BBC series *Amazing Hotels* has featured the journalist Giles Coren and the TV-chef Monica Galetti, who "roll up their sleeves to work alongside staff" when they portray individual hotels. The image accompanying the promotional blurb shows them presenting spectacular cloches—state-of-the-art hotel service which is also a stock image with a nostalgic view of the institution. Such tableaux respond to the ideal image of well-ordered modernity steeped in tradition. Meanwhile, in German interwar literature and film, the employees' experiences showcase the relentless pressure and anxiety associated with

180 Ulrike Zitzlsperger

modernity. They serve to ground the experiences of customers and guests and illustrate the unholy workings in the "Cathedrals of Modernity."

Notes

1 This was a common metaphor and catchphrase during the interwar years, signifying industrial or urban buildings linked to progress and consumerism: factories, railway stations, museums, hotels, and department stores. For a discussion of "Cathedrals of Modernity" in Berlin, see Zitzlsperger 2016. See also Lorente 1998 for a relevant analysis of museums.
2 See also Matthias, Chapter 4, and Heynickx, Chapter 13, on Kracauer and the hotel lobby.
3 In this chapter, the terms "staff" and "employee" are seen as interchangeable, though "staff" refers in the first instance to the member of a specific group.
4 Leitner made her name as an undercover newspaper reporter motivated by her belief in socialism and the redemption it offered.
5 *Feuilletons* were newspaper or magazine essays of cultural, political, or social criticism. The series of the "Hotelworld" essays are collected under the title "Hotels" in the English translation, *The Hotel Years* (2016).
6 See also Heynickx, Chapter 13, on Roth's discussion of hotels.
7 For an analysis of US hotel modernity, see Giles (2002, 212–14).
8 On revolving doors, see Heynickx, Chapter 13.
9 See, for example, the 1925 novel *Metropolis* by Thea von Harbou, made into a film in 1927 by Fritz Lang.

Works Cited

Anderson, Wes (dir.). 2014. *The Grand Budapest Hotel*. United States: Fox Searchlight Pictures.
Baum, Vicki. 2016. *Grand Hotel*. Translated by Basil Creighton with revisions by Margot Bettauer Dembo. New York: New York Review Books.
Baum, Vicki. 2018. *Es war alles ganz anders. Erinnerungen*. Cologne: Kiepenheuer & Witsch.
Baum, Vicki. 2021. *Der große Ausverkauf*. Cologne: Kiepenheuer & Witsch.
Demps, Laurenz, and Carl-Ludwig Paeschke. 2004. *The Hotel Adlon*. Berlin: Nicolai.
Dudow, Slatan. 1932. *Kuhle Wampe*. Germany: Prometheus-Film-Verleih und Vertriebs-GmbH.
Giles, Paul. 2002. *Virtual Americas: Transnational Fictions and the Transatlantic Imaginary*. Durham: Duke University Press.
Goulding, Edmund (dir.). 1932. *Grand Hotel*. USA: Metro-Goldwyn-Mayer.
Gruber, Eckhard. 1994. *Fünf Uhr-Tee im Adlon. Menschen und Hotels*. Berlin: Fannei und Walz.
Haffner, Ernst. 2013. *Blutsbrüder*. Berlin: Metrolit.
Knoch, Habbo. 2005. "Das Grandhotel." In *Orte der Moderne. Erfahrungswelten des 19. und 20. Jahrhunderts*, edited by Alexa Geisthövel and Habbo Knoch, 131–40. Frankfurt and New York: Prestel.
Knoch, Habbo. 2016. *Grand Hotels. Luxusräume und Gesellschaftswandel in New York, London und Berlin um 1900*. Göttingen: Wallstein.

Kracauer, Siegfried. 1977a. "Die Hotelhalle." In *Das Ornament der Masse*, 157–69. Frankfurt/Main: Suhrkamp.
Kracauer, Siegfried. 1977b. "Die kleinen Ladenmädchen gehen ins Kino." In *Das Ornament der Masse*, 279–94. Frankfurt/Main: Suhrkamp.
Kracauer, Siegfried. 2010. *Die Angestellten*. Frankfurt/Main: Suhrkamp.
Lehnert, Gertrud. 2011. "Einsamkeiten und Räusche. Warenhäuser und Hotels." In *Raum und Gefühl. Der Spatial Turn und die neue Emotionsforschung*, edited by Gertrud Lehnert, 151–72. Bielefeld: Transcript.
Leitner, Maria. 2020. *Hotel Amerika*. Berlin: Continator.
Lindner, Rolf. 2016. *Berlin. Absolute Stadt. Eine kleine Anthropologie*. Berlin: Kadmos.
Lorente, J. Pedro. 1998. *Cathedrals of Urban Modernity: Creation of the First Museums of Contemporary Art*. Aldershot: Ashgate.
Mäder, Ueli, and Andreas Schwald, eds. 2017. *Dem Alltag auf der Spur. Zur Soziologie des Alltags*. Zürich: edition 8.
Murnau, F. W. 1924. *Der letzte Mann*. Germany: UFA.
Nagel, Otto. 2017. *Die weiße Taube oder das Nasse Dreieck*. Bern: Walter Frey.
Price, Dorothy. 2015. "The New Woman in 1920s Berlin." In *Berlin Metropolis, 1918–1933*, edited by Olaf Peters, 274–93. Munich: Prestel.
Roth, Joseph. 1989-1991. *Die Kapuzinergruft*. Vol. 6. In *Werke*. Ed. by Fritz Hackert and Klaus Westermann. 6 vols. Cologne: Kiepenheuer & Witsch, 225–346.
Roth, Joseph. 1989-1991. *Hotel Savoy*. Vol. 4. In *Werke*. Ed. by Fritz Hackert and Klaus Westermann. 6 vols. Cologne: Kiepenheuer & Witsch, 147–243.
Roth, Joseph. 2002. "The Very Large Department Store." In *What I Saw. Reports from Berlin, 1920–1933*. Translated by Michael Hofmann, 95–101. New York: W. W. Norton & Company.
Roth, Joseph. 2016. "Hotels." In *The Hotel Years. Wanderings in Europe between the Wars*. Translated by Michael Hofmann, 142–70. New York: Granta.
Schivelbusch, Wolfgang. 2007. *Geschichte der Eisenbahnreise. Zur Industrialisierung von Raum und Zeit im 19. Jahrhundert*. Frankfurt/Main: Fischer.
Spiekermann, Uwe. 2005. "Das Warenhaus." In *Orte der Moderne. Erfahrungswelten des 19. und 20. Jahrhunderts*, edited by Alexa Geisthövel and Habbo Knoch, 207–17. Frankfurt, New York: Prestel.
Vehling, Paul. 2019. *Die Moral des Hotels: Tischgespräche*. Bremen: Inktank.
Walther, Gabriele M. 1990. *Hotels. Geschichte in Geschichten*. Cologne: vgs.
Wilson, Ben. 2020. *Metropolis: A History of the City, Humankind's Greatest Invention*. London: Vintage.
Zitzlsperger, Ulrike. 2013. *Topografien des Transits. Die Fiktionalisierung von Bahnhöfen, Hotels und Cafés im zwanzigsten Jahrhundert*. Oxford: Peter Lang.
Zitzlsperger, Ulrike. 2016. "Berlin: Flesh and Stone, Space and Time." In *The Palgrave Handbook of Literature and the City*, edited by Jeremy Tambling, 165–82. London: Palgrave Macmillan.

12 White Women and Cheap Hotels

Tyler T. Schmidt

In the spring of 1950, the Poet Laureate Consultant in Poetry, Elizabeth Bishop, was living at the Black-owned Slaughter Guest House near Dupont Circle. Writing to poet Robert Lowell she described it as a "hotel—sort of—called 'Slaughter's'?—run entirely by colored people for Eurasians, strange gray people, poets, etc." (Bishop 1994, 204). The place is "gloomy," she tells another friend (200). The temporary, however sustained, nature of her housing reflected Bishop's ambivalence about her post. She was on her way back to Yaddo that summer and, she hoped, to more productive seasons. She had spent the previous spring at Blythewood, an exclusive psychiatric hospital, and was growing increasingly anxious about her duties as poetry consultant.[1]

Lesbian bard of Key West (where she would rent a hotel room when distractions at home got too high) and later Brazil, Bishop, a fervent traveller, wrote often of hotels in her poems, letters, and dream journals.[2] Her queer attention—her ambiguous, precise phrasing—to the "strange gray people" at Slaughter's hints at some of her sadness but also points to the aesthetic questions of hotel life that this essay pursues. Both the elderly and other folks marked by strangeness are the sort of residents one expects to find in these boarding houses, guesthouses, and other alternative domestic spaces. I imagine the homosexual man or woman of the 1950s rejected by their families as part of such a tribe. But as is so often the case with Bishop, her description of the lodgers' "strangeness" is coupled with a mention of racial and cultural difference.

Hotels, as critics of Bishop know, mattered deeply to her poetic imagination and creative output. She quipped to Lowell in January 1949 that she should become a "scullery maid" at Key West's Casa Marina where her friend Selden Rodman, the writer and "folk" art collector, stayed among the visiting tennis stars (Bishop 1994, 181). And Bishop's hotel histories run long. She stayed at the Hotel Chelsea for much of the fall of 1936. In August 1937, she wrote to Marianne Moore from the Hôtel Foyot in Paris, reporting a terrible automobile accident in Burgundy with Louise Crane and Margaret Miller, her college friends.[3] And there is this: in July 1938, Bishop stayed at La Residencia, located at 523 West 113th

DOI: 10.4324/9781003213079-16

Street in New York City. Writing to poet Marianne Moore, her steady correspondent, Bishop reports:

> This [dormitory] seems to be a very good place to work. I have done a lot the last four days, and it is certainly amusing – the animation at mealtime is quite overwhelming. I am even saying "Pass me the sugar" and "The boy has my pen" in Spanish.
>
> (1994, 76)

The hostel-like communal sleeping, dining, and evidently writing offer another version of cheap accommodations. Bishop embraces the dormitory, her thrifty hotel, as a classroom of linguistic pleasure. "Easy adaptability" is how the African-American novelist Ann Petry would characterize white women's peculiar occupancy of cheap rentals. Thrift permitted these women both adventure and remove from the prying eyes of polite society.

Ann Petry's fiction also examines the geographies of our racial histories and the stories a city holds. Her intricate 1953 novel *The Narrows* (recalling the storytelling of James Joyce) creates a mosaic of small-town Connecticut life, including an interracial romance between Link Williams, a Black barman stuck in his hometown after graduating from Dartmouth, and Camilo Sheffield, a white married woman and heiress to the family empire. Petry's treatment of the nameless "Harlem hotel" where Link and Camilo carry on much of their affair has long held my interest. This collection's shared investigation into the meanings of the modernist hotel provides the welcomed opportunity to put Bishop and Petry, and their depictions of racialized hospitality, into closer conversation, and to attend more closely to the questions of class and labour raised by Bishop's poem "In a cheap hotel" and Petry's sociologically rich visit to a Harlem hotel in *The Narrows*. Their citations of the hotel as structure for the nation's civil unrest and mundane civil responsibilities reflect a world in which the modern woman is re-imagining herself. These literary depictions of hotel life, as I read them, both respond to and reflect a postwar anxiety about interracial sexuality, women's more public expressions of sexual desire, and re-imagined gender identities facilitated by the rapid social changes that followed World War II. Within the modern city, full of social possibility and deviance, Petry and Bishop document the intimate spaces of aesthetic exchange and sexual exploration found in hotel rooms.

My essay pays attention to the ways that white women occupy the hotel as a space of sexual possibility and racial transgression. My close readings examine some of the ways white women, whether poet laureate or love-smacked heiress, inhabit the hotel, not solely as a site of utopian possibility, but as a space of racial-sexual fantasy and shame often made possible by the labour of African-American workers. Much of what I will have to say here is about the affective labour of the hotel for its occupants and its workers, figures of the literary imagination often burdened with or by white guilt and privilege, but I am also interested in broader critiques of labour and the objects of hospitality that surround these literary and literal places. While not exactly a Marxist reading of Petry's and Bishop's hotel vignettes, my thoughts on race and the erotic lives of the modernist hotel are not negligent to the questions of economy and care raised in these texts. Petry and Bishop both allude to but avoid a full, deserved scrutiny of African Americans' manual and affective labour in the hotel industry. The fantasies of modernism, in fact, often avoid thinking about the invisible systems of hotel staff that make the hotel's promise of escape, of alternative subjecthood, possible.[4]

Utopia on the Cheap

The architectures of the hotel—lobby, bar, elevators, rooms—invite social connections across race that are both revelatory and crushing. In his canonical "The Hotel Lobby" (1932), Siegfried Kracauer is attuned to the sinister as well as sublime power of this cultural space, writing, "But if a sojourn in a hotel offers neither a perspective on nor an escape from the everyday, it does provide a groundless distance from it which can be exploited, if at all, *aesthetically*." For him, the lobby dweller is at risk of a "disinterested satisfaction in the contemplation of a world creating itself" (Kracauer 2004, 35).[5] Wayne Koestenbaum, in his loving gloss and admonishment of Kracauer ("I wish that Kracauer were more tolerant of the hotel lobby's 'tinge of exoticism' "), shudders with pleasure at the hotel's "indifferent populatedness" (2007, 67). It is the cheap hotel's promised indifference, a busyness that distracts from deviance, that these white women seek. For Bishop, it is the hotel's cheapness that ignites the erotic; for Petry's leading lady it is a state to transform, a space to sidestep social scrutiny.

Scott Herring, in his reading of Willa Cather's "Paul's Case," describes the luxury hotel as one of the "abstracted cosmopolitan spaces," a location "indifferent to modern constructions of sexual knowledge" (2007, 16). The Waldorf-Astoria is revealed as a space where "queerness functions as situated dislocation," creating a different form of community, one not grounded in sexual identification (101). These literary citations of the cheap hotel highlight a similar indifference but also explore queerness of a different sort: interracial intimacies and other sexual "perversions." The hotel room, whether luxury or budget, facilitate forms of sexual knowledge related to racialized desires and their historical, including compositional, taboos.[6]

Many of the enduring fantasies of the hotel as utopia, as escape, as space of public–private possibility are informed by modernism's fetishistic love for the "new" city as the site of social possibility, technological terror, and spiritual alienation. As Emma Zimmerman writes in her treatment of Jean Rhys's spatial poetics: "The hotel is a key space of modernity as it embodies the confusion of the private and public spheres that is so crucial to the development of the modern city" (2015, 79). Imani Perry directs us to points where these public spaces and the poetic imaginary meet, places where gender and queerness make contact in the modernist city. Writing of the social changes that marked public spaces of the late nineteenth-century city, Perry writes: "In the public imaginary the 'new woman' was twinned with the images of 'dandies': decadent and deviant men, feminine men, who were likewise a threat for their visible transgression of gender ideals" (2018, 68). My reading of cheap hotels and white women's occupation of them builds on this earlier period of modernism and urbanization. I am particularly interested in the ways Petry's and Bishop's postwar portraits of interracial intimacy rethink the relationship between womanhood and social deviance in a cultural moment of sociological scrutiny of race and sexuality in the United States.[7]

Rather than meditate on the modern city in the abstract or on these literary texts of the late 1940s and early 1950s as iterations of a "late modernism," I take the cue to "focus our attention on the nature of the particular modernity in question" (Friedman 2010, 487), in this case to the emerging interracial relationships being fostered in inter-war and postwar cheap hotels. These literary depictions of hotel life, as I read them, both respond to and reflect postwar anxieties about interracial sexuality, women's more public expressions of sexual desire, and re-imagined gender identities facilitated by the rapid social changes that followed World War II. Within the modern city, full of social possibility and deviance, Petry and Bishop render the intimate spaces of aesthetic exchange and sexual exploration found in hotel rooms.

Night Clerk Dream Book

Bishop's "In a cheap hotel" provides the first proper accommodations for thinking through this essay's questions of white womanhood and the economies of race and sex. I return to, check myself back into, "In a cheap hotel" in order to more fully engage the racial politics of labour that I argue structure the poem as well as many modernist fantasies about the hotel. This cheap hotel sits ambiguously in poetic space. The poem's lack of geographical specificity and even its temporal uncertainty mimics a hotel room's tendency to suspend time and place to become a kind of neutral playground or dreamspace.[8] The poem's first half:

> In a cheap hotel
> in a cheap city
> Love held his prisoners   or my love
> brought the pitcher of ice—
> dropped the quarter in the spidery old electric fan—

> Love the Night Clerk, the Negro bell-boy
> I remember the horrible carpet
> & its smell, & the dog-eared telephone book
> with its ominous look
> full full of the names
>   of strangers close to my head,
> my head with our name in it
>   or nameless embarrassment—
>   (Bishop 2006, 83)[9]

Bishop's poem centres on Love, the "Night Clerk": capitalized and a figure of capital. He is hailed by the labour we name as "hospitality." Hospitable: to entertain strangers as the *Oxford English Dictionary* suggests. This is the work of generous (an economy implicit in this definition) hospitality, a word that looks so close to hospital, another favourite haunt in Bishop's poetics.[10] Rich connections can be made between the care we seek in each space. "In a cheap hotel" raises questions about the labour of the night as well as what we might call sexual sickness, certainly psychic disease. The after-hours staff are there to turn on fans and offer iced pitchers just perfect for gin. Alice Quinn, who included the unpublished (and unfinished) poem in *Edgar Allan Poe & The Juke-Box*, speculates that its origins might be found in Bishop's notes for her essay "The U.S.A. School of Writing" about a chained-up love. I see this poem staged somehow after a visit to New York where Bishop has taken up lodging in the racial imagination, part diary, part dream journal.

The fragmentary, unfinished quality of Bishop's drafting of the poem is lost in its anthologizing and my reproduction here. Bishop's hotel poetry begins in middle-of-the-night scribblings of an itchy memory or equally racial fantasy. The mind goes back to the motor-court memory. The spacing, her dashes, and the tentative brokenness of the poem must matter to our reading of it. Bishop dreams up a Black "bell boy," "boy" the charged infantilizing of Black men common on Jim Crow streets but also in the job title itself. Bell Boy with his icy pitcher. But as he is named Love we can't help but twin him with the night visitor at the end of Bishop's poem who "chains me & berates me." In her room, Bishop waits for her Night Clerk.

>   Six
> Five yrs. ago   still
> Almost every night   —frequently
> [every night] he drags me
> back to that   bed
> the ice clinks, the fan whirs.
> He chains me & berates me—
> He chains me to that bed & he berates me.
>   (2006, 83)

These night visits are animated by bondage and submission. This annual ritual of debasement in the hotel reminds readers of its role in our ritualistic escapes as empty stages (again the labour invisible) for our sexual-romantic-erotic desires. Bishop's cross-race encounter, with its slippage between worker and lover, is imagined as taboo. She calls it a "nameless embarrassment" which hints at both interracial intimacy (even the spectre of a Black night-time visitor into the sleeping space is provocative) and sexual kink. The shame that animates the poem and its nightly revisiting "every night he drags me back to that bed" mimics the violence of dream, perhaps the dominance of our subconscious drives. For Bishop, and as we will see with Petry, the hotel is foremost a site of sexual transgression of symbolic, but also corporal, explorations of submission and dominance that are notably framed in economic or material terms. Modernism's purported drive to unsettle taboos is questioned in Bishop's "cheap hotel." Her tableau demonstrates the way seemingly progressive or "risky" portraits often reify the taboos of interracial sex, inter-class intimacies, and sexual kink they seek to question.

In revisiting the poem, I got caught in the phone book, "dog-eared," and the paltry library that the hotel often offers. In the unpublished poem "Miami," which Quinn places in the late 1950s but finds shared language and images from "In a cheap hotel," written at least a decade earlier, Bishop writes of "two soiled telephone books / filled with their thousands of names/and none of them are ours thank God" (2006, 118).[11] She goes on to contemplate "in the dark drawer undoubtedly a Gideon Bible," the literature of the American hotel. Koestenbaum in his own thoughts on "Hotel Bishop" ventures:

> The point of <u>hotel reading</u> is freedom to interpret, to wander, to have perverse (and wrong) ideas. Bishop dreams of lacking choices. She imagines—a darkly utopian fantasy—that her liberties are curtailed and that she must rely on her own imagination's resources.
>
> (2007, 62)

The Night Clerk provides the poet with another narrative beyond a list of strangers' names, but there is no compensation for this imaginative labour. And Bishop's characterization of the Negro-Night clerk *is* perverse: "wrong" in its gaze and her imagined rituals. In both poems, the phone book with its thankful anonymity illogically seems to be a source of embarrassment for Bishop. These books are "stuffed" with names "beside our heads," she writes in another version of "Miami." It is a potent image of intimate (sleeping close) anonymity and one I find radiating with erotic possibility. In "In a cheap hotel," Bishop speaks of "Strangers in a phone book"; for us today this anonymous intimacy is found in the sex apps that ding across our cities in hotels, hostels, and rented bedrooms.

On Camilo's Dime

Writer of the bestseller *The Street* (1946), Petry is associated equally with her sociological portraits of Harlem life and modernist portraits of New England, drawing from her childhood in a family of pharmacists in Old Saybrook, Connecticut. Farah Jasmine Griffin reads Petry within a tradition of left-leaning American writers "who depicted social problems as a means of encouraging readers to address and alleviate them" (2013, 115). The violent currents of social change are evident in Petry's short story "In Darkness and Confusion" (1947) where she imagines the unfolding of the 1943 Harlem riot from the perspective of William Jones, casual witness to a confrontation in the lobby of the Braddock Hotel in Harlem. On that first day of August, Robert Brandy, a Black soldier, intervened when Marjorie Polite, a Black woman, was assaulted by a white police officer. Thousands of Harlem residents took to the streets in the two days of unrest that followed.[12] The rumour that Brandy had been killed spread and heightened Harlemites' anger over the treatment of Black soldiers and veterans. In Petry's fictionalized account, William has just learnt that his son, stationed at a Southern base, is locked in a military prison for a physical altercation with a white officer after he challenged Jim Crow humiliations. Petry uses the riot as both backdrop and catalyst for her meditation on a modern Harlem family shaken by racial violence and shaped by the postwar city's less visible systemic oppressions. She also recognizes that the modernist hotel as murky site of social change, particularly when the nuances of gender, race, and class are factored in, holds much more than a utopian promise.

In contrast to the Braddock Hotel, the fictional Harlem hotel in *The Narrows* is a site of less overt forms of racialized violence, ones connected to hotel labour, including the facilitation of white women's fantasies. Petry's journals in her archive reveal her interest in unravelling the psychology of interracial relationships, a central concern of *The Narrows*.[13] The Harlem hotel is foundational to that inquiry. In the vaguely named "The Hotel," we again take the elevator to a hotel room in the postwar city, in this case one outfitted by Camilo, a wealthy woman stepping out on her husband, to accommodate her liaisons with Link. The novel's extended meditation on the "The Hotel" renders the establishment as a microcosm of both white privilege and commodified blackness. Petry writes:

> She called it The Hotel, just like the rest of Harlem, easily, casually, taking it for granted that you would know that she was talking about this one particular hotel, not needing to identify it by name. She makes everything hers, he thought. Part of that easy adaptability which he had once liked and admired and even envied in her, and which he now found irritating.

She owned everything: people, cars, houses, establishing her ownership quickly; she bought bellboys, desk clerks, elevator men, doormen. Bought 'em up fast. Had bought him, too.

"What's the matter?" she repeated.

(1999b, 283)

These hotel scenes position white womanhood within Black sociality, centred and marginal in a liminal space that mirrors the hotel room's porous border between public and private. These scenes reflect a larger cultural moment of changing sexual attitudes, including around interracial intimacies, and shifting (though deeply entrenched) racial protocols. Rather than solely a liminal space away from the strictures of both segregation and marital (heteronormative) obligation, the hotel room also provides a structure, a desired privacy, for interracial intimacy and other scrutinized relationships.

In trying to tease out white women's attraction to, perhaps identification with, blackness, Carla Kaplan notes her debt to queer theory for its exploration of "how so-called private emotions and feelings, seemingly inchoate longings and desires, can be understood as a form of political resistance and political critique" but a resistance often overlooked and running below the surfaces of more overt forms of political expression (2013, 359). Petry's depiction of Camilo and Link's affair, including a wealthy white woman's attempt to claim a hotel within a Black community to overstep social barriers, dispels the simple idea that private desires can enact resistance, revealing these actions as their own kind of social fantasy. The idea that how we feel and who we fuck holds an implicit political subversion is intertwined with the narratives of the hotel as a site of transient, modernist liberation that I referenced earlier. Indeed, white women's liberation from the suburbs and the conventional gender roles of white, heteronormative marriage often includes a transgression of racial and class lines. Yet the spaces that host these transgressions rely on their own racial hierarchies of labour. If as historian Wini Breines has argued, "The feminine mystique was white as the suburbs, a code to ensure white women's segregation from and dependence on men and their differentiation from black women" (2001, 49) then some white women, seeking liberation, found possibility with Black men and within desegregated, however fleeting, places that could accommodate interracial and other forms of deviant intimacies.

Both Bishop and Petry ponder what it means for white women to encroach on Black spaces or deracialized spaces of hospitality as a rejection of those racial codes and sexual boundaries. Bishop's unsettling, queer hotel encounter and Petry's Harlem hotel are presented as an escape from corrosive whiteness. Shane Vogel has argued that entertainment districts (and certainly white New Yorkers sought Harlem nightlife as an alternative to more racially and sexually rigid sectors of the city) "provided opportunities for the expansion of middle-class subjectivity" (2009, 55). White women's adaptability to these spaces, and the allure of the cheap as central to these sexual desires, also connects to their fantasies of erotic submission or transgression. Bishop's letters and notebooks remind us that hotels, particularly cheap ones, were a part of this network of entertainment and intra-class sociality that many women artists explored.

Petry's portrait of hotel sex recognizes whiteness as a privilege often to make oneself at home anywhere, or at least believe that one has a right to do so. Link's irritation at Camilo's "easy adaptability" is connected to a larger critique of the ways black masculinity, like a weekend escape to a hotel, is used to spice up the doldrums of bourgeois married life. Petry's use of "easy adaptability" exists in an economics of social control and racial stratification. Camilo's repeated question "what's the matter?" also underscores the oblivion of white privilege that Petry's hotel episode also seeks to interrogate. Link is surprised to learn that the room was paid for by the month, reflecting a more permanent domestic situation that recalls the central role apartment hotels played for gay/queer persons seeking alternative domestic spaces or simply stability in a hostile world.

Link soon discovers that their room in a third-rate hotel was transformed to justify its Waldorf-Astoria prices on Camilo's dime. He finds a "Kingside bed. Sheets made to order. Blankets made to order. Millionaire's bed" (Petry 1999b, 284). Petry stresses the material conditions of the hotel: "cheap," in the neglected parts of the city, and in need of comforts—imported goods in Camilo's case. Of course, this comfort and her aesthetic imperative to make over the hotel room relies on the staff—the porters, maids, and maintenance men. The hotel simultaneously becomes both transitory—a respite from the domestic structure—and a facsimile of home. Harlem both exists and does not outside their door. In both texts, the erotic encounter must be addressed aesthetically. "I remember the horrible carpet / & its smell," writes Bishop. The humble comforts of fan and ice in Bishop's poem are central to her easy adaptability. These shabby surroundings are essential to these scenes which ultimately raise questions not only about the racialized labour of the hotel that I have already signalled but also the ethics of interracial intimacies and the articulations of white womanhood that rely on blackness to take their form.

Queer Guests

America's anxiety about interracial intimacies and other bonds across racial lines were part of a larger postwar attention to sexual perversions of all sorts. The citation of queerness informs these hotel stays: Bishop's lesbianism, the kink implied in the chained-up humiliations, Camilo's thrill of breaking social codes and Link's own shame at his objectification. Petry, in fact, explicitly names the role that the hotel, tucked away in a marginalized neighbourhood, plays in queer expression, fugitivity, and survival.

> The Hotel knowing that these rooms would be used for assignations, for the consummation of illicit relations between males, between females, between males and females, for rape, for seduction, sexes arranged and rearranged, mixed up, mismatched, and so charged Waldorf-astoria prices for thirdrate and fourthrate accommodations, but the next night, ah, miracle of wealth, miracle of gun money, miracle of being an heiress.
>
> (1999b, 283-84)

Petry's democratic catalogue of the sexualities housed in the hotel is rather stunning. This passage—a sort of Kinsey report as Whitmanesque list—illustrates that the postwar city and novels about it often folded in a growing public discourse about sexuality including increasing attention to its "deviant" forms. Notably, Petry doesn't shy away from the sexual violence that the seeming anonymity and transience of the hotel makes possible. Within her expansive demarcation of sexuality, Petry renders the hotel as an extra-legal place, a chaotic space outside the law that accommodates a variety of social-sexual deviances and subjectivities.

Alongside white women seeking cheap hotels, gay men were another population upsetting social norms of home and family. For these men, the hotel has been both employer and home. Historian George Chauncey has argued, for example, that "The increasing number and respectability of apartment houses and hotels helped make it possible for a middle-class gay male world to develop" (1994, 158).[14] Samuel Delany has famously explored the social-sexual possibilities of a pre-gentrified Times Square, positing that "[c]ontact is likely to be at its most useful when it is cross-class contact" (1999, 142). The public spaces of porn theatres and parking lots that Delany savours were, of course, off limits to white women of the middle and leisure classes. Hotels, often in neighbourhoods where "vice" was overlooked, and to a lesser extent residential hotels, provided spaces for single women to explore a life with less racial and sexual strictures. These cultural histories (including the important role YMCAs played in building sexual and artistic networks for gay men in postwar Chicago and New York) document the ways hotels in various forms are central to queer history by securing intimacy and re-imagining domesticity to accommodate social-sexual difference.[15] My sense of these hotel scenes are informed by queer cultural studies projects, including Chauncey's as well as Kevin Mumford's pioneering work on sex districts, that recognize the role hotels and boardinghouses have played not only in modern urbanization, but in providing spaces for queer existence and expression and for social connections across racial and economic lines.

Michel Foucault included "honeymoon hotels" in his list of "crisis heterotopias," which he describes as "privileged or sacred or forbidden places, reserved for individuals who are, in relation to society and to the human environment in which they live, in a state of crisis" (1986, 24–25). We have seen the ways crisis still animates the modern hotel: from Link's confrontation with being a kept man in a space where he is surveilled by Black employees to the hotel occupant's humiliations by the Night Clerk in Bishop's poem. In his spatial taxonomy, Foucault also identifies a shift to "heterotopias of deviation," those spaces where "individuals whose behavior is deviant in relation to the required mean or norm are placed" (25). My interest in Bishop's cheap hotel and Petry's vignette lies in the centrality of race—the navigating of it, the claiming of its desires, its exploitative tinges—to these expressions of deviance. The Harlem hotel in *The Narrows* occupies a queer position between Foucault's two social-spatial categories, a space of sexual initiation (or an indulgence of a taboo as some might have seen it) and a space of purchased acceptance of social deviance—both racial and sexual in nature. While it is tempting to read these narratives of interracial liaisons in hotels within a framework of social risk and as relational experiments made possible by urbanization, the rigid racial lines both inside the hotel and the city around it point to a consolidation of social roles as much as a rupture of them. The staff in Petry's hotel know their place; it is Camilo who tramples the invisible lines of race with her intimate banter. John, the elevator man. Ralph, the doorman. She knows the staff by name. The staff fawn over Camilo, enraging Link with their "undemanding, humble" demeanour, but they also mutedly judge her recklessness (Petry 1994b, 282). Money smooths over these transgressions.

Knight of the Bags

While these writings provide a historical look at some of the sexual attitudes and racial anxieties that defined World War II and the Cold War that emerged from it, I would not want my largely fanciful examination of the formal choices Bishop and Petry made in their representations of white women and the sexual desire they explore in the hotel room to overlook the relevance of these literary portraits to today's workers in hotels, cheap and otherwise. This precarious workforce, which faces class elitism, real threats of sexual violence and often backbreaking work, is represented, though marginal and largely invisible, in these portraits.[16] This invisibility begins to unravel through the act of naming. Bishop names her Night Clerk "Love" as I read it. This symbolic nomenclature is contrasted by Petry's precision when she (in a novel brimming with details and the extraneous) writes of Roland, "Knight of the Bags," the bellboy/porter with whom Camilo had obviously curried favour (1999b, 284). She has even connected him with a doctor to help his ailing mother. He is caught "looking at Camilo with a mixture of awe and gratitude"

(282). Unlike Bishop's Night Clerk, Petry offers a portrait in quick strokes of the economic disparities beneath these exchanges.

There is, in fact, a subtle capitalistic critique in Petry's staging of this interracial relationship. Beyond the secret affair between white heiress and Black man, Petry, for example, notes "the miracle of gun money" in transforming the Harlem hotel from third-rate to luxury (1999b, 284). Camilo's family is in the ammunition business, a particularly American industry and Link's discontent (his musings at the hotel bar) are based in his disgust at being a "kept man," a "toy-plaything" (286). He is bought in a sense with the funds of racial violence. Link's interior monologue draws a line from the white woman enslaver to contemporary humiliations (compromised masculinity, in a sense, makes Link "queer") and the complexities of interracial sex in modern life. "Bought and sold, he thought. Bought at an auction, sold again at the death of the owner" (280). "His long line of bought and paid for ancestors." "Looking for men, black men" (288). The hotel promises a space for private racial performance, but the more public racial and sexual prohibitions and the nation's often underwritten history of racialized sex intrude with persistence. Modernism is often marked and marred by a nation's economic and erotic transformations. To be modern is to be fiscally autonomous, to seek a "self-madeness" often undergirded by white power structures. It is the lack of economic autonomy in his interactions with Camilo that rattles Link. In many ways their affair reverts to old racial scripts of the white mistress and the objectified enslaved man.

Link undergoes a quiet resistance at the hotel's bar—a deeply attuned portrait of a man grabbling with his own sexual objection and the ghosts of slavery that haunt his relationship with Camilo. Link's brandy break reminds us of the hotel bar's role, as Petry reports it, as a space where one engages in affective labour, where one dons the psychological armour to continue with compromised intimacies. Petry explores an extended metaphor of a hawk needing to be hooded to examine this self-medicated containment of desire. The Harlem hotel is positioned as a sanctuary and stage for sexual-racial transgression, but the ghosts of American racism and its gendered-sexual protocols trouble its modernity and promises of transient encounters and identities. Marxist critic Marshall Berman writes: "To be modern, I said, is to experience personal and social life as a maelstrom, to find one's world and oneself in perpetual disintegration and renewal, trouble and anguish, ambiguity and contradiction" (1983, 345). He goes on to argue that this impulse "to survive and create in the maelstrom's midst" is what connects modernists across eras and cultures. While the work of Bishop and Petry, vibrant in the decade after World War II, might be stretching the timeframe of America's High Modernism to its edges, their interest in locating the modern white woman in the maelstrom of the nation's both rigid and evolving racial systems highlights capitalism's imprint on these emergent forms of whiteness and racial intimacy. Both Bishop and Petry question the modernist romance with the hotel as a waystation, an ark for dreaming. Animated by its racial dimensions and the social permissiveness this purchased privacy affords, the hotel is yet another nuanced space of racialized labour, one at work to make a cheap space, one costly for the labourers who facilitate it, for white women's desires and their racial mischief.

In "Blueprint for Negro Writing" (1937), Richard Wright exalts literature for its power to go where history cannot: "The imaginative conception of a historical period will not be a carbon copy of reality. Image and emotion possess a logic of their own" (1994, 105). In her modernist rendering of a private history of civil rights, Petry makes the hotel workers visible; she names them and gives them a sprinkling of dialogue. It feels insignificant but also importantly distinct from the voices we can't hear in Bishop's Night Clerk poem. These moments direct us to a larger reading of invisible labour in the literature and lived realities of hotels. The affective labour made visible in both texts holds my interest, but we need not ignore the more material and proletarian critiques we might discover latent in these authors' work. Bishop took interest, troublesome for some, in the Black and Cuban workers who laboured in her Key West home. Petry's short stories and novels almost always paid attention to the ways we work, including the domestic workers and the cashiers labouring to make lives and loves of their own. Wright's call for an alternative history rooted in image and emotion must necessarily include our affective histories, stuffed like Bishop's telephone pages with erotic possibility and its racial resonances, in this case an under-written history of white women lodging in cheap hotels, fiddling to find comfort, and adapting to its quiet pains.

Notes

1. See Bishop (1994), 185–86, and Lombardi (1995), 107–08. "I was the most snooty and unpopular person at Blythewood," Bishop confesses (Bishop 1994, 190).
2. For discussions of Bishop's hotel stays and travels more broadly, see Koestenbaum (2007), MacArthur (2008), Schmidt (2013), and Miller (1995).
3. See Bishop (1994, 60–61). Louise Crane, of the Crane Paper fortune, was both Bishop's Vassar classmate and girlfriend. Margaret Miller, a visual artist and later a curator at MoMA, would lose her arm from this accident.
4. Matt Brim's important work on the material conditions that produce "queer ideas" is on my mind here. His reminder to pay attention to "our embodiments and our built environments" resonates with the labour of the hotel worker to which I want to draw our attention (Brim 2020, 16). This essay is only a start to an inquiry into modernist texts that explore the transitions between the domestic and work spheres of their working-class characters. A "literature of the break room" would be central to an investigation. The elevator exchanges that Petry writes of in her Harlem hotel scene, as one quick example, seek to bring the hotel worker into some form of embodiment; in contrast, the Night Clerk in Bishop's poem stays tellingly disembodied and unvoiced. For a

discussion of the experience and literary rendition of hotel staff in the context of 1920s and 1930s Germany, see Zitzlsperger, Chapter 11, in this volume.
5   On Kracauer's "The Hotel Lobby," see also Heynickx, Chapter 13, in this volume.
6   See also Cray, Chapter 8, for a discussion of hotels and sexuality in Djuna Barnes and Anaïs Nin.
7   As narratives of late modernism—and unconventional episodes of female interiority—the work of Bishop and Petry can be productively situated within the emergent field of American Studies, a discipline taking form in the late 1940s and 1950s. In addition to the work of F. O. Matthiessen and Lionel Trilling, I am thinking here of Gunnar Myrdal's *American Dilemma: The Negro Problem and Modern Democracy* (1944), Alfred Kinsey's *Sexual Behavior in the Human Male* (1948) and *Sexual Behavior in the Human Female* (1953), and W. E. B. Du Bois's "An Appeal to the World" (1947). These monumental works shaped mid-twentieth-century public conversations about race and sexuality and find contact points in the work of Bishop and Petry written in this same period. Bishop, as one example, mentions Karen Horney's *The Neurotic Personality of Our Time* in a May 1942 letter to Marianne Moore, reminding us of the enduring influence of psychoanalysis on Cold War literary representations of sexual perversion (1994, 108).
8   Alice Quinn, editor of these unpublished poems, discusses her uncertainty over composition dates in an interview with Tess Taylor (Taylor 2006).
9   The poem "In a cheap hotel" and the excerpt from "Miami" are from *Edgar Allan Poe & The Juke-Box* by Elizabeth Bishop, edited and annotated by Alice Quinn. Copyright © 2006 by Alice Helen Methfessel. Introduction copyright © 2006 by Alice Quinn. Reprinted by permission of Farrar, Straus and Giroux and Carcanet Press, Manchester UK. All Rights Reserved.
10 "Visits to Saint Elizabeths" and "Mercedes Hospital" are her most famous poetic excursions to medical institutions.
11 See Taylor (2006) and Quinn's extensive note for "Miami" which offers several sources and composition dates for the poem as well as its shared imagery with "In a cheap hotel" (Bishop 2006, 319–20).
12 Historians often stress the property damage and stolen goods in their discussions of the August 1943 riots, but six Black Americans were killed, the arrests neared 500, and the injured, including some white residents, neared 200. See Capeci (1977) for an essential account of the events.
13 For a discussion of Petry's compositional process and interest in situating the relationship of Link and Camilo in a cultural moment of shifting public attitudes about race and sex, see Schmidt (2013, 152–55).
14 For a deeper dive into rooming houses and private residences as important parts of a city's sexual geography, distinct from vice districts, see Robertson (2012).
15 As Albert Reiss writes,

> Queers and peers typically establish contact in public or quasi-public places. Major points of contact include street corners, public parks, men's toilets in public or quasi-public places such as those in transportation depots, parks or hotels, and "second" and "third-run" movie houses (open around the clock and permitting sitting through shows.
> (1961, 106)

16 For a starting point, see Guerrier and Adib (2000).

Works Cited

Berman, Marshall. 1983. *All That Is Solid Melts Into Air: The Experience of Modernity.* London and New York: Verso.
Bishop, Elizabeth. 1994. *One Art.* New York: The Noonday Press.
Bishop, Elizabeth. 2006. *Edgar Allan Poe & The Juke-Box: Uncollected Poems, Drafts, and Fragments.* Edited by Alice Quinn. New York: Farrar, Strauss, Giroux.
Breines, Wini. 2001. *Young, White, and Miserable: Growing Up Female in the Fifties.* Chicago: University of Chicago Press.
Brim, Matt. 2020. *Poor Queer Studies.* Durham: Duke University Press.
Capeci, Dominic J., Jr. 1977. *The Harlem Riot of 1943.* Philadelphia: Temple University Press.
Delany. Samuel. 1999. *Times Square Red, Times Square Blue.* New York: New York University Press.
Foucault, Michel. 1986. "Of Other Spaces." Translated by Jay Miskowiec. *Diacritics* 16 (1): 22–27. https://doi.org/10.2307/464648
Friedman, Susan Stanford. 2010. "Planetarity: Musing Modernist Studies." *Modernism/Modernity* 17 (3): 471–99.
Guerrier, Yvonne, and Amel S. Adib. 2000. "'No, We Don't Provide That Service': The Harassment of Hotel Employees by Customers." *Work, Employment & Society* 14 (4): 689–705. www.jstor.org/stable/23747724
Griffin, Farah Jasmine. 2013. *Harlem Nocturne: Women Artists of Progressive Politics during World War II.* New York: Basic Civitas.
Herring, Scott. 2007. *Queering the Underworld: Slumming, Literature, and the Undoing of Lesbian and Gay History.* Chicago: University of Chicago Press.
Kaplan, Carla. 2013. *Miss Anne in Harlem: The White Women of the Black Renaissance.* New York: HarperCollins.
Koestenbaum, Wayne. 2007. *Hotel Theory.* New York: Soft Skull Press.
Kracauer, Siegfried. 2004. "The Hotel Lobby." In *The City Cultures Reader*, edited by Malcolm Miles, Tim Hall, and Iain Borden. 33–39. London: Routledge.
Lombardi, Marilyn May. 1995. *The Body and the Song: Elizabeth Bishop's Poetics.* Carbondale: Southern University Press.
MacArthur, Marit J. 2008. "'In a Room': Elizabeth Bishop in Europe, 1935–1937." *Texas Studies in Literature and Language* 50 (4): 408–42.
Miller, Brett C. 1995. *Elizabeth Bishop: Life and the Memory of It.* Oakland: University of California Press.
Perry, Imani. 2018. *Vexy Thing: On Gender and Liberation.* Durham: Duke University Press.
Petry, Ann. 1999a. *Miss Muriel and Other Stories.* New York: Mariner Books.
Petry, Ann. 1999b. *The Narrows.* New York: Mariner Books.
Reiss, Albert J. 1961. "The Social Integration of Queers and Peers." *Social Problems* 9 (2): 102–20. JSTOR, www.jstor.org/stable/799006
Robertson, Stephen, Shane White, Stephen Garton, and Graham White. 2012. "Disorderly Houses: Residences, Privacy, and the Surveillance of Sexuality in 1920s Harlem." *Journal of the History of Sexuality* 21 (3): 443–66. www.jstor.org/stable/23322010
Schmidt, Tyler T. 2013. *Desegregating Desire: Race and Sexuality in Cold War American Literature.* Jackson: University of Mississippi Press.

Taylor, Tess. 2006. "Paper Trail." *The Atlantic.* January 2006. www.theatlantic.com/magazine/archive/2006/01/paper-trail/304557/
Vogel, Shane. 2009. *The Scene of the Harlem Cabaret: Race, Sexuality, Performance.* Chicago: University of Chicago Press.
Wright, Richard. 1994. "Blueprint for Negro Writing." *Within the Circle: An Anthology of African American Literary Criticism*, 97–106. Durham, NC: Duke University Press.
Zimmerman, Emma. 2015. "'Always the Same Stairs, Always the Same Room': The Uncanny Architecture of Jean Rhys's *Good Morning, Midnight.*" *Journal of Modern Literature* 38 (4): 74–92.

Theory, Design

13 *Rota Moderna*

Vortex Force in Viennese Hotel Lobbies

Rajesh Heynickx

Like all hotel lobbies, the lobby of the Hotel Royal, situated in the heart of Vienna,[1] just a few minutes away from Vienna State Opera, is an interstitial space, a place to meet, to wait, and to move through (see Figure 13.1). It introduces and disengages at the same time. Images and artefacts, spread all over this lobby, offer the contemporary hotel visitor bits of information about the past.

At one end of the lobby, those who are checking in can have a look at a painting of Vienna around 1683. In this painting, the city lights up as a distinct spot, its surrounding land unaffected by the urban sprawl. It shows a concentric ensemble of picturesque houses, safely situated behind medieval walls. At the other end of the lobby space, the visitor can stop at a couple of display cabinets. Here, a set of shattered memorabilia like city stamps, stone cups, pieces of ironwork, old pictures, and newspaper articles chronicle the hotel's past. The background music played is Johan Strauss's waltz music that, as Marshal McLuhan once noted, in the early nineteenth century broke through "the formal feudal barriers" of courtly dance styles (1966, 22).

The use of history in the lobby of Hotel Royal is far from unique. Vienna's grand hotels often attribute prestige to their lobbies with the help of fake historical columns. In the Imperial Hotel and Hotel Bristol, portraits of emperors of the Habsburg Monarchy still try to capture the visitor's attention. And up to this day, traces of famous past visitors, mainly in the form of pictures or signatures in guest books, are given the status of relics in lobbies. All this is done to accentuate a lineage: new guests feel flattered when they seem to belong to a prestigious pedigree. Yet, in the Hotel Royal a visitor might also fall under the spell of a different, less comforting aesthesis. From the moment his or her gaze moves from the panorama of the painting to the dispersed set of remnants in the cabinets, the idea that Vienna is irrevocably transformed takes hold. Still, this visitor, even when he or she is enjoying the rolling rhythm of the waltz that fills the lobby, can conjointly discover something else. With the traffic jam during the trip from the airport fresh in mind, she/he might realize that modernization also leads to spatial congestion. And at the moment that this idea, namely that a modern world of movement also

DOI: 10.4324/9781003213079-18

Figure 13.1 The lobby of Hotel Royal in 2019. The painting on the right depicts Vienna around 1683. © Wolfgang Thaler.

implies obstruction, emerges, the feeling of a slowing down, or inaction in the face of over-stimulus, can settle in the visitor's mind.

Whether the contemporary hotel guest reflects on the congestion of a modern world or is charmed by a genealogy of former visitors, the image of a vortex fits in both cases the description of the underlying modernization process. As we know, from the nineteenth century on, "all that is solid melts into air."[2] A maelstrom of change produced tons of cultural wreckage that, if not totally dissolved through time, washed up in later eras where it became gradually discarded or partially integrated. This *Denkbild* (thought-image) of a vortex perfectly applies to Vienna. The city that saw itself as the headquarters of the Old World of Central Europe became in the last decades of the nineteenth century a crucible of modernity. It then got jammed with original minds embracing experiments with visuality (Oskar Kokoschka) and tone (Arnold Schoenberg), producing the first stream-of-consciousness narrative (Arthur Schnitzler), or revolutionizing ideas about the life of the mind (Sigmund Freud). In order to suggest such dizzying novelty, Carl Schorske's landmark book *Fin-de-siècle Vienna* starts with a dissection of Maurice Ravel's *La valse*, in which a Viennese waltz spins towards chaos and splinters apart (Schorske 1980).[3]

Vienna's multifarious modernism interacted with the changing form of the city. As Anthony Alofsin and Joseph Leo Koerner demonstrated, Viennese architecture affected and reflected changes in sociopolitical

Figure 13.2 The Corso on the Ringstrasse in Vienna. Print after a painting by Theo Zasche, c. 1900. © Schloss Schönbrunn Kultur and Betriebsges.m.b.H.

identities and cultural values (Alofsin 2008; Koerner 2016). Besides Adolf Loos's well-known 1910 provocative attack against the highly ornamental style of the day with his lecture "Ornament and Crime" (1985, 100–103), one setting stands out in this story: the Ringstrasse, a new grand boulevard dating from 1865 (see Figure 13.2). In that year, the ancient walls that had kept out the Turks for so many centuries were demolished and replaced by a passage encircling the historical core and opening on the cleared lands. Over the years, public buildings, luxurious apartment houses, parks, and, not least, hotels emerged around it. Besides opening up the city, the area enclosed by the bustling avenue became the fashionable quarter for a burgeoning middle class. The Ringstrasse, finally, triggered heavy debates between architects who subscribed to a communitarian take on the built environment and those who preferred a functionalist approach (Schorske 2014, 157–71).[4]

Being a semipublic gateway to the private space of the hotel room, the hotel lobby, I will argue, acted, just like the Vienna Ring Road, as a centrifuge, a space that was part and parcel of modernity's maelstrom. But how was the lobby perceived and represented by those who used this centrifuge? And how did that centrifuge of modern life actually function? Firstly, I will concentrate on how the lobby became linked to a mythical whole, namely the Austro-Hungarian Empire. It turns out that during the interwar period the hotel was an excellent place to muse about the bygone world of the *Späten Kaiserzeit* (the Late Empire). Here, the writings of Joseph Roth will reveal a desperate attempt to give meaning to history's turmoil. Secondly, I will focus on a non-human actor. I will unpack the idea that the revolving door, a "machine" invented in the nineteenth century for hotel buildings, facilitated a world in constant motion. Our main guide in understanding this wheel of modernity, this crucial component of the lobby centrifuge, will be another famous Austrian author, Robert Musil.

A Sunken World

Already before the Ringstrasse era, grand hotels in Vienna were known for being sites of transit and exchange, offering entries to other worlds. For example, the Hotel National, Vienna's first grand hotel, built in 1848, had its own telegraph office (see Figure 13.3).

Also there, and only there in Vienna, one could read the London *Times* (Hoffman 2018, 92). Standing at the crossroads of multiple lives, entailing a criss-cross of destinies and unexpected encounters, hotels mixed bodies and stories, luggage and language. In the lobby, where new guests arrived

Figure 13.3 The Grand Hotel National was a modern luxury hotel with a telegraph, two hundred rooms, central heating, and several dining rooms and lounges, a semicircular courtyard and a garden terrace. The different languages used in this advertisement reveal its international visitors. © Vienna Museum.

constantly, transience dominated. In his iconic 1925 essay "The Hotel Lobby," Siegfried Kracauer argued that those sitting in the lobby's club chairs vanished "into an undetermined void." Lingering in a "groundless distance" from both the everyday and one's own home, hotel guests were immersed in a peripatetic universe (2005, 183–84). According to this German cultural theorist, what happened in the lobby pointed to a broad sociological process: a world characterized by traditional practices and a sense of belonging (*Gemeinschaft*) became overwhelmed by a more individualistic, competitive, and impersonal organization of mere society (*Gesellschaft*).[5]

In a dark reflection on living in the post-1945 world, the philosopher Theodor W. Adorno, a friend of Kracauer, radicalized this insight. He stated that hotels epitomized an existential homelessness (1999, 38–39). Still, Adorno's reflection does not stand when we read how the Austrian author Joseph Roth looked at hotels. For Roth, who lived during long periods of his life in hotels all over Europe (including Vienna), hotels did not only embody a staggering alienation. On the contrary, he detected a homelike environment in the hotel. Exactly because of its anonymity, the impersonal hotel could offer him a form of personal relief:

> I love the "impersonal" quality of that room, as a monk may love his cell. And as other men may be happy to be reunited with their pictures, their china, their silver, their children and their books, so I rejoice in the cheap wallpaper, the spotless ewer and basin [...] and that wisest of books: the telephone directory. [...] I am by myself but not isolated, alone but not forgotten, private but not abandoned. I have only to open the window, and the world steps in. [...] I am a hotel citizen, a hotel patriot.
>
> (Roth 2015, 156, 158)

Here is a gloss on the old home from home adage: for Roth, it is possible to set up one's own private space in a hotel. At the same time, the passage shows that the line between public and private spaces is one of the most delicate and subtle, yet also one of the most massive boundaries in modern history. As the economist and historian Albert Hirschman demonstrated in his book *Shifting Involvements: Private Interest and Public Action* (1982), when the term "private" emerged between the sixteenth and nineteenth centuries, it primarily functioned as a negative concept. Derived from the Latin *privare*, which means to deprive someone of something, the term "private" stood for an act of subtraction, that is, a carving out of one's own (mental) space. Yet, such an act of subtraction was equally aligned with public affairs. The pursuit of private interests and a harmonious social order were not unavoidably antithetical, contrary to what Kracauer and Adorno thought. And that is exactly the idea that undergirds Roth's final sentence when he identifies himself as a "hotel citizen, a hotel patriot," by which he presupposes a larger fabric.

Moreover, as we can read elsewhere in his work, the lobby is for him a platform on which to realize his international mindset:

> It is there, in the lobby, that I sit all day. This is my home and my world, the faraway and the nearby, my unsuspecting gallery. This is where I begin writing about the hotel's employees, my friends. They are all characters! Citizens of the world! Judges of character! Experts of languages and the soul! Nobody is more international than they. They are the real internationals.
> (1956, 234; my translation)

When subscribing to an ideal of international mobility and cultural variety, Roth is proclaiming the values of a world he mourned: the Danube Monarchy. This Old Empire was, as Karl Schlögel remarked, a "unique imperial complex that had all the features of a heterogeneous conglomerate" (2016, 314). Vienna, the Empire's capital, was a multi-ethnic metropolis and the capitals of the Kingdoms and the crown lands were no less multi-confessional and multilingual. However, this conglomerate was held together by astonishingly strong forces of cohesion and integration. Through sharing the same routines and standards, two dozen peoples and ethnic groups succeeded in living underneath the same political roof.

In order to consolidate a cultural homogeneity in a world of religious, cultural, and linguistic *mélanges*, the creation of a unified time-space was necessary. A central administration and a common architectural language were evident tools. But also railroads and trains, transporting people all over the Empire constituted an Empire in its own right. For example, travellers often read the same guide, the Baedeker, and that established its own axes of communication which, eventually, amounted to an Empire. Hotels, installing timetables of trains in their lobbies, became crucial nodes in a grid, facilitating contacts between very remote parts. In a period when tourism diminished "the world to the space of a hotel lobby and a picture postcard, and rendered travel the exercise of running in place," as the historian Paul Fussell once wrote (1979, 32), the Viennese hotel and its lobby actually was a miniaturized Danube Monarchy. It was a hotspot, a hub for connections and intermixtures (see Urry and Rojek 1997, 5–20).

By the time Roth behaved as a full-time *Hotelmensch*, the Monarchy was gone. What was left were the remnants of its townscapes and façades, gestures and habits. The interwar lobbies of Vienna became vestiges. Although primarily shaped by a frantic present, they equally pointed to a past missed by many. As Roth complained in his 1932 novel *The Radetzky March*, in which he chronicled the decline and fall of the Austro-Hungarian Empire:

> That was how things were back then. Anything that grew took its time growing, and anything that perished took a long time to be forgotten. But everything that had once existed left its traces, and

people lived on memories just as they now live on the ability to forget quickly and emphatically.

(2000, 102)

For sure, sitting in lobbies Roth tried to launch a counterattack. While drinking and writing behind one of its small tables, the lobby offered him an Archimedean point from which to unhinge the world that was blown apart by the shots at Sarajevo.

The Inner Machinery of Modernity

Roth's hotel writings can illustrate why and how the Viennese lobby spaces possessed a political and cultural DNA. His musings clearly show that space is made of time: the lobby grounded in a continuous (re)assembling of temporal regimes. Some people patiently waited in the lobby and reflected on the past (as Roth did); others only quickly rushed through it. Of course, Roth was not the only person who encountered this multifarious temporality in Vienna, nor was he alone in focusing on how a feverish modernization was responsible for it. In *The Man Without Qualities* (*Der Mann ohne Eigenschaften*, 1930–1943), a modernist novel in three volumes, Robert Musil came to similar conclusions when he tried to unpack what the Austro-Hungarian monarchy's last days, Vienna in 1913, had looked like:

Time was on the move. People not yet born in these days will find it hard to believe, but even then time was racing along like a cavalry camel, just like today. But nobody knew where time was headed. And it was not always clear what was up or down, what was going forward or backward.

(1997, 7)

In his magnum opus, Musil had a particular concern with the way in which society forged ideas about life and itself. The plot often veers into allegorical digressions on a wide range of existential themes, constantly oscillating between a confusing novelty and a seemingly stable past. Because that is the key point: "nobody knew where time was headed" (7). What was "forward" or "backward"? What was "up" or "down"?

Unveiling the doubt and uncertainty of the modern world was Musil's literary trademark. Already in his earliest diaries, written between 1898 and 1902, he developed for himself the artistic persona of "Monsieur le vivisecteur" ("Mister Vivisectionist"), one who explored states of consciousness and emotional relations with an intellectual scalpel (Coetzee 2007, 30–34). Also, in a series of essays written around 1925, multiple topics, like inflation or publicity, were subjected to a vivisection. When reflecting on the modern built environment, Musil noted that the smooth surface of modern architecture did not come as a surprise:

> Since man is born in a clinic and dies in a hospital, he likewise requires aseptic restraint in the design of his living space. We call this sort of phenomenon a spontaneous architectural development born out of the spirit of the times.
>
> (1987, 58–59)

In the modern built environment, Musil thought, it was especially threshold architectures, such as gates, doors, and portals, which had effected the most drastic transformations:

> The only original door conceived by our time is the glass revolving door of the hotel and the department store. In former times, the door, as a part of the whole, represented the entire house, just as the house one owned and the house one was having built were intended to show the social standing of his owner. The door was an entrance into a society of privilege.
>
> (59)

When lamenting that "the great age of doors is behind us," and talking about "sweet illusions that creep up on us with a sentimental longing every time we look at an old-fashioned portal," Musil did not just map the changes at the surface of modern times. What mostly interested him was how architecture's underlying cultural codes had become recoined. Architecture became increasingly dictated by transit, not by dwelling. Where for a very long time the operations of opening and closing coincided with a clear human act, namely establishing the distinction between outside and inside, the revolving door stood for a continuum, the action of moving along in a steady, continuous stream. Bettina Matthias therefore called the revolving door "the most striking metaphor for a hotel's basic operational principle: that of change and flow" (2006, 54).

The revolving door was developed in 1888 by the American inventor Theophilus Van Kannel (see Figure 13.4).[6] In his first advertisement, the slogan "Always closed" aired the paradox Musil hinted at: a revolving door allows people to walk through a door which is permanently closed.

Of course, the primary goal of this apparatus was to control the stream of bodies entering the lobby. It was a differentiation barrier, designed to control, even discipline the circulation (Stalder 2009). That direct effect did not stay unnoticed. Its enormous potential was quickly picked up. In 1909 the Austrian architectural critic Joseph Lux, for a long time based in Vienna, argued that future hotel design could perfectly align with the modern world in the form of "a synthesis of hospitals, wagons-lits and machinery." Still, although his prophecy was a direct one, an exact prediction was not given by him: "Maybe in 50 years we will reach such excellent hotels" (1909, 17).

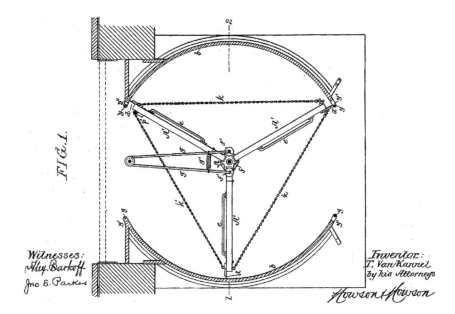

Figure 13.4 Technical drawing of the revolving door by Theophilus van Kannel from the patent specification for patent number 387571 dated August 7, 1888. www.google.com/patents/US387571?hl=d.

Rota Fortunae

When noting down his prophecy, Lux seems to have realized that predicting the future is a risky business. It is like spinning a Wheel of Fortune. In medieval and ancient philosophy, the Wheel of Fortune, or *Rota Fortunae*, was a symbol of the capricious nature of fate. The wheel belonged to the goddess Fortuna who spins it at random, changing the positions of those on the wheel: some suffer great misfortunes, others gain windfalls. Hollywood movies have used hotels to visualize this surprise of coincidence. Probably the best known is Edmund Goulding's (1932) film *Grand Hotel*, based on the 1929 novel *Menschen im Hotel* (published in English as *Grand Hotel in* 1930) by Vicky Baum who was born in Vienna. When she died of leukaemia in Hollywood in 1962, aged 72, she was a modern bestselling author. Her difficult youth in the Austrian capital, "the city of paradoxes" as Allan Janik and Stephen Toulmin called it (1973), had become a distant memory, a past she had overcome but which would resonate in her novel on which the 1932 MGM film would be based.

In the film, in which Baum had a cameo role, the reception desk in the lobby has a circular form and stands at the centre. Around the desk a bold pattern of alternating black and white squares forms a vortex. To the tune of a Viennese waltz, the film starts off as a cosmogenesis; out of a fusion of bodies, sounds, objects, practices, and rituals a unique universe emerges. At the same time, the hotel is a casino of fate. Poor people become rich; rich people face bankruptcy or end up in jail. An old aristocracy is no match for those who practise modern stenography. All these plots start and end in the lobby. Only one person seems to stand outside this series of dramatic collisions and interlocking histories: the disfigured war veteran Dr Otternschlag. Day after day, he sits in the lobby, reading a newspaper. There are no messages for him, although he doesn't stop asking the people behind the lobby desk if there are any. His famous quote "Grand Hotel [...] always the same. People come, people go. Nothing ever happens" pinpoints what living in a modern world meant: finding a place in a vortex.

Musil and Roth both evoked and analysed the restless standstill Dr Otternschlag embodied. Both were fascinated by how the hotel, a privileged site of exchange and connection, became a production locus for the modern self. For both, the lobby and its revolving door captured and defined an unavoidable reconfiguration of old habits or customs. Whereas the historian and sociologist Michael Pollak (1992) could state that ballrooms and concert halls probably were the only places where the multi-ethnic Austrian Empire really existed, the lobby might be seen as a place where a longing for unity became both fabricated *and* eradicated. Just as the dance partners in a Viennese waltz need to each do their part to balance the centrifugal forces they generate, the persons who strolled through Viennese lobbies were condemned to position themselves in a rapidly changing world.

Those who visit Vienna nowadays are still in the grip of a *rota moderna*. Of course, they don't identify, as Baum, Roth, and Musil did, with an epochal change resulting from the dissolution of the Danube Monarchy. What for them was of the essence has nowadays become an add-on. When they have used their smartphones to find a nearby latte bar with Sachertorte, and just before they inform a friend that Sissy, the actor of that mushy movie seems to have had a meet-and-greet in the hotel—the text message being "Her image is all over the place"—the contemporary hotel visitors drop their belongings in a generic hotel room. They will never know who was married to Emperor Franz Joseph I.

Notes

1 A minute's walk from Stephansplatz square with its iconic cathedral and U-Bahn station, this polished family-run hotel is for many contemporary tourists the perfect starting point from where to explore Vienna.
2 This famous line from the first section of *The Communist Manifesto* by Karl Marx and Friedrich Engels (1976, 487) serves as the title of Marshall Berman's seminal study of twentieth-century modernity (1982).

3 Other studies, with catchy titles like *L'apocalypse joyeuse* (Clair 1986), or *Nervous Splendor* (Morton 1981), further helped to promote the insight that the path Vienna took at the end of the nineteenth century was one of old orders being replaced by new systems. For a broad view on this rising modernity, see Clair (1986); for a splendid introduction to this era, see Gronberg (2007).
4 Today the Ringstrasse symbolizes the era of the late Monarchy, as the scene of the rise of the upper middle classes, a locus of seeing and being seen. Originally no hotels had been planned for the Ringstrasse; the projected buildings were intended to be a mix of public edifices, private town palaces, and apartment blocks for the wealthy. However, Vienna's hosting of the World Exhibition in 1873 gave rise to an imperative need for high-quality accommodation, and many luxurious hotels were duly built on the Ringstrasse.
5 On behavioural frameworks of belonging in a transnational context, see Matthias, Chapter 4, in this volume.
6 Van Kannel came with a design that he referred to as the "New Revolving Storm Door." The design spaced out four doors equally on a pivot, with two of the doors always making contact with the wall. As a result, there was little transfer of interior and exterior air, as well as limited amounts of noise and fumes entering the building.

Works Cited

Adorno, Theodor W. 1999. *Minima Moralia: Reflections from Damaged Life*. Translated by E.F.N. Jephcott. London: Verso.

Alofsin, Anthony. 2008. *When Buildings Speak: Architecture as Language in the Habsburg Empire and Its Aftermath, 1867–1933*. Chicago: University of Chicago Press.

Berman, Marshall. 1982. *All That Is Solid Melts into Air: The Experience of Modernity*. New York: Simon & Schuster.

Clair, Jean. 1986. *Vienne 1880–1938. L'apocalypse joyeuse*. Paris: Editions du Centre Pompidou.

Coetzee, J. M. 2007. *Inner Workings. Literary Essays, 2000–2005*. New York: Penguin Books.

Fussell, Paul. 1979. "The Stationary Tourist." *Harper's Magazine* (April): 31–38.

Grand Hotel. 1932. [film] Directed by Edmund Goulding. Metro-Goldwyn-Mayer Corp.

Gronberg, Tag. 2007. *Vienna: City of Modernity, 1890–1914*. Oxford: Peter Lang.

Hirschman, Albert. 1982. *Shifting Involvements: Private Interest and Public Action*. Oxford: Robertson.

Hoffman, Thomas, and Beppo Beyerl. 2018. *Die Stadt von Gestern. Entdeckungsreise durch das verschwundene Wien*. Vienna/Graz: Styria Verlag.

Janik, Allan, and Stephen Toulmin. 1973. *Wittgenstein's Vienna*. New York: Simon & Schuster.

Koerner, Joseph Leo. 2016. "The Ringstrasse at 150 years." *The Burlington Magazine*, 158 (January): 26–31.

Kracauer, Siegfried. 2005. "The Hotel Lobby." In *The Mass Ornament: Weimar Essays*, edited and translated by Thomas Y. Levin. Cambridge: Harvard University Press.

Loos, Adolf. 1985. "Ornament and Crime (1910)." In *The Architecture of Adolf Loos: An Arts Council Exhibition*, edited and translated by Wilfried Wang and Yehuda Safran, 100–03. London: The Council.
Lux, Joseph August. 1909. "Das Hotel ein Bauproblem." *Der Architekt* (15): 17–20.
Marx, Karl, and Friedrich Engels. 1976. *Collected Works*. Vol. 6. London: Lawrence & Wishart.
Matthias, Bettina. 2006. *The Hotel as Setting in Early Twentieth-Century's German and Austrian Literature. Checking in to Tell a Story*. Rochester: Camden House.
McLuhan, Marshall. 1966. *Understanding Media: The Extensions of Man*. New York: New American Library.
Morton, Frederic. 1981. *A Nervous Splendor: Vienna 1888/1889*. Harmondsworth: Penguin.
Musil, Robert. 1987. "Doors and Portals." In *Posthumous Papers of a Living Author*. Translated by Peter Wortsman. New York: Penguin.
Musil, Robert. 1997. *The Man Without Qualities*. London: Picador.
Pollak, Michael. 1992. *Vienne 1900. Une identité blessé*. Paris: Gallimard.
Roth, Joseph. 1956. *Panoptikum. Gestalten und Kulissen.* (Vol. 3 of Gesammelte Werke in drei Bänden). Cologne/Berlin: Kiepenheuer & Witsch.
Roth, Joseph. 2000. *The Radetzky March*. Translated by Joachim Neugroschel. London: Penguin.
Roth, Joseph. 2015. *The Hotel Years*, edited and translated by Michael Hofmann. London: Granta.
Schlögel, Karl. 2016. *In Space We Read Time: On the History of Civilization and Geopolitics*. New York: Bard Graduate Center.
Schorske, Carl E. 1980. *Fin-de-Siècle Vienna: Politics and Culture*. New York: Alfred A. Knopf.
Schorske, Carl E. 2014. *Thinking with History: Explorations in the Passage to Modernism*. Princeton: Princeton University Press.
Stalder, Laurent. 2009. "Turning Architecture Inside Out: Revolving Doors and Other Threshold Devices." *Journal of Design History* 22 (1): 69–77.
Urry, John, and Chris Rojek. 1997. "Transformations of Travel and Theory." In *Touring Cultures: Transformation of Travel and Theory*, edited by John Urry and Chris Rojek, 1–20. London: Routledge.

14 Grand Hotel Theory

John Hoffmann

In one of the more memorable insults in the history of critical theory, Georg Lukács alleged in 1962 that German intellectuals had checked into what he called "the Grand Hotel Abyss" (1963a, 17). Lukács's remark appeared in the preface to a new version of *The Theory of the Novel* [*Die Theorie des Romans*], which had originally been published in 1916; and the targets of his criticism are usually taken to be members of the Frankfurt School, Theodor W. Adorno in particular.[1] In his classic history of the Institut für Sozialforschung, Martin Jay comments that "Lukács voiced his and other Marxists' disdain for the Frankfurt School by dubbing it the 'Grand Hotel *Abgrund* (Abyss)'" (1973, 296). A more recent history of the School has gone so far as to use the phrase "Grand Hotel Abyss" for its title (Jeffries 2016). Persistent as this attribution has been, the connection between the Hotel Abyss and the Frankfurt School is misleading since Lukács in fact censures "a considerable part of the leading German intelligentsia, Adorno included" before laying out a critique of Ernst Bloch, a writer who never belonged to the Institut für Sozialforschung and was at times in open conflict with its members (Vidal 2007).[2] Despite their personal friendship, Bloch and Lukács became intellectual antagonists in the late 1930s, when they participated in the famous Expressionism Debate, which weighed the political merits of modern art during Stalin's show trials and the militant rise of the Third Reich; and the fact that Bloch had recently emigrated from East to West Germany after the building of the Berlin Wall in 1961 was likely on Lukács's mind as he formulated his broadside against (presumably West) German intellectuals.[3] What is more is that the first time Lukács publicly deployed the metaphor of the Hotel Abyss in print, it had nothing to do whatsoever with the Frankfurt School, Bloch and Adorno, or any other members of the postwar German intelligentsia. It appeared in Lukács's 1954 treatise *The Destruction of Reason* to refer to the system of Arthur Schopenhauer.

Once the conventional associations have been cleared away from the Grand Hotel Abyss, several modernist and para-modernist allusions become apparent: the 1932 MGM blockbuster *Grand Hotel*, for example, which Mark Goble has used to show how modern media technologies influenced both Hollywood cinema and the modernist prose of Gertrude

DOI: 10.4324/9781003213079-19

Stein (2010, 85–149).[4] The Grand Hotel Abyss also calls to mind the setting of Thomas Mann's *The Magic Mountain* [*Der Zauberberg*], an allusion that is particularly apt since Lukács has frequently been seen as a model for the character of Leo Naphta in the novel (Löwy 1979, 59–65). Redolent of Mann's sanatorium, the depiction of the grand hotel in *The Theory of the Novel* reads as follows:

> a beautiful hotel equipped with every comfort on the edge of the abyss, of nothing, of senselessness. And the daily sight of the abyss, between the pleasant delights of meals or artistic productions, can only heighten the pleasure of these refined comforts.
> (Lukács 1963a, 17)

This scene evokes both the lavish meals Hans Castorp enjoys at the sanatorium and the long, lazy days residents spend staring out at the alpine landscape while reclining in conspicuously comfortable lounge chairs. Thus, the image of the Grand Hotel Abyss calls to mind the cultural decline that Mann identified with bourgeois society before World War I as well as the decadence, absurdity, and even madness that Lukács famously associated with modernism.

This essay reassesses Lukács's use of the Hotel Abyss by comparing its original formulation in *The Destruction of Reason* with its later deployment in *The Theory of the Novel*. More specifically, the metaphor of the Hotel Abyss will serve as a focal point for considering another passage from the preface to *The Theory of the Novel*, which takes aim at what Lukács calls a "coupling of a left ethics and right epistemology" (1963a, 18). The main problem with the Hotel Abyss—and the reason why it carries critical force in Lukács's attack on the German intelligentsia—is the way the hotel represents this fusion of left ethics and a right epistemology born of material luxury and political privilege. In other words, the metaphor of the Hotel Abyss "equipped with every comfort" embodies a left/right fusion whose relevance obtains both for German cultural politics, irrespective of the Frankfurt School, and also for the history of modernism and its critical legacy as it took shape in the latter half of the twentieth century.

Right Epistemology

Written nearly a decade after Lukács had returned to Hungary from wartime exile in the Soviet Union, *The Destruction of Reason* is best known for its critique of Friedrich Nietzsche, who epitomizes what Lukács sees as an irrationalist strain in philosophy descending from German idealism to National Socialism (Aronowitz 2011, 57–62; Brown 2018, 379–97). Yet the treatise, which employs Marxist methodologies for the sake of a sweeping, and frequently tendentious, intellectual history, can be more fruitfully considered as part of a genre of books by mid-century intellectuals who were trying to reckon with the intellectual roots of Nazism. Other famous examples in this genre would include Max Horkheimer and Theodor Adorno's *Dialectic of Enlightenment,* Hannah Arendt's *The Origins of Totalitarianism*, or in the cultural sphere, *From Caligari to Hitler,* Siegfried Kracauer's book on Weimar cinema. Coming at the end of a fifty-page dismantling of the Schopenhauerian project, the metaphor of the Hotel Abyss in *The Destruction of Reason* diverges slightly, albeit significantly, from the version presented in *The Theory of the Novel*: "So Schopenhauer's system, brilliant in its architectural form and clearly structured, rises up like a beautiful, modern hotel, equipped with every comfort on the edge of the abyss, of nothing, of senselessness" (Lukács 1974, 218–19). When read alongside the passage from *The Theory of the Novel*, two crucial differences jump out. First, the original formulation highlights the formal characteristics of Schopenhauer's system and, as a consequence, the Hotel Abyss: both possess an "architectural form" that is "brilliant" and "clearly structured." The later version reworks these details, omitting the architectural references and describing simply a "beautiful hotel equipped with every comfort" (1963a, 17). Thus, the features of the metaphorical hotel that align it with Schopenhauerian philosophy—its systematic architectonics, its brilliance—are left out while the description of the hotel's beauty remains. More striking still, in *The Destruction of Reason,* the Hotel Abyss is not grand. Rather, it "rises up like a beautiful, modern hotel." In its first iteration, then, the Hotel Abyss lacks its later grandeur and manifests instead the clear, clean lines of modern architecture.

Although the depiction of a "beautiful, modern hotel" includes only a few details regarding architectural design, the imaginary edifice does betray certain affinities with the modern architecture discussed by Lukács in *The Specificity of the Aesthetic* (1963b), his late tome on aesthetic theory.[5] Towards the end of a chapter on architecture, Lukács discusses modernism in predictably unfavourable terms, targeting one tendency in particular, geometrism (*Geometrismus*), which is made to stand for modern architecture as a whole. Buildings that call attention to geometrical shapes are denounced as antihuman (*gegenmenschlich*) because abstract form dictates appearance rather than function or use value for inhabitants (Lukács 1963b, 456). Once geometry becomes the dominant motif, a structure "allows itself—with respect to its usefulness—to be realized with every comfort, without determining an external or internal space that would make it [i.e. usefulness] visually apparent" (456). According to Lukács, forfeiting functionality does not entail a loss of luxury. Modern architecture in a geometrical mode may be furnished with every convenience—"*mit allem Komfort*" —in the same way that the Hotel Abyss is "equipped with every comfort [*mit allem Komfort ausgestattet*]." What is lost in the process of architectural abstraction, however, is the distinct purposiveness of exterior and interior spaces—the specificity of their aesthetic, as it were—which would otherwise manifest visually. As a result, "a public pool can look like an office," Lukács states, "and a factory like a church" (456). Even though a hotel is not mentioned in this list, it would not have been out of place. Under the sign of modernism, at least on Lukács's account, a building, any building, sacrifices its architectural function for the sake of pure form.

Surprisingly enough, one of the figures Lukács cites in support of his treatment of modern architecture is Schopenhauer, who argued in *The World as Will and Representation* [*Die Welt als Wille und Vorstellung*] that architectural symmetry and geometrical regularity must be subordinated to the basic imperative that a structure support weight (1947, III.468–477). That is to say, Schopenhauer believed that architectural design should reflect a fundamental purposiveness inhering in all buildings, a claim that allows Lukács to cast him as an antiformalist. Yet the Hotel Abyss, as has already been noted, is significant for precisely its formal properties—"architectural form" that is "brilliant" and "clearly structured." This tension between Schopenhauer's anti-formalist theory of architecture and Lukács's architectural metaphor for the formalism of Schopenhauerian philosophy does not indicate that Lukács had undertaken a revision of his views in the decade separating *The Destruction of Reason* and his later treatise on aesthetics. If anything, his positive estimation of Schopenhauer in *The Specificity of the Aesthetic* is an exception that brings his overwhelmingly negative appraisal in *The Destruction of Reason* into sharper relief.

Lukács begins his critique in *The Destruction of Reason* by laying out the socio-economic circumstances that accompanied Schopenhauer's rise, tracing the history of class struggle in the nineteenth century and casting Schopenhauer as a reactionary critic of the revolutions of 1848. Here at least, Lukács was on firm ground. One of the better-known facts from the life of Schopenhauer is that he stipulated in his will that his assets should go to a fund for the support of disabled soldiers, as well as their families, who had helped suppress the revolution (he also allowed troops to fire upon a demonstration from his apartment and filed an official police report informing on revolutionaries) (Safranski 1987, 479–82). Lukács places additional weight on the scales by pointing out that Schopenhauer, son of a Danzig merchant, benefitted from a privileged upper-bourgeois background, which leads to him being labelled "the first irrationalist on a purely bourgeois foundation" (1974, 177). Armed with these biographical observations, Lukács then performs a political interpretation of a central tenet of Schopenhauerian thought, namely, its pessimism. And it is on this point that the argument shifts away from Schopenhauer's personal politics, reactionary as they may have been, to the "right epistemology" later exemplified by the Hotel Abyss.

For Schopenhauer, pessimism reflects definite metaphysical commitments in his philosophical system while opening out onto a general worldview that beholds the wretchedness of human existence and refuses to look away or countenance ideological palliatives. Although the sources for Schopenhauer's pessimism were manifold, they were rooted in a scepticism about optimistic philosophies that offer reassuring tales about the order of things while failing to reckon with the suffering that attends the human condition. "If the most obdurate optimist were led through the hospitals, wards and surgical torture chambers, the torture chambers of prisons, and slave quarters," Schopenhauer, channelling Voltaire, writes in *The World as Will and Representation*, "he would finally realize what kind of best of all possible worlds this is" (1947, II.383). One particularly noxious sort of optimism for Schopenhauer was religious dogma that propounded a divine sanction for the universe. Another was the implicit optimism of Hegel—Schopenhauer's rival and, for a time, colleague at the University of Berlin—who construed human history as the progressive unfolding of a rational World Spirit (Copleston 1975, 74, 91). In contradistinction to Hegel's dialectical reason, Schopenhauer argued that the world is driven by a blind, implacable, and manifestly irrational will. The metaphysical engine of the Schopenhauerian world, the will manifests most visibly in acts of human agency; yet natural forces such as electricity and magnetism also evince the impetus of the will. As Schopenhauer explains, such perpetual wilfulness cannot be abolished any more than human desires can find permanent satisfaction. There is only endless striving, which may ebb but can never cease outright. Only in exceptional cases, exemplified by the ascetic practices of Christian monasticism or the withdrawal from worldly affairs found in Buddhism and other eastern philosophies, might enlightened individuals pursue what Schopenhauer calls a "negation of the will [*Verneinung des Willens*]," a process of curbing egoistic impulses that promises more lasting relief from the incessant dictates of wilfulness (1947, IV.446–487).

In Lukács's estimation, this worldview has definite political consequences since defining the human condition as a form of implacable willing vitiates the warrant for ameliorating suffering through concrete political action. If life is at bottom the unending experience of desire, longing, and privation, as Schopenhauer in his pessimistic mood very often makes it seem, then why should individuals or groups undertake to better their station when it only means a displacement and ultimately futile reprieve from the yearnings of the will? In any event, it can hardly be denied that prescribing conscious withdrawal from the world, stoic endurance amid general misery, and extinguishing the teleological motivations of the will have little in common with the progressive political engagement, to say nothing of revolutionary action, favoured by Lukács. Thus, Schopenhauer and philosophers like him are said "to educate their followers in social passivity" (Lukács 1974, 188)—a passivity that may gaze upon human anguish with sympathy, as in the above rumination on slavery and torture, but does little or nothing to bring it to an end. For his part, Schopenhauer was awake to these implications, admitting that his pessimistic disposition does qualify as a form of resignation (1947, II.181–182). For Lukács, though, pessimism constitutes a deeper conviction than mere fatigue or resigned disillusion. It entails an intentional disavowal of worldly action. In effect, on Lukács's account, the pessimist is a quietist, a person who knowingly accepts suffering as an unalterable reality and remains inactive in the face of social ills. This is the first major plank of Schopenhauer's "right epistemology." Instead of trying to correct the woes of the world, Schopenhauerian philosophy furnishes the intellectual means to accommodate them.

Several spatial metaphors in the closing paragraph of *The World as Will and Representation* convey the psychological as well as metaphysical consequences of the negation of the will expounded by Schopenhauer, who comments on the seeming "passage into empty *nothingness* [*Übergang in das leere* Nichts]" that his philosophy encourages (1947, II.483, emphasis in the original). For instance, Schopenhauer extols the "complete oceanic calmness of the mind [*gänzliche Meeresstille des Gemüts*]" that follows from negating the will (486); and in his book's final sentence, he presents a spatial motif that Lukács would later use as a template for the Hotel Abyss: "for those in whom the will has been turned and denied, this world of ours, so very real with all its suns and milky ways, is—nothing" (487). This passage contains an implicit commentary on Immanuel Kant, Schopenhauer's most esteemed philosophical predecessor, who famously pursued a "Copernican Revolution" in his critical philosophy by making the mind the basis for constructing reality instead of having the world furnish the empirical grounds for mental operations. But instead of cultivating reverence for "the starry sky above me and the moral law within me" as Kant declared in the *Critique of Practical Reason* (1902, V.288), Schopenhauer denies the primacy of either mind or world, reducing both to epiphenomena of the will and replacing Kantian admiration of the heavens with serenity in the face of nothingness.

Shortly before deploying the metaphor of the Hotel Abyss in *The Destruction of Reason*, Lukács reflects on this concluding flourish, summing up his analysis by asserting that the Schopenhauerian system collapses into an "abyss of nothing, the dismal background of the senselessness of existence" (1974, 218). Therefore, when he immediately goes on to describe a hotel perched "on the brink of the abyss, nothing, senselessness," Lukács is repurposing the terms from his more expansive critique of Schopenhauerian pessimism and reconfiguring its spatial parameters. Placed on the edge of the void, but not within it, the hotel becomes a vantage point for observing empty space. Hence, the world is not negated in this depiction. It instead becomes a matter for aesthetic contemplation. A resident of Hotel Abyss—a proxy for the Schopenhauerian philosopher—may gaze upon a sublime landscape and behold only the bleak vastness of blank, vacant nothingness. And far from practising an ethos of austerity in the face of such emptiness, the guests console themselves with all the comforts of modern refinement. Indeed, the poverty of the world around them only enhances the pleasure they take in their more immediate environs.

For all the theoretical weight placed on Schopenhauer's pessimism, the right epistemology imputed to the philosopher cannot be restricted to withdrawal from the world. Lukács inaugurates a second line of critique just before introducing the metaphor of the Hotel Abyss, which accuses Schopenhauer of "aristocratism [*Aristokratismus*]," a concept denoting a class-based feeling of superiority over the masses (1974, 218). This aristocratic tendency is on display when Schopenhauer elevates the philosopher—and elsewhere, the artistic genius—into a kind of hero or saint who presides over the hoi polloi. So, for example, Lukács notes "that the strongly pointed aristocratism of Schopenhauer's philosophy raises its followers, in their imagination, high above the miserable rabble that is so narrow-minded to fight and suffer for an improvement of social conditions" (218). Tellingly, in both the passage indicating the aristocratic disposition that supposedly plagues Schopenhauer and the description of the Hotel Abyss perched above a chasm, Lukács employs the same verb, *erheben*, to designate elevated detachment. The hotel "rises up [*erhebt sich*] [...] on the edge of the abyss" just as Schopenhauerian philosophy hoists its followers aloft on a cloud that floats above the masses. Hence, the metaphor of the Hotel Abyss stands for a particular kind of class conflict, representing the discord between aristocrats and the proletariat, upper classes and lower, through the actual physical elevation of the hotel.

Aristocratism brings out other political connotations of the Hotel Abyss, particularly with regard to modernist cultural politics. In light of Lukács's status as one of modernism's most trenchant critics, the depiction of a "beautiful, modern hotel" entails a very specific kind of disparagement rooted in the critique of modernism he developed in the 1930s. In his contribution to the celebrated Expressionism Debate, Lukács burdens modernism with many sins: its experiments with form distracted from important matters of content; its criticisms of bourgeois society and capitalism were self-indulgent illusions; and its disregard for a popular audience aligned it with elite tastes, at least when compared to Lukács's own preference for the realist novel.[6] That is all to say, modernism was an artistic movement cut off from the masses; it was an aristocratic movement elevated above the people much in the manner already discussed in reference to Schopenhauer.

Examining Lukács's reading of Schopenhauerian aesthetics in *The Destruction of Reason* gives these associations a more concrete grounding, since Lukács construes the theory of art contained in *The World as Will and Representation* as an ideological precursor of modernism. In brief, Schopenhauer considered art to be a vehicle for specific configurations or "objectifications [*Objektivationen*]" of the will that he likened to Platonic ideas because they constituted the essence of reality underlying the shadowy appearances revealed to the phenomenal subject (1947, II.199–316). Thus, intuiting the nature of the will through art, especially music, affords a deeper insight into the true lineaments of the world than rational reflection and logical inference. Although Lukács devotes only two paragraphs of his exegesis to aesthetics, strikingly little given the significance of art for his own philosophy, he is keen to dissociate Schopenhauer's aesthetic theory, which relies on a highly idiosyncratic reading of Plato, from writers such as Goethe and Schiller, who also believed that art provided a privileged path to higher truth. Within German classicism, Lukács concedes, "a strong element of the isolation of art, an element of escape from social reality and praxis" does indeed make itself felt (1974, 206). Schiller's conception of aesthetic education prescribes distance from society; and Kantian disinterestedness explicitly distinguishes judgements of aesthetic value from determinations of moral or political worth.

Yet Lukács insists that both Kantian and Schillerian aesthetics can be recuperated for social purposes: aesthetic education, for example, allows subjects to retreat from the world in order to engage with art's higher unities before then returning to social reality more attuned to aesthetic harmony. With Schopenhauer, though, the situation is entirely different. "With Schopenhauer (and before him in reactionary Romanticism), this flight becomes the central problem of aesthetics" (Lukács 1974, 206). For Schopenhauer, in other words, this escape from the social world becomes a more persistent feature of the philosophy of art. And as a result, Lukács continues, "Schopenhauer is also an important forerunner of the later European decadence" (206). In this passage, the decadence that need not speak its name is, of course, modernism. Lukács indicates as much when he then notes that the "complete flight from social action" typified by Schopenhauerian aesthetics "is necessarily connected with the distortion of humanity through that sort of aesthetic activity" (206). Though the point is awkwardly put, its sense is clear enough: escapism reflects a decadent, distorted humanism that must necessarily be expressed in cultural production. That Lukács had used the same language in the Expressionism Debate to describe the "distortion [*Verzerrtheit*]" of modernist style practiced by Joyce that Bloch then transformed into a "distorted picture [*verzerrten Bildes*]" of modern reality is by no means incidental (Lukács 1973, 199). Lukács means to convey that a distorted, as opposed to realist, humanism is a Schopenhauerian legacy that later came to fruition in the antirealist tendencies of modern art.

To be fair, Lukács was not above offering occasional, grudging praise of modernism. In the same critique published during the Expressionism Debate, he lauds Surrealism, a designation that included Joyce, for its ability to "create charming and interesting means of expression" (1974, 203). But whatever brilliance modernism may have achieved in its rhetorical effects, it was ultimately a coterie affair unable to capture social truths as could the realist novel. Therefore, when Lukács criticizes Schopenhauer for his aristocratic tendencies before immediately turning to a metaphor of a "beautiful, modern hotel" that is "brilliant in its architectural form," he is applying the same critical scruples developed in his earlier estimations of modern art. When he mentions Schopenhauer in *The Specificity of the Aesthetic* as a sceptic regarding architectural formalism, that momentary sign of agreement does not mitigate his overarching critique of Schopenhauerian philosophy as a harbinger of modernist decadence. That is to say, at the Hotel Abyss, all the guests are aristocrats. Having shunned social action and withdrawn from the world, they spend their days enjoying luxurious meals and "artistic productions" that, it may safely be inferred, were distinctly modernist in style.

In light of the foregoing analysis, it is now possible to make some provisional comments about the political associations of the Hotel Abyss and its residents: "a considerable portion of the German intelligentsia, Adorno included." On the one hand, all of the features of the right epistemology identified with Schopenhauer—pessimism, aristocratism, modernism—found their place in the writings of the Frankfurt School, not least Adorno: the legendary pessimism of *The Dialectic of Enlightenment*; the mandarin tastes of the School's leading theorists; the corresponding valorization of modern art as a negation of the cultural industry and a one-dimensional society. Indeed, both Max Horkheimer and his later associate at the Institut für Sozialforschung Leo Lowenthal belonged to the Schopenhauer Gesellschaft during their undergraduate years in Frankfurt (Jay 1973, 44). Thus, the cultural politics represented by the Frankfurt School shows every sign of what Lukács would describe as a "right epistemology" notwithstanding the efforts of Adorno, Horkheimer, and their colleagues to revitalize Marxism for a new generation of leftists.

On the other hand, narrowing the implications of the Hotel Abyss to the Frankfurt School does a disservice to Lukács's social theory, which has a far more expansive investment in the meaning of "right epistemology." For Lukács, modern capitalism inculcated a very specific kind of intellectual temperament, namely, contemplation, which a radical philosophy committed to revolutionary praxis must overcome. Konstantinos Kavoulakos has recently elaborated on this contemplative disposition, explaining that for Lukács, subjects within a capitalist order tend to withdraw into a reflective posture once that socio-economic system hardens into a reified ideology, a "second nature" (2018, 137–41). As soon as capitalism and its ideological fruits seem to be ineluctable truths, the features of that false reality may be studied as though they were natural phenomena, which forecloses the possibility of acting against vested interests or making reforms according to more rational ends. In short, capitalism generates a particular kind of epistemological praxis, contemplation, that insulates it from practical threats. As such, the "social passivity" that Lukács identifies explicitly with Schopenhauer and implicitly with the residents of the Hotel Abyss is part and parcel of this eminently capitalist praxis—a right epistemology whereby subjects assume a contemplative attitude that reflects on the world instead of changing it, as Marx believed was the true task of philosophy.

Such contemplation may become thoroughly reactionary, as when Schopenhauer fulminated against revolutionaries out of fear of losing the assets that allowed him to devote his life to philosophy free from the encumbrances of the marketplace (Safranski 1987, 478); or the contemplative disposition may take the form of a tamer agnosticism regarding the established economic order, a comfortable complicity with capitalism that easily shades into de facto acceptance. When levelling his charge that German intellectuals, particularly those residing in the ascending capitalist superpower of West Germany, had taken up residence in the Hotel Abyss, Lukács is effectively alleging that those guests are guilty of this decadent form of epistemological praxis. Comforted by luxury and material privilege, the aristocrats at the Hotel Abyss enjoy "the pleasant delights of meals or artistic productions" (1963a, 17) while contemplating the emptiness of their surroundings beyond the brink.

Left Ethics

Thus far the left/right fusion implied by the metaphor of the Hotel Abyss has been considered entirely in terms of the former of the two parts, the right epistemology. This emphasis is warranted by the fact that Lukács intended his statement as a swipe at the German intelligentsia, thereby rendering the right-leaning elements the more significant of the pairing. But appreciating the substance of the claim that German intellectuals, Adorno included, have checked into the Hotel Abyss requires acknowledging that the ideological constellation Lukács seeks to diagnose does contain leftists elements, if only a left ethics. It will now be argued that this ethics may be identified with a single concept that was central not only for Lukács in *The Theory of the Novel* but also for Ernst Bloch, one of the main targets of Lukács's critique and a leftist committed to his own heterodox Marxism. That concept is utopia.[7] Hence, if right epistemology combines pessimism, aristocratism, and modernism into a coherent, though ultimately objectionable, philosophical programme, then the left ethics signified by the Hotel Abyss entails a utopian disposition that may not satisfy Lukács's political demands but at least does not offend them in the manner of Schopenhauer.

At various points in *The Theory of the Novel*, including its preface, Lukács reflects on utopia as both a philosophical and a literary concern. The sentence immediately following the amended description of the Hotel Abyss, for example, redirects the reproach from the German intelligentsia and Adorno to Bloch, Lukács's old friend and erstwhile adversary from the Expressionism Debate. "That Ernst Bloch, untroubled up till now, stands by his synthesis of left ethics and right epistemology does honor to his character," Lukács writes, "but cannot mitigate the anachronism of his theoretical attitude" (1963a, 17–18). Thus, Bloch represents the paradigmatic ethical-epistemological synthesis at hand; and the characteristic attitude that Bloch was clinging to in the early 1960s, Lukács makes clear, had already been worked out in his early work *The Spirit of Utopia* (1918). In fact, Lukács singles out *The Spirit of Utopia* in his preface as a text "in which a left ethics aligned with radical revolution appears paired with a traditional-conventional interpretation of reality" (1963a, 17). So *The Spirit of Utopia* is identified as an example of a left/right synthesis. Moreover, Lukács begins to elucidate the specific character of a left ethics and suggest how it might combine with a right epistemology. To wit: a left ethics entails a radicalism committed to revolutionary change while nevertheless being amenable to a retrograde conception of reality. The Hotel Abyss, as will be shown shortly, comes to represent this disjunction between radical change and comfort with convention.

To his credit, Lukács subjects his own work to the same scrutiny he levels against Bloch. Casting a retrospective glance on the book he wrote nearly fifty years earlier, Lukács writes in his preface that "*The Theory of the Novel* is not conservative in character but explosive. At the same time, it is based on a highly naive and wholly unfounded utopianism" (1963a, 15). Just as Bloch's revolutionary ethics was compromised by a conventional, and thereby false or at least incomplete theory of reality, the subversive force of *The Theory of the Novel* suffered from its own limitation, a naive utopianism. In fact, these two assessments should be read together inasmuch as they are making largely the same point in reference to different authors: in their early years, both Lukács and Bloch lacked a suitable theory of reality, which led them to fall back on utopian thinking to fill the intellectual void. For the late Lukács looking back, utopia functioned as a placeholder for the theory of reality he would later find in Marx and a properly materialist understanding of the world.

With this background in place, Lukács then spells out precisely what he means by utopia: "the hope that from the disintegration of capitalism, from the selfsame disintegration of the lifeless, life-denying socio-economic categories, a natural, dignified life can emerge" (1963a, 15). It would be going too far to call this utopian mindset optimistic. Its point of departure is recognition of the bleakness of life under the prevailing socio-economic conditions; and even though hope is summoned in the face of those conditions, there seems little confidence that such a new order might emerge. But this mindset surely cannot be squared with the pessimism of Schopenhauer. On the contrary, where Lukács claims that Schopenhauerian pessimism "rejects life in every form and brings it face to face with nothingness" (1974, 218)—a nothingness epitomized by the beautiful, modern Hotel Abyss—the utopianism advanced in *The Theory of the Novel* insists on holding open the possibility for a renewal of life that will restore dignity to the human condition. Hence, the left ethics limned in Lukács's preface requires maintaining an openness, a utopian hopefulness for a better world, however unrealistic such a hope may be.

Before returning to the Hotel Abyss and applying this left ethics of utopia to its cultural politics, Lukács's examination of utopian writing in the body of *The Theory of the Novel* must be examined as a complement to his comments in the preface. Written in 1914 while Kant and Hegel were its author's primary philosophical guides, *The Theory of the Novel* is divided into two parts: the first considers works of art as expressing the metaphysical condition of particular cultures at distinct periods in history, the integrated culture of classical antiquity epitomized by Homeric epic and the so-called problematic culture that results from the decline into modernity and the fracturing of classical unities. The second part, "Typology of the Novel Form," includes Lukács's reflections on utopia and is therefore of more immediate interest for our purposes. To summarize briefly a rather complex argument, the general aim of this part of *Theory of the Novel* is to classify modern fiction according to a distinct schema, which Lukács refers to as a misalignment (*Unangemessenheit*) between soul and world that takes two paradigmatic forms: "the soul is either narrower or wider than the world given to it as a forum and basis for its actions" (1963a, 96). This formulation makes the debts to Hegel clear. Soul and world—or in more conventional Hegelian terms, *Geist* and *Welt*—furnish the operative vocabulary for understanding the metaphysical condition of a given culture and, by consequence, the artists and artworks those cultures produce. Where integrated cultures—the classical world of Homer and his heroes—enjoyed a harmonious unity between internal life and external world, problematic cultures, by contrast, find the modern soul falling out of alignment with its environs.

Utopia pertains to the second kind of misalignment, when the soul is wider than the world. This metaphysical situation leads to a variety of novelistic attributes: the robust internal life of characters that is typical of nineteenth-century fiction indicates enlargement of the soul, for instance; or, to take two other examples, extended reflections on mood and ruminations on the infinite shadings of subjective impressions reflect this amplified interiority. Such elaborate inwardness stands in stark contrast to the other kind of misalignment, when a narrow soul enters the wide world. This relationship leads to action, adventure, and plots motivated not by a reflective, deliberating protagonist but by the contingency and risk of a lively external environment. For Lukács, the quintessential example of this form of misalignment is *Don Quixote*. And whereas Quixote's knight errantry eventuates in "an excessive and uninhibited activity outward" due to the shrunken nature of the soul, the enlarged interiority of nineteenth-century novels brings about the opposite characteristics: "the tendency is more towards passivity, the tendency to avoid external conflicts and struggles and rather to accept them, the tendency to resolve everything within the soul that has to do with the soul" (1963a, 115). This latter disposition should be familiar in light of the foregoing discussion of right epistemology. Although he is primarily concerned with the artistic products of *Geist* in the nineteenth century, Lukács may as well be describing Schopenhauerian philosophy, an exact contemporary of the novelists associated with excessive interiority.

This inflated inwardness does not collapse into a void of pessimistic meaninglessness—an abyss of nothing—because the soul finds an outlet in utopia. Lukács introduces the concept of utopia by positing a somewhat sudden shift in the basic terms of his argument: "this aesthetic problem is however at its deepest roots an ethical problem" (1963a, 117). In other words, the aesthetic problem of how to render an overabundant internal life in the form of the novel is in truth a question of ethics, a question of how the world ought to be arranged as opposed to the expression of a metaphysical condition. Lukács, in his characteristically crabbed early style, explains:

> the hierarchical question of super- and subordination between inner and outer reality is the ethical problem of utopia; the question, to what extent the capacity to think of a better world can be ethically justified, to what extent a life may be constructed that is complete in itself and a point of departure for shaping life.
> (1963a, 117)

What was a misalignment between soul and world has become a hierarchical problem, a matter of better and worse, implying that an ethics of utopia concerns how the external world should be constructed according to an inner standard that restores something of the lost wholeness possessed by integrated cultures. Even though Lukács refrains from politicizing this kind of utopian thinking as either "right" or "left," the relationship between inner and outer life is at odds with the passivity of Schopenhauerian pessimism, which prescribes deliberate restraint or conscious resignation amid the vicissitudes of the will. For Lukács, utopia entails a fundamentally active disposition that seeks to create out of the interiority of the self a model for the world that promises a better life than the one it has inherited.

To what extent, then, does the Hotel Abyss embody this hope for a better world? And more to the point, how does this utopian spirit intersect with a conservative epistemology? Before addressing these questions with a reading of the Grand Hotel Abyss, it is worthwhile to restate the theme:

> a beautiful hotel equipped with every comfort, on the edge of the abyss, of nothing, of senselessness. And the daily sight of the abyss, between the pleasant delights of meals or artistic productions, can only heighten the pleasure of these refined comforts.
> (Lukács 1963a, 17)

The image of the Hotel Abyss perched above an empty expanse reflects the concepts that Lukács derived from Schopenhauer: senselessness, nothingness, and nihilism. These are foundational attributes of the world—the external world, that is—where the Hotel Abyss is located. Beyond the confines of this modern edifice, there is no potential for purposeful action, no chance for interacting with others, instigating or resolving conflict, or creating meaning through the development of character. The world has shrunken into oblivion, generating precisely the misalignment between inner and outer life that Lukács identifies with the problematic condition of modernity.

Indeed, a left ethics reveals how the internal condition of the hotel is correspondingly enhanced—rendered in all its grandeur, one might say. Fully equipped with the comforts and amenities befitting a luxury establishment, the Grand Hotel Abyss could well qualify as a kind of utopia. It is beautiful; its guests do not suffer from hunger or material privation; on the contrary, the aristocrats that dwell there enjoy delicious meals. Furthermore, their spiritual needs are provided for. They enjoy artistic productions, and Lukács even notes their delight in those spectacles. In sum, their comforts are refined, their pleasures are heightened, and their material provisions are plenty. The guests enjoy a dignified life, of a sort, even if their diversions bear only the most tentative relationship to reality.

This reading makes plain the limitations of the synthesis of left ethics and right epistemology and why Lukács used the metaphor of the Grand Hotel Abyss to chide German intellectuals. To the extent that this hotel embodies a utopia, its dreams for dignity and the dissolution of "life-denying socioeconomic categories" are restricted to the comfortable confines of a grand hotel. Only those aristocrats who can afford to pay for their stay may enjoy the pleasure of its comforts. Accordingly, resolving the disjunction between a left ethics and right epistemology—a problem of critical praxis no less than critical theory—cannot be accomplished by staring out at the abyss and contemplating its emptiness. It requires checking out of the hotel and turning towards reality—going back down the mountain, as it were. In such a way, a left ethics, instead of being a mere matter for the soul, might then become a left politics.

Acknowledgement

The research for this chapter was funded by the Deutsche Forschungsgemeinschaft (DFG, German Research Foundation), with grant number 427978369.

Notes

1 All translations in this essay are my own. The works are cited in their German editions but referred to with English titles.
2 If anything, the qualification "including Adorno" indicates that the Frankfurt School was not the primary target of Lukács's critique since any connection between the German intelligentsia at large and the Institut für Sozialforschung, or at least one of its members, had to be made explicit. Late in life, Bloch vehemently denied connections with the Frankfurt School. Although his reaction

was coloured by bitterness at the fact that Horkheimer declined to assist him after his emigration to the United States, his words are nevertheless revealing. He insists in a late interview "that I had nothing to do with the Frankfurt School!" Responding to an article that nevertheless counted him as a member of the School, Bloch responded: "complete nonsense" (Reinicke 1979, 80, 78). For a general account of Bloch and the Frankfurt School, see Vidal (2007). Tyrus Miller (2022, 18) has noted that an even earlier use of the phrase "Grand Hotel Abyss" appeared in an unpublished essay of 1933.
3   For Lukács's intellectual relationship to Bloch, see Radnóti (1983, 63–74). Bloch, at the very least, suggests his awareness of Lukács's critique in a letter dated some three years later. See Bloch to Lukács, 4 September 1965 (Bloch 1985, I.205). The Expressionism Debate began with the publication of polemical articles by Klaus Mann and Alfred Kurella in the September 1937 issue of *Das Wort*. These articles occasioned major responses by Herwarth Walden, Béla Balasz, Rudolf Leonhard, and of course Lukács and Bloch. The exchange is sometimes referred to as the "Brecht/Lukács debate" even though Brecht's contribution was only published posthumously (see Schmitt 1973).
4   For Lukács and modernist studies more broadly, see Esty (2009).
5   For discussion of the relevance of *The Specificity of the Aesthetic* and Lukács's theory of architecture for post-World War II debates in Hungary, see Moravánszky (2019, 1–12).
6   See Lukács, "Es geht um Realismus" (1973, 192–230).
7   Bloch's first major contribution to a theorization of utopia was published as *Der Geist der Utopie* in 1918. He later expanded his arguments into his magnum opus *Das Prinzip Hoffnung* (1954). For recent discussions of utopia in literary and cultural studies, see Jameson (2016), Kotin (2017), and Mao (2020).

Works Cited

Aronowitz, Stanley. 2011. "Georg Lukács' *Destruction of Reason*." In *Georg Lukács Reconsidered: Critical Essays in Politics, Philosophy and Aesthetics*. London: Continuum.

Bloch, Ernst. 1985. *Briefe: 1903–1975*, edited by Karola Bloch et al. Frankfurt: Suhrkamp Verlag.

Brown, Alexander. 2018. "In Defence of Reason? Friedrich Nietzsche in Thomas Mann's 'Nietzsches Philosophie im Lichte unserer Erfahrung' and Georg Lukács' *Die Zerstörung der Vernunft*." *Nietzsche-Studien*, 47 (1): 379–97.

Copleston, Frederick. 1975. *Arthur Schopenhauer: Philosopher of Pessimism*. London: Search Press Ltd.

Esty, Jed. 2009. "Global Lukács." *Novel: A Forum on Fiction*, 42(3): 366–72.

Goble, Mark. 2010. *Beautiful Circuits: Modernism and the Mediated Life*. New York: Columbia University Press.

Jameson, Fredric. 2016. *An American Utopia: Dual Power and the Universal Army*, edited by Slavoj Žižek. New York: Verso.

Jay, Martin. 1973. *The Dialectical Imagination: A History of the Frankfurt School and the Institute of Social Research 1923–1950*. Boston: Little, Brown and Company.

Jeffries, Stuart. 2016. *Grand Hotel Abyss: The Lives of the Frankfurt School*. New York: Verso.

Kant, Immanuel. 1902- (v.1, 1910). *Kants gesammelte Schriften*, edited by Königlich Preussischen Akademie der Wissenschaften. Berlin: G. Reimer.
Kavoulakos, Konstantinos. 2018. *Georg Lukács's Philosophy of Praxis: From Neo-Kantianism to Marxism*. London: Bloomsbury Academic.
Kotin, Joshua. 2017. *Utopias of One*. Princeton: Princeton University Press.
Löwy, Michael. 1979. *Georg Lukács: From Romanticism to Bolshevism*. Translated by Patrick Camiller. London: New Left Books.
Lukács, Georg. 1963a. *Die Theorie des Romans: Ein geschichtsphilosophischer Versuch über die Formen der großen Epik*. Neuwied am Rhein: Hermann Luchterhand.
Lukács, Georg. 1963b. *Die Eigenart des Ästhetischen*. Neuwied am Rhein: Hermann Luchterhand.
Lukács, Georg. 1973. "Es geht um den Realismus." In *Die Expressionismusdebatte: Materialien zu einer marxistischen Realismuskonzeption*, edited by Hans-Jürgen Schmitt. Frankfurt: Suhrkamp.
Lukács, Georg. 1974. *Die Zerstörung der Vernunft*. In *Georg Lukács Werke*, Band 9. Darmstadt und Neuwied: Hermann Luchterhand Verlag.
Mao, Douglas. 2020. *Inventions of Nemesis: Utopia, Indignation, and Justice*. Princeton: Princeton University Press.
Miller, Tyrus. 2022. *Georg Lukács and Critical Theory: Aesthetics, History, Utopia*. Edinburgh: Edinburgh University Press.
Moravánszky, Ákos. 2019. "The Specificity of Architecture: Architectural Debates and Critical Theory in Hungary, 1945–1989." *Architectural Histories* 7(1), no. 4: 1–12. https://doi.org/10.5334/ah.315
Radnóti, Sándor. 1983. "Lukács and Bloch." In *Lukács Revalued*, edited by Agnes Heller, 63–74. Oxford: Basil Blackwell.
Reinicke, Helmut, ed. 1979. *Revolution der Utopie: Texte von und über Ernst Bloch*. Frankfurt: Campus Verlag.
Safranski, Rüdiger. 1987. *Schopenhauer und die wilden Jahre der Philosophie: Eine Biographie*. München: Carl Hanser Verlag.
Schmitt, Hans-Jürgen, ed. 1973. *Die Expressionismusdebatte: Materialien zu einer marxistischen Realismuskonzeption*, edited by Hans-Jürgen Schmitt. Frankfurt: Suhrkamp.
Schopenhauer, Arthur. 1947. *Sämtliche Werke*. Seven Volumes. Second Edition, edited by Arthur Hübscher. Eberhard Brockhaus Verlag: Wiesbaden.
Vidal, Francesca. 2007. "Ernst Bloch in, gegen und mit Frankfurt." In *Das Feld der Frankfurter Kultur- und Sozialwissenschaften vor 1945*, edited by Richard Faber and Eva-Maria Ziege, 137–48. Würzburg: Königshausen & Neumann.

15 Prototype Hotels for the Jet Age

Bruce Peter

This chapter concentrates on the architecture, interior design, and promotion of new American-financed international business and tourist hotels of the late 1940s, analysing these as transcultural spaces of modernity on the cusp of the jet age. It reflects upon the origins of the International Style and its dissemination through hotel architecture, interior design, and promotion to represent a new postwar vision of America as a technologically progressive and powerful nation. It shows how in developing nations, the International Style was quickly adopted for hotel design by local architects and that in the Caribbean, new hotel resorts were planned as symbols of progressiveness and modernity. It focuses on the Statler hotel in Washington, DC, which was mainly aimed at accommodating governmental and business guests, and on the Hotel Jaragua in Ciudad Trujillo in the Dominican Republic and the Caribe Hilton at San Juan in Puerto Rico, which were tropical resort hotels for tourists. These three hotels, it will be shown, were precedents for the subsequent development of American and international postwar hotel design more generally.

The International Style took its name from a 1932 exhibition at the Museum of Modern Art in New York, curated by Henry Russell Hitchcock and Philip Johnson, which displayed images and models of avant-garde European modernist buildings constructed during the preceding decade. The museum itself had been founded in 1929 by the very wealthy New York philanthropist Abby Rockefeller (wife of John D. Rockefeller Jnr. of the oil dynasty) and her friends—the modern art collector Mary P. Bliss and the art writer and critic Mary Quinn Sullivan. Their main motive was to promote modernism in art and visual culture to ensure that the USA would not fall behind Europe and Soviet Russia in aesthetic matters. With regard to how modernist architecture was promoted through the International Style exhibition, in contrast with many leading European and Russian theoreticians and practitioners, Hitchcock and Johnson (1932) placed emphasis only on its visual and spatial characteristics and ignored its associations with radical leftist politics. In any case, Johnson's personal politics at that time were of the extreme right and he was a vocal admirer of Nazism (Ockman 2009, 56–58). From an American point of view, architectural modernism was

DOI: 10.4324/9781003213079-20

promoted as being more efficient than other styles in terms of its logical use of space and its incorporation of up-to-date technologies to speed up construction and provide superior environments with more sophisticated services to users. These supposed benefits were potentially attractive to commercial clients, including hotel entrepreneurs. Above all, it was modernism's clean-lined aesthetic, involving asymmetrical façade composition, repeated structural elements, and the extensive use of glazing, which was to prove highly seductive to businesses wishing to promote up-to-date public images and thereby hopefully gain commercial advantages over their competitors.[1]

The International Style exhibition took place at a time when America and the western world were in the throes of the Great Depression. Consequently, there was initially a lack of capital for commercial building work and, moreover, the American commercial world already had taken to heart the modern decorative design styles popularized in the wake of the Exposition Internationale des Arts Décoratifs et Industriels Modernes, which had taken place in Paris in 1925. Buildings ranging from giant skyscrapers—and major public projects enacted under President Franklin D. Roosevelt's New Deal, such as the Hoover Dam—to the new, though quite small, hotels of Miami Beach were all variations of what would later on come to be termed as "Art Deco." Due to the Depression and World War II, it would take somewhat longer for the International Style to percolate from the rarefied world of the Museum of Modern Art and into the American commercial design mainstream.

The International Style, however, also represented a much more radical break with tradition than Art Deco. After all, to embrace modernism was to accept and adopt a range of elite, intellectualized, and distinctly non-mainstream stances with regard to aesthetics, space, culture, society, and politics, and these positions almost invariably represented the obverse of the kinds of popular taste that hotel operators, among many other commercial service providers, sought to offer. Modernist architects typically strongly encouraged their clients to accept minimalist aesthetics with unadorned surfaces and strictly controlled details when those clients' own instincts usually were to supply decorative excess so that their premises would appear as luxuriously aspirational and offering the best possible value for money. In short, the International Style's aims of visual and material restraint were seemingly at cross-purposes with those of the existing American hotel industry.

On the other hand, as the International Style looked futuristic, it clearly had potential to signify to viewers and users that a property was the most up-to-date, and, besides, in a hotel, unlike in a domestic environment, it was possible to sample new design ideas only for the limited duration of a stay and without having to live with them all of the time. Furthermore, while on holiday and during leisure time, guests were encouraged to relax, and, through exposure to up-to-date design while enjoying eating, drinking, and poolside sunbathing, they thereby perhaps became more open to novel aesthetic concepts which, in these circumstances, would even appear to have taken on a heightened glamour.

By the mid-twentieth century, when international modernism first began to affect American hotel design, the USA's hospitality industry was the world's most advanced. Leading developments was the extensive Statler chain, which was often referred to as the "Statler System," and which had brought high-capacity, well-appointed, and equipped hotels aimed at the mid-market to America's burgeoning industrial and commercial cities. The chain had been founded by the entrepreneur Ellsworth M. Statler, who had first built a temporary wooden hotel in Buffalo, New York, accommodating each night up to 5,000 guests visiting the 1901 Pan-American Exhibition. In 1907, a permanent Statler Hotel replaced it, every one of its 300 rooms being fitted with a private bathroom, something never previously attempted on such a scale and achieved through rigorously standardized planning. Bathrooms for adjoining rooms were situated back-to-back adjacent to the corridor, thereby enabling each pair on every storey to share the same plumbing shafts, which were accessed from service hatches in the corridors (Pfueller Davidson 2005). Statler's intent was not to compete with the luxury hotels, but rather to offer clean, comfortable, and moderately priced rooms for the average traveller and his means of achieving this goal were eventually emulated worldwide in the planning of hotels and, later on, also of mass-market cruise ships.

During the interwar years, the Statler chain expanded, building large hotels in many of America's biggest cities and charging as little as $1.50 per room per night. Its properties invariably were strictly rectilinear in plan, filling whole blocks of the urban grid. On smaller sites, bedroom accommodation and associated corridor circulation was arranged around the perimeter with a rectangular central courtyard, enabling daylight to reach the inward-facing rooms. Hotels occupying bigger plots, by contrast, typically had bedroom storeys laid out with sequences of identical wings coming off a spinal central corridor. In each approach, the idea was to maximize the length of external walls so that every room would have a window, while maintaining a regular modular pattern to enable the inclusion of standard *en suite* units. Viewed from the street, Statler hotels appeared as giant monoliths of facing brick, rising from rusticated stone bases and usually with deep cornices at roof height—the typical Beaux Arts-inflected "look" of American commercial architecture of their era.

By the 1940s, the idea that commercial efficiency could best be expressed through "functionalist" architectural solutions had begun to take root in the USA among the leading architectural firms designing for the hotel trade. This did not at first mean fundamentally changing the layout or construction of buildings but merely removing any Beaux Arts, Art Deco, or "moderne" forms and detailing from their facades and interiors, leaving pure rectilinear volumes with flat surfaces punctuated by regularly spaced windows.[2]

The 850-room Washington Statler of 1943, designed by the Chicago-based architectural firm of Holabird, Root, and Burgee—which since its establishment in 1880 as Holabird and Root had made hotel design a key speciality—was considered to be of strategic importance by the United States government as it offered the potential to accommodate securely the many additional officials and dignitaries in the capital on account of the war effort (see Figure 15.1). It was therefore one of few large building projects to which permission for completion was granted during these years.

The hotel was the work of one of Holabird's senior architects, Richard Smith, who was assisted by a recently employed Harvard architectural graduate, William B. Tabler. The latter displayed a prodigious talent for hotel design and subsequently established himself in independent practice as one of the leading specialist hotel architects working internationally. According to the American journal *Architectural Forum*, one innovation of the Washington Statler was a layout intended to privilege guests arriving and leaving by car over pedestrians, the hotel's main entrance being at the rear and accessed from a covered "motor drive" ("Washington Statler" 1943). Within the building, there was an automobile elevator to lift cars up to the second floor where the ballroom was located so that when, for example, President Franklin D. Roosevelt visited, he could be brought there directly, and, moreover, cars could be displayed during trade exhibitions. On the interior, cold cathode lighting was used throughout, and the bedrooms were both smaller and lower-ceilinged than in previous Statler hotels ("Washington Statler" 1943).

To an extent, the hotel's austere aesthetic was a reflection of a culture generated by Depression and wartime economics. Making a virtue

Figure 15.1 Hotel Statler, Washington, DC. Bruce Peter personal collection.

out of necessity, American commercial entrepreneurs such as Statler promoted this minimalistic "look" as being very up-to-date. Yet, in key locations upon which guests' attention was focused, the actual finishes used were quite lavish. For example, the cream limestone blocks cladding the exterior were costlier than the bricks with which previous Statlers had been covered (Pflueller Davidson 2005, 98–100). The lobby, meanwhile, was entirely lined with flat sheets of marble, just as in Ludwig Mies van der Rohe's Barcelona Pavilion. These smooth finishes were, however, applied as veneer upon an underlying design that was essentially neo-classical and with a high degree of symmetry in all of its elements ("Washington Statler" 1943).

While war raged in Europe and in South-East Asia, within the Americas the development of networks of airline routes and the financing of the construction of hotels to accommodate increasing numbers of travellers were seen as prime ways of binding North and South more closely together. In the 1940s, Pan American World Airlines was operating frequent services to the Caribbean and South America, with several departures per day from Miami to Havana in Cuba and to San Juan in Puerto Rico—both favourite American holiday destinations. There were also daily flights to Rio de Janeiro, though the journey took five days with overnight stops *en route* in San Juan, Port of Spain in Trinidad, and at Belem and Recife in Brazil. However, it was predicted that soon a new generation of fast, high-altitude "jetliners" would supersede the existing propeller planes, reducing such trips to a matter of hours (Potter 1996, 12).[3]

Just as in the USA, since the 1920s, the Art Deco and modern styles had significantly impacted the design of commercial, residential, and public buildings alike in Central and South America. Again similarly, the International Style began to emerge in the 1940s as a consequence of influential figures arguing that the construction of futuristic-looking and spatially innovative buildings would symbolize national development and progress to the wider world. Leading politicians in the region were not necessarily equally progressive about democracy or respect for citizens' rights, however, and, indeed, much like in 1930s Europe, dictators would prove to be among modernist architecture's most enthusiastic patrons in the Caribbean in particular.[4]

Encouraging tourism was an obvious way to achieve economic growth in places where few already had sufficiently high levels of education or advanced technical skills to enable full-scale industrialization to take place, but where the climate was tropical, the beaches pristine and expansive, and the seas azure blue. New resort hotels were thus required, but the Spanish colonial styles, which had typified many such developments in the recent past, did not align with national images now seeking to emphasize self-determination and to convey messages of progress and renewal, however contrived these were in actuality. Moreover, their façades were required to be symmetrically composed and to have particular recognizable design features that were historically precedented,

Figure 15.2 Hotel Jaragua, Ciudad, Trujillo, poolside view. Bruce Peter personal collection.

whereas modernist composition was freer, enabling buildings to respond better to geographical and climatic circumstances. Although modernism's colonialist resonances were perhaps less obviously apparent, modernist resort hotels could be viewed as representing another more covert colonialist approach.

The first Modern Movement hotel in the Caribbean was the Hotel Jaragua in Ciudad Trujillo (formerly Santo Domingo) in the Dominican Republic (see Figure 15.2). Designed by the American-educated local architect Guillermo González Sánchez and completed in 1946, the 66-bedroom hotel very successfully demonstrated the attractiveness of modernist open planning and contrasts of lightness and cool shade in a tropical context. The years preceding the hotel's development had been turbulent ones for the Dominican Republic. Independent from Spain since 1821, it had been occupied by the USA in 1916 to ensure cooperation due to its prime strategic importance in relation to the Panama Canal. In 1924 it gained independence once more but during the 1930s came under the brutal military dictatorship of Rafael Trujillo, who ordered the renaming of the capital after himself. Trujillo was also an enthusiastic modernizer, and, with American support, significant economic growth was achieved under his leadership. A hurricane had badly damaged Santo Domingo in 1930, and the construction of Ciudad Trujillo as a modern replacement was viewed by him as a prestigious national project.[5]

Guillermo González Sánchez's architectural career had begun in the wake of the American occupation when he was employed as a draughtsman in the Dominican Islands' Office of Public Works. During the 1920s, he studied through a scholarship at Yale University, during which time he also visited Europe where, in addition to observing buildings featuring the Beaux Arts detailing favoured by his tutors at Yale, he had his first encounters with modernism. These had a profound impact upon him. Upon commencing practice in 1936 under the Trujillo dictatorship, it was the approaches of Le Corbusier and Walter Gropius that he sought to emulate. Although he completed a number of notable urban planning and public building projects in the late 1930s, the Hotel Jaragua was his first major work to attract international attention and acclaim ("Jaragua Hotel" 1946).

The hotel's accommodation block was of five storeys, with the public rooms on the ground floor arranged along the seaward side, where they faced an outdoor swimming pool at one end and a terrace equipped with a bandstand and dance floor at the other. Projecting outwards between these was the ballroom, which was purely Corbusian in manner; its first floor was extruded on slender piloti and surrounded by an outdoor terrace accessed from the exterior via a cantilevered stairway. Indeed, nearly the entire edifice was remarkably advanced for its time and place—much more so than comparable hotels in Miami, for example, which continued to be designed in the Art Deco idiom. The hotel was built by a contractor owned by Sánchez's brother, Alfredo, their close cooperation ensuring that precise attention could be paid to the detailing. The gleaming white concrete planes, lush green lawns, turquoise pool, and cool, air-conditioned interior altogether created a very appealing image of tropical modernity. Yet, in the two-storey foyer, the scene was dominated by a marble bust of Trujillo, whom the unnamed critic from *Architectural Forum* described as "iron-fisted" ("Jaragua Hotel" 1946). The interior décor was generally light and simple with tiled floors and mirror-clad walls to increase the sense of illumination in otherwise shaded corners. In the centre of the ballroom's ceiling, a large baroque-style chandelier, designed by the architect, was one of the few instances of more traditional signifiers of hotelier luxury.

Late in 1949, a much bigger 300-room resort hotel of even more advanced design was completed in San Juan in the United States' Caribbean territory of Puerto Rico. It too was the work of relatively young and unknown American-trained local architects, Osvaldo Toro, Miguel Ferrer, and their assistant, the civil engineer Luis Torregrosa-Casellas, of Toro y Ferrer, whose design was the winner of a competition. Toro and Torregrosa-Casellas were both graduates of Cornell University in 1937 and 1938, respectively, whereas Ferrer had studied at Columbia University, from which he too had graduated in 1938. A further member of the team designing their entry was a close friend and former student colleague of Toro's, Charles H. Warner, who was a founding partner of

Warner-Leeds in New York with existing hotel design experience and who was brought in to help make their scheme seem more credible, particularly as the intention was to appeal particularly to American tourists ("Jaragua Hotel" 1946).

Toro and Ferrer's decision to enter practice together in San Juan was timely as, after some turbulent recent incidents of public disorder and mass killings by the police, the United States government of Franklin D. Roosevelt was determined to bring to the territory some "New Deal" prosperity, which included money for new architectural projects. In 1941, Roosevelt dispatched one of his political advisers, the progressive academic and politician Rexford Tugwell to govern the island, by enacting constitutional reforms and commencing a programme of development. Among Tugwell's early initiatives was to establish the Puerto Rico Industrial Development Company (PRIDCO) in 1942 with a mandate to develop tourism and manufacturing industries, hopefully leading to new wealth, long-term prosperity, and peace. As part of this strategy, Puerto Rico urgently needed a large, new resort hotel to accommodate mainly American holidaymakers and businessmen for whom San Juan was now reachable by plane in as little as six-and-a-half hours from the USA ("The Caribe Hilton" 1950, 74).

Toro y Ferrer's design for the hotel was state-of-the-art; located on a rocky and wind-swept promontory on Puerta de Tierra, an offshore island linked to the main town of San Juan by a bridge, its massive ten-storey accommodation block, containing 300 bedrooms, was to become the prime local landmark. In terms of layout, the design was indebted to proposals by Le Corbusier from the interwar era for the type of edifice that subsequently took form in Marseille as the Unité d' Habitation apartment block—though the completion of the hotel in 1949 preceded it by four years. Just as with Corbusier's proposals, the hotel's accommodation block was held aloft on piloti, which in a hot and humid climate allowed sea breezes to circulate through the open-sided but shaded area beneath. The reinforced concrete structure was massively strong to withstand hurricanes. Heavily framed by the main volume, a grid of open projecting balconies was, like the piloti, contrastingly slender. To avoid there being a "landward" side, the hotel was orientated with one end facing the sea and the balconies twisted at an angle so that all were exposed to refreshing sea breezes. On one side, adjacent to the main entrance, their regular rhythm was interrupted two-thirds of the way along by a service tower for the lifts and stairs, at the summit of which the hotel's name would be mounted. On the roof, the water tank and air-conditioning plant formed a related vertical accent. The overall design approach represented a "world first" for a large resort hotel, providing a model design solution that would be endlessly replicated around the world in the ensuing decades, albeit rarely quite so convincingly. The fact that the hotel's grounds contained picturesquely ruinous historic defences in rough local stone that were part of the Fort San Geronimo only served to emphasize all the more greatly its pristine cream-painted smoothness, the rectilinearity and rigorous repetition of its elements ("Spectacular Luxury" 1950).

Just as at the Hotel Jaragua in Ciudad Trujillo, from which Toro y Ferrer also took inspiration, the hotel's ground floor and the immediate surroundings of the accommodation block were designed as a series of open-plan and inter-linked spaces in which activities flowed from one to another; for example, there could be poolside dining and entertainment. So as to make full use of the dramatic potential of the triangular headland at the seaward end, however, the circulation, social and recreational spaces were orientated towards the headland at right angles to the accommodation block. The articulation of the two elements was resolved by an open foyer with a feature staircase, enabling horizontal and vertical connectivity. According to the reviewer from the journal *Interiors*, these elements were planned to be "part of the landscape," with the main block above merely shading them from the sun ("The Caribe Hilton" 1950, 74).

Most unusually, the service spaces were in the bottom of the accommodation block's landward end, where a single kitchen served all of the catering outlets which were on the same level. Such an unconventional but eminently practical arrangement could not have been achieved in a hotel of traditionally symmetrical design. Upon completion, the *Architectural Forum*'s critic wrote admiringly of the "impression of broad, windswept porches, built expansively for the true luxury of use" and contrasted these with the "pompous colonial style, charm-conditioned by a posh decorator" of other recent tropical hotel resorts ("Spectacular Luxury" 1950, 98). *Interiors*, meanwhile, commented approvingly that the building was "thoroughly penetrated by spur walls, overhangs, and far-flung stairways. The chief spaces are in reality as sketchy as they appear on the plan, resulting in an unimpeded flow of traffic and vision which connects the building to the landscape" ("The Caribe Hilton" 1950, 86).

Operating such a hotel to a standard necessary to attract the desired clientele required American hotelier expertise, and so the Puerto Rican developers contacted various potential operators and also placed advertisements in the hospitality trade press. Although various contenders apparently responded, the choice fell upon an up-and-coming American hotel entrepreneur, Conrad N. Hilton—whose name at that time was far less known even in the USA than many others in the trade, but was one that henceforth would be closely associated with the accommodation of jet age travellers. As Hilton recalled in his 1957 autobiography, *Be My Guest*:

> I replied at once in their own graceful Spanish tongue and with all the enthusiasm I felt [...] We would operate their hotel under a long-term percentage rental agreement with renewal options, two thirds of the gross operating profits to go to the owners and one third to us. We

would also hire Puerto Ricans for a large percentage of our staff and work out a program of on-the-job training in our United States hotels where their own people could learn the best we knew in techniques of modern hotel management.

It seemed a very good basic plan to me. I was immensely pleased with it. I was even more pleased when they wrote back at once accepting my terms.

(1994, 233)

Hilton's useful bilingualism resulted from his being born and brought up in San Antonio, a small village in New Mexico that in his formative years had retained much of the character of the old "Wild West." His father was a migrant from Germany and his mother was of Norwegian parentage but born in Iowa, and so his inheritance and habitus were from the outset multi-cultural (Hilton 1994, 58).

Hilton served in France during the closing months of the First World War and first saw Paris at its liberation. His experiences there had a profound effect on his consciousness; the cosmopolitan French capital proved electrifying after a life lived only in rural New Mexico. Upon returning home, Hilton felt the restlessness of a "displaced person" as his encounter with Paris had vastly expanded his horizons. Ambitious from the outset of his business career, he travelled to Cisco in Texas—which was in the throes of an oil boom. When he initially sought lodgings in a hotel called the Mobley, he found that it was booked solid with the guests sleeping in three eight-hour shifts. Despite this remarkable turnover, the owner was very keen to sell up as he believed that he could make more in oil than in hospitality; Hilton therefore offered to buy the property but only just managed to raise the necessary capital from family members, friends, and a local bank (Hilton 1994, 92–111).

As the 1920s progressed, Hilton rode an economic boom, acquiring further hotels in Texas. Later, when the American economy recovered from the Wall Street Crash, he bought luxury hotels in northern cities in the USA, and in 1942 he made his first overseas foray, operating the newly completed, though architecturally traditionalist, Palacio Hilton in Chihuahua in Mexico as an all-inclusive resort hotel, offering American tourists week-long "package" holidays. This model provided the prototype for the hotel he would be running on behalf of PRIDCO in Puerto Rico (see Figure 15.3). Hilton Hotels Corporation was incorporated in 1946, and a new division, Hilton International Hotels, was established two years thereafter specifically to run the San Juan hotel and other subsequent overseas properties (Hilton 1994, 171–222).

Named the Caribe Hilton, the hotel was scheduled for inauguration in December 1949. Its interiors were outfitted to Hilton's specifications by Toro y Ferrer's American colleague Charles H. Warner, their detailing successfully harmonizing with the hotel as a whole. Together, the architects produced an overall colour system for the exterior and interior. Each

Figure 15.3 Caribe Hilton exterior, San Juan, Puerto Rico. Bruce Peter personal collection.

vertical stack of bedrooms, their curtains and the balconies were coloured in bright pastel shades so that when the hotel was viewed from a distance, a subtle kaleidoscopic effect was realized, which contrasted with the cream paint applied to the surrounding structure. On the inside, the walls of the lobbies on each floor were likewise colour-coded, but they used a horizontal scheme instead and this matched similar colours for guests' baggage labels. As *Interiors* pointed out,

> A guest with a Caribe pink tag, for example, need not bother to read the first part of the number (which would tell him that he belongs on the tenth floor). All he has to do is concentrate on numbers indicating which room is his and unless he is color-blind or drunk he should have no trouble getting home.
>
> ("The Caribe Hilton" 1950, 78)

Toro, Ferrer, and Warner were determined to employ local artists and craftspeople to decorate the hotel. The German-born, though Puerto Rico-based architect Henry Klumb, a former employee of Frank Lloyd Wright and Louis Kahn, designed some of the furniture. Klumb had moved to San Juan in 1944 at the suggestion of Rexford Tugwell, who wanted him to become involved in designing schemes to realize his plans for the island's development (these were to include a municipal library and university buildings). Other items of the hotel's furniture were produced in the USA by a number of leading manufacturers such as Knoll and Herman Miller to drawings by, among others, the critically acclaimed Danish designer Jens Risom. Upholstery fabrics, rugs, blinds, curtains, and murals were also designed and made locally, as were the polished coloured cement floor tiles used throughout the interiors which, unlike more conventional flooring solutions for hotels, were completely resistant to humidity—and indeed pretty much everything else that might be dropped upon them ("The Caribe Hilton" 1950, 76–78).

Arriving by car or taxi from the hotel's landward end, the drive ran parallel to the accommodation block, half way along which it terminated at a porte-cochère. The lobby was accessed up a shaded, gently sloping ramp. A feature stairway accessing the first floor had wide open mahogany treads and glazed balustrades. On the adjacent wall, there was a large abstract mural by J. Torres Martino while the wall on the stair landing was panelled in polished black marble with white veining. The lobby merged seamlessly with the lounge and with the pool terrace which, in turn, merged with shops and a soda bar. On either side of the accommodation block's seaward end were pools with a mix of shallow and deep water for bathing or swimming. The restaurant and casino were on the first floor, the former having floor-to-ceiling windows around three sides giving impressive views across the surrounding coasts and seascape, the latter being dark and intimate with each table illuminated from a hanging lantern ("The Caribe Hilton" 1950, 85). The bedrooms on the floors above were, however, quite compact and many had sofa-beds that were converted each morning by the hotel's cleaning staff for daytime use and back for sleeping each evening. By this means, a daytime living room atmosphere was created with an impression of greater space than there actually was ("The Caribe Hilton" 1950, 81).

A very important aspect of the Caribe Hilton's design and atmosphere was its carefully landscaped surroundings, designed by the Texan-born, though San Juan-based, garden specialist Hunter Randolph. The manicured lawns, informal pathways and patios lined with palm fronds which began within the building and spread out into its surroundings added greatly to the tropical allure. Achieving these involved substantial labour; as *Interiors* records,

> an area called "The Garden of Eden" has been filled with representative specimens of the island's more exotic flowers and trees, and a beach was blasted out of the coral reef and covered with imported sand guaranteed not to stick to clothing.
> ("The Caribe Hilton" 1950, 80)

The hotel's signage and graphic signature for use on all printed matter, tableware, and other items were devised by the Florida-based advertising agency of Erwin Harris, who recently had produced similar packages for the most up-to-date of the resort hotels at South Miami Beach. Indeed, it was reputedly Harris who suggested the name "Caribe Hilton," as well as the stylized hand-written font for the hotel's identity. In an increasingly mediatized world, having a distinct and readily associable brand became increasingly important, not least in the hospitality and leisure sectors. As Harris explained, "The logotype must reveal the style of the hotel, it must establish a feeling and a personality. More important, when it runs in the newspapers and magazines, it must be highly legible and immediately identifiable" (quoted in End 1963, 214). Graphics for resort hotels, such as the Caribe Hilton, needed to conjure what he described as a "romantic remembrance," achieving "high style [...] without getting into high fashion" (214). Romanticism was in his opinion best achieved through a slightly feminized approach, whereas city hotels aimed at attracting the convention trade needed a masculine identity appealing to businessmen (214). Harris's position with regard to resort hotels echoes what had been common knowledge in the travel trade since the late nineteenth century: that in bourgeois households, it was very often women who made decisions about where to go on holiday.

Conrad Hilton launched the Caribe Hilton by flying two plane-loads of Hollywood celebrities, society journalists, and public figures to the hotel for a glitzy party, the details of which filled newspaper columns across the USA and thereby encouraged Americans to book holidays there. Living in Beverly Hills, Hilton was in regular contact with numerous leading stars of stage and screen who were delighted to be involved in the launch of the hotel and to meet their Puerto Rican admirers (Hilton 1994, 241–42).

Altogether, the Caribe Hilton project cost 7.3 million dollars, which was considered as extraordinarily good value, given how much accommodation it contained and what an impressive diversity of facilities it provided. During the hotel's first five years of operation, tourists staying there reputedly boosted the local economy by an average of 20 million dollars per annum and, in 1956, this figure reached 25 million ("The Caribe Hilton" 1950, 74).[6] For Puerto Rico, the completion of the hotel was a most notable achievement, especially as not far away from it, but separated by a thick tropical forest, was a shanty town more typical of the island as it was then. A total of 18,000 Puerto Ricans applied for the 450 places to work at the hotel and those who passed Hilton's aptitude test could, at least according to *Interiors*, consider themselves fortunate as "at least one knows that the bellboy would rather be carrying one's luggage than say, be working on a sugar plantation" ("The Caribe Hilton" 1950, 80). *Interiors* furthermore records that, upon arrival, guests were given the "Welcome Caribe Hilton" cocktail, served in a fresh coconut in which the content was mixed with rum, lime juice, sugar, apricot brandy, and ice while, in the basement, a machine was producing for this purpose 15,000 ice cubes per hour. Meanwhile, strolling musicians wearing hats fashioned from palm leaves played folk tunes while the bars, restaurant, and casino prepared to part guests from their dollars ("The Caribe Hilton" 1950, 74). The *Architectural Forum*'s critic, however, focused on what could be learnt from the hotel's slick design and stylish appearance, observing, "this is the kind of hotel which should be built in Florida and California, but never has been" ("Spectacular Luxury" 1950, 98).

In May 1952, the first commercial jet flight occurred and, very quickly, international jetliner route networks were established. The Caribe Hilton greatly influenced the design of practically every subsequent resort hotel built globally during the jet age. The type of facilities it offered soon was replicated in important Hiltons built in locations as diverse as Beverly Hills and Istanbul (both opened in 1955). Even in the mid-1960s, Hilton still was continuing to use the Caribe Hilton as an exemplar to be emulated—for example, sending the Dutch architects of the Amsterdam and Rotterdam Hiltons, Hugh Maaskant and Frederik Wilhelm de Vlaming, to stay in it to gain inspiration and to familiarize themselves with what was wanted (Provoost 2013, 281–82). Osvaldo Toro, meanwhile, was employed by Hilton as a consultant and advisor for hotel projects around the world. The Tel Aviv Hilton of 1965 by the Israeli architect Ya'acov Rechter, for example, benefitted from his input, its layout closely copying that of the Caribe Hilton (Rechter 2020). Architectural modernism tended to develop archetypes—universal solutions based on successful precedents that could be widely applied—and the Caribe Hilton provided a very effective one.

The Hilton International-operated hotels that followed the Caribe Hilton were flagship developments in a broader campaign of the expansion of American business and political influence in the American continent and around the world. For the host countries, they were also iconic projects of modernization. More generally, postwar modernist luxury hotels were associated with—and possibly helped to justify—a very broad diversity of political systems, ranging from dictatorships such as in the Dominican Republic in the case of the Hotel Jaragua, to democracies and they came to appear in nations from across the ideological spectrum.

Notes

1 See Matthews (1994, 43–59) for a detailed analysis of the aims and context of the International Style exhibition.
2 See "Washington Statler" (1943); "Hotel Statler" (1948); "The Statler Hotel" (1949); and "Commercial hotels" (1950).
3 Outwith the Americas, Pan American also had a daily flight to London as well as less frequent ones to Lisbon and to Leopoldville in the Congo (Potter 1996, 12).
4 Fidel Castro was a big fan of modernist system-building in Cuba, while his predecessor Fulgencio Batista also had many modernist buildings erected.
5 See Derby (2009) for a detailed analysis of Trujillo's policies.
6 See also Hilton (1994, 262).

Works Cited

"Commercial Hotels: A Study of Planning Method Used by Architects Holabird, Root and Burgee for International Adaptation, e.g., Statler Hotel, Washington,

DC; Talmanaco and Del Lago Hotels, Venezuela; Hotel at Bogota, Colombia." 1950. *Architectural Forum* (June): 90–101.

Derby, Lauren H., ed. 2009. *The Dictator's Seduction: Politics and the Popular Imagination in the Era of Trujillo.* Durham: Duke University Press.

End, Henry. 1963. *The Interiors Book of Hotel & Motor Hotels.* New York: Whitney Library of Design.

Hilton, Conrad. 1994. *Be My Guest.* New York: Fireside Press. [Original edition Prentice Hall Press, 1957].

Hitchcock, Henry Russell, and Philip Johnson. 1932. *The International Style.* New York: Museum of Modern Art.

"Hotel Statler, Washington, D.C.; Architects: Holabird and Root." 1948. *Builder* (July): 36–42.

"Jaragua Hotel: Dictator Trujillo Builds a Luxury Hotel in the Reconstructed Caribbean Capital which Today Bears His Name." 1946. *Architectural Forum* (September): n.p.

Matthews, Henry. 1994. "The Promotion of Modern Architecture by the Museum of Modern Art in the 1930s." *Journal of Design History*, 7 (1): 43–59.

Ockman, Joan. 2009. "The Figurehead: On Monumentality and Nihilism in Philip Johnson's Life and Work." In *Philip Johnson: The Consistency of Change*, edited by Emmanuel Petit, 56–58. New Haven: Yale University Press.

Pfueller Davidson, Lisa. 2005. "Early Twentieth-Century Hotel Architects and the Origins of Standardisation." *Journal of Decorative and Propaganda Arts, The American Hotel*, 25: 72–100.

Potter, James E. 1996. *A Room with a World View: 50 Years of Inter-Continental Hotels and Its People 1946–1996.* London: Weidenfeld and Nicolson.

Provoost, Michelle. 2013. *Hugh Maaskant: Architect of Progress.* Rotterdam: nai010.

Rechter, Amnon (son of Ya'acov Rechter). 2020. Interview by Bruce Peter by telephone on 24 January.

"Spectacular Luxury in the Caribbean—the Caribe Hilton Hotel at San Juan, Puerto Rico." 1950. *Architectural Forum* (March): 98–102.

"The Caribe Hilton: An Object Lesson in What You Can Do with $7,000,000." 1950. *Interiors* (April): 74–85.

"The Statler Hotel, Washington, DC; Architects: Holabird and Root." 1949. *Architecture Illustrated* (July): 81–90.

"Washington Statler." 1943. *Architectural Forum* (June): 61–76.

Index

Note: Endnotes are indicated by the page number followed by "n" and the note number e.g., 107n1 refers to note 107 on page 1.

abjection 43, 138, 143, 148
Adorno, Theodor W. 23, 26, 205, 211, 213, 215, 221–22, 226
Ahmed, Sara 51, 63, 151
Allen, Douglas E. 72, 77
Alofsin, Anthony 202–03, 211
Anderson, Elizabeth 114, 119, 121
Anderson, Paul F. 72, 77
Anderson, Wes 171, 180
Appadurai, Arjun 97, 108
Aragon, Louis 23, 27
Archive 26, 52, 60, 97, 188
Aronowitz, Stanley 214, 227
Art Deco 230–31, 233, 235
Ashcroft, Bill 97, 108
Auric, Georges 49, 59, 62
Auslander, Philip 59, 63
Austria *see* Vienna
"autobiografiction" 137
Avermaete, Tom 5, 9, 46

Bacon, Julie Louise 52, 63
Baedeker 100–01, 104, 107, 206
Balbec; *see also* Cabourg 12–14
ballet 49, 51, 57–59, 62
Ballets Russes 49–50
Barnes, Djuna 2–3, 124–30, 134–35; *Nightwood* 7, 124–29
Bates, Charlotte 113, 121, 124, 135
Baudelaire, Charles 22, 26
Baum, Vicki 169–70, 172, 174–78, 180; *Grand Hotel* 169–70, 172, 174–77, 180; *Es war alles ganz anders. Erinnerungen* 170, 180; *Der große Ausverkauf* 170, 174, 176–77, 180
Beaumont, Matthew 156, 166

Benjamin, Walter 1, 4, 6, 9, 14, 21–23, 26, 27–28, 140, 143, 151; *The Arcades Project* 9, 21–22, 26, 27; *Origin of the German Trauerspiel* 140, 151; "On Some Motifs in Baudelaire" 143, 151; "On the Image of Proust" 14, 21–22, 27; "Paralipomena to 'On the Concept of History'" 27; "Surrealism: The Last Snapshot of the European Intelligentsia" 26, 27; *The Writer of Modern Life: Essays on Charles Baudelaire* 22, 27
Benstock, Shari 124, 126, 130, 134, 135
Bérard, Christian 55, 59
Berger, Molly W. 2, 9
Berman, Jessica 9, 99, 108, 155, 166
Berman, Marshall 193, 196, 210, 211
biopolitical 6, 37, 40
Bishop, Elizabeth 2, 8, 182–87, 190, 192–96; "In a cheap hotel" 8, 183, 185–87, 192–95; "Miami" 187, 195
Black, Barbara 2, 9
Blake, William 60–62
Bloch, Ernst 214, 220, 222–23, 226, 227
Blondel, Nathalie 53, 55, 61, 62, 63
boarding house 22, 37, 95, 100, 182
Bollery, Franziska 33, 46
Bourdieu, Pierre 72, 77
Braddock Hotel, New York 188
Breines, Wini 189, 196
Breton, André 2, 23–24, 26–27, 124, 130, 135; *Nadja* 23–24, 26, 27
Brown, Alexander 214, 227
Brown, Kevin 37, 46

Budgen, Frank 155, 166
Burgess, Anthony 90, 91
Butt, Nadia 98, 108
Butts, Mary 2, 3, 6, 49–63; "The House Party" 6, 50–53, 56–58, 60, 62

Cabourg 11–12, 14
Calmette, Gaston 11
Camp 84, 136, 139–41, 143, 145–50
Caribbean 9, 98, 233–35
Caribe Hilton, Puerto Rico 229, 237–43
Carlson, Marvin 51, 52, 63
Cavafy, C. P. 84, 91
Caws, Mary Ann 126, 127, 135
Cecil Hotel, Alexandria 79, 81–83, 90
Chalk, Bridget T. 9, 10, 98, 108
Chanel, Coco 49, 56, 59, 61
Cheng, Vincent 160, 166
City Arms Hotel, Dublin 155, 159–63
Clarke, Matthew 138, 149, 151
Clifford, James 23, 26, 28
Cocteau, Jean 4, 6, 49–50, 52–63; *The Blood of a Poet* 50, 55; *The Difficulty of Being* 50, 55, 60, 63; *Opéra* 60; *Orphée* 50, 55, 60
Coetzee, J. M. 207, 211
Cold War 192, 195
Colvile, Georgiana M. M. 127, 129, 135
Connellan, Kathleen 43, 46
conspicuous consumption 68, 69, 71; *see also* Veblen, Thorstein
Copjec, Joan 42, 46
Copleston, Frederick 217, 227
Corfu 110, 113–14, 117, 118
Cray, Josie 7
Crispi, Luca 159, 160, 162, 163, 164, 166
Crump, James 62, 64

Dale, Daphne 74, 77
dance 50, 55, 57, 58, 59, 61, 69, 71, 72, 75, 128, 144, 145, 210, 235; *see also* ballet
Danzer, Ina 125, 136
Davidson, Robert A. 2, 4, 10
Debo, Annette 110, 121
De Certeau, Michel 50, 63
De-la-Noy, Michael 137, 151
Delany, Samuel 191, 196
Demps, Laurenz 178, 180
Denisoff, Dennis 83, 91
department stores 7, 8, 168–74, 176, 178, 179, 180

dérive 17
Derrida, Jacques 39, 46
Despotopoulou, Anna 3, 10, 72, 73, 77
dialectical image 22, 26
Diboll, Mike 86, 89, 91
Dimakis, Athanasios 6
Dudow, Slatan 176, 180
Dufy, Jean 58
Dufy, Raoul 58
Dumas, Alexandre 73
Duncan, Isadora 49, 50, 54, 55, 59
Durrell, Lawrence 2, 4, 79–91; "Alexandria, Cairo and Upper Egypt, 1977" 91; *Balthazar* 80, 81, 85, 91; *The Alexandria Quartet* 79–81, 84, 86, 87, 89, 90, 91; *The Black Book* 88, 89, 91

Edmunds, Susan 114, 121
Edwards, Amelia B. 90n2, 91
Eells, Emily 25n5, 28
Egypt 79–92
Elbert, Monika M. 2, 10
Eliot, T. S. 60, 125–26, 130
Ellison, David R. 15, 28
Emerson, Kent 114, 121
End, Henry 241, 243
Ernaux, Annie 24, 28
Expressionism 213, 219, 220, 222, 227

Farfan, Penny 51, 63
Felder, Martijn 38, 39, 47
Feys, Torsten 36, 37, 46
Fieni, David 83–84, 91
Flandria Palace Hotel, Ghent 40–42, 44
Florence 95–109
Forster, E. M. 3, 7, 79, 92, 95–109; *Alexandria: A History and Guide* 79, 92; *Pharos and Pharillon* 81, 92; *A Room with a View* 95–109; "A View without a Room: Old Friends Fifty Years Later" 106, 108; "The Story of a Panic" 104–05; *Two Cheers for Democracy* 108
Foster, Hal 131, 132, 136
Foucault, Michel 67, 77, 192, 196
Foy, Roslyn Reso 61, 63
Frankfurt School 213, 214, 221, 226–27n2
French Riviera 6, 49–64
Freud, Sigmund 12, 16, 114, 130, 131, 140, 147, 202
Friedman, Susan Stanford 110, 114, 115, 121, 185, 196
Fussell, Paul 22, 28, 206, 211

Garrity, Jane 56, 63
Gibson, Andrew 161, 166
Gifford, James 91n7, 92
Goble, Mark 213, 227
Goldring, Douglas 49
Goodlad, Lauren M. E. 107n1, 108
Gouda, Frances 39, 46
Goulding, Edmund: *Grand Hotel* 177, 180, 209–10, 211
Graham, Sarah 110, 121
"Grand Hotel Abyss" 213–28; see also Lukács, Georg
Grand Hôtel Cabourg 11, 12, 14
Grand Hôtel d'Angleterre et Belle Venise 110, 113, 120
Grand Hôtel des Bains 65, 67
Grand Hotel National, Vienna 204
grand hotels 2, 7, 14, 33, 34, 45, 65–71, 73, 74, 77, 88, 95, 96, 111, 157, 168, 171, 173, 174, 179, 201, 204, 213–14, 226
Great War *see* World War I
Gregory, Eileen 110, 111, 121
Griffin, Farah Jasmine 188, 196
Griffiths, Gareth 97, 108
Grosvenor Hotel, Dublin 156
grotesque 12, 87, 88, 143, 144, 145, 146, 147
Gruber, Eckhard 175, 180
Guest, Barbara 111, 122
Guggenheim, Peggy 53

Haag, Michael 80, 92
Haffner, Ernst 177, 180
Halim, Hala 91n5, 92
Hankins, Gabriel 98, 109
Harlem 1, 8, 183, 188–90, 192, 193, 194n4
Harrison, Jane Ellen 59, 63
hasard objectif, le 126
Hawkes, Joel 6
Hayner, Norman S. 25n3, 28
Hayward, Cecilia 11
H.D. 2, 3, 7, 110–23; "H.D. by Delia Alton" 110; *Magic Mirror, Compassionate Friendship, Thorn Thicket: A Tribute to Erich Heydt* 111, 113, 115, 120, 122; "Mira-Mare" 7, 110–22; *Notes on Thought and Vision* 7, 110, 117, 121; "Secret Name: Excavator's Egypt (circa A.D. 1925)" 112, 122; *Tribute to Freud* 7, 110, 111, 114, 117, 122; *The Mystery* 111
Hember, Polly 7

Herring, Scott 185, 196
Hext, Kate 91n3, 92
Heynickx, Rajesh 8, 33, 46
Hilton, Conrad 237, 241, 243
Hirsch, Marianne 19, 28
Hirschman, Albert 205, 211
Hirsh, Elizabeth A. 114, 122
Hitchcock, Alfred 77
Hitchcock, Henry Russell 229, 243
Hoffman, Thomas 204, 211
Hoffmann, John 8
Hollywood 209, 213, 241
hospitals 32–45
Hotel: architecture 8, 33, 39, 52, 77, 168, 169, 184, 208, 215, 229–43; child 25n3; see also Hayner, Norman S.; culture 6, 70–75; design/interiors 3, 7, 8, 33–38, 40, 67, 83, 84, 162, 168, 171, 208, 209, 215, 229–43; discipline 6, 42, 208; labour/staff 8, 19, 41–42, 112, 156–59, 162, 168–80, 183–84, 184–90, 192, 194, 195n4, 238, 240; lobby 2, 8, 18, 19, 66, 69, 81–83, 162, 171, 172, 173, 174, 176, 184, 188, 201–10, 233, 240; luxury 3, 8, 12, 68, 71, 83, 143, 184, 193, 204, 214, 215, 222, 226, 231, 235, 237, 238, 242; rooms 1, 3–5, 7, 12–19, 22, 26n17, 33, 37–38, 42–43, 50, 52, 55, 58–59, 62, 79, 84, 87–88, 89–90, 95–109, 116–17, 125–34, 144–46, 161, 174, 183, 185, 187–92, 231, 232, 236, 239, 240; routines 5, 45, 72, 156, 174, 177–79, 206
hotel *as*: heterotopia 67, 192; see also Foucault, Michel; landmark 1, 9, 168, 236; metaphor 7, 8, 41, 84, 88, 105, 113, 180n1, 208, 213–27; palimpsest 5, 21; prison 6, 38, 40, 43, 60, 177; transcultural space 1, 3, 7, 9, 83, 95–108, 229; transnational space 1, 6, 9, 66, 83, 71–75, 77, 83, 98; utopia 183, 184–85, 187–88, 222–26, 227n7
hotels *and*: affect 2, 7, 8, 19, 36, 38, 112, 113, 115, 138, 140, 142, 145–46, 150, 183, 184, 193, 194; allegory 137–51; class 2, 6, 7, 8, 12, 38, 65–77, 95, 126, 155–66, 170, 183, 187, 188–94, 203, 216, 219; community 1, 5, 6, 35, 49–50, 54, 56, 61–62, 66, 77n4, 97, 165, 184; cosmopolitanism 12, 25n2,

39, 71, 73, 77, 80, 90n2, 99, 238;
death 1, 7, 15, 16, 42, 45, 54,
85–86, 88–89, 125, 127, 129, 130,
140, 142–44, 146, 149, 150, 156,
159–60, 176; dwelling 1, 4, 22,
131, 208; empire 2, 6, 8, 79–91,
203–07, 210; gender 1, 2, 6, 7,
23–24, 61–62, 76, 87, 103–06,
125–35, 137–40, 144–47, 155–59,
176–78, 182–95; homelessness 107,
161, 176, 205; hospitality 3, 4, 6,
12, 20, 36–37, 38–39, 75, 183,
184, 186, 189, 231, 237, 238, 241;
immigration 36–40, 45; intimacy
5, 8, 68, 145, 185–90, 191, 193;
leisure 3, 6, 8, 38, 65, 66, 68–77,
171, 230, 241; memory 2, 6, 11–14,
16–19, 21–25, 115, 132, 143–45,
186; mobility 1–6, 8, 39–40, 43, 70,
95, 96, 99, 104–07, 160, 173, 206;
performance 4, 6, 7, 49–62, 66, 69,
70–76, 144, 176, 179, 193; privacy
2, 5, 6, 22, 66, 83, 84, 88, 96, 103,
113, 126, 128, 133, 144–45, 159,
162–65, 176, 185, 189, 193, 194,
203, 205; race 182–94; sexuality 1,
2, 7, 53, 58, 60, 105–06, 124–29,
155–59, 164, 165, 183, 185,
191; surveillance 3, 40, 156, 163;
tourism 6, 8, 95–97, 99, 101, 106,
107, 106, 233, 236; violence 7, 45,
124, 138, 163, 187, 188, 191, 192,
193; war 4, 6, 8, 36, 43, 44, 45,
80, 81, 88, 90, 210, 214, 232, 233;
women 3, 23–26, 58, 70, 71–73,
75–77, 95–107, 124–35, 156–59,
163–65, 176, 182–95
Hotel Adlon, Berlin 178–79
Hotel Bristol, Lugano 111–13
Hotel Bristol, Vienna 201
Hotel Carlton, Frankfurt 26n11
Hotel Chelsea, New York 182
Hotel Danieli, Venice 111–12
Hotel Europa, Venice 15
Hôtel Floridor, Paris 21
Hôtel Foyot, Paris 182
Hotel Jaragua, Dominican Republic
229, 234–37, 242
Hotel Matschakerhof, Vienna 19
Hôtel du Midi, Paris 21
Hotel NASM, Rotterdam 6, 36–39
Hotel National, Washington D.C. 33
hôtel particulier 22
Hôtel Pimodan, Paris 22
Hôtel Ritz, Paris 34

Hotel Royal, Vienna 201–02
Hotel Statler, Washington DC 229,
232–33, 242n2
Hôtel de Suède, Paris 24; *see also*
Sphinx Hôtel
Hotel Welcome, Villefranche 6,
49–54, 56–58, 61–62
Hutchison, Sharla 128–29, 136

Ibrahim, Tarek 80, 92
Inglin, Meinrad 6, 71, 74–75, 77;
Grand Hotel Excelsior 71, 74–75, 77
International Style 8, 229–30, 233, 242
Ippolito, Christophe 91n5, 92
Isarlo, Georges 52
Italy 63n2, 95–96, 99–102, 106–07,
111

James, Henry 1, 3, 10, 6, 65, 71–75,
162; *The American Scene* 1, 3, 10;
"Daisy Miller" 3, 10, 71–74, 75
James, Kevin J. 2, 3, 4, 10, 40, 46, 89,
90, 92
Jameson, Fredric 9, 10, 22, 28, 141,
151, 227
Janik, Allan 209, 211
Jay, Martin 213, 221, 227
Jazz 52, 57, 115
Jeffries, Stuart 213, 227
Jennings, Michael W. 22, 26n12, 28
Johnson, Philip 229, 243
Jones, Charlotte 40, 44, 46
Joyce, James 2, 7, 86, 91n3, 155–67,
183, 220; *Ulysses* 7, 155–67

Kahn, Louis 239
Kant, Immanuel 70, 142, 151, 218,
220, 224, 228
Kaplan, Carla 189, 196
Katz, Martin 67, 77
Kavoulakos, Konstantinos 221, 228
Kisacky, Jeanne 34, 47
Kloepfer, Deborah Kelly 110, 114, 122
Klumb, Henry 239
Knoch, Habbo 168, 171, 180
Koerner, Joseph Leo 202–03, 211
Koestenbaum, Wayne 23–24, 28, 184,
187, 194n2, 196
Kolocotroni, Vassiliki 6
Kracauer, Siegfried 66, 77, 168, 170,
181, 184, 196, 205, 211, 215;
Die Angestellten 170, 181; "Die
Hotelhalle" ("The Hotel Lobby")
66, 77, 168, 181, 184, 196, 205,
211

Lacan, Jacques 140, 146, 151
Laurencin, Marie 58
Laurens, Henri 49
Lee, Gregory B. 97, 109
Lehnert, Gertrud 170, 181
Leitner, Maria 169, 172, 177, 180n, 181; *Hotel Amerika* 169, 172, 177, 181
Leslie, Esther 21, 22, 26n13, 28
liberal humanism 96, 98, 102, 107n1
Lindner, Rolf 177, 181
Lomas, David 128, 136
Loos, Adolf 203, 212
Lost Generation 56
Löwy, Michael 214, 228
Lukács, Georg 1, 2, 8, 213–26, 226n2, 227n3–6, 228
Luna Park Hotel, Cairo 80
Lupton, Ellen 34, 47
Lusty, Natalya 135, 136
Lux, Joseph August 33, 208, 209, 212
Lyford, Amy 125, 135n2, 136

MacCannell, Dean 51, 63
Macmillan, Rev. Hugh 52, 63
Mäder, Ueli 174, 181
Mahfouz, Naguib 90n1, 92
maisons de passe 23
Malabou, Catherine 141, 145, 148, 150, 151
Mallarmé, Stéphane 73
Malt, Johanna 23, 28
Mann, Thomas 65, 66, 67–69, 72, 77n2, 175–79, 214; *Confessions of Felix Krull, Confidence Man* 69, 175–76; "Death in Venice" 65, 66, 67–68, 72, 77n2; *The Magic Mountain* 214
Mao, Douglas 97, 109, 227, 228
Mara, Miriam O'Kane 157, 166
Markel, Howard 36, 47
Martin, Nicholas 163, 166
Marx, Karl 210n2, 212
Marxism 26, 184, 193, 213–28
Massey, Anne 5, 9
Matthias, Bettina 2, 4, 10, 124, 136, 208, 212
McCabe, Susan 110, 122
McLoughlin, Kate 56, 64
McLuhan, Marshall 201, 212
McNaugher, Heather 98, 109
Merleau-Ponty, Maurice 139, 151, 161, 157
Milhaud, Darius 49
Miller, J. Abbott 34, 47

Miller, Henry 80, 91n7
Minca, Claudio 37, 38, 39, 47
modernist party 56
Monte Carlo 52, 53, 110, 114, 115, 116, 120, 121n1
Montgomery, Maureen E. 73–74, 78
Moore, Robbie 2, 4, 6, 10
Moraru, Christian 98, 109
Morris, Adalaide 110, 114, 122
Morris, Cedric 49, 62
Morse, Daniel Ryan 98, 108n2, 109
Morton, Frederic 211n3, 212
Mukherjee, Narugopal 98, 109
Mullin, Katherine 159, 166n2, 167
Mumford, Kevin 191
Munro, Hector 40
Murnau, F. W. 169, 172, 173, 174, 181
Murray, Alex 91n3, 92
Musil, Robert 2, 8, 204, 207–08, 210, 212; "Doors and Portals" 208; *The Man without Qualities* 207–08

Nabholz, Ann-Catherine 89, 92
"Nadja" (Léona Camille Ghislaine Delcourt) 27n19
Nagel, Otto 176, 181
Nazism 215, 229
New York 170, 182–92, 229, 231, 236; *see also* Harlem
Niemeyer, Carl 159, 160, 167
Nightingale, Florence 34, 47
Nijinska, Bronislava: *Les biches* 50, 51, 57–58, 60; *Les noces* 49, 60; *Le train bleu* 49, 50, 59
Nin, Anaïs 3, 124; *House of Incest* 124, 125, 130–34; *The Novel of the Future* 130
Nora, Pierre 21, 25n8, 28

Oatlands Park Hotel 137
Ockman, Joan 229, 243
Ong, Chin-Ee 37, 47
opium 50, 53, 59, 60, 61, 62
Orientalism 83, 84, 86
Ormond Hotel, Dublin 7, 155, 159, 164, 165
Ostriker, Alicia 111, 114, 122

Paeschke, Carl-Ludwig 178, 180
Parade 62
Parezanović, Tijana 80, 92
Paris 21–23, 24, 26n14, 26n16, 58, 61, 62n1, 89, 111, 124, 126, 134, 182, 230, 238
Parsons, Deborah 155, 167

Pater, Walter 149, 151
Peirce, Henry Davis 36–38, 47
Peleggi, Maurizio 80, 89, 92
Pension Bertolini 7, 95
pensions 99, 100, 101, 103, 107
Pero, Allan 7
Perry, Imani 185, 196
Peter, Bruce 4, 8
Peters, Arthur King 56, 64
Petry, Ann 2, 3, 8, 183–85, 187, 188–94, 194n4, 195n7, 195n13, 196; "In Darkness and Confusion" 188; *The Narrows* 8, 183, 188–93
Pfueller Davidson, Lisa 231, 243
Phenomenology 2, 138, 139, 143, 170; see also Merleau-Ponty, Maurice *and* Ahmed, Sara
Phillips, Terry 44, 47
Picasso, Pablo 49, 58, 59
Pohorilenko, Anatole 62, 64
POOL group 112, 120n1, 121n2
Poore, George Vivian 33, 47
porte battante 23, 26n17
postmemory 19
Potter, James E. 233, 242n4, 243
Poulenc, Francis 57, 58, 64
Prendergast, Christopher 25n5, 28
Price, Dorothy 176, 181
Proust, Marcel 2, 6, 11–17, 21, 22, 25n8, 143, 145; *À la recherche du temps perdu* II, 12–14; *À la recherche du temps perdu* IV 14; *À la recherche du temps perdu* V 15–17
Provoost, Michelle 242, 243
psychoanalysis 44, 125, 130, 134, 195n7

queerness 62, 139, 184, 185, 190, 125–30, 138–39, 182–94
queer space(s) 2, 7, 51–54, 61–62, 112

Raitt, Suzanne 40, 43, 44, 47
Rathwell, Richard 99, 109
Ray, Man 49
Rechter, Ya'acov 242, 243
Reichard, Ruth D. 33, 47
Reiss, Albert J. 195n15, 196
revolving door 2, 8, 174, 204, 208–10
Risom, Jens 240
Ritz, César 34
Ritz, Marie-Louise 34, 47
Ritz Hotel, London 35, 147
Roosevelt, Franklin D. 230, 232, 236

Rose, Francis 49, 54–55, 56, 59, 64
Rosemont, Penelope 27n20, 29, 135n1, 136
Ross, Shawna 7
Roth, Joseph 2, 4, 8, 169, 170, 171–72, 175, 204, 205–07, 210, 212; "Hotelwelt" 4, 169, 173–75, 176; "The *Patron*" 25n2, 169; *The Radetzky March* 206; "The Very Large Department Store" 169, 178
Rousseau, Henri 127–28
Ruskin, John 14–15, 16, 17, 22, 25n5, 29

Sanatoria 35, 138
Sandwirth Hotel, Venice 19
Saunders, Max 137, 151
Schelling, F. W. J. 141, 142, 151
Schivelbusch, Wolfgang 171, 181
Schlögel, Karl 206, 212
Schmidt, Tyler T. 8
Schneider, Rebecca 51, 64
Schnitzler, Arthur 65, 67, 202; "Fräulein Else" 67, 69, 73, 78
Schopenhauer, Arthur 213, 215–19, 220, 221, 222, 223, 224, 228
Schopenhauerian pessimism 216–17, 218
Schorske, Carl E. 202, 203, 212
Sebald, W. G. 2, 6, 17–20, 21, 25n6, 25n7, 29; *Vertigo* 17–20
Sedgwick, Eve Kosofsky 51, 61, 64, 141, 151
Seferis, George 80
Seymour, Miranda 86, 92
Shaw, David Zane 142, 151
Shelbourne Hotel, Dublin 156, 157
Shepheard's Hotel, Cairo 80–82, 89, 90n2, 91n6
Short, Emma 2, 3, 7, 10, 113, 115, 124, 136
Simmel, Georg 67, 70, 78
Sinclair, May 2, 4, 6, 36, 40–45, 47–48, 124; *A Journal of Impressions in Belgium* 6, 40–45; "Where Their Fire Is Not Quenched" 42
Sontag, Susan 17–18, 21, 29
Souhami, Diana 111, 122
Soupault, Philippe 11, 29
Soviet Union 214
Spacks, Patricia Meyer 164, 165, 167
Sphinx, The 23, 26n18, 129, 135

Sphinx Hôtel 24
Spoo, Robert 115, 122
Statler, Ellsworth M. 231
Stein, Gertrude 213–14
Steiner, George 84, 92
Stravinsky, Igor 49, 59, 62n1
Surrealism/Surrealists 11, 23, 24, 26n16, 62, 91, 124, 126, 127, 129, 130, 131, 134n1
surrealist aesthetics 6, 55, 58, 124–36
Symons, Arthur 87, 92
synaesthesia 13, 144

Tadié, Jean-Yves 11, 12, 15, 29
Taxidou, Olga 50, 64
Tellman, John 41–42, 48
Tiffin, Helen 97, 108
Tomes, Nancy 33, 48
Toulmin, Stephen 209, 211
transgression 3, 7, 124, 129, 183, 185, 187, 189, 190–93
Tregarthen's Hotel, Scilly Isles 110, 113, 117, 120
Trois Couronnes Hotel, Vevey 71, 72
Trollope, Anthony 90n2, 92
Turner, J. M. W. 15

uncanny 18, 24, 35, 52, 60, 62, 85, 112, 142, 147, 150

van Lennep, D. J. 4, 10, 161, 167
Veblen, Thorstein 68, 69, 70, 71, 78
Vehling, Paul 171, 181

Venice 14–16, 17, 19, 22, 65, 111, 112
Vienna 1, 8, 17, 18–19, 76, 201–11
Villefranche 1, 49, 52, 53–59, 61, 62n1
Vogel, Shane 189, 197
Vortex 8, 202, 210

Wagner, Richard 15
Walkowitz, Rebecca L. 97, 109
Walsh, Joanna 35, 38, 48
Warren, Andrew 165, 167
Waugh, Alec 49, 59, 64
Welch, Denton 2, 3, 7, 137–51; *In Youth Is Pleasure* 7, 137–51
Werfel, Franz 65, 67, 69, 78; "The Staircase" 67, 69
Wescott, Glenway 50, 52, 56, 58, 62
Wharton, Edith: "Terminus" 5, 9n2, 10
Wood, Christopher 49, 50, 58, 59
Woolf, Virginia: *Mrs Dalloway* 4–5
World War I 4, 6, 8, 107, 121n3, 170, 175, 214
World War II 77, 80, 81, 88, 106, 107, 183, 185, 192, 193, 230
Wright, Frank Lloyd 239
Wright, Richard 194, 197

Zahlan, Anne Ricketson 82, 92
Zimmerman, Emma 184–85, 197
Zitzlsperger, Ulrike 8
Zweig, Stefan 2, 3, 6, 65, 67, 70, 71, 75–76; *The Post Office Girl* 65, 67, 70, 71, 75–76